SINGAPORE 1942

# Singapore 1942

## Britain's Greatest Defeat

Alan Warren

Hambledon and London
London and New York

Hambledon and London
102 Gloucester Avenue
London, NW1 8HX

838 Broadway
New York
NY 10003–4812

First Published 2002

ISBN 1 85285 328 X

A description of this book is available from the
British Library and from the Library of Congress.

Typeset by Carnegie Publishing, Lancaster
Printed on wood-free paper and bound in
Malaysia by SRM Production Services

# Contents

# Illustrations

*Between Pages 210 and 211*

# Maps

# Introduction

At Singapore, early in 1942, under a hot tropical sun, thousands of soldiers were drawn up on parade for inspection. The men stood in ranks either side of stretches of road. They were from many corners of the British Empire, the largest empire the world had ever known. Among the soldiers were kilted Scotsmen, Englishmen in drill shorts and sun helmets, and Australians wearing bush hats. Also on parade were many men from the so-called 'martial races' of India. There were tall, bearded Sikhs in turbans, short, sturdy Gurkhas from Nepal, and Muslim and Hindu soldiers from the Punjab.

As the cars carrying the inspecting party drove by, the paraded men stood to attention. A pennant fluttered in the breeze on the bonnet of one of the leading vehicles. Some of the men standing to attention wore shallow steel helmets, but otherwise they were unarmed and dressed only in simple uniforms designed for service in hot weather. At the head of the parade were the British commanders of the troops, including several senior generals. Rows of medal ribbons on their breasts signified long and successful military careers.

The car carrying the inspecting party halted and several men got out. As they approached the officers at the head of the parade, the latter saluted. Most of the salutes were smart, others were a touch weary or perfunctory. Two senior British generals stood in front of the others, Lieutenant-General Arthur Percival, a tall, slim man wearing a standard flat cap, and Lieutenant-General Lewis Heath.

As cinema cameras recorded the event, and onlookers took photographs, a tall and heavily-built general wearing a dark uniform and a sword walked towards Percival. He saluted the British commander and stepped up to shake his hand. Lieutenant-General Tomoyuki Yamashita, the commander of the Japanese XXV Army, had on 15 February successfully completed his invasion of Malaya by the capture of Singapore Island. The army drawn up on parade was a part of what was left of the defeated and disarmed British force. The ceremonial inspection was a publicly imposed loss of face on the British. But it also marked more than just another defeat: it was in fact the greatest single defeat the British Empire had ever suffered.

The Japanese triumph was also a great victory for non-Europeans over a European empire.

This book attempts a fresh study of the campaign in Malaya and the fall of Singapore. The armies of the British Empire melted away before a numerically inferior Japanese force. The command decisions that lost an army comprised mostly of keen volunteers were a root cause of the problem, but the lack of adequate air and naval support did not help matters. Failings in long-term strategic preparation were also so serious that the campaign to defend Malaya may have been doomed from the outset.

The story of the Malayan campaign remains a fascinating one, and the passage of time makes it easier to probe the wounds of such a bad defeat. In other Allied campaigns defeat was turned into victory, but this did not happen at Singapore. The study of an institution in the context of defeat may tell us more about its strengths, weaknesses and salient characteristics than a similar study of a long string of successes won by overwhelming weight of resources.

No professional history of the tactical campaign, drawing on both British and Australian archives, has been written since the official histories were published in 1957. Military history is seldom at its best when accounts of defeats are written by the defeated. Memoirs and regimental histories are also often vague or narrow in focus. While the evidential base for the campaign leaves much to be desired, the case for a reconsideration of the Malayan campaign has been immeasurably increased by the release of new material by the British Public Record Office and the Australian War Memorial during the 1990s. Indeed anyone now writing an account of a Second World War campaign, and seeking to reconstruct events from the bottom upwards, now benefits from access to as complete a set of records as is ever likely to be available.

A full account of the campaign needs to absorb sources on all the troops involved, British, Indian, Australian and Malayan, as well of course as Japanese. It should be remembered that half of the troops in Malaya were drawn from the Indian army. Australians also played a prominent role in the campaign. In London, the National Army Museum, Imperial War Museum, Public Record Office and India Office collections all contain valuable material. Unit histories, headquarters diaries, unpublished memoirs, private records and intelligence files provide a great deal of new information. In Canberra, the Australian War Memorial holds equivalent records for Australian forces and copies of British material. In contrast, the archives of Imperial Japan were largely destroyed between the surrender of Japan and the arrival of the American occupation force. Japanese archival sources available in English consist mostly of reports compiled by Japanese officers after the war ended, often at the request of United States officials.

This book is narrative in style and sets out to give a complete account of the key events and engagements in the campaign, setting them in the wider context of the Second World War. Britain's loss of Malaya and Singapore to the Japanese is one of the Second World War's most compelling stories and marked a turning point in the history of the twentieth century.

For permission to reproduce illustrations I am grateful to the Australian War Memorial (8-9, 12, 16-17, 19-20, 22, 24-25, 29) and the Imperial War Museum (1-7, 9-11, 14-15, 18, 27-28). I am also grateful to the Australian War Memorial in Canberra and to an Australian Army History Research Grant for enabling me to pursue my research in London, Singapore, Kuala Lumpur and Canberra. I would like to express my thanks to all those who have helped me during the preparation of this book. Whilst in London I received help from the staffs of the British Library, the Imperial War Museum, the National Army Museum and the Public Record Office. Brian Farrell of the National University of Singapore has been an invaluable support, as have my colleagues at Monash University, in particular Ian Copland, David Cuthbert and Eleanor Hancock. Lastly, my publisher and editor, Martin Sheppard, has been encouraging and appropriately critical throughout.

# 1

# British Malaya

The Malay Peninsula lies astride the route between India and China. The peninsula is roughly the size of England and Wales, and is four hundred miles long from north to south, and sixty to two hundred miles wide from east to west. The northern frontier of Malaya shares a border with Thailand's Isthmus of Kra. To the east of Malaya is the South China Sea. Singapore Island lies off the southern tip of the peninsula, and less than sixty miles away to the south west, across the Strait of Malacca, is Sumatra.

A rugged series of jungle-clad mountain ranges and highlands run down the spine of the Malay Peninsula. Primary jungle is the term used to describe jungle in its native form, untouched by human hand. Straight tree trunks strain upwards towards the light. At a height of 100–150 feet the trees burst into a canopy that blocks out the sky. A garden of mosses and ferns grow in the treetop canopy, and creepers and vines wrap themselves around the trunks of trees, or hang down to the ground. The giant roots of the trees are covered by a carpet of dead leaves, small trees and palms.

Secondary jungle is created when primary jungle is cleared to make way for cultivation or dwellings, and the land later abandoned for the jungle to grow back. Secondary jungle is thicker at ground level than primary jungle, and bamboo thickets, vines and giant thorny grass impede human movement. Swathes of secondary jungle are frequently found in rural districts at unpredictable intervals.

Wild pigs, deer and the occasional tiger live deep in the jungle. Chattering monkeys, large lizards and a kaleidoscope of bird species can also be found. Midges, malaria-carrying mosquitoes, leeches, biting red ants and frogs are a general nuisance to humans. A cacophonous medley of nocturnal noises breaks the silence at night.

Coastal plateaus on either side of the central Malayan ranges are the natural focus of human settlement. On the west side the plain is up to forty miles wide. On the east coast the plain is narrower and interrupted by encroaching wilderness. Rivers and streams run out of the ranges towards both the east and west coasts of the peninsula. Rivers may be shallow and meandering at times but can be quickly transformed into raging torrents by heavy rain.

The climate of Malaya is constantly humid. Lying just north of the equator, the temperature near the coast is a warm 22–33 degrees centigrade. The steady winds of the north-east monsoons roll across the South China Sea from November to January, and the less severe south-west monsoons blow from June to August. The monsoons bring especially heavy rain storms.[1]

Asian traders plied the seas around Malaya for centuries prior to the arrival of Europeans in the region. Malays from Sumatra emigrated across to the peninsula to trade and mine. Europeans reached what they would call the 'Far East' during the 1400s. The Portuguese seized Malacca in 1511, and were supplanted by the Dutch in the 1600s. The British, through the agency of the East India Company, had gained a foothold in the region at Bencoolen, on the south-west coast of Sumatra, by the late seventeenth century. They leased Penang Island, off the north-west coast of Malaya, in 1786 to establish another major trading station. In 1819 Sir Thomas Stamford Raffles, the new Governor of Bencoolen, arranged a treaty with a local ruler to acquire Singapore for the East India Company. Raffles was looking for a new base from which to protect and aid British merchant ships sailing to China. Malacca was soon added to Britain's territories in the Malay Peninsula. The free trade ports operated by the British came to dominate trade in the region. Chinese junks turned their backs on the principal Dutch port of Batavia.[2]

Singapore became an important staging post for ships trading between the ports of China and India. Encouraged by the opening of the Suez Canal, and the invention of the steamship, Singapore grew dramatically. From a negligible population when Raffles landed in 1819, and 52,891 in 1850, the census of 1911 counted 311,303 people present at Singapore. From 1826 Penang, Province Wellesley, Malacca and Singapore became a single administrative unit called the Straits Settlements. The Straits Settlements remained under Indian control until 1867, when they were transferred to the custodianship of the Colonial Office and became a crown colony. Fort Canning was built to protect the government at Singapore from rebellion. The Royal Navy's command of the seas was the colony's principal line of defence.

The Malay peninsula had for generations been divided into sultanates. There was a certain balance between these rulers as none was all-powerful. Some sultanates were autonomous, and others in the peninsula's north owed a nominal allegiance to Siam. The sultans were supported by subordinate chieftains, and a general populace that lived mainly by fishing and agriculture. In Malay villages (kampongs) groups of houses on stilts with thatched roofs were sited amid groves of fruit trees, coconut palms, vegetable gardens and flowering shrubs.

The Malay states changed rapidly from the 1820s onwards. Merchants, mostly from the Straits Settlements, and with the cooperation of local chieftains, began to develop mines in the traditional tin-mining districts of western Malaya. Large numbers of Chinese immigrants were brought in to work in the tin mines. The East India Company meddled in the affairs of the sultanates on occasion, but on the whole tried to remain aloof from the peninsula. From the 1870s, however, acting on Colonial Office instructions, British officials administering the Straits Settlements began to move aggressively to turn the Malay states into protectorates.

A severe bout of civil war within the states, piracy, smuggling, the growing wealth of the mines, the safety of British-protected subjects working the mines and a fear of other European rivals provided a number of justifications for the informal annexation of the peninsula. British expansion into Malaya was backed by threats and inducements – little military force was required.

British residents were appointed to advise the sultans in all matters except Malay religion and custom. A civil service was established to preside over the building and management of a western infrastructure and administration throughout Malaya. Government revenues boomed, and the British did much to shore up the position of the sultans and Malay aristocracy during a period of great change. Several states banded together to form the Federated Malay States with a capital at Kuala Lumpur. These arrangements had been largely put in place by the first decade of the twentieth century, a decade that saw spectacular growth in the rubber industry. Before long rubber exported from Malaya, mostly to the United States to feed the growing tyre business, accounted for half the world's production. Significant advances in public health were also made under colonial administration. There was no cure for malarial fever, but suppressant drugs were available. In the space of a few decades the British had unified the Malayan Peninsula, transformed the economy, drawn the Malay elite into the western world and sponsored a massive surge of Chinese and Indian immigration. (The Indians were mostly Tamils.) At the foot of the peninsula, Singapore's growth was boosted by the economic development taking place on the mainland.

Malaya's defence and foreign relations were entirely in the hands of Britain. As the strongest of the European colonial powers, Britain's possessions in the Far East were relatively secure during the latter half of the nineteenth century. But the rise of Japan as an industrial nation, with western imperial ambitions, had by the turn of the twentieth century introduced a long-term threat to the European empires east of India.

An Anglo-Japanese alliance had served Britain well during the First World War, but the alliance was permitted to lapse in 1923 out of respect for the

1. The Far East.

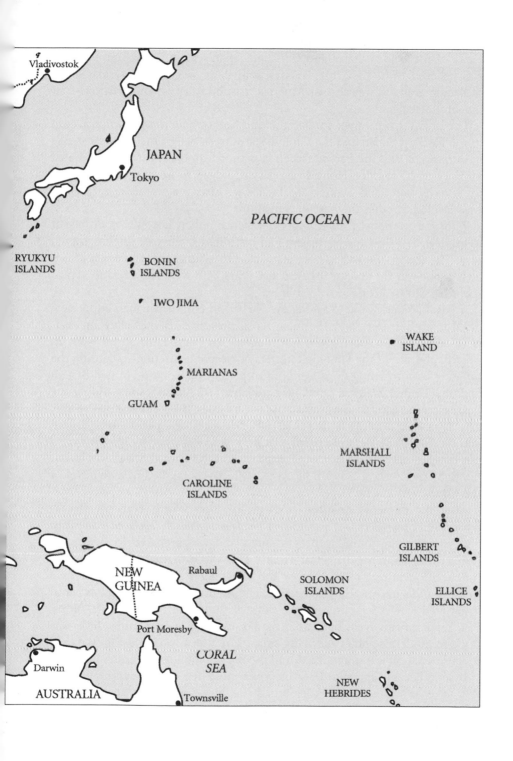

Vladivostok

JAPAN

Tokyo

PACIFIC OCEAN

RYUKYU
ISLANDS

BONIN
ISLANDS

IWO JIMA

WAKE
ISLAND

MARIANAS

GUAM

MARSHALL
ISLANDS

CAROLINE
ISLANDS

NEW
GUINEA

Rabaul

GILBERT
ISLANDS

SOLOMON
ISLANDS

ELLICE
ISLANDS

Port Moresby

Darwin

CORAL
SEA

AUSTRALIA

Townsville

NEW
HEBRIDES

views of the United States and Canada.[3] Japan's most likely future enemy was believed to be the United States, and there was never any likelihood of Britain going to war against America in support of Japan, irrespective of the circumstances.

The British government studied the question of building a new naval base in the Far East. Japan and the United States were two of the three strongest naval powers, and the Pacific Ocean was therefore the most likely arena of a future naval conflict. Hong Kong was adjudged to be too close to Japan for a naval base, and Sydney too far away. After lengthy deliberations, it was decided to build the base at Singapore.

Plans for a rational British imperial defence policy, however, soon began to unravel. The British government had instituted a 'ten-year rule' in August 1919. The service ministries were instructed to assume that there would not be a major war for at least the next ten years, and were subjected to savage spending limits. Worse was to follow.

A naval conference at Washington opened in November 1921, and a new naval treaty was signed by the main naval powers early the following year. A system of arms control was introduced that pegged the Royal Navy at roughly the size of the United States Navy. Severe restrictions regarding the building of new capital ships were put in place. The treaty permitted Britain and the United States a tonnage equivalent to fifteen capital ships, the Japanese nine capital ships, and France and Italy five capital ships apiece. The Japanese, displeased they had not been granted parity with Britain and the United States, were partly placated by a deal whereby Britain would not develop naval bases east of Singapore, and the United States would not develop bases west of Hawaii. Japan was effectively granted naval control of the north-west Pacific.

After the immense financial costs of the First World War, the British government feared that it would not be able to match declared American and Japanese ship-building programmes, and was prepared to accept the terms of the Washington Naval Treaty. This was a dramatic reversal of the nineteenth-century policy whereby the Royal Navy had to be at least equal to the world's next two largest navies.[4] The signing of the Washington Naval Treaty led to the scrapping of the bulk of the Royal Navy's capital ships. Few replacements were built and, thanks to defence economies, little was done to modernise older surviving ships. The Royal Navy's lead in the field of naval aviation was squandered, and the big ship building industry crippled.

It soon became apparent that the governments of America and Japan did not have any intention of carrying through the grandiose ship-building programmes that had frightened the British into signing the Washington Naval Treaty. Successive American administrations took their country into diplomatic isolation. The Japanese embarked upon an extended period of civilian-dominated government during the 1920s, and had neither the political will nor the economic wherewithal for grand naval building.

In reality the British Empire was the second strongest economic power on earth, and was more than capable of paying for a programme of arms spending that made the creation of a two hemisphere battle fleet a high priority. Britain had a genuine need for a powerful navy given its global responsibilities. Britain's enthusiasm for its navy had, however, always been inspired by the threat that other European navies posed to the United Kingdom. Traditionally, by dominating the United Kingdom's home waters in Europe, the Royal Navy could also shield the Empire from naval interference by other European powers. The signing of the Washington Naval Treaty, however, destroyed the Royal Navy's ability to shield the Empire, and indicated that Britain was not prepared to take seriously a naval threat that was directed against the Empire rather than the United Kingdom. Britain would have to send the bulk of its capital ships to the Far East merely to meet the Japanese on even terms. This would obviously be impossible if any other threat existed elsewhere.[5] The Empire's shield was thus removed almost immediately after the Dominions, India, and the colonies had sacrificed so much during the First World War to fight land battles in France and Flanders on Britain's doorstep.

The Admiralty was directed to come up with a workable grand strategy, despite the fact that it did not have enough ships to defend the Empire. The plan decided upon was that the main fleet would sail to Singapore only if a definite threat emerged in that region. It was expected that Singapore would have to hold out for several weeks until the fleet arrived. It is debatable whether informed individuals at the Admiralty ever believed that the strategy was workable. The 1930 London Naval Treaty led to the imposition of new treaty restrictions on the building and replacement of warships. The numbers of cruisers and submarines were restricted and a battleship construction 'holiday' extended. These new arms limitations further damaged the interests of the British Empire.

A naval base at Singapore was slowly built during the 1920s and 1930s. Plans to build a base large enough to hold the Royal Navy's main battle fleet were shelved to save money. The base being built was actually too small to accommodate a large fleet.[6] New Zealand, Hong Kong, the Straits Settlements, the Federated Malay States and Johore state made contributions towards the cost of the base. Australia was going to make a sizeable contribution, but the funds were diverted to building cruisers after the base was temporarily cancelled in 1924.[7]

By 1939 Malaya's population had grown to 5,500,000 people, of whom

43 per cent were Chinese and 41 per cent Malay. The rest of the population was mostly Indian, or European and Eurasian. Aboriginal people lived in the deep jungle of the central ranges. A small Japanese community worked in the tin and rubber industries, or as barbers, photographers, dentists and shopkeepers in the towns. The division of Malaya into separate states, mass immigration, prosperity and sharp racial divisions all combined greatly to retard the development of a nationalist movement. The nationalism of Indians and Chinese was mainly focused on their respective homelands. The British found the Malays to be well-mannered and easy going. At the start of the Second World War the imperial sun over Malaya was still at high noon.

At this time, perhaps 70 per cent of Malaya was covered by jungle, particularly down the mountainous spine of the peninsula. In the coastal plains there were many forests of primary and secondary jungle, but the landscape had been altered by human habitation and economic development, especially in the western coastal plain. Alongside roads and railway lines rubber plantations had been established, some developed by large European-owned public companies, others by Chinese or Malay farmers and entrepreneurs. The rubber trees were planted in neat rows. It was relatively easy to move through a well-tended estate under a high canopy of mature trees. Tracks running in the estates were passable for vehicles when the ground was firm. Palm oil and banana estates had similar characteristics.

A colonial society had long existed in the Straits Settlements and Malay States. In the towns European clubs became the centre of official social and sporting life. Swimming, tennis, golf and bridge were staple activities. Eurasian, Malay, Chinese and Indian elites had less influential parallel organisations. The courts of the Malay princes were another centre of power. The high status of Europeans was maintained by not employing Europeans in government or European-owned businesses below a certain grade, and by seldom allowing Asians to rise above that level. Hill stations were built inland, servants were plentiful, and there was little in the way of income tax for expatriates to concern themselves with. Mostly baseless stories of whisky-sodden planters, and government officials softened by years of luxurious living, abounded in the popular culture of the period.[8]

Singapore was a crowded, polyglot city in which extremes of wealth and poverty existed side by side in the steaming heat. The wealthy lived in beautiful residential suburbs surrounding the central town area. Abundant greenery gave a hint of jungle to the suburban fringe. Ethnic minorities had their own quarters in the city. Overcrowded Chinatown held an immense number of people. In Chinatown tiny shops displayed their wares and the streets were festooned with washing strung out on poles. Secret societies still existed. Carts and trishaws met the transport needs of ordinary people. Singapore River was jammed with hundreds of barges and boats. The harbour area was full of warehouses and goods waiting for shipment to other parts of the world.

A spacious and ordered government and business district dominated the centre of the town. Raffles Hotel was one of a number of prestigious hotels. Near the Singapore Club, the Padang, a large field by the seafront, served the sporting needs of its members. The spire of St Andrew's Cathedral rose above its neighbouring buildings. Government House, fronted by a splendid lawn, looked down on the town from rising ground. By 1939 Singapore had a new domed Supreme Court building and one 'skyscraper', the Cathay Building. Small villages dotted Singapore Island and were connected to the metropolis by a good road network.

Upon the outbreak of war in Europe in 1939, the Governor at Singapore, Sir Shenton Thomas, received Colonial Office instructions that the management of Malaya's economy, the rubber and tin industries in particular, was to be his top priority. 38 per cent of the world's tin and 58 per cent of the world's rubber came from Malaya. The bulk of these materials was exported to the United States and earned valuable dollars. Despite the war, there was almost no rationing in Malaya. The news media avoided upsetting the populace at the government's request. The 'business as usual' feel to the colony persisted even when the war news from Europe grew gloomy. At Singapore the Chinese Communist Party was outlawed. Due to Japan's war in China, the bulk of the Chinese community in Malaya remained staunchly anti-Japanese.

At Singapore the Naval Base had finally been opened in 1938. The Naval Base was a fenced off town with rows of depots, magazines and barracks. A large floating dock had been towed all the way from Britain, and there was another graving dock large enough to hold a battleship. Batteries of coastal artillery had been built to command the approaches to the Naval Base and commercial harbour, where large merchant ships anchored in the outer roads. Singapore Island was not a fortress, but a great deal of official propaganda was generated to broadcast news of Singapore's impregnability. The 'Gibraltar of the Far East' was portrayed as a cornerstone of empire.

Officially the period Singapore was expected to withstand a siege before relief arrived in the form of the Royal Navy's main battle fleet was forty-two days. By 1939 this period had been raised to seventy and then ninety days. In September 1939 the 'period before relief' was raised to 180 days. It was clear that the army and RAF were going to have to shoulder a greater burden of Malaya's defence in the navy's absence. The senior army and air force officers, Lieutenant-General Sir Lionel Bond and Air Vice-Marshal Sir John Babington, did not help matters by feuding furiously on both a personal and a professional level. In the opinion of the local naval commander, the chief cause of the friction was Babington's great faith in the effectiveness of his gravely under strength RAF command.

Military thinking in Malaya during the late 1930s had turned to the problem of defending all of the peninsula, rather than just Singapore and the adjacent mainland. But General Bond was aggrieved that he had not been consulted on the location of new aerodromes under construction in the north and east of Malaya. After all, once the aerodromes had been built, the army would be required to defend them.[9] RAF commanders claimed that the limited range of 1930s aircraft, and the poor weather over Malaya's central range, meant that aerodromes had to be built close to the peninsula's northern frontier and east coast. In April 1940 Bond estimated that he would need between thirty-nine and forty-two battalions if the army was to defend Malaya. He had only nine battalions at the time, but suggested that twenty-five might suffice if the RAF was strongly reinforced.[10]

By the onset of the Second World War a good deal had been done to improve the local defences of Malaya. But there was still a long way to go before the colony could be considered secure, were it ever to be seriously threatened with assault by a major power.

## 2

# The Rise of the Japanese Empire

Early in the twentieth century the British Empire was at its zenith. Naval power, colonial settlement, annexation and mercantile expansion had taken Britain to many corners of the globe. As a rule the most far-flung parts of the British Empire were safe from Britain's European enemies so long as Britain was in a robust condition in Europe. Indeed, at the turn of the twentieth century, a European adversary of Britain had not been able to send strong and effective forces to menace Britain's colonial possessions since the late eighteenth century, the period of the American and French Revolutions.

Yet, late in the nineteenth century, the rise of Japan as a major power with imperial ambitions in Asia introduced a new threat to the British Empire that originated beyond Europe. Japan was determined to become a modern, industrial nation to avoid the fate of China, the coast of which was dominated by European trading posts. The state of British military preparedness in Europe would not necessarily have a strong bearing on operations against a major power located east of the Suez Canal.

Japan, at the north west of the Pacific Ocean, had for several centuries been a 'hermit kingdom'. The shoguns and their professional military retainers, the samurai, had kept a tight grip on the country. During the early decades of the nineteenth century United States whaling ships had worked the waters around Japan. Shipwrecked crews were treated harshly by Japanese authorities as having breached Japan's self-imposed isolation. Finally in 1853 a United States naval squadron, commanded by Commodore Perry, arrived at Nagasaki and, among other demands, issued an ultimatum that Japan give trading and diplomatic rights to foreign nations. Perry said he would return the following year for an answer to the ultimatum. Japanese observers were most impressed by Perry's steam-driven warships. In 1854 the Shogun was forced to sign a treaty opening Japan to American traders. Other powers soon secured similar rights.

By the middle of the nineteenth century European powers had forced the weakened Chinese empire to open its doors to trade. To some extent the opening of Japan was an extension of the same process. After the Opium wars the Chinese Emperor was made to sanction the establishment of a series of treaty ports up and down China's coast, from which European traders used their privileged status to expand their influence into the hinterland. The British were the leading power on China's coast, and Hong Kong and Shanghai became the most famous of the treaty ports.

In Japan influential people were alarmed and impressed by the position the European powers were building in east Asia. There was strong xenophobia in Japan among the leading clans, and the Shogun was blamed for acceding to the demands of the western powers. Nevertheless, opponents of the shogunate were quick to adopt new weapons and military techniques from Europe. The shogunate was overturned and in 1868 a new system of government was introduced under the authority of the Emperor Meiji. The Emperor, or Mikado, had been a semi-captive of the previous regime.

Rather than risk Japan becoming another plaything of the west, the Japanese ruling class set out to modernise their country. Rather like Great Britain, Japan had the tremendous natural advantages of a common language, ethnicity and culture, combined with good communications, basic education and a large population in a compact land mass. The pace of change proved extraordinary. Feudalism was done away with rapidly, though its mentality carried on for decades. The great landowners returned their fiefs to the Emperor and the samurai lost their exclusive right to bear arms.

Many reforms were introduced after the return of high level missions sent to Europe to learn all they could of western technology and organisational techniques. Naval reform was based on the Royal Navy, and military and constitutional practices were borrowed from France and Germany. An industrial economy, heavily dependent on imported raw materials, was built up. A national army, general staff and western-style military academies were established, and a limited parliamentary system put in place. On a more ideological plane, the ancient religion of Shinto was made the state religion. It was emphasised that the imperial family was of divine origin. Love of and obedience to country and Emperor were central Shinto principles.

The nearness of the Asian mainland had always been a threat to Japan's security. In 1860 the Russians had obtained the Pacific coast port of Vladivostok from China. During the 1890s the Russians began building the Trans-Siberian Railway to Vladivostok. There was no economic justification for building the railway. Its purpose was overtly strategic, as it would enable Russia to transport and maintain a large army near its Pacific coast. Fear of Russia became a dominant feature of Japanese foreign policy from this time on.

The Japanese government rid itself of any threat from China during an eight month war in 1894–95. China sued for peace and Japan became the most influential power in Korea. But intervention by France, Germany and

Russia in support of China severely modified the peace treaty between Japan and China. The Japanese annexed Formosa (Taiwan), but they were forced to renounce their claim to the Liaotung Peninsula and Port Arthur, a strategically vital Chinese Manchurian port to the south of Korea. To add insult to injury, in 1898 Russia leased Port Arthur from the Chinese, and in 1899 began building a branch of the Trans-Siberian railway to Port Arthur.

These Chinese concessions to Russia, and a number of other fresh concessions to European powers, led in part to the 1900 Boxer 'Rebellion', whereby the foreign legation area in Peking was besieged by Chinese forces. More than half the troops involved in the western expedition to raise the Boxer siege were Japanese.

In 1902 Britain formed an alliance with Japan to establish jointly a commanding presence in the western Pacific aimed principally at Russia. The Russians had done much to build up their strength in Manchuria during the time of the Boxer revolt. Before long the Russians had based a fleet in the Far East at Port Arthur, and had further obvious territorial ambitions in the region. The Anglo-Japanese treaty was essentially defensive in orientation, and neither party was obliged to go to war if the other party attacked a third nation.

With the qualified support of Britain, Japan launched a war against Russia in 1904. The war began with a surprise attack on the Russian fleet at Port Arthur on the night of 8/9 February. Japanese forces from Korea landed on the Manchurian coast and moved swiftly to isolate Port Arthur. In a series of fierce land battles Russian forces were pushed northwards across Manchuria towards Mukden. After a bloody siege, Port Arthur fell early in January 1905.

The closing dramatic chapter to the war was the Russian decision to sail its Baltic Fleet half way around the world to take part in operations in the Far East. The fleet left Europe late in 1904 and only steamed past Singapore on 8 April 1905. It sailed on to reach the Tsushima Straits, close to the southern tip of Korea. On 27 May the Japanese fleet under Admiral Togo won a historic victory at the Battle of Tsushima. The battle was won by a navy created with British technical assistance, and warships built mainly in British shipyards.[1] Tsushima was, at the time, the greatest naval battle of the post-sail era.

Beaten at sea, with stalemate on land, and revolution brewing at home, the Tsarist government signed a peace treaty in September 1905. After the war Japan secured the rights in Manchuria that had been Russia's, including Port Arthur and the southern section of the Manchurian railway. Korea, which had been partly occupied by Japan during the emergency of the war with Russia, was eventually annexed in 1910.

With the Russian Far Eastern fleet at the bottom of the ocean, the Royal Navy was able to withdraw its battleships in the Far East to Britain to augment a fleet being built up to face the Germans across the North Sea.[2] During the First World War the Anglo-Japanese alliance encouraged Japan to enter the war against Germany. The Japanese seized German territory in China and the Pacific, in particular the treaty port of Tsingtao in November 1914, and the Caroline, Marshall and Mariana Islands. Japanese forces also helped Britain to supress a mutiny at Singapore in 1915.

Yet Japan's relations with the western powers were damaged during the war by the extent of Japan's imperial ambitions in China. In 1911 the last Manchu Emperor had been deposed and a Chinese republic was proclaimed the following year, though in practice the country fell into the hands of local warlords as the regions broke away from the control of Peking. In 1915 Japan presented China's new authorities with a set of twenty-one demands designed to further Japanese influence. It took American-led intervention drastically to limit Japan's attempt to secure new rights in China. (The United States's annexation of Hawaii and the Philippines at the close of the nineteenth century had by now made the Americans a central player in the scramble for Chinese trade.) Japan's military adventurism continued with a substantial intervention in Russia's civil war. Troops were stationed deep in Siberia from 1918–22.

During the 1920s China continued to lie in the grip of its warlords. This began rapidly to change following the founding of the National Party of China – the Kuomintang – in south China in the early years of the decade. The Kuomintang, under Chiang Kai Shek, steadily expanded its control beyond its initial power base. In 1927 Nationalist forces captured Peking, and a central government was established at Nanking in 1928. The founding of the Communist Party of China in 1922 further complicated the political environment.

In Japan of the 1920s civilian politicians with a cautiously internationalist outlook enjoyed a rare period of political ascendancy. For instance, Japan was an active participant in the League of Nations. Between 1921 and 1927 military spending fell from 49 per cent to 28 per cent of the government's budget.[3]

The economic crisis of the Great Depression from 1929 onwards greatly changed the international situation. The concept that international co-operation was the pathway to prosperity was dealt a severe blow by the collapse of international trade and the subsequent erection of trade barriers between nations and imperial blocs.

The Japanese government had believed for several decades that it had special rights in China, due to geographic proximity. Japanese nationalist ideologues had also developed a body of thought concerning an empire in Asia. With Japan's export-orientated economy hit hard by the collapse of world trade, the military became increasingly convinced the nation needed guaranteed access to new markets and raw materials on the Asian mainland. Japan's population had more than doubled since the Meiji Restoration and China was a large land mass. The army's quasi-feudal links with small landowners and the rural peasantry made Japan's generals only too well aware how much pain the trade depression was causing.

Japan's constitutional arrangements had always been dangerously weak so far as responsible parliamentary government was concerned. The Japanese cabinet and military were separately responsible to the Emperor and not to Parliament. In addition, the military could control the cabinet through its nominees to the posts of army and navy minister, who by imperial edict could only be servicemen (the prime minister, foreign and finance ministers were the other members of the inner cabinet). The services could therefore bring down a government whenever they chose by withdrawing their ministers and refusing to name successors. In theory Emperor Hirohito, who had come to the throne in 1926, held in balance the government and military command, but in practice the Emperor's warm approval of the military's line of thinking gave the generals enormous influence.

With the assassination of Prime Minister Hamaguchi in November 1930, partly because he had pushed through Japanese acceptance of the London Naval Treaty, militarism arrived on the stage of Japanese politics as a major force. Secret societies with ultra-nationalist agendas flourished among army officers. Another Prime Minister was assassinated in 1932 and civilian party government was brought to its knees. Military extremists regularly accused the government of trampling on the link between the armed forces and the imperial throne, violating the position of the Emperor.[4]

At this juncture, a crisis developed in Manchuria when the local warlord recognised the Nationalist government in Nanking, and began to obstruct the Japanese presence in southern Manchuria. Manchuria was a rich source of coal and iron ore, and an important new export market. The Japanese had been developing economic ties in Manchuria for some years, and by the late 1920s three-quarters of the region's economy was in Japanese hands. (Ninety per cent of Manchuria's inhabitants were ethnic Chinese.)

With Japan's position in Manchuria at risk, officers of the Kwantung army (Japanese forces in Manchuria) took matters into their own hands and staged a bombing incident on the railway they were guarding near Mukden on 18 September 1931. The Kwantung army claimed that local Chinese forces were responsible and a campaign was launched against them.

Man for man Chinese soldiers were seldom a match for the Japanese. China's fractured social system was an unsound basis upon which to build a loyal and united army.

The Tokyo government was not informed of the Kwantung army's intentions, though some officials knew of the plans, but the government was forced to rubber-stamp the army's actions after the event. The Chinese appealed to the League of Nations, of which the Nanking government was a member. Late in October 1931 the League of Nations passed a resolution calling on Japanese forces to return to their original positions in southern Manchuria. The Japanese argued that they were acting in self-defence in a lawless country. A League of Nations Commission of Inquiry investigated the war in Manchuria and condemned Japanese aggression. After the league's council passed a vote of censure on Japan's conduct in Manchuria, the Japanese responded by resigning from the league. No sanctions, however, were imposed on Japan. But Japan's isolation from the community of nations was well underway. Manchuria was overrun during 1932 and further gains were made in northern China. The Japanese set up a new puppet state in Manchuria.

Yet there was further fighting in China for Japan. Early in 1932 a large Japanese expedition was sent to Shanghai to counter anti-Japanese riots. Heavy fighting lasted a period of weeks. Only in May 1933 was a general truce signed between the Japanese and the Chinese Nationalists. A line was drawn across north China roughly along the Great Wall, with a demilitarised zone south of the wall. Japan had clearly become the most influential foreign country in the affairs of China.

Massive increases in Japanese military spending continued throughout the 1930s. An attempted military coup in Tokyo on 26 February 1936, led by young officers from one particular army faction, resulted in a series of assassinations of officials before the rising was suppressed three days later. The failed revolt further intimidated civilian opposition to the will of the military in government circles.

In Europe Hitler had come to power in January 1933. Nazi Germany left the League of Nations that year, and repudiated the military clauses of the Treaty of Versailles the following year. The system of naval disarmament instituted after the First World War soon crumbled as well. In June 1935 an Anglo-German naval treaty was negotiated. Britain agreed that Germany could build a fleet up to 35 per cent of the Royal Navy's surface tonnage. With the rebirth of the German fleet it became unlikely that the Royal Navy would ever be able to send a large force to the Far East, and Malaya in particular. The general naval treaties were due to expire in 1936 anyway. Although another conference at London was held in 1935–36 to draw up a new round of treaties, Japan withdrew from negotiations and launched a new capital ship building programme. The London conference was adjourned indefinitely in January 1936.

Britain's military response to the rising threat of Germany and Japan was half-hearted. Although in 1932 the ten year rule was suspended, it was only in the mid-1930s, after the final collapse of the disarmament conferences, that an expansion programme for the Royal Navy and RAF was set in motion. Yet because at least half the Royal Navy's battleships and aircraft carriers were unmodernized or obsolete, the new ships launched in the late 1930s and early 1940s merely replaced old ships. They did little to enhance Britain's ability to meet its responsibilities in both European and Far Eastern waters.

The international situation only grew more dangerous as the 1930s moved forward. Crises over Abyssinia (October 1935) and Spain ( July 1936) strained and complicated relations between the great European powers. In November 1936 Germany and Japan signed an anti-Comintern (anti-Communist) Pact. A month previously the Rome-Berlin axis had been formed to cement German-Italian cooperation in European affairs.

Meanwhile, in east Asia the truce between China and Japan was speedily unravelling. Chiang Kai Shek had been coming under pressure from various Nationalist factions to end his campaign against the Communists and form a united front opposed to further Japanese encroachment in northern China. (The Communists had been driven into the north west interior – the so-called 'Long March'.) Chiang feared the Japanese might reduce him to no more than a provincial warlord. His regime had built up an army of thirty divisions, trained by German advisers, quite apart from other regional Chinese forces acting under the umbrella of the Nationalist movement.

Renewed war between Japan and China erupted in an unexpected fashion. On the night of 7 July 1936 a Japanese company on night manoeuvres near Marco Polo Bridge at Peking was fired at. (Under the 1901 Boxer Protocol Japanese troops were part of the international force guarding the route between Peking and the sea.) Fighting erupted between Japanese and Chinese troops. Within a few days local representatives had worked out a cease fire, but the governments of both sides to the dispute subsequently ignored these negotiations and reinforced their armies in north China. Japanese troops were transferred southwards from the Kwantung army.

On 17 July Chiang publicly called on the Chinese people to resist Japan and ordered his forces into the demilitarized zone in north China. Throughout mid to late July there was intense debate within the upper reaches of the Japanese military and government as to how they should respond to the crisis. The government, with Prince Konoye Fumimaro as Prime

Minister since June, was not keen on renewed conflict, but news that the Chinese were moving forces northwards helped to tip the balance in the cabinet in favour of sending to China a stream of divisions from Japan. Japanese leaders had faced a series of crises since 1931 and had become accustomed to taking assertive military decisions. What is more, China was seen as weak and divided between several political groupings. In Tokyo a successful conclusion to a brief war was expected. Indeed, by the end of July Japanese troops were already in control of the Peking-Tientsin region. Over the next few months Japanese forces made extensive territorial gains in north China. (Lieutenant-General Tojo Hideki, chief of staff to the Kwantung army, commanded part of the forces engaged.)[5]

The conflict soon grew into a general Sino-Japanese war. In August a force of Japanese marines at Shanghai, stationed to protect civilian Japanese working in the city, was confronted by a large Chinese army. The Yangtse valley was the core of the Nanking regime and provided its main financial support. The best Nationalist formations were posted within well-prepared defences around Shanghai, one of the largest cities in the world. Skirmishing soon led to heavier fighting. On 14 August Chinese aircraft bombed Japanese shipping off Shanghai and the following day Japanese naval aircraft bombed Nanking and Shanghai.[6]

On 23 August the first Japanese reinforcement division made an assault landing on the Yangtse River to relieve pressure on the embattled marines. Japanese reinforcements arrived piecemeal until there were five divisions under General Iwane Matsui holding a large bridgehead. Yet the network of creeks, canals and swampland at the mouth of the Yangtse favoured the defender. When the Japanese advanced inland, beyond the support of naval gunfire, they became bogged down. During September and October a huge battle raged around Shanghai.

The Japanese High Command eventually decided to launch a new offensive in central China to break the deadlock. After weeks of bitter conflict in and around Shanghai, on 5 November the Japanese landed the three divisions of X Army in Hangchow Bay, south of the city, to turn the southern flank of the Chinese cordon. Another Japanese division from north China was landed on the Yangtse north of Shanghai on 13 November, using purpose-built landing craft. It had taken nine divisions to break the Chinese grip on Shanghai. The three month campaign had been expensive. Japanese casualties amounted to 40,672, of whom 9115 were killed.[7]

The Chinese retreated inland along the Yangtse basin towards the Nationalist capital of Nanking, which lay two hundred miles upriver from Shanghai. Japanese mechanized columns and aircraft pressed the Chinese but there was a pause in operations. There was still uncertainty in the

Japanese government as to how far the war should be extended. Peace negotiations mediated through the German ambassadors in Tokyo and Nanking were under consideration for much of November. Chiang, though, procrastinated in the face of relatively moderate Japanese peace terms. Tokyo lost patience and finally authorized an advance on Nanking on 1 December.

Japanese forces were soon at Nanking and on 8 December the Chinese army left behind to defend the city was instructed to surrender by noon on 10 December. A Japanese division crossed the Yangtse upstream of Nanking to isolate the city. The Chinese commander responded by ordering that buildings outside the city walls be set on fire. A ring of smoke stained the sky around Nanking as the Japanese prepared for their final assault. The attack began on 10 December and two days later resistance began to crumble. The Japanese entered the city on 13 December. The Chinese military had taken a terrible beating since the commencement of hostilites.

For a month an officially sponsored terror was waged by the Japanese against the population in and around Nanking. What began as an operation to round up and kill Chinese soldiers turned into a frenzied, drunken orgy of murder and rape. For days the sound of sporadic machine gun and rifle fire filled the air in Nanking. Bodies were dumped in the Yangtse and washed up on the banks. Photographs of Japanese soldiers using Chinese prisoners for bayonet practice before a crowd of onlookers made compelling evidence of atrocity. Bayoneting of prisoners often took place under officer supervision. There were beheading competitions among Japanese troops. Infants were thrown into the air and impaled on bayonets. The gang rape of thousands of women, old and young, showed that the Japanese had no respect for women, who were often promptly shot after they had been raped.

Chinese propagandists later claimed that upwards of a quarter of a million people were killed at Nanking. Appalled western observers were certain that this was an exaggeration but the death toll must have run to many tens of thousands.[8] Estimates of the death toll depend on how many of Nanking's population are believed to have fled the city prior to the arrival of the Japanese. It is likely that the majority had fled westwards.

Why was the sack of Nanking so ferocious? To start with, Japanese soldiers had been conditioned not to value any life but that of the Emperor. The Japanese military's contempt for the Chinese was virulent, and many soldiers were keen to avenge their comrades fallen in the Shanghai fighting. There were few military police on hand to stop events running out of control as discipline broke down amongst Japanese troops.

Moreover, much of the impetus for the atrocities at Nanking came from the top of the chain of command. There was an element of strategic calculation to the whole exercise.[9] Orders seem to have been given to eliminate all captives, possibly both to remove potential guerillas and to relieve pressure on the army's supply train. The lack of any clear war aim may have encouraged senior Japanese generals to view the campaign in the lower Yangtse as a war of plunder and devastation, a giant punitive expedition intended to do as much damage as humanly possible. The whole advance towards Nanking had been marked by burning, plundering and murder in many towns and villages. Millions of refugees from the lower Yangtse fled their homes, many of whom would perish from famine and disease. Japan's international reputation was ruined by news of the Nanking campaign. After the Nanking atrocities it was all but impossible for Japan to be still accepted as a respectable member of the international community.[10] Japanese conduct in the capital of Asia's most populous nation did not presage the 'dawn of a new renaissance for Asia'.

Japanese troops upstream from Nanking had been ordered to fire on all shipping trying to escape from the city. On 12 December the USS *Panay* was sunk by aircraft on the Yangtse, and the British gunboat HMS *Ladybird* was shelled by artillery. The event received a great deal of hostile newspaper coverage in the United States. Within two weeks of the sinking of the *Panay* the Japanese government had apologized for the incident and agreed to pay an indemnity. The United States and British governments took no punitive action against Japan, but this was not the only significant infringement of the rights and property of Anglo-Americans in China during this period. For instance, in August 1937 the British Ambassador in China had been seriously wounded by a Japanese air attack on the road between Shanghai and Nanking.[11]

After the loss of Nanking the Chinese Nationalists were more ready to come to terms with the Japanese, but in the wake of their victories the Japanese stiffened their terms and there was little hope of a settlement. In January 1938 the Konoye cabinet declared that they would not accept Chiang Kai Shek's government as a party to any diplomatic settlement.

During 1938 the Japanese military extended the war and pushed inland across northern and central China. The fighting did not all go Japan's way. A column of the 10th Division rashly advancing south from the Yellow River towards Hsuchow, near the Peking-Nanking railway, was encircled on 6 April. A relief force from the 5th Division failed to fight its way through the cordon and eight thousand Japanese were killed. The setback was only temporary; Hsuchow was taken on 19 May. Retreating Nationalist forces blew the dykes of the Yellow River in places to flood vast areas of the countryside to block the Japanese advance on Hankow, four hundred miles up the Yangtse from Nanking. Millions of civilians were made homeless and untold death and suffering caused. But by late October Hankow had fallen.[12]

About the same time, on 12 October, a surprise landing was made near Canton in south China by a three division Japanese force. The city, which was inland from Hong Kong, was taken swiftly, cutting the Nationalists' main external supply route. In February 1939 Hainan Island was occupied. Japanese forces also took Chinese territory adjacent to the frontier of French Indo-China to cut the rail link leading to Hanoi and other French ports. The Japanese held nine-tenths of China's railway system, and had reached the fringe of South-East Asia, but Japanese forces lacked the logistic support to penetrate into the deep interior of China and a stalemate set in. At Chungking, nine hundred miles up river from Hankow, Chiang's main army and government was virtually invulnerable except to bombing raids.

In December 1938 Prime Minister Konoye spoke in a radio broadcast of a 'New Order in East Asia'.[13] Yet, at the start of 1939 the Konoye cabinet resigned over the quagmire in China, and internal disagreements over Japan's relations with Germany. Chiang Kai Shek's forces continued to receive some outside aid from Soviet, American, British and French sources. In those parts of China occupied by the Japanese, rather as in Manchuria, Japanese officials set out to monopolize the drug industry to help fund their campaigns. Within Japan the military's control over the country increased as the war effort absorbed more and more of the economy. Steps were begun to establish a puppet Chinese government, and the Japanese settled down as a quasi-permanent army of occupation within their own zone of China. The Japanese tried to treat Chungking as just another troublesome local regime. Japanese forces in China would later reach 850,000.[14]

Ever since the start of the Sino-Japanese war Tokyo had kept a watchful eye on the Soviets. There had been regular skirmishes between Soviet and Japanese troops along the Manchurian-Siberian frontier, but in the summer of 1938 a pitched battle took place only fifty miles from Vladivostok. There was even heavier fighting across the summer of 1939 near Nomonhan and the frontiers of Manchuria and Outer Mongolia. A skirmish begun on 11 May escalated sharply. In this undeclared border war Japanese forces suffered a serious defeat at the hands of a force twice their strength. General Zhukov's mechanized and armoured formations enveloped their Japanese opponents. Of 56,000 Japanese involved, 8500 were killed and a similar number wounded.[15] Some units were annihilated. An armistice was concluded in September of that year. At Nomonhan the Japanese army learnt that the capacity of Soviet forces was not to be underestimated. To make matters worse, late in August the Soviets and Germans signed a non-aggression pact. The Soviet threat in east Asia loomed larger than ever.

In June of 1939 the Japanese blockaded the British concession at the north Chinese port of Tientsin over a minor dispute, though at heart lay the issue of ongoing western trade with the Nationalists. The British offered to negotiate a settlement and were forced to make concessions regarding Japan's special law and order needs in China. Later in the year British naval forces left the Yangtse valley and British troops were pulled out of Tientsin and Peking to avoid any further incidents.

On 26 July 1939 the United States gave notice that it was cancelling the United States-Japan Treaty of Commerce and Navigation, a decision partly influenced by Japan's actions at Tientsin. Senior figures in the White House, Congress and the press were becoming increasingly critical of Japan's actions in China. American exports of oil and iron had underpinned Japan's war industries, but America's tolerance of Japanese aggression was wearing thin. At the end of 1938 Washington had even given Chungking a small loan for military aid. The irony of Japan's China policy was that, far from making it self-sufficient, the demands of the conflict were making Japan more dependent than ever on imports from the west, and from America in particular. The commercial treaty was terminated at the start of 1940. This changed little in practice, though it did create uncertainty in the minds of Japan's leaders, and meant that Japan was now vulnerable to punitive American trade sanctions. Nonetheless, the half-heartedness of British and American responses to Japan's China war encouraged Japanese leaders to believe that the western democracies lacked resolve. The Japanese, on the other hand, were becoming battle-hardened and ruthless as the war in China dragged on.

# 3

## The Defence of Malaya

In Europe general war broke out in September 1939 after Germany invaded Poland. Britain and France declared war when Germany refused to halt the invasion. The war was not a surprise. Europe had come perilously close to war in 1938 at the time of the Munich Agreement. Britain was now less able to play a major role in the affairs of the Far East. Still, at the outset, during the 'Phoney War', the Second World War's direct impact was confined to Europe.

The fall of France and the entry of Italy into the war in June 1940 had a decisive impact on the theoretical plan for defending the Far East. The French fleet was lost to the Allied cause, and the Italian fleet in the Mediterranean joined the Axis. The Royal Navy soon became badly over-stretched in the North Atlantic and Mediterranean. There was now no chance of the main fleet heading to the Far East. The plan had always been a fair weather scheme that would only work in the most favourable of circumstances. An appreciation by the British Chiefs of Staff in August 1940 acknowledged that a fleet could no longer be sent to the Far East, and belatedly ordered that the army and RAF be built up to defend Malaya.

In September 1940 Winston Churchill, Prime Minister since May, dictated the opinion: 'The defence of Singapore must ... be based upon a strong local garrison and the general potentialities of sea power.'[1] Churchill believed that 'the Japanese would never attempt a siege of Singapore with a hostile, superior American fleet in the Pacific'.[2] The belief that the United States could and would contain Japan became the basic assumption behind the British Empire's defence policy in the Far East. Given the Royal Navy's inability to deploy force east of the Suez Canal, there was little alternative to that kind of wishful thinking.

In the latter half of 1940 Britain's position in the Far East continued to spiral out of control. The fall of France had presented Japan with a golden opportunity for action. On 26 July an emboldened Japanese cabinet approved a policy to develop a 'new order in Greater East Asia' centred on Japan, Manchuria, China and other unspecified parts of Asia necessary to the formation of a self-sufficient bloc. Japan took advantage of Britain's problems in Europe to demand the closure of the road through Burma to China from July to October 1940. Some weeks earlier, the Japanese had also tried to pressure the Dutch authorities in the East Indies to supply them with oil. More dramatically, Japanese troops entered northern Indo-China after the Vichy French government capitulated to Japanese demands on 25 September. This effectively cut the supply route to China through the Hanoi delta. Japan sought further to penetrate South-East Asia by involving itself in a border conflict between Thailand and the French.

Germany's conquest of most of continental Europe had demonstrated in no uncertain terms that it was the strongest power in Europe. Japan had been building closer relations with Germany across the late 1930s. With Germany at the summit of its power, the moment seemed ideal to forge an alliance with the European Axis. A new cabinet under the leadership of Prince Konoye took Japan into the Axis pact on 27 September. (The new Army Minister in the Konoye cabinet was General Tojo.) Germany, Italy and Japan agreed to aid each other if one of their number was attacked by a power not involved in a current conflict.

Membership of the Axis pact ensured that Germany recognised that east Asia was a Japanese sphere. The Germans had appeared to have half an eye on French and Dutch colonial possessions in Asia. But now, according to Prince Konoye: 'Germany and Italy intend to establish a New Order in Europe and Japan will do likewise in Greater East Asia.'[3] As part of the Axis Japan also had the prospect of assistance in the event of war with the United States. Foreign Minister Matsuoka Yosuke, a strong supporter of a German alliance, stated quite directly at a meeting of Japan's leaders that the Axis was 'a military alliance aimed at the United States'.[4] The Germans hoped that Japan would restrain the Americans whilst they dealt a final blow to the British. Japan's entry into the Axis meant that observers in America and Britain increasingly saw Germany and Japan as a joint threat. The pact also caused Japan's leaders to consider the possibility of war with America and Britain more seriously.

The fall of France had caused the Roosevelt administration to recast its foreign policy strongly in favour of helping the British Empire. American factories worked on orders for the British military. In September 1940 the 'destroyers for bases' deal signalled a deepening American involvement in Britain's war. In light of American opposition to German policy, it made sense to adopt a less generous attitude towards Japan, the new Asian wing of the Axis. In late July the Americans prohibited the export of aviation grade gasoline, lubricating oils and certain grades of scrap iron to Japan.[5] After the Japanese entry into northern Indo-China the Americans embargoed the export to Japan of all types of scrap iron.

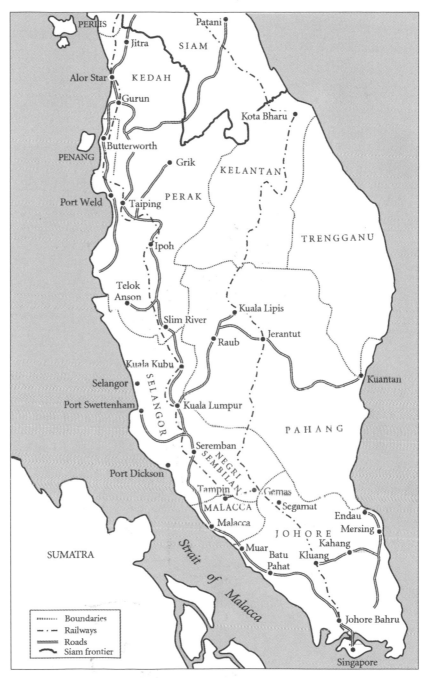

PERLIS
Patani
SIAM
Jitra
Alor Star
KEDAH
Gurun
Kota Bharu
Butterworth
PENANG
Grik
KELANTAN
Port Weld
Taiping
PERAK
Ipoh
TRENGGANU
Telok
Anson
Kuala Lipis
Slim River
Raub
Jerantut
Kuala Kubu
Selangor
SELANGOR
Kuantan
Port Swettenham
Kuala Lumpur
PAHANG
Seremban
NEGRI
SEMBILAN
Port Dickson
Tampin
Gemas
Segamat
MALACCA
Endau
Malacca
Mersing
JOHORE
Kahang
SUMATRA
Muar
Batu
Kluang
Pahat
*Strait of Malacca*

.......... Boundaries
– · – Railways
——— Roads
‿‿‿ Siam frontier

Johore Bahru

Singapore

2. Malaya.

During the spring of 1940 the United States Pacific Fleet shifted its main base from California to Hawaii. Later that year, Congress authorised funds to build a greatly expanded two-ocean navy. The Selective Service Law was also passed to introduce peacetime conscription to America. On 30 November 1940 it was announced that the United States government was to loan $100,000,000 to the Chinese Nationalists to help them resist Japan. The slumbering giant of America was awakening from a long period of relative international isolation.

At Singapore, a joint defence appreciation prepared in October 1940 by British commanders in the Far East suggested that the better part of 566 aircraft and an army garrison of three divisions would be needed to defend the colony. The commanders also requested that British forces be permitted to advance into southern Thailand if the Japanese entered that country.[6] In the Chiefs of Staff's response to the appreciation, the Air Ministry stated that 336 aircraft was the highest target they could work towards during 1941.

In Europe, the threat of the German army across the Channel in northern France was a perpetual anxiety for the British government. All responsible British military leaders were concerned about the possibility of an invasion during the autumn of 1940. By early 1941, however, Churchill and the RAF's Air Chief Marshal Portal were inclined to discount the threat of invasion, believing that the Germans lacked the air and naval superiority required to make a serious attempt. The Chief of the Imperial General Staff, General Sir John Dill, and the First Sea Lord, Admiral Sir Dudley Pound, supported by the Home Force's General Sir Alan Brooke, were nevertheless still of the view that 'the possibility of a German invasion could not be set aside and still existed in a very potent form'.[7]

Throughout 1940–41 Dill was loath to send troops away from Britain. He was one of the leading advocates of continuing to hold the great bulk of the British Army's divisions in the United Kingdom. Yet Dill had claimed in a memorandum written in June 1940 that Singapore was, after the United Kingdom, 'the most important strategic point in the British Empire'. Dill certainly believed in building up the Far East's garrison, but the troops despatched to Malaya were mainly from India and Australia. The 12th Indian Brigade had been added to the garrison late in 1939. The 6th and 8th Indian Brigades arrived late in 1940, and the 22nd Indian and 22nd Australian Brigades arrived early in 1941.

In a directive issued on 28 April 1941, Churchill stated that the chance of war with Japan was remote, and that the Middle East was the second most important theatre behind the United Kingdom. Dill again protested that Singapore was second to Britain and that the Far East's defences were sub-standard. Dill later wrote to Churchill: 'Quite a small addition at Singapore will make all the difference between running a serious risk and achieving full security.' The trouble, though, was that Dill only wanted a better sharing of the Empire's manpower between the Middle East and the Far East.[8] Nobody in London wanted to send formations from Britain to the Far East, least of all Dill. Churchill had to fight hard against his senior military advisers just to get men and equipment out of Britain to the Middle East.

The failure to send British Army formations to Malaya was also a root cause of the RAF's failure to send units to the Far East. The RAF's leaders were still a long way from realizing that their responsibilities in respect to army cooperation applied to formations of the Indian and Dominion armies, as well as the British Army.

In November 1940 a General Headquarters Far East was opened at Singapore. Air Chief Marshal Sir Robert Brooke-Popham was appointed to command both the army and RAF in the Far East. His responsibilities included Burma, Borneo and Hong Kong, in addition to Malaya. Brooke-Popham had no control over the Royal Navy, despite the fact that the Singapore Naval Base was Malaya's principal strategic asset. The appointment of a RAF officer to be the new Commander-in-Chief reflected the air force's importance in the defence of Malaya. Brooke-Popham was sixty-two years old, and had begun his career in the army. After transferring to the infant Royal Flying Corps, he had gone on to hold several of the RAF's highest posts, before retiring to become Governor of Kenya in 1937. He had a high-pitched voice, thinning blond hair and a friendly manner. One of his first tasks was to oversee an improvement in relations between the local RAF and army commanders at Singapore.

In practice Brooke-Popham's arrival saw the army increasingly subordinated to the RAF's plans. Brooke-Popham backed the RAF's scheme to build new aerodromes across Malaya. Given the expanding network of aerodromes, increasing pressure was applied to the army to deploy its strength northwards from Singapore to defend them. The air marshal was also keen to develop an existing plan, if a Japanese attack was imminent, to advance into the Kra Isthmus in southern Thailand. If the army could stop an enemy from establishing aerodromes in the Kra Isthmus there was much to be gained. To clear the air amongst senior commanders at Singapore, Brooke-Popham had Lieutenant-General Bond relieved of his post as GOC Malaya in May 1941. He had found Bond to be uncooperative.[9] The tempestuous Air Vice Marshal Babington was also replaced by Air Vice-Marshal C. W. H. Pulford. In London General Dill was aware of the circumstances of Bond's relief. He decided to send out as replacement a general who had recent experience at Singapore, and who, as a graduate of the Royal Naval Staff College and the Imperial Defence College, understood the need for inter-service cooperation.

The new General Officer Commanding (GOC) Malaya was Lieutenant-General A. E. Percival. Percival had been a protégé and friend of General Dill for some years.[10] Arthur Percival had been born in 1887 in Hertfordshire. After attending Rugby school, he had worked for a trading company in the City of London before volunteering to join the army in 1914, on the outbreak of the First World War. Percival served in France and Flanders from 1915 to 1918 with the 7th and 2nd Bedfordshires, and saw extensive action. In September 1916, during the Somme offensive, he had been wounded by shrapnel in four places leading his company in a general assault on the Schwaben redoubt, beyond the ruins of Thiepval village. After a period in hospital Percival had returned to his battalion the following spring. After another year's grinding combat he had become a battalion commander, and acted as brigade commander on more than one occasion during 1918. In April 1918 Percival's battalion cooperated closely with neighbouring Australian units, a useful experience given what life would later hold for him.

After the First World War Percival saw further service with British forces in north Russia and the Irish Civil War. In 1923 he attended the Staff College. He returned to the Staff College in 1931 as an instructor, having spent time at the Naval Staff College in the intervening period. Percival made a great impression on Dill, who was Staff College commandant. After a spell as commander of the 2nd Cheshires, he went on to attend the Imperial Defence College. In 1936 he was sent to Malaya as GSO 1 on the recommendation of Dill, who had now become Director of Military Operations and Intelligence at the War Office. As Malaya Command's chief staff officer, Percival travelled extensively in the colony and examined the possibilities of an overland attack on Singapore from the north.

Percival returned to England at the end of 1937 to become Brigadier General Staff at Aldershot under Dill's command. The Aldershot corps went to France in 1939 as I Corps. Following promotion to major-general, Percival returned to Britain in February 1940 to command a division under training. By the end of April he had transferred to the War Office as one of three assistants to the CIGS. (Dill was Vice-CIGS at the time.) Percival became GOC 44th Division after its return from Dunkirk, a posting away from the War Office at his own request. At the end of March 1941 he was told of his promotion to lieutenant-general. He left Britain for Malaya on 1 May.

Even a good friend was to concede that 'Arthur Percival was not an easy person to get to know, nor was he in any way a striking personality'. Dill wrote of Percival in a 1932 report: 'He has not altogether an impressive presence and one may therefore fail, on first meeting him, to appreciate his sterling worth.' But Percival, though somewhat reserved, was a courageous and responsible man who had taken his profession very seriously.[11] In appearance he was tall, buck-toothed and lightly built.

In Singapore, at Malaya Command, Percival was assisted by a small staff, most of whom had not undertaken formal staff training. Malaya Command's administrative staff was adequate. The troops would not have been fed, clothed, housed or armed if that had not been so. Likewise there were sufficient operations staff to direct the movements of formations under Percival's command, but training and intelligence gathering were badly neglected due to a shortage of officers to carry out those duties.

III Indian Corps's headquarters was set up in Malaya to control the growing number of Indian formations in the colony about the time of Percival's arrival. The army officer sent to command III Corps was the Indian Army's Lieutenant-General Sir Lewis Heath. Heath was senior to Percival in date of rank but Percival's subordinate in Malaya. This was because Percival had been appointed by London, Heath by New Delhi. The two appointments had been made independently of each other.

Lewis Heath had been born in India in 1885, and had been educated at Wellington. He had joined the Indian Army in 1906, and had suffered a permanent injury to an arm and lost an eye in Mesopotamia during the First World War. Heath never attended the Staff College, but he had been an instructor at the Senior Officers' School at Belgaum during the mid 1930s. He went on to command a brigade in Waziristan during one of the North-West Frontier's frequent tribal revolts. After the outbreak of war, he commanded the 5th Indian Division in a victorious campaign against the Italians in Eritrea in 1940–41. Heath was one of the first Indian Army generals to win a corps command in an overseas theatre during the Second World War. He was very highly regarded in Indian circles.

According to Percival, Heath never showed any outward signs of resenting his relegation. The two men were on friendly but distant terms. It was not unusual for general officers of the British and Indian Armies to work together in a unified command structure. A proportion of senior appointments in the Indian Army were always held by British service officers. Heath, a handsome widower, was soon joined in Malaya by his new fiancée, a New Zealand nurse some years his junior whom he soon married.

General Percival had been placed in command of an army comprising troops drawn from across the British Empire. The parent army of all the Empire's armies and contingents was the British Army. The British Army's regimental system, command structure, operational and training doctrine, senior leadership, staff procedure, equipment and logistic organization set the standard for all other imperial armies. It would have been difficult to build a coherent army out of units from Britain, India, the Dominions and the colonies if they had not had so many things in common.

During the years of peace the bulk of the British Army's Far East garrison was based at Singapore. Officers mixed in the same circles as European businessmen, up-country planters and government officials. Regular 'home' leave meant that by the interwar period service in the colonies was no longer a semi-permanent exile from Britain.

In a parallel world, 'other ranks' lived a far more disciplined and structured existence. Life was unhurried but the army had evolved a routine to fill in a day that commenced early in the morning. There were endless parades for any number of reasons. There was even a church parade on Sundays. Men still wore a pith helmut (sun helmut or *sola topi*) that had been part of a soldier's equipment in the tropics since Victorian times. The hottest hours of the day were spent indoors in large, airy barracks with only limited privacy. A bed, kit box and mosquito net was the full extent of each private soldier's kingdom. Electric fans hanging from the ceiling of the barracks at Tanglin, Changi and elsewhere had replaced the old swinging punkahs. A good deal of sport was played in the late afternoon and early evening. Sunset was at 6.30 p.m. every evening of the year and was swiftly followed by the onset of the equatorial night.

Junior British servicemen were by a considerable margin the poorest Europeans living in the colonies. They certainly did not take part in the high life. Many of the best hotels were out of bounds to other ranks. Yet, in small ways, junior servicemen enjoyed a social status higher than they might have enjoyed in Britain. Native staff were employed for menial tasks around the barracks. Off duty men could visit cinemas, bars, amusement parks, dance halls and the red light districts. Local travel leave was available if a man could afford it, though many could not. Under such conditions marriage was rare among privates, but more common among NCOs and warrant officers, who took up almost all the married quarters available.

In September 1939 the principal infantry units of the Malayan garrison were the 2nd Loyals, 1st Manchesters, 2nd Gordon Highlanders, 2/17th Dogras and 1st Malays. The Manchesters had seen recent active service fighting Arab guerillas in Palestine and had been converted into a machine gun battalion. The 2nd East Surreys arrived from China in 1940 and Major-General F. Keith Simmons, formerly commander of British troops at Shanghai, became GOC Singapore Fortress. Simmons was a tactful and courteous man who did not intrude upon Malaya Command.

Singapore Island was a cramped environment from the standpoint of military training. There were none of the wide open spaces of India or mainland Malaya where large-scale exercises might be conducted. Observers had long noted that the standard of training of units stationed at Singapore declined over time. During 1939–41 British units were forced to send large drafts of regular soldiers back to the United Kingdom to serve in other units of their regiment or corps, and accept less suitable national service conscripts as replacements.[12] During 1940 troops began to clear and wire posts on the beaches along the south coast of Singapore.

Most of the troops who had arrived in Malaya after 1939 were from India. As in the First World War, the Indian Army was deployed overseas to support Britain's war aims. The Indian Army of the interwar period was not a national or nationalist army in the contemporary western sense. Within its ranks there was, however, a sense of region, district and community. At the outbreak of war the Indian Army was a little over 200,000 strong, but by the end of 1941 it had expanded by means of voluntary recruitment to almost 900,000 officers and men (and would expand to over 1,800,000 by the end of 1942). The 4th and 5th Indian Divisions were sent to the Middle East during 1939–40.

After the fall of France the Government of India offered to raise an extra five divisions for overseas service, and planned to raise five more once those first five had departed. During 1940–41 the 6th, 8th and 10th Divisions set sail for the Middle East. The 9th and 11th Divisions were dispatched to Malaya. Expanding any army in a hurry presents problems. In India young recruits had to be taught many elementary skills. Peasants who had grown up amid bullock carts had to become accustomed to lorries, bren gun carriers, mortars, machine guns and radio sets. There were particular problems associated with creating a first-class army out of colonial material, but the British had had generations of experience. Of the colonial powers only the French could hope to do it so well.

The Indian Army was organized on a similar basis to the British Army. An infantry battalion had four rifle companies comprising three platoons each, plus a headquarters company made up of several specialist platoons. Indian Army units had a complex social profile. Indian races noted for their physique, martial self-image and political reliability, such as Dogras, Garhwalis, Mahrattas, Sikhs, Jats, Rajputs, Pathans and Punjabi Muslims, were heavily recruited. Large numbers of Gurkhas were recruited from Nepal, beyond the northern border of India. In rural communities military service was an honourable profession, and brought an important supplement to a family's agricultural income.

In practice the peacetime Indian Army was drawn from less than 5 per cent of the Indian population, and had very strong ties to the Punjab province. Carefully targeted recruiting in districts with strong associations with the British-Indian government made up for the fact that both crown and nation were hazy concepts. Soldiers ('sepoys') were often enlisted from the same families and villages as existing soldiers. Sepoys were usually recruited young, subject to strict physical standards. They grew to manhood within the world of the army. Training, discipline, group pride, tradition, careerism and known leaders made up the glue that held Indian units together. During the world wars traditional recruiting areas, and similar ethnic groups in neighbouring districts, were recruited to saturation point. These men dominated the infantry. Recruiting was later extended to parts of India not usually enlisted; these men generally went into the support arms.

Most infantry battalions comprised a mix of different Indian races and religions, each organised into a separate company as a safeguard against mutiny. The Gurkhas, 17th Dogras and 18th Garhwal Rifles were the principal exceptions to this arrangement. (Even the 11th Sikhs contained a Punjabi Muslim minority). Each community had its own holidays, eating arrangements and reinforcement stream. But this complex structure was mostly unnecessary. The only significant mutiny in the Indian Army between the famous 1857 mutiny and 1941 had been when half the 5th Light Infantry had run amuck at Singapore in 1915. (Almost a hundred mutineers were killed or executed in the course of crushing the mutiny.)

The senior half of an Indian battalion's officers were holders of a King's Commission, twelve to sixteen at full strength. KCOs came out to India from Britain. They were all British apart from a small number of Indians who had attended Royal Military Academy Sandhurst, and a small minority from the Dominions. Officers of the Indian Army had high responsibilities given their lack of numbers. They were given pay bonuses for passing compulsory Indian language exams, and gradually learnt a great deal about their sepoys by living amongst them.

At the close of the First World War Indians began to receive King's Commissions. A small number of places were made available for Indians at Sandhurst from 1919. But the 'Indianisation' of the officer corps was a very slow process between the world wars, though it was appreciably speeded up when an officer training academy was opened at Dehra Dun in 1932. Graduates from Dehra Dun were known as 'Indian Commissioned Officers'. By 1939 one in seven officers serving with the Indian Army was an Indian, and these were concentrated in certain units. (The 'Indianised' units to serve in Malaya were the 5/2nd Punjabis, 5/11th Sikhs, 1/14th Punjabis,

4/19th Hyderabads and 3rd Cavalry). In Malaya the segregation of races was more vigorously practised than in India. Indian officers who had expected to be treated like their British counterparts of the same rank were often offended to varying degrees.

Two special types of officers, called jemadars and subedars and holding a Viceroy's Commission, comprised the junior half of an Indian unit's officers. VCOs were Indians promoted from the ranks, usually after at least ten years' service. These men were junior to all officers with King's or Indian commissions, but wore the same rank insignia as lieutenants and captains. Jemadars commanded platoons, and a subedar was the senior VCO in a company. The senior VCO in a battalion was the subedar-major. VCOs were the principal link between the army's mostly British officers and the sepoys. So far as the sepoys were concerned the VCOs were fully-fledged officers in every sense. One shortcoming of the VCO system was that, without the western education that British and Indian officers took for granted, even the most talented VCO was to some extent isolated from his superiors by culture, language and some aspects of training.

Prior to 1939 a single Indian battalion had been attached to the peacetime garrison of Malaya (2/17th Dogras). The first of a steady stream of Indian formations to arrive in Malaya was the 12th Indian Brigade, deployed late in 1939. The 12th Brigade's British infantry unit was the 2nd Argyll and Sutherland Highlanders. The Argylls had left the United Kingdom back in 1927 and had been posted to the West Indies, Hong Kong, China and various stations in India. They had seen active service against tribesmen of the North-West Frontier of India in 1935 and again in 1937. In October 1940 the 6th Brigade arrived, followed by the 8th Brigade in November, the 15th Brigade in March 1941, the 22nd Brigade in April, and the 28th (Gurkha) Brigade in September 1941. The 15th Brigade's British battalion was the 1st Leicesters, which had left Britain in 1925 for Egypt, Cyprus and India, including active service in tribal Waziristan in 1938–39.

As already noted, Lieutenant-General Heath's III Indian Corps headquarters was established in Malaya in May 1941. The 11th Indian Division's headquarters became operational late in 1940 to control the 6th, 15th, and later the 28th Brigades. The 11th Division's commander was Major-General D. M. Murray-Lyon, an expert bagpiper and keen smoker of cigarettes imported from Aden. He had spent the First World War with a British regiment, prior to transferring to the Indian Army and the 4th Gurkhas in 1925. Murray-Lyon had won the Distinguished Service Order and the Military Cross, but he had not attended the Staff College. In a campaign against tribesmen in Waziristan in 1937 he had been a successful battalion commander. Rather like Heath, Murray-Lyon had been promoted a general

on the basis of his practical record as a troop leader. The headquarters of
the 9th Indian Division was opened early in 1941 to command the 8th and
22nd Brigades. The 9th Division's commander was Major-General Arthur
Barstow, a graduate of both the Staff and Imperial Defence Colleges.

In February 1941 the first Australian troops arrived at Singapore on the
*Queen Mary* – the 22nd Brigade of the 8th Division. Australia was one of
the Dominions of the British Empire, and had immediately followed Britain
into war with Germany in September 1939. To Australia Britain was very
much the mother country. As in the First World War, Australians had
flocked to volunteer for the armed forces. Almost all Australians were of
relatively recent British descent. Britain was Australia's main source of culture, information, trade and diplomatic representation. Australians drew
great strength from the knowledge that they inhabited a privileged province
of the greatest empire on earth.[13]

During the 'Phoney War' period, prior to the German invasion of France,
recruitment to the Australian Imperial Force (AIF) was slow. In January
1940 there were only 811 enlistments, and a mere 217 the next month.
Meantime the Royal Australian Air Force was besieged by applicants. But
as France fell, and the British Expeditionary Force was evacuated at Dunkirk,
recruitment shot up to 48,496 in June 1940, 21,022 in July, and 32,524 in
August.[14] In a crisis, conscription was unnecessary. Officers and NCOs
transferred across from the militia to give the AIF a cadre of trained men.
By early 1941 the 6th, 7th and 9th Australian Divisions had left for the Middle
East. In North Africa, Greece, Crete, and later Syria, Australian divisions
played key roles in a series of battles to augment the military reputation
acquired by their fathers in the 1914–18 war.

The appointment of the AIF's senior officers had presented difficulties.
Australia had no regular army formations, and it was no longer acceptable
to appoint a British general to command Australians directly. Senior Australian militia officers, and a handful of Australian regulars holding down
administrative appointments, were thus the only candidates.

Lieutenant-General T. Blamey was chosen to command the AIF in the
Middle East. He had been chief staff officer of the Australian Corps in France
in 1918. But Blamey was no Monash. His chief accomplishment in the Middle
East was to upset the British by demanding the premature withdrawal of
the 9th Division from Tobruk in order to reassert his personal command
over the formation. Yet the Australian divisional commanders in the Middle
East, Mackay, Lavarack and Morshead, were all adjudged to be successes.

One of the most senior generals on the Australian Army List at the outbreak
of war was Major-General H. Gordon Bennett. In 1939 Bennett had probably

hoped to command the AIF. During the early months of the war Bennett was passed over for command on several occasions. Command of the 6th, 7th and 8th Divisions all went to other officers promoted over Bennett's head. Bennett's argumentative temperament alarmed those familiar with the level of cooperation and trust demanded of senior generals in an allied command. On 13 August 1940, however, the Australian Army's Chief of the General Staff was killed in an aeroplane crash, and the GOC 8th Division was promoted to take his place. Bennett was in turn appointed to the 8th Division. He finally got command of a formation bound for 'overseas'.

Bennett had been born in 1887 in Melbourne, his grandparents having emigrated from England in the 1850s. After leaving school, he became an actuarial clerk. As a young man of middling height and thinning red hair, he had joined the militia in 1908. When the federal government introduced compulsory military service, Bennett, a wiry and energetic man, secured rapid promotion in the expanded militia. He had become a major at the age of twenty-five, whereas a competent British regular officer might not have reached that rank until he was over forty.

Upon the outbreak of war in 1914 the AIF's 6th Battalion was raised within the area of Bennett's militia regiment, and he became its second-in-command. At Gallipoli the 6th Battalion suffered appalling losses. Bennett was shot in the shoulder and wrist on the opening day of the landing, and his younger brother was killed as a sergeant in the same unit. He became commander of the 6th Battalion before the end of the Gallipoli campaign and led it to France in 1916. During 1917–18 he commanded a brigade with distinction.

Bennett had a successful business career between the world wars, and had at various stages been an assistant actuary, a public accountant, company director, sole commissioner of the city of Sydney, and president of the Associated Chambers of Manufacturers of Australia. *The Times* correspondent, Ian Morrison, later wrote of Bennett: 'He was a rasping, bitter, sarcastic person, given to expressing his views with great freedom. As a result he quarrelled with a great number of people. But he did have a forceful personality. He was imbued with a tough, ruthless, aggressive spirit.' [15] Bennett had little time for staff-trained officers, and believed that only a citizens' militia could breed well-rounded fighting leaders. He had had little military training or experience since the First World War. On the unattached list since the early 1930s, he had upset a number of senior officers by attacking the organization of the Australian military in the press in 1937.

The arrival of the 8th Australian Division's advance guard introduced a new element to Malaya. Lieutenant-Colonel C. G. W. Anderson heard a wife of a British official claim that the local inhabitants had sent their wives, children and goats to the hills when they got news that the Australians were coming.[16] Major M. Ashkanasy of the 8th Division's headquarters recorded:

> the Australians were very much glamorised and out of this developed the anta-
> gonism towards Australians on the part of British troops that many of us tried
> to combat at every point. It was not overt but you began to sense that the people
> who'd been there a long while did not like the idea that now the Australians had
> arrived everything would be alright.[17]

Press reports, fuelled by government propaganda designed to talk up Malaya's defences, spoke of the arrival of 'a huge force of matchless Australians, the peerless Anzacs', 'the finest shock troops in the world'. Disparities in pay and the level of aid given by comfort funds and leave clubs further strained Anglo-Australian relations in Malaya. Captain G. Round noted that Australian soldiers on leave ran foul of British military police intent on enforcing strict dress and behaviour regulations designed to preserve the prestige of the white man in Asia.[18]

Of course many people were pleased to see the Australians arrive. After his first visit to the 22nd Brigade, Brooke-Popham noted that, although the Australians had different standards regarding smartness of turnout, and were rather sparing in the use of 'sir', their fresh outlook was stimulating. He thought that 'the real reason is that they regard the preparation for war not as a sort of incident in normal peace-time routine, which is somewhat the attitude of the professional soldier, but as a practical reality which is at present the sole aim and object of their life'.[19]

The social composition of the AIF was profoundly influenced by the practice of voluntary recruitment. In Britain conscription systematically diverted the best and the brightest into the air force, navy, munitions industry and the technical arms of the army. The infantry ran almost last in the manpower stakes. The beauty of voluntary recruitment was that it enabled the infantry to get a fair share of the keenest servicemen.

Australian battalions had anonymous number titles, and large recruiting zones, but the men who chose to enlist had much in common. The 2/20th Battalion is believed to have had twenty-six sets of brothers. In another battalion a former commanding officer later calculated that his unit had had nineteen pairs of brothers, of whom one or both of almost all the pairs was destined to die, including a father and two sons.[20] This was only the tip of the iceberg. Each unit contained a network of relationships based on family, friends, school, work, shire and suburb that could never have existed if non-territorial conscription had been enforced.

Voluntary recruitment permitted an infantry battalion to assemble a set of high calibre NCOs who could genuinely act as another level of combat leaders. NCOs capable of more than just drill and administration could transform a unit's drive and flexibility. Half the AIF's men were twenty-five or over. Junior officers had to be older than in the British Army. The less formal social manner of the Australians altered relations between junior officers and men, as did the almost complete absence of regular soldiers. Junior officers had to be more consultative than might otherwise have been the case. Open communication between officers and men was, however, a godsend for tactical innovation. Australian soldiers enjoyed above average physique, though no better than men from other Dominions and the United States. When men were operating at the absolute limit of human endurance, good physique was a real advantage.

The 8th Australian Division's sector was in Johore state. A great deal of time was devoted to weapons training, field craft and tactics. With less of an emphasis on drill and turnout, the discipline of an Australian unit depended on intensive field training. Officers sent to visit British and Indian units soon found that nobody, with the possible exception of the 2nd Argylls, had thought much about how best to fight a war in dense plantation and jungle. British officers were still a little too keen to keep their men out of the midday sun.

Until the 27th Australian Brigade's arrival in August 1941, Brigadier H. B. Taylor's 22nd Australian Brigade was General Bennett's only formation. (The 23rd Brigade remained in Australia, and was later sent to Darwin and the Dutch East Indies.) Taylor was a distinguished scientist in civilian life, and had been an infantry captain in the AIF in the First World War. Tension quickly developed between Taylor and Bennett. Bennett noted in his diary in March: 'Had words with Taylor. He resents receiving orders and does his best to thwart me. He stated that he was well equipped mentally for his job, that I knew nothing and that the last war was useless experience.'[21] Taylor, who possessed a first-rate mind, took a keen interest in the mostly unstudied tactical problems of jungle warfare. He had trouble taking a commander seriously who took little care to follow developments in contemporary warfare. This view is entirely borne out by the contents of Bennett's diary, which reveal a man mostly concerned by promotional intrigue, ceremony and day to day trivia. A company commander in the 22nd Brigade, Major C. B. O'Brien of the 2/18th Battalion, later claimed he only saw Bennett three times in Malaya.

> On one occasion at the conclusion of a brigade exercise under divisional direction, the GOC made a criticism which consisted practically entirely of the deplorable training of officers' batmen and of the necessity of running a school for officers' batmen. That was the only criticism I heard him give of any of our exercises.

Taylor even suspected that Bennett paid attention to the movements of 'the stars' when making military decisions.[22]

The 27th Brigade's commander had fallen ill prior to its arrival at Singapore. The senior battalion commander in the brigade, Lieutenant-Colonel F. G. Galleghan, assumed that he would take over. Galleghan was the son of a Newcastle wharf crane driver, and was to a small extent of West Indian origin. He had been a sergeant in France and Flanders in 1917–18, but was commissioned in the militia after the war and had become a lieutenant-colonel by 1932, in addition to working his way up to a middling rank in the civil service. A big martinet of a man, Galleghan was furious when he heard that Bennett had promoted Lieutenant-Colonel D. S. Maxwell of the 2/19th Battalion to command the brigade. Bennett favoured Maxwell as the latter had already been in Malaya for several months. Maxwell, an AIF captain in the First World War and at 6 foot 3 inches a giant of a man for his generation, had trained as a doctor in the 1920s and had only recently returned to combatant duty in the militia. Maxwell later recounted: 'When I went aboard [the ship from which the 27th Brigade was disembarking] Galleghan welcomed me with, "Well you needn't expect me to congratulate you on the red flannel you're wearing"'.[23] Internecine conflict within the hierarchy of the 8th Australian Division was well underway at more than one level.

# 4

## *Preparations for War*

As 1940 made way for 1941, the prospects of peace in the Far East went from bad to worse. Japan's Foreign Minister Matsuoka left for Europe on 12 March 1941. Matsuoka achieved little of substance in Berlin and broke his homeward journey at Moscow. On 13 April a five-year neutrality pact was signed between Japan and the Soviet Union. Matsuoka did not even bother to consult his colleagues in Tokyo before signing the pact. As Germany had a non-aggression pact with the Soviets, why should not also Japan?

On 22 June the Germans invaded the Soviet Union. Japan was given little advance warning of Germany's attack, otherwise Japan might have supported its Axis partners by attacking the Soviet Union in the Far East. Indeed, Matsuoka wanted to go to war with the Soviets and help defeat them before any sort of United States-Soviet alliance could be formed. But other key figures in the government advocated a wait and see approach. The army was not keen on opening a second major land war in Asia.

There is no question that the German invasion of the Soviet Union changed the situation in east Asia. With the Russians occupied fending off the Nazis, Japan was now free to consider a more aggressive penetration of South-East Asia. Japanese diplomacy in east Asia during the opening months of 1941 had been cautious, possibly in anticipation of a German attempt to overwhelm Britain.[1] But now that the Soviet menace had receded, it was the time for action. On 2 July, the Imperial Conference in Tokyo agreed to 'construct the Greater East Asia Co-prosperity Sphere regardless of the changes in the world situation'.[2] Japan would continue the war in China, await developments in regard to the Soviets, and prepare for expansion into South-East Asia. The next step into South-East Asia was to be the establishment of bases in southern Indo-China. Part of the motivation behind that step was the need to prepare for a possible war with the western powers.

On 14 July 1941 the French authorities in Indo-China were given another set of Japanese demands, which were accepted on 23 July. The first of tens of thousands of Japanese troops began to enter the southern part of the colony. Japanese warships were based at coastal ports, and the air force stationed units around Saigon. Once ensconced in southern Indo-China the

Japanese were closer to Singapore, the Philippines and Dutch East Indies than ever before. In the meantime a new Konoye cabinet was formed in Tokyo without Matsuoka, who had been removed from office as he was believed to be too pro-German.

The United States reacted strongly to Japan's latest act of aggression on the Asian mainland. On 25 July the United States effectively banned the export of oil and other materials that had been fuelling the Japanese war machine for years. An asset freeze was introduced, which meant in practice that Japan could not obtain the dollars needed to buy American goods, many of which were now subject to a system of export licensing.[3] Surprised British and Dutch governments quickly followed suit. During the 1930s half of Japan's oil had been imported from America. But by 1940–41 Japan was importing 80 per cent of its oil from America, and another 10 per cent from the East Indies. The Japanese had been stockpiling oil, but had only enough for eighteen months usage at normal rates.

The American imposition of trade sanctions was a terrible surprise to the Japanese government. They had not regarded the occupation of Indo-China as a *casus belli*. Some influential government figures had felt that America would only stir when British interests were directly threatened. But American actions had been taken in the context of recently made decisions to provide additional aid to Britain, the Soviet Union and China. The Americans could not keep 'subsidising' the Japanese war effort whilst opposing diplomatically and economically both German expansion in Europe and Japan's presence in China. About this time it was also decided to station volunteer American airmen in China, and reorganise and reinforce a new Far East Command in the Philippines.

An increased level of support from the United States, and the entry of the Soviets into the war, improved Britain's strategic position in Europe, but senior British generals did not substantially change their assessment of the situation during 1941. Late in June the CIGS, General Dill, was telling his colleagues that an invasion of Britain was still a distinct possibility, and that no further risks could be run in home defence.[4] As Major-General John Kennedy, the War Office's Director of Military Operations and Intelligence, explained in his memoirs, the War Office did not expect the Soviets to last long against the might of the German army that had so easily conquered France. In theory there was ample time for the German army to beat the Soviets and return to western Europe to invade Britain before winter. General Sir Alan Brooke, GOC Home Forces, noted that the opinion 'shared by most people, was that Russia would not last long, possibly three or four months, possibly longer'.

As 1941 wore on it became apparent that the Soviets were holding on, and that no invasion of Britain would be possible that year. In September Vice-CIGS Lieutenant-General Sir Henry Pownall agreed with that view, 'But I think it probable that an attempt will be made in the spring'.[5] The War Office was determined not to run any risk in so far as the defence of the United Kingdom was concerned. In December 1941 there were twenty-nine mobile divisions in the United Kingdom, all of which were British but for two Canadian divisions. Of nineteen divisions outside Britain, and principally in the Middle East, all but five divisions were from the Empire.[6]

*Deployment of Mechanised British Empire Army Divisions,*
*December 1941*

|                     | United Kingdom | Middle East | Persia-Iraq | Far East |
|---------------------|----------------|-------------|-------------|----------|
| Armoured Divisions  | 6              | 3           | 0           | 0        |
| UK Infantry         | 21             | 2           | 0           | 0        |
| Dominion Infantry   | 2              | 6           | 0           | 1        |
| Indian Infantry     | 0              | 2           | 3           | 2        |

As the Germans advanced further into the Soviet Union, the British government decided to send military aid to Russia. Convoys carrying aircraft, tanks and other equipment began sailing to Russia via the Arctic Circle. It has been claimed that this made it difficult to send equipment to other theatres, including the Far East. But there were never any concrete plans in 1941 to send armour to the Far East, despite rising tensions with Japan. Given the reluctance of Dill, Brooke and other generals to deploy British formations overseas, it was very much to Churchill's credit that a tank force was built up in Egypt large enough to relieve Tobruk successfully towards the end of 1941. The tanks and other army equipment sent to Russia were taken from the Home Forces. Likewise the shipping of aircraft to Russia from reserve stocks had little bearing on the movement of formed units out of the United Kingdom.

The trouble with the War Office's strategic assessment of 1941 was that British aerial and naval forces enjoyed superiority around the United Kingdom, and there was little practical prospect of invasion. Indeed the Germans had not seriously considered invading Britain since the spring of 1940. Dill was told in November 1941 that he would be relieved the following month when he reached the age of sixty. He was very tired, but Admiral Sir Dudley Pound, the First Sea Lord, was already sixty-four and in genuinely bad health. Churchill had finally run out of patience with Dill's lukewarm suport for the Middle East theatre. Dill later spoke to his successor Brooke about the possibility of Japan entering the war.

> He [Dill] had told me [Brooke] frankly that he had done practically nothing to meet this threat. He said that we were already so weak on all fronts that it was impossible to denude them any further to meet a possible threat. I think he was quite right in his dispositions and that he could not have done more to meet the probable Japanese entry into the war.[7]

As Brooke so wholeheartedly agreed with Dill, the War Office's institutional neglect of the Far East was unaltered by the former's replacement of the latter.

Dill had been replaced, but his protégé Percival was just beginning his posting at Singapore. Early in August 1941 Percival had told the War Office that his minimum requirements in Malaya were five divisions and an armoured brigade. In late August and September the 27th Australian and 28th Indian Brigades reached Singapore, the last significant formations Percival's army was due to receive that year. III Corps's divisional reconnaissance regiment, the 3rd Cavalry, arrived in October. The 5th, 88th and 137th Field Regiments, and 80th Anti-Tank Regiment, were due to arrive late in November and early December. By November 1941 Percival had only four under strength divisions under his command.

The RAF was even less supportive of the Far East than the War Office. Brooke-Popham was displeased that the Air Ministry was doing little to make good its promises to build up the RAF in Malaya. The elderly air marshal complained that the army would receive little aerial support if the situation did not quickly improve. A handful of new fighter squadrons forming in Malaya were still equipped with American-built Buffaloes, which had been rejected for service in Britain. The Air Ministry belatedly informed Brooke-Popham that it would not be possible to do much before the end of 1941:

> we have had to face disappointments in production both at home and in USA and to undertake accelerated programme of expansion in the Middle East. At present time we are having to reinforce Middle East still further to meet probable scale of attack in Spring. Necessity to provide aircraft to support Russia and offset her loss of production capacity likely to impose further strain on British and American resources. In these circumstances it is not possible (repeat not possible) to give you firm programme of air force reinforcements but it is clear that we shall not repeat not be able to complete target programme nor indeed to give you any substantial reinforcement before the end of the year.[8]

The Air Ministry's list of excuses was both lengthy and comprehensive. RAF strength in Malaya would only reach 158 aircraft towards the end of 1941, with another eighty-eight in reserve.[9]

During September 1941 Duff Cooper, formerly the Minister of Information, was sent out to Singapore to study the problems of civil-military coordination. On 5 November Brooke-Popham was informed by Churchill that he was to be relieved of command by 'an army officer with up-to-date experience'. As far back as August the Governor of Burma, Sir Reginald Dorman-Smith, had asked that Brooke-Popham be replaced by a younger man, and Duff Cooper in October had penned the view that the Commander-in-Chief was 'damned near gaga'.[10] After some discussion, it was decided to send Vice-CIGS Pownall to Singapore to take Brooke-Popham's place. Pownall did not want the post, and suspected that he was being pushed out of the way to free up his billet at the War Office for one of Churchill's favourites. It was, however, going to take many weeks to ship and fly Pownall to the Far East. In the meantime Brooke-Popham, his confidence badly shaken, remained at his post. His impending departure was still a secret, yet news of it leaked out and was widely known in senior official circles.

Since late August Churchill had been urging the Admiralty to send a small force of capital ships to Singapore. It took a good deal of arm twisting at the Admiralty and Defence Committee to push the plan through in the face of considerable service opposition. The Admiralty's preferred plan had been gradually to build up a fleet in the Indian Ocean during 1942. By the latter half of October the modern battleship *Prince of Wales* had been ordered to join the old battlecruiser *Repulse*, already heading towards the Far East.

Churchill always conceded that the creation of a Far Eastern Squadron was as much a political as a naval gesture. The *Prince of Wales* and *Repulse* 'had been sent to those waters [the Far East] to exercise that kind of vague menace which capital ships of the highest quality whose whereabouts is unknown can impose upon all hostile naval calculations'. The *Bismarck* had been sunk in May 1941, but as the German warships *Scharnhorst*, *Gneisenau* and *Prinz Eugen* were at Brest on the west coast of France, and the *Tirpitz* and *Admiral Scheer* were believed to be ready to sail, the Royal Navy was hard pressed to spare more than two capital ships after meeting the needs of the Home Fleet, Gibraltar and the Mediterranean Fleet. The fleet aircraft carrier *Indomitable* was to join the battleships but she ran aground at Jamaica on 3 November and had to undertake repairs. No other large carrier was available.

The Vice-Chief of the Naval Staff, Sir Tom Phillips, was appointed to command the Far Eastern Squadron (Force Z). He was promoted two steps from rear-admiral to acting admiral. Phillips was pallid in colour, five feet two inches tall, and weighed barely nine stone. He was, however, decisive, opinionated, a hard taskmaster, at times abrasive, yet sociable enough to have a wide network of friends and contacts throughout the navy. Phillips had served on cruisers in the Mediterranean and Far East during the First World War, and was a protégé of Admiral Pound, the First Sea Lord, who had already promoted Phillips out of turn to be Vice-Chief of the Naval Staff.

News of Phillips's appointment to Force Z straight from a long string of staff postings was not popular in naval circles.[11] Vice-Admiral Sir Andrew Cunningham, the Commander-in-Chief in the Mediterranean, commented: 'What on earth is Phillips going to the Far Eastern squadron for? He hardly knows one end of a ship from the other.' Vice-Admiral Sir James Somerville, in command of H Force at Gibraltar, 'shuddered to think of the Pocket Napoleon' going out to the East. 'All the tricks to learn and no solid sea experience to fall back on.'[12] Phillips's promotion had been necessary partly because the Royal Navy of 1941 was so small. In an earlier generation an experienced seagoing vice-admiral in command of one of the Home Fleet's battle squadrons could have been appointed, but the Home Fleet of 1941 had only a handful of capital ships.

Phillips was old-fashioned doctrinally in so far as he still believed the battleship to be the supreme weapon of war at sea. Back in 1938 'Bomber' Harris had quipped: 'Tom, when the first bomb hits, you'll say, "My God, what a hell of a mine".'[13] Like many senior Royal Navy officers, the losses suffered off Norway and Crete had caused Phillips to modify his views. But none of the Royal Navy's capital ships lost at sea during the war so far had fallen prey to aircraft. There was reason to believe that the cripplingly high level of losses around Crete had been due to freakishly heavy German attacks.

The *Prince of Wales* left the Clyde on 25 October, arriving at Cape Town on 16 November. A newly launched ship, she was very hot aboard in a tropical climate, as she had been designed for service in the North Atlantic. She had been with the battlecruiser *Hood* when the latter exploded during an engagement with the *Bismarck* and *Prinz Eugen* in May 1941. Under the command of Captain John Leach, she had scored the hit on the *Bismarck* which had caused an oil leak that set in motion the chain of events that led directly to the German ship's destruction. After repairs, the *Prince of Wales* had taken Churchill to a meeting with President Roosevelt in August 1941. The battleship's crew had also had some useful live anti-aircraft gunnery practice on a convoy run into the western Mediterranean in September.

The *Repulse*, an aged veteran launched in 1916, was already in the Indian Ocean on convoy duty. The *Repulse*'s Captain W. G. Tennant had been Beachmaster during the Dunkirk evacuation, but the ship herself had seen little action in either war against Germany. The old 'R' Class battleship

*Revenge* was also in the Indian Ocean, but it was not planned to add her to Phillips's squadron as she was too slow and poorly built to fight a modern capital ship. The small aircraft carrier *Hermes* was due for a refit at Simonstown in South Africa, and she was also considered too old to work with Force Z.[14]

At Singapore, Force Z's ultimate destination, Percival was busy disposing his army to defend Malaya. The 9th Indian Division's two brigades, the 8th and 22nd, were posted on the west coast at Kota Bharu and Kuantan respectively, principally to defend the aerodromes recently built there. In north-east Malaya the 11th Indian Division's 6th and 15th Brigade's were based near Jitra, from where they could either advance into Thailand towards Singora, as part of an operation code-named Matador, or take up a defensive position to shield Alor Star aerodrome. They would be joined by the 28th Indian Brigade in either eventuality. Operation Matador was believed to need four brigades in dry weather, but was feasible with only three brigades in the wet season. The 12th Indian Brigade was in reserve south of Kuala Lumpur. The dispositions of III Indian Corps had thus been heavily determined by the RAF's requirements.

The two Australian brigades, the 22nd and 27th, were stationed in Johore, and at Singapore the garrison fielded another two brigades of regular troops. By 1 December the army garrison of Malaya had reached over 91,000, and would be boosted by the arrival of another small convoy before 7 December.[15]

Throughout 1941 the training of the forces gathering in Malaya had been handicapped by a lack of direction from Malaya Command, and by the need for troops to do extensive labouring work on defences being built in their areas of responsibility. Formations in Malaya were also still in the process of having their equipment upgraded to a standard taken for granted in other theatres of war. An officer of a Punjabi regiment noted that his unit was forced to train with wooden anti-tank rifles and to maintain a supply of Molotov cocktails. Instead of using radio sets, signallers often trained with lamps, flags and heliographs. There was also little practice ammunition for mortars. Some weapons did not arrive until very late in 1941. Units arriving from India were particularly behind in terms of acquiring new equipment. Bren gun carriers, sub-machine guns and large lorries all had to be absorbed by infantry units accustomed to a far narrower range of equipment. Matters were not helped by the inexperience of many units' officers and NCOs. One battalion had only two officers with more than seven years' experience. All the rest had less than four years' service.[16]

At Malaya Command's headquarters Brigadier Simson, Percival's Chief Royal Engineer, found bundles of War Office pamphlets on the subject of anti-tank defence lying in cupboards. When informed, Percival told Simson to produce a single booklet summarizing the pamphlets, but the resulting booklet was only incompletely distributed at the eleventh hour.

Outwardly at least the garrison of Malaya remained optimistic. The commander of the 2nd Argyll and Sutherland Highlanders told Brooke-Popham, 'I do hope, Sir, we are not getting too strong in Malaya because if so the Japanese may never attempt a landing'. An Australian battalion commander opined that his men deserved a better enemy than the Japanese.[17] Early in September 1941 an officer arriving in the Far East noted:

> Entering Singapore produced a comforting feeling of security. Uniforms of all kinds were to be seen everywhere. Aeroplanes droned incessantly overhead, and at night the sky was streaked with the pale beams of searchlights. There was the great Naval Base ... By day and night one heard firing practice from the fifteen-inch guns which defended the island.[18]

In lectures troops were told that the Japanese were small, myopic and technically backward. Popular cartoon images of the Japanese promoted the idea of tiny, strutting men in glasses brandishing swords, with buck-toothed grins and slanted slits for eyes. The British military attaché at the Tokyo embassy complained after a visit to Malaya: 'our chaps place the Japs somewhere between the Italians and Afghans'. There were few British experts on the Japanese military, and the Imperial Japanese Army's relative isolation from European military culture made it difficult to assess its efficiency.[19] Japan's failure to defeat China had not impressed European soldiers. Even in Anglo-American governmental circles there was a feeling that Japan had only a fragile economy that was falling towards bankruptcy due to a shortage of raw materials and the morass of the war in China.

On 1 October Brooke-Popham reported hopefully to the War Office:

> Japan is now concentrating her forces against the Russians and cannot suddenly change this into a concentration in south although she could still dispatch a sea-borne expedition from Japanese waters without our knowledge. Nevertheless we reiterate our view that the last thing Japan wants at this juncture is a campaign in the south.[20]

Preparations for Operation Matador, a pre-emptive invasion of southern Thailand to forstall a Japanese occupation, still continued. Upwards of thirty officers were sent into Thailand with civilian identities for reconnaissance purposes.

The state of Anglo-Japanese relations, however, was of limited importance compared with the ongoing diplomatic problems between Japan and America. Britain took for granted American leadership in the western powers confrontation with Japan. President Roosevelt and Prime Minister Churchill met at Newfoundland from 9 to 14 August 1941 – the 'Atlantic Conference'. In the course of the discussions Churchill proposed that the United States, Britain and the Dutch issue parallel warnings to the Japanese regarding further aggressive action in the region. The United States delegation agreed with the proposal but in practice the American government was opposed to any further provocation of the Japanese. Ultimately only a vague warning was given to the Japanese Ambassador in Washington.[21]

In north-east Asia, the Japanese supreme command built up its strength in Manchuria in preparation for war with the Soviet Union. But German operations in western Russia had not been decisive and Soviet forces in Siberia remained strong. Early in August the military accepted that war with the Soviets was not practical that year.

At a 6 September meeting of the Imperial Conference, in the presence of the Emperor, it was decided to complete war preparations by the end of October, whilst negotiations with the United States continued. Admiral Nagano Osami, the Chief of Naval Operations, explained that Japan could do nothing and collapse in a few years, or go to war whilst there was still a 70–80 per cent chance of initial victory.[22] The only alternative to being slowly strangled by the trade embargo, or bowing to the Americans' demands, was to fight a war against the western powers to seize the raw materials of South-East Asia, in particular the oil of the Dutch East Indies.

Prime Minister Konoye was keen to pursue negotiations with the United States. Across the closing months of 1941 the United States and Japan tried to reach an agreement to end the trade embargo. But the United States would not let Japan have oil unless they undertook a humiliating withdrawal on the Asian mainland. The Americans' terms were harsh as they did not want to let down the Chinese Nationalists. On 14 October Army Minister Tojo firmly told the cabinet that widespread troop withdrawals in China were not acceptable to his service. Retreat would endanger Japan's position in Manchuria, Korea and any benefits reaped from the 'China Incident'. The nation would return to being the 'Little Japan' before the Manchurian Incident.[23] On 16 October the cabinet resigned, as it was unwilling to launch a fresh war.

On 17 October General Hideki Tojo became Japanese Prime Minister. He also continued as War Minister. That an army general was made Prime Minister, at the direction of the Emperor's advisers, reflected the true power the army had built up in Japanese politics over the past decade. The army had become Japan's collective dictator.[24] Tojo was the army's representative at the summit of power.

At a conference in Tokyo on 1–2 November the civilian foreign and finance ministers were against war with the United States, but both the army and navy were in favour. The navy was concerned about the falling oil reserves and the army foresaw ever-increasing American aid to China. It was decided to pursue negotiations only until midnight 30 November.[25] The timing of the attack on South-East Asia and the Pacific was also partly determined by the approaching winter monsoons. At an Imperial Conference on 1 December, General Tojo advised that war was necessary to preserve the Japanese Empire. Subordinate headquarters were sent orders to confirm that hostilities would commence on 8 December (or 7 December east of the international date line).

Japan's war planners wanted to build an empire so large that the western powers would be unable to stomach the cost of retaking it inch by inch. The Japanese government hoped their Axis partners would prevail over the Soviets and Britain in Europe, after which a negotiated peace could be made with an isolated United States and a withered Chungking regime. The anti-war rhetoric and apparent divisions in American politics suggested that Washington might be amenable to a negotiated peace. The Japanese plan depended to a dangerous degree upon the Germans triumphing in Europe. It was a tremendous gamble.

A key figure in the planning process was Admiral Yamamoto Isoroku, the Commander-in-Chief of Japan's Combined Fleet. Yamamoto knew that Japan had only a limited chance of winning a prolonged conflict. He was not enthusiastic about the idea of war with America. But the change of base of the United States Pacific Fleet to Hawaii had opened up the possibility of a pre-emptive strike. If Japan could in one blow knock out America's main offensive weapon, it might buy enough time to forge a viable Pacific empire.

Could a surprise attack across three thousand miles of ocean succeed? Yamamoto remembered Japan's surprise attack on Port Arthur, in the 1904 war with Russia. The admiral had a background in naval aviation, and the recent success of British carrier biplanes against the Italian fleet at Taranto on 11 November 1940 lent further encouragement. Plans were set in motion to develop a torpedo that could be dropped to run in the shallow waters of Pearl Harbor. Yamamoto was confident of initial success, but he was not optimistic in the medium term. Yamamoto told a senior politician: 'If I am to fight, I shall run wild for the first six months or a year, but I have utterly no confidence for the second or third year of the fighting.' If the attack on Pearl Harbor was a success, the Imperial Japanese Navy's eleven battleships and ten aircraft carriers would be more than a match for Allied naval forces, and could be relied on to shield the army's invasion convoys sailing for South-East Asia.

*Warships stationed in the Pacific, 7 December 1941*

|  | battleships | aircraft carriers | cruisers | destroyers | submarines |
|---|---|---|---|---|---|
| British Empire | 2 | 0 | 8 | 13 | 0 |
| United States | 8 | 3 | 24 | 90 | 60 |
| Netherlands | 0 | 0 | 3 | 7 | 13 |
| Total | 10 | 3 | 35 | 110 | 73 |
| Japan | 10 | 9 | 35 | 127 | 86 |

In late 1941 a headquarters for Japan's Southern Army was established at Saigon. For the purposes of the campaign Southern Army was divided into four smaller armies, each with its own designated objective. A Japanese army was the equivalent of a European corps-sized formation. Under the command of Count Terauchi, Southern Army's XIV Army was to invade the Philippines, XV Army was to take Thailand and Burma, XXV Army was to seize Malaya, and XVI Army was to overrun the Dutch East Indies. The conquest of South-East Asia was to be accomplished at breakneck speed. In planning the campaign the Japanese aimed to capture Hong Kong in three weeks, Manila in the Philippines in seven weeks, Singapore in about three and a half months, and Java in about five months.

Southern Army comprised only ten of the Imperial Japanese Army's fifty-one divisions. (The Japanese army also had many independent brigade-sized formations, and some of these would join Southern Army.) The bulk of Japan's forces remained in China and Manchuria. In fact, in December 1941 the Japanese army numbered roughly two and a quarter million men. Of these only 400,000 were made available for the drive to the south.

The capture of Singapore was Southern Army's principal objective, as the island was the most important naval base in South-East Asia. For the invasion of Malaya, XXV Army headquarters was allotted the 5th, 18th and Imperial Guards Divisions, and the brigade strength 3rd Tank Group. Elements of these divisions had conducted training exercises in landing operations in China during the year. The 56th Division was available in reserve at Japan if required.

The 5th and 18th Divisions, from Hiroshima province and Kyushu respectively, were experienced formations, and had seen heavy fighting in China. By 1941 those two formations had already accumulated as much operational experience as most Anglo-American divisions would acquire in the entire 1939–45 war. The 5th Division had taken part in fierce combat in north and central China in 1937–38, and had spearheaded the coastal assault landing that preceded the seizure of Canton in October 1938. The 5th Division had also taken part in the occupation of northern Indo-China in September 1940, and was thus well acquainted with the jungles, rubber plantations and climate of South-East Asia. The 18th Division had taken part in the Shanghai-Nanking campaign of 1937 and other campaigns in China. The 18th Division's General Mutaguchi Renya was the regimental commander of the detachment involved in the Marco Polo Bridge Incident. On the other hand, the Imperial Guards Division had seen only limited action. The Guards were raised from all Japanese military districts, and comprised officers of leading families and men of above average physique. The 3rd Air Division and the navy's 22nd Air Flotilla, fielding over 500 aircraft, were to support both the XV and XXV Armies.

The Japanese army was not heavily equipped in terms of weaponry, nor were its transport, medical service or general logistic support particularly well developed. This was probably a consequence of not having fought a war against a developed nation since 1905. Japanese artillery was less plentiful than in a European army, and Japanese tanks were smaller than their European equivalents. But, thanks to the fighting in China, the Japanese military had been given the opportunity to update its methods. In China commanders had learnt to manoeuvre their forces quickly, often at night, in a bid to envelop their enemy. The Japanese approach to war placed an emphasis on stealth, surprise and infiltration.

The strength of the Imperial Japanese Army lay in its tremendous endurance and spirit of self-sacrifice. Officers and men drew heavily upon a reinterpretation of the samurai ethos and the code of Bushido – the Way of the Warrior. The morale of the Japanese soldier seemed unbreakable, and displays of the highest level of bravery were routine. The Japanese soldier was taught to hate his enemy. A pamphlet distributed to some Japanese troops advised them:

> When you encounter the enemy after landing, think of yourself as an avenger come face to face at last with his father's murderer. Here is the man whose death will lighten your heart.

Japanese troops felt obliged to fight to the death for their divine Emperor, and were indoctrinated in what – by western standards – might be termed a cult of death. The Japanese military code looked upon surrender as a dishonourable and treasonous act. As a foreign observer was later to comment, even when a surrounded Japanese soldier was alone on the battlefield, he seemed to fight on as if his ancestors were watching. There was little decorative panache about Japanese soldiery, yet that masked a heroic outlook and offensive spirit. There were rigid distinctions between ranks and severe punishments were imposed for any disciplinary infraction. The brutality of army discipline caused ordinary soldiers to vent their frustrations on civilians and prisoners that fell into their hands.

The general appointed to command the vital XXV Army was Lieutenant-General Tomoyuki Yamashita. Yamashita, the son of a doctor, had been born in 1885 in an isolated mountain village. At the age of fifteen he had entered cadet school at Hiroshima. He later attended the Central Military Academy in Tokyo, which was under the personal patronage of the Emperor. Having missed the war of 1904–5 with Russia, the first notable milestone in his military career was graduation from the War College at the age of thirty-two, after which he was sent to the Japanese Embassy in Switzerland as assistant military attaché. (Captain Hideki Tojo was also posted in Switzerland at the time.) Yamashita later spent three years in Vienna as military attaché. Yamashita's rise in the army was steady and by 1936 he was Chief of Military Affairs at Imperial Headquarters. During the Young Officers Revolt that year Yamashita played a mediating role in its suppression. Service in Korea as a major-general was followed by a spell as a divisional commander in China.

Late in 1940 Yamashita led a military mission to Germany and Italy. Now a lieutenant-general, he met Hitler in Berlin. After a posting to Manchuria, he was recalled early in November 1941 to take command of XXV Army. A dignified man with a large, shaven head and broad neck, Yamashita was tall by Japanese standards, enjoyed good relations with his subordinates, and was noted for his stoicism and lack of public emotion. He always began the day with a bow and prayer facing the Emperor. A senior staff officer described Yamashita as a 'clear headed type of politician'.[26]

Yamashita arrived at his new post as XXV Army commander on 15 November. Lieutenant-General Sosaku Suzuki was to be XXV Army chief of staff. But other Japanese officers had been working on preparations for the campaign in South East Asia for a considerable time. Yamashita's Chief of Planning and Operations, Lieutenant-Colonel Masanobu Tsuji, had been studying the problems of fighting in tropical jungle for many months. Born in 1903, the spartan and energetic Tsuji had graduated from the army's staff college top of his year. He had seen extensive service in China during the 1930s and against the Soviets in 1939. At the start of 1941 Tsuji had joined a research unit set up in Formosa by army headquarters to study the problems of waging war in tropical climates. Training exercises were held in south China and on Hainan Island to study questions of sea landings, transport, equipment and supply. Tsuji's research unit prepared a pamphlet entitled *Read This Alone and the War Can Be Won* summarizing their findings. It was approved by Imperial General Headquarters and 40,000 copies were printed for distribution.

Japanese officers disguised as commercial travellers had been sent
to South-East Asia by the General Staff, War Ministry and other bodies to
gather intelligence throughout 1941. (In Thailand British and Japanese agents
sometimes stayed in the same hotels.) Every town in Malaya had its Japanese
businessmen, shopkeepers, photographers and dentists. In time these would
be seen as an advance guard of the invasion. This view was an exaggerated
one, but the Japanese did have a well-established espionage network in
South-East Asia. For instance, Japanese residents provided aerial photographs
of Singapore.

In general, Japanese agents had concluded that Singapore's southward
defences were solid. Intelligence sources were less forthcoming, though, on
the state of military preparations on the north coast of Singapore and in
Johore on the mainland. One of Tsuji's deputies, Major Asaeda, travelled
in disguise to southern Thailand to investigate local airfields, the shore line
at prospective landing points, and the state of roads leading south to Malaya.[27]
Japanese forces bound for Malaya had few detailed maps. Outline maps,
distributed down to regimental level, had been obtained mainly through
the military attaché at Bangkok. Australian and British newspapers and
magazines were among the best sources of information regarding Malaya.

In southern Indo-China new aerodromes were hurriedly built to support
the oncoming offensive. Tsuji flew as an observer in an unarmed twin-
engine aircraft on a reconnaissance flight over southern Thailand and
northern Malaya. Tsuji and his pilot, Captain Ikeda, flew over the town
of Kota Bharu in north-east Malaya, but could see nothing below for fog.
Two days later another flight was made in fine weather. There were three
Royal Air Force aerodromes near Kota Bharu and Japanese planners feared
that enemy aircraft might smash their shipping if a landing was made at
Singora, a nearby port in southern Thailand. Flying through storms and
rain the aircraft flew over the northern Malayan aerodromes of Alor Star,
Sungei Patani and Kota Bharu. The aerial photographs taken failed to come
out, but it was clear to Tsuji that the British aerodromes were large and
well-developed.[28]

The finalized XXV Army plan was to land the 5th Division at Singora and
Patani in southern Thailand, whilst the 18th Division's 56th Regiment landed
at Kota Bharu in north-east Malaya to seize the nearby aerodromes. There
was some concern regarding the rough seas of the Thai and Malayan coasts,
as local fisherman did not put to sea at that time of year. Motorized steel
landing barges, however, were sturdier than native boats. The Imperial
Guards Division was to take part in the invasion of Thailand, and then
move down into Malaya by road. The 18th Division's 124th Regiment and
the 35th Brigade's headquarters were earmarked to occupy Borneo, leaving

the rest of the 18th Division available to support the 5th Division's landing or conduct fresh landings on the east coast of Malaya, depending on how the campaign developed.

General Yamashita left Saigon for Hainan Island on 25 November. At Samah, a Hainan port where part of XXV Army was assembling, the general stayed at a hotel called 'The Golden Night'. The proprietress kept geisha girls and there were drinking parties into the night. According to Yamashita's biographer:

> One night the proprietress tried to pay a typical Japanese compliment. She sent her daughter dressed in her best clothes and said: 'This girl will wait on you and I have ordered her to do anything you want.' Yamashita called one of his staff and said: 'Take this girl away. She is a victim. When I am going to fight against the enemy so soon how can I take a virgin tonight?' [29]

The next day the general moved to his headquarters ship.

Yamashita was aware that, once in Malaya, he would have to push his troops southwards swiftly, improvising a plan of campaign from one week to the next. XXV Army had the relative luxury of lorries and bicycles, instead of the animal transport units were often equipped with on the Asian mainland. It also had strong engineering support as Malaya was criss-crossed by rivers and streams, although its thick jungle was pierced by an excellent road and railway system that led directly to Singapore, Yamashita's and XXV Army's main objective.

Whilst Japan was completing final preparations before embarking on war in the Pacific and South-East Asia, the western powers were carefully watching developments in the region. American code breakers were consistently intercepting some types of Japanese signals. On the basis of that information, on 24 November 1941 the United States Chief of Naval Operations signalled Pearl Harbor:

> Chances of favourable outcome of negotiations with Japan very doubtful. This situation coupled with statements of Japanese Government and movements of their naval and military forces indicate in our opinion that a surprise aggressive movement in any direction including attack on Philippines and Guam is a possibility.[30]

The commanders at Pearl were not given all the background intelligence gathered in Washington, but they had been warned to be ready for war.

On 29 November the War Office in London passed on to Air Chief-Marshal Brooke-Popham at Singapore the contents of a message they had just received from the RAF's delegation in Washington.

> Joint planning staff have been informed verbally this afternoon by War Plans

Division War Department that USA Army Commanders in Far East have been informed that Japanese negotiations have reached stage when their final breakdown or offensive action by Japan against Thailand, Netherlands East Indies or Philippines may be expected at any time. USA Commanders have been instructed to await initial offensive move by Japanese and carefully to avoid overt action on their own part.[31]

Unlike at Pearl Harbor, British commanders at Singapore acted on their war warning. On 1 December the Volunteer Forces in Malaya were mobilized, and the European community quickly realized that a crisis was imminent. On 3 December the Admiralty told Singapore that the Japanese Embassy in London had destroyed its cypher machine.[32] With the possibility of invasion so real, daily RAF reconnaissance sorties were flown deep into the Gulf of Siam and the South China Sea.

In Washington President Roosevelt assured British diplomats that the United States would support the British Empire in a war against Japan. Roosevelt told Lord Halifax that if Japan attacked British or Dutch territory 'we should obviously all be together'. Thus on 5 December the Chiefs of Staff in London advised Brooke-Popham that he could launch Operation Matador on his own initiative if a Japanese convoy was sailing for the Kra Isthmus in southern Thailand, or if the Japanese attacked any other part of Thai, British or Dutch territory. Major-General I. S. O. Playfair, Brooke-Popham's chief of staff, told the latter: 'They have now made you responsible for declaring war.'[33]

With the military situation in the Far East so uncertain, senior officers at Singapore had heaved a sigh of relief on 2 December when the *Prince of Wales* and *Repulse* arrived amid a blaze of orchestrated publicity and genuine local enthusiasm. The warships steamed around the island and up the eastern channel of the Johore Strait to the Naval Base. The Governor, Brooke-Popham and other dignitaries turned out to greet the ships. Admiral Phillips had flown on ahead of Force Z from Colombo, and had arrived at Singapore on 29 November. Vice-Admiral Sir Geoffrey Layton's appointment as commander of the China Station was ended upon Phillips's arrival. Earlier in the war, the pugnacious Layton had commanded a cruiser squadron in the Norwegian campaign, and he had briefly been second-in-command of the Home Fleet. Layton was very disappointed to be superseded by Phillips. Rear-Admiral E. J. Spooner remained in command of the Naval Base.[34]

Phillips had been ordered by the Admiralty on 28 November to fly from Singapore to the Philippines to confer with the American Admiral Hart at Manila. Despite a new crop of war warnings, Phillips insisted on flying to Manila on 4 December as originally planned. At Singapore Force Z soon lost its teeth, as the *Prince of Wales* was temporarily immobilized by running repairs, while the *Repulse* set out for Darwin on 5 December. Phillips's decision to dispatch the *Repulse* southwards may have been influenced by a suggestion from Admiral Pound that the two big ships should go to sea to thwart a possible surprise attack at Singapore. Pound may though have expected Phillips to keep his fleet at sea near Singapore. Phillips, partly because he had only just arrived at Singapore, did not fully understand that war might start within days. During a vital period, neither Phillips nor his capital ships were ready for action.

The first Japanese transports bound for Thailand and north-east Malaya left Hainan Island, off the coast of China, at dawn on 4 December. A second convoy left Saigon the next day. The two forces were scheduled to join up on the morning of 7 December in the Gulf of Siam. Vice-Admiral Kondo Nobutake's Southern Force was in charge of all naval forces in South-East Asia. Southern Force's principal units were two pre-1914 battleships, the *Kongo* and *Haruna*. (The *Kongo* was British built, the *Haruna* a Japanese-built copy of the same design). Vice-Admiral Ozawa Jisaburo's Malaya Force was responsible for the protection of the convoys heading for Thailand and Malaya. Rear-Admiral Kurita Takeo's 7th Cruiser Squadron formed the main component of Ozawa's command. Ten Japanese submarines had also been deployed in a patrol line off western Malaya.

The transports sailed close to the coast of Indo-China to avoid detection. General Yamashita and his headquarters were aboard the transport *Ryujo Maru*. In total there were 26,640 XXV Army soldiers in the first flight of convoys. Yamashita intended to go ashore at Singora close behind the first wave of invaders. Lieutenant-Colonel Tsuji, also on the *Ryujo Maru*, later wrote: 'Never had I wished so earnestly for heavy rain as I did then.'[35] The voyage was going to take over two days, and the Japanese were relying on the bad weather of the breaking monsoon to shield the convoys from prying eyes.

Bad weather had in fact prevented British reconnaissance aircraft from flying on 4 December, and only limited operations were possible the following day. On 6 December, for the first time in three days, twin-engine Hudson bombers of No. 1 Squadron Royal Australian Air Force took off from a rain-swept Kota Bharu aerodrome. The intention of the pilots was to fly all the way to Cambodia Point. About midday the aircrew of Flight Lieutenant J. C. Ramshaw's Hudson sighted three transports and a cruiser steaming around Cambodia Point into the Gulf of Siam, 185 miles from Kota Bharu. Shortly afterwards, Ramshaw's crew discovered the main Japanese convoy and counted about twenty transports. The Hudson flown by Flight Lieutenant J. G. Emerton also saw the main convoy about this time. Ramshaw's Hudson flew up and down the convoy at less than a thousand feet. There was no doubt as to what the aircrew was seeing. Ramshaw flew into the clouds when the convoy launched a seaplane, and his radio operator signalled their findings back to base.[36]

At Singapore an anxious Brooke-Popham received the information, but he was not prepared to violate another country's neutrality whilst there was still some question as to the convoys' destination. The convoys might have been an elaborate ruse to entice the British into invading Thailand first. A message was sent to Admiral Phillips at Manila informing him of the situation.

Luck was with the Japanese. Very heavy weather closed in again on 7 December. Rain squalls, fog and dense cloud greatly reduced visibility. Not long after 9 a.m. the combined convoy split into several smaller ones, one bound for Kota Bharu, another for Singora and Patani, and the others for destinations further north in Thailand. Admiral Ozawa had decided to go ahead with the Kota Bharu landing, as there had been no sign of opposition from the Royal Navy. Later that morning Japanese aircraft shot down a Catalina flying boat before it could send a message back to base. During the afternoon ships were sighted by RAF aircrew closing on Singora, but this information did not reach headquarters at Singapore until 9 p.m. that night. It was clearly too late to launch Operation Matador, and with some relief Brooke-Popham further postponed a decision on that subject. During the day the British Ambassador in Bangkok had contacted Brooke-Popham to implore him not to violate Thai neutrality before the Japanese.

As British commanders at Singapore dithered over the probable approach of an invasion force, other Japanese fleets were moving out across the Pacific Ocean. A fleet of six Japanese aircraft carriers and support ships had put to sea on 26 November and sailed across the empty, stormy north Pacific in total secrecy towards Hawaii. Early on Sunday 7 December, from the pitching decks of Admiral Nagumo's carriers, 183 aircraft were launched for an attack on Pearl Harbor. Just after 7 a.m. an American radar operator at Hawaii saw a huge flight of aircraft on his screen to the north. He alerted his superior but was told that the planes were American B–17s on route from California. There was no coordinated American scheme of aerial reconnaissance in place despite the war warnings. The warships in harbour were not protected by torpedo nets.

Just before 8 a.m. the first wave of Japanese navy bombers, torpedo bombers and fighters swooped in, taking advantage of complete surprise.

Some Japanese aircraft headed for the military airfields where hundreds of machines stood unprotected, parked on runways. The largest group zoomed in on Pearl Harbor, home to the United States Pacific Fleet. Within a short space of time numerous torpedo hits were scored on the big ships moored in Battleship Row. A forward magazine of the *Arizona* exploded from a bomb hit and a column of smoke shot high into the air. Four hundred men were trapped when the *Oklahoma* capsized after flooding caused by torpedo strikes. The *West Virginia* was engulfed by fire. The *California* settled to the bottom of the harbour in shallow water. The other four battleships in port were also damaged; the crippled *Nevada* had to be beached. At 8.40 a.m. the second wave of Japanese aircraft arrived to add to the turmoil. By the time the assault had finished, eight battleships and a number of smaller ships were sunk or damaged. 2403 Americans had been killed and 1178 wounded.[37]

The raid on Pearl Harbor was certainly a fine tactical victory for the Japanese, but strategically the benefits of the attack were less significant. The fuel dumps at Hawaii were still intact and, more importantly, American aircraft carriers away at sea escaped damage. Admiral Nagumo elected to withdraw his fleet to safety rather than stay near Hawaii to hunt down the American carriers, or launch further strikes against Pearl's shore installations. Above all else the Pearl Harbor raid brought America into the war in the Pacific and Asia. And also in Europe when later the Germans quixotically declared war on America in support of Japan.

Meanwhile Japanese forces were ready for an immediate assault on the colony of Hong Kong. On China's coast, already surrounded by Japanese troops, Hong Kong had never been expected to hold out long. A small army garrison of six battalions, artillery and some volunteer force units had been left in the colony for the sake of prestige. The authorities could not just run off without a fight. In the days immediately after the outbreak of war British, Indian, Canadian and local Chinese forces were quickly pushed off the Chinese mainland by the Japanese 38th Division. A siege of Hong Kong Island began.

In the Philippines, the war also started badly for General Douglas MacArthur's Filipino-American forces. Unlike at Pearl Harbor, the Philippines were not taken by surprise. When it was 10 a.m. at Pearl on 7 December it was 4 a.m. at Manila on 8 December. Yet despite full knowledge that a war was already underway, the United States Army Air Force was crippled on the opening day. Many American bombers and fighters were destroyed on their aerodromes, parked wing to wing for fear of saboteurs. From bases in nearby Formosa (Taiwan), Japanese troops of General Homma's XIV Army landed at several points along the Philippines coast line. Military and political leaders in Washington knew they could do little to help MacArthur's command.

With several Japanese armies starting their assault on South-East Asia, the outlook for Allied forces in the region was grim.

# 5

# The Japanese Onslaught

In the Thai-Malayan theatre of the vast new Pacific war, the main Japanese convoy anchored off Singora about 2.20 a.m. on 8 December, not long after the start of the attack on Pearl Harbor on the other side of the international date line. The ships were rolling in heavy seas, but the bright lights of Singora guided landing craft towards the shore. Tsuji was on dry land by 4 a.m. Sporadic Thai resistance ended within hours.[1]

Confirmation of a state of war soon reached Singapore. At 3.30 a.m. radar stations at Changi and Mersing picked up unidentified aircraft 140 miles from Singapore. Just after 4 a.m. Japanese bombers glided across a clear sky, beneath a full tropical moon. The lights of Singapore were still blazing as the Air Raid Precautions (ARP) headquarters was not manned, and the civil authorities could not be passed a warning. The Japanese twin-engine naval bombers had flown all the way from Indo-China. Almost two hundred casualties were caused by bombs falling in the centre of Singapore town. Chinatown suffered hits, and among the bombed out buildings was Robinson's restaurant in Raffles Place. Bombs also landed on two of the island's aerodromes, but at another aerodrome three Buffaloes stood waiting. They were refused permission to take off for fear of being hit by friendly anti-aircraft fire. The raid was a rude shock to both official and civilian morale. The next morning crowds gathered to look at the bomb craters. The Japanese population remaining in Malaya was swiftly rounded up and interned by the colonial authorities. Within the next few days a Far East War Council was formed at Singapore. Duff Cooper was appointed Resident Minister for Far Eastern Affairs. The War Council was intended to deal with political and emergency matters, but not interfere with the service commanders.

The Japanese convoy bound for Kota Bharu, on Malaya's north-west coast, dropped anchor before midnight on 7/8 December. The main unit of Major-General Takumi's detachment was the 56th Regiment of the 18th Division. With the addition of other support troops, Takumi's force comprised 5300 men. The landing had been timed to coincide with the raid on Pearl Harbor, but it actually commenced over an hour earlier.

The Japanese transports had been guided to Kota Bharu by the lights of

the town, though absurd tales of fifth columnists shining lanterns out to
sea would later be told and retold. Troops ashore had noticed the shadowy
presence of three large ships, and by 1 a.m. the news had been relayed to
Singapore. When the Governor, Sir Shenton Thomas, was informed, he
allegedly said: 'Well, I suppose you'll shove the little men off.'

Kota Bharu was a small town close to the mouth of the Sungei Kelantan,
a short distance from the Thai frontier. The main task of the local defending
force, the 8th Indian Brigade, was to protect the three aerodromes located
south of the river. Brigadier B. W. Key's brigade was deployed across over
thirty miles of beach. The 3/17th Dogras held ten miles of beach south of
the Sungei Kelantan, and the 2/10th Baluchis had an even longer sector to
guard further south. In reserve to the rear were the 1/13th Frontier Force
Rifles, and the 2/12th Frontier Force Regiment (on loan from the 22nd
Brigade). The second-line 1st Hyderabads and 1st Mysore State Force Infantry guarded the aerodromes from parachute landings.

The beaches near Kota Bharu were laced with barbed wire, and a line of
concrete pillboxes had been built at thousand yard intervals. A second line
of reserve posts to the rear covered the gaps between the first line of posts.
Further south, in the Baluchis' sector, the defences were less developed, and
one ten mile stretch was guarded only by dummy emplacements. There
were few mangrove swamps on this part of the Malayan coast, but behind
the main sandy beaches there was a tangled belt of palms and streams that
greatly interfered with human movement. To the north west of the Sungei
Kelantan, across which a boom had been placed, there was only a handful
of Indian troops.

The Japanese transports had anchored off Badang and Sabak beaches, just
south of the river mouth. These were the closest beaches to Kota Bharu
town. Each beach was held by a company of Dogras. On Badang beach A
Company occupied a front of three miles, and B Company on Sabak beach
had three miles of sand to defend. This was the brigade's strongest concentration of troops, and the best place for the Japanese to land from Brigadier
Key's viewpoint. The Japanese chose to come ashore at this dangerous place
as they knew that Kota Bharu aerodrome was in constant use barely two
miles inland. The aerodrome had to be quickly neutralised for the landing
to succeed.

Armour-plated barges crewed by engineers, and packed with drenched
and seasick Japanese soldiers, were lowered from the transports into the
rolling sea. Around 12.45 a.m. the barges headed shorewards. Eighteen-
pounder guns on the beach fired the first shots at the dark silhouettes out
at sea. The pillbox machine gun posts were a long way apart, but the
defenders were alert and ready, and a withering fire was directed towards

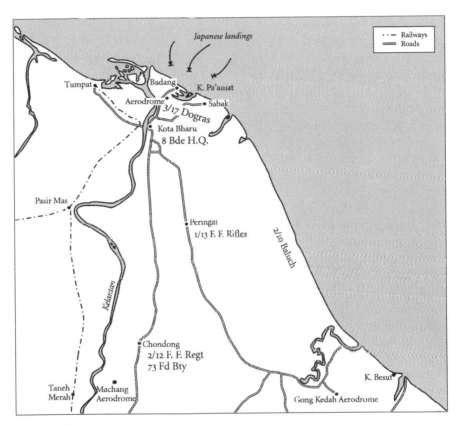

3. Kota Bharu.

the shapes looming ahead on the water. Several barges were sunk or damaged, but the others pressed onwards with determination, mostly towards the inner ends of Badang and Sabak beaches. The beaches were divided by a creek mouth that opened into an inlet behind the inner ends of the beaches. The crews of several barges intrepidly motored their craft into the creek mouth.

The first wave of assault troops, who landed amid a chaos of gunfire and shouting, suffered heavily trying to force a passage through the barbed wire on the beach. But the barges that had penetrated into the inlet landed men behind the beach defences. Assailed from the front and rear, the pillboxes either side of the creek mouth were soon captured. Japanese troops advanced up the beach in both directions, and a 2000 yard strip fell under the control of the invaders. Japanese and Indian soldiers burrowed into sand blown into high banks by monsoonal winds. The surf crashed over the bloody corpses littering the shore.

News of the landing soon reached Kota Bharu aerodrome. Airmen could hear sounds of gunfire coming from the beach. Hudson bombers of Wing Commander R. H. Davis's No. 1 Squadron RAAF began taking off at two to three minute intervals. The Hudsons did not have far to travel to reach the transports off Badang and Sabak beaches. Attacking at mast-top height, the Hudsons bombed and strafed any shipping or barges they could see on the sea below. Deadly anti-aircraft fire, however, soon took its toll. According to a Japanese source, the first Hudson downed by the shafts of coloured tracer crashed onto a landing barge. Flight Lieutenant Ramshaw's aircraft returned from its opening bombing run in less than the time it takes to smoke a cigarette, but was shot down on a second mission.[2]

Bombing set the transport *Awagisan Maru* on fire from stem to stern. The ship was later abandoned to sink. Several hits were also scored on the other two transports. The aerial assault badly disrupted the disembarkation of the third and final wave of infantry. The naval commander had wanted temporarily to withdraw out to sea, but Takumi's headquarters insisted that the landing continue as planned. The barges reloaded and headed shoreward again as best they could during lulls between air attacks. The two remaining transports and their naval escort withdrew northwards from Kota Bharu before dawn, with the intention of returning again the following night.

By daylight the Japanese had opened a deep hole in the Dogras' line of posts. On Badang beach the Dogras' reserve company and a company of the 2/12th Frontier Force Regiment battled to contain the Japanese. On Sabak beach the invaders advanced southwards, but another Frontier Force Regiment company counter-attacked to relieve a threatened post.[3]

After being informed that the Baluchis had had an undisturbed night,

Brigadier Key ordered the rest of his two reserve battalions to counter-attack and push Takumi's men back into the sea. Given the size of Key's command the body of troops he was sending forward to shore up the Dogras' line was a strong one, and a sensible concentration of force at a critical point on the battlefield. In many places, though, the balance of the 2/12th Frontier Force Regiment and 1/13th Frontier Force Rifles were held up in the tangle of deep, swollen streams and islands behind the beaches.

As dawn broke at Singapore Brooke-Popham was still waiting for the results of RAF reconnaissance flights to Singora. By 9.45 a.m. news of a mass of Japanese shipping at Singora had reached the Commander-in-Chief. Brooke-Popham was finally able to cancel Operation Matador. The Japanese had obviously won the race for Singora. The army commander, General Percival, who had gone to attend a meeting of the Legislative Assembly, did not receive word of the cancellation till 11 a.m. Half an hour later Percival ordered General Heath to man the Jitra position, and to send Kroh column ('Krohcol') into Thailand to seize the Ledge feature on the road leading to Patani. These orders did not reach Heath until 1 p.m., after which Heath rang Percival for confirmation. Heath's orders to his formations were not issued until 1.30 p.m. Half a day had been lost.[4]

The 8th Indian Brigade was not alone in seeking to repel the invaders. At 6.30 a.m. Hudsons of No. 8 Squadron RAAF and Blenheims of No. 60 Squadron RAF left Kuantan for Kota Bharu. The aircraft dropped more bombs on the disabled transport and barges crowding the shore line. Hudsons of No. 1 Squadron returned to the fray, supported by other squadrons based elsewhere in Malaya. A number of bombers were damaged by ground fire, and two Blenheims were shot down.[5]

Japanese aircraft arrived at Kota Bharu soon after 9 a.m. for the first of a series of attacks on the aerodrome. Wing Commander Davis was surprised by the acrobatic agility of the Navy Zeros and Army 97s that swooped down low to strafe men, machines and buildings. There were few casualties among the ground staff, but by afternoon, unsettled by repeated air attacks, the airmen began to believe that Japanese snipers were firing across the aerodrome. The stray rounds were almost certainly 'overs' from the direction of the beaches, but nerves were wearing thin. Late in the afternoon a report was sent to Air Headquarters Singapore advising that the Japanese had reached the aerodrome boundary. Air Vice-Marshal Pulford gave permission to evacuate the aerodrome. There was a good deal of confusion during the evacuation. The station's buildings were set on fire, but neither the munitions nor petrol dump were destroyed.

At 6 p.m. Major-General Barstow, GOC 9th Indian Division, told Key that he could retire from Kota Bharu at his own discretion, and that he was not to risk the annihilation of his command. With the aerodromes abandoned there was no good reason for the isolated brigade to remain at Kota Bharu. It had never been intended to fight a prolonged battle in defence of the town. Key ordered his troops to withdraw through a dismally rainy night to a new line roughly four to five miles inland. As the retirement was getting under way, the petrol dump at Kota Bharu aerodrome was set alight by British artillery fire to prevent it falling into Japanese hands. Japanese troops nearing the aerodrome opened fire on the figures outlined by the red and white glare. The commanding officer of the 1st Hyderabads, Lieutenant-Colonel C. A. Hendricks, and his adjutant were killed amidst the tumult, and their battalion quickly fell apart.

Despite darkness, rain, broken communications, flooded streams, swamps and marauding Japanese patrols, most of the brigade had retreated inland by dawn of 9 December. Further skirmishing followed, and parties of Japanese began feeling around the brigade's right flank. Over the next two days, Key ordered a further withdrawal to Machang, over thirty miles from the invasion beaches.

According to Lieutenant-Colonel Tsuji, on land and sea Takumi Detachment lost 320 killed and 538 wounded at Kota Bharu. By the evening of 10 December the 8th Brigade's battalions had rounded up most of their stragglers and had over six hundred men each. Three days later, the brigade's casualties were listed as sixty-eight killed, 360 wounded, and thirty-seven missing, significantly fewer than Takumi Detachment's losses.[6]

Whilst the action at Kota Bharu had been taking place, the campaign began to unfold elsewhere. On 8 December the Japanese disembarked troops at Singora in Thailand, and Japanese aviators began an assault on Alor Star and Sungei Patani, the RAF's two principal aerodromes in north-west Malaya.

Sungei Patani aerodrome was heavily bombed. A warning that unidentified aircraft were approaching had been received, but the station commander missed the opportunity to scramble his fighters. Two Buffaloes took off through bursting bombs, but upon closing with Japanese bombers the pilots found that their guns would not work: they were not carrying any ammunition. Whilst ground staff took shelter in drainage ditches, no less than ten Buffaloes and Blenheims were destroyed or damaged on the ground by phosphorous-charged incendiary bombs. It had been difficult properly to disperse the aircraft given the waterlogged state of the grass aerodrome. Sungei Patani station's headquarters was also hit, and the main runway badly damaged.[7]

At 10.45 a.m. another twenty Japanese bombers raided Sungei Patani. More damage was inflicted, and No. 21 Squadron was reduced to only four serviceable Buffaloes. Blenheims of No. 62 Squadron at Alor Star aerodrome were also caught on the ground by Japanese bombers, after returning from an early morning mission to Kota Bharu. Four Blenheims were destroyed by falling bombs, another five were damaged, and the station's buildings and fuel dump were set ablaze.

The remaining aircraft at Sungei Patani and Alor Star were ordered back to Butterworth aerodrome that evening or early next morning. By the end of 8 December the RAF in northern Malaya had lost over half its flying strength, yet it was opposed by between four and five hundred Japanese aircraft based in Indo-China.[8]

In RAF circles stories began to circulate of fifth columnists sending messages to the Japanese by radio. With this information the Japanese were alleged to have been able to time their attacks to catch RAF aircraft on the ground. The real reason for the staggered timings of the Japanese onslaught on northern Malaya was that heavy monsoonal showers had rendered their aerodromes in Indo-China unserviceable for varying periods. The weather had prevented a mass take off at dawn by all squadrons.

Nonetheless an air liaison officer based in northern Malaya, Captain Patrick Heenan of the 3/16th Punjabis, was later arrested and executed for espionage. Apparently Heenan had spent part of a six month furlough in Japan in 1938–39, and he had continued to mix with Japanese at Singapore in 1941. Heenan had been in the habit of making clandestine trips into Thailand, and he was caught in possession of a small, disguised radio transmitter. Heenan may have flirted with Japanese intelligence, but exaggerated estimates of his effectiveness have little basis. Small radios in 1941 barely worked in jungle over any distance. The idea that the Japanese based their plans around the messages of a British traitor at a vital stage of the war is preposterous.[9]

Admiral Phillips had returned to Singapore before midday on 7 December, having flown out of Manila the previous evening. The *Repulse* returned from her cruise to Darwin shortly after, and the *Prince of Wales*'s crew readied their ship for sea after patching up unfinished engineering repairs. But when the Japanese landed at Kota Bharu that night, Phillips's fleet had yet to leave the Naval Base.

Had Phillips been able to take Force Z to sea during the night of 6/7 December, after the first reports had been received that a Japanese fleet was heading into the Gulf of Siam, it is hard to say what might have happened. Force Z might have been quickly sunk, but events are just as likely to have taken a different course. The approach of Force Z might have compelled the Japanese to divert the landing at Kota Bharu to Singora. Force Z might have intercepted Japanese shipping off Kota Bharu, or an engagement with Japanese forces covering the Singora and Patani convoys might have taken place. Either way Phillips had by 8 December missed his opportunity to have any impact on the Japanese invasion of Thailand and northern Malaya. Phillips was himself responsible for this error as he had dispersed his squadron during a critical period.

Yet Phillips was in no doubt as to what he should do next. He decided to take Force Z to sea late on 8 December for a belated foray northwards to attack Singora after first light on 10 December. To remain at Singapore was unwise, as the Naval Base was vulnerable to bombing, and to sail south would have left Phillips and the Royal Navy open to a charge of leaving the army and Malaya in the lurch. Phillips believed that he was taking a calculated risk, and he only intended going through with his plan if Force Z remained unsighted during 9 December. The admiral hoped that the monsoon would shield Force Z from observation.

Phillips had no fear of high-level bombing or dive bombers. He believed that well-handled ships and anti-aircraft fire could deal with those threats. He was more concerned by the prospect of attack by torpedo bombers. But, as the Captain of the Fleet, Captain L. H. Bell, later explained, Phillips trusted that if Force Z achieved surprise those Japanese aircraft immediately available would be armed for land operations, and would not be carrying anti-shipping bombs and torpedoes. As the ships retreated towards Singapore Phillips assumed they would only face 'hastily organized' bombers flying from Indo-China. Whilst the risk of torpedo attack within 200 miles of enemy aerodromes was considered great, the risk was believed to decrease at longer ranges until it diminished to almost zero at a range of 400 miles. British intelligence had no idea that the twin-engine bombers that had flown 600 miles from Indo-China to bomb Singapore the previous night could be readily rearmed as torpedo bombers. The range of Japanese torpedo-carrying aircraft was actually as great as a thousand miles. According to Bell, current intelligence assumed that the Japanese were no more competent at warfare than the Italians.[10]

Brooke-Popham had no control over Phillips's actions, while likewise the admiral's seniority, and known authoritarian tendencies, kept opposition to his plans to a minimum in naval circles. Bell later wrote that Phillips, Force Z's chief of staff Rear-Admiral A. F. E. Palliser, Captains Tennant and Leach, and himself were

> unanimous that it was impossible for the Navy to attempt nothing while the army and air force were being driven back, and that the plan for a sudden raid, though hazardous, was acceptable. There was also the psychological effect of the fleet putting to sea in this grave emergency.[11]

But some officers had their doubts. The now unemployed Vice-Admiral Layton did not expect to see Force Z again after it sailed. The Fleet Engineering Officer, Captain O. W. Phillips, was told by Rear-Admiral Palliser to stop spreading despondency when he expressed his dismay about the impending operation. Somewhat prophetically Captain Leach of the *Prince of Wales* told his midshipman son at the Naval Base pool, shortly before sailing: 'I am going to do a couple of lengths now – you never know when it mightn't come in handy.' [12]

On the morning of 8 December Phillips requested Air Vice-Marshal Pulford to provide air reconnaissance ahead of the fleet. The admiral also asked for fighter protection off Singora after dawn on 10 December. Phillips had no aircraft carrier, but the aerodromes scattered across Malaya meant that the peninsula was potentially one giant aircraft carrier. Pulford and Phillips met in person later in the morning. But by afternoon, in light of the disaster unfolding for the RAF in northern Malaya, and the nagging need to maintain Singapore's air defences, Pulford informed Phillips that, while reconnaissance was possible, fighter protection off Singora on 10 December was unlikely. Of the four Buffalo squadrons at Singapore (No. 243 RAF, No. 453 RAAF, No. 488 RNZAF, and a Dutch squadron), only one was allocated to fleet defence. The protection of Force Z was not the highest of the RAF's priorities so far as Pulford was concerned, and may have been as low as third priority behind the battle in northern Malaya and the air defence of Singapore.

The cause of naval-air cooperation was not helped when the commander of the squadron allocated to fleet defence, No. 453 Squadron, met Phillips's air liaison officer. The squadron's commander offered to put in place a flight roster whereby several aircraft were over Force Z at all times in daylight hours. That scheme would have required Force Z to sail close to Malaya's western coast. Phillips, reasonably enough, could not agree to that. In fact, due to the admiral's stern determination to maintain radio silence at sea as much as possible, no workable arrangement of any kind could be agreed upon. The failure of Phillips and the RAF to come to an agreement for cooperation also meant that Pulford was given no incentive or reason to assist Force Z by shifting fighters northwards to Kuantan aerodrome. Palliser, who remained ashore, later signalled Phillips at sea to confirm that Pulford could not provide fighter protection off Singora. Pulford had at least made the situation clear to Phillips.

Force Z sailed at 5.30 p.m. on 8 December with four destroyers: the modern *Electra* and *Express*, and the elderly *Tenedos* and *Vampire*. Three old cruisers were at Singapore but only the *Durban* was ready to sail, and Phillips decided to leave her behind. The next day, 9 December, Force Z steamed northwards towards the Gulf of Siam. The day was rainy and cloudy, classic monsoon conditions. Visibility was down to half a mile at times. Force Z had sailed around the Anambas Islands out into the South China Sea to minimize detection, but at 1.45 p.m. the Japanese submarine *I–65* spotted the British squadron and shadowed it for over three hours. Later in the afternoon the skies cleared and Japanese aircraft were sighted.

At 6.30 p.m. the destroyer *Tenedos* turned back towards Singapore as she was running short of fuel. At 6.55 p.m. Phillips steered north west. He turned west at 7.30 p.m., and finally turned back for Singapore at 8.15 p.m. Phillips knew that aircraft had spotted Force Z, and that all hope of surprise off Kota Bharu or Singora was gone. He had only maintained course till he was sure his shadowers had departed. The squadron's sally northwards had been somewhat of a disappointment. Phillips had not found any Japanese shipping. But as the Japanese invasion convoys had reached Singora two days previously that was not altogether surprising.

Phillips was unaware of the fact, but Force Z had closed to within twenty-five miles of the Japanese cruisers and destroyers covering the invasion of Thailand and Malaya before turning away. If Phillips had continued northwards for another fifteen minutes contact might have been made. Admiral Kondo's battleships were still well to the north east. Kondo had hoped that the cruisers might tempt the British northwards for an action the next morning.[13]

After receiving reports that a hostile squadron had been sighted, the Japanese 22nd Air Flotilla attempted to intercept Force Z during the evening of 9 December. The pilots were unable to locate their target on the broad expanse of the ocean, and many were turned back by bad weather. Flares were dropped over a Japanese warship, but the error was realised in time to prevent an attack.

On 9 December the RAF in Malaya had another bad day, beginning a sequence of events that would have a critical impact on Admiral Phillips and Force Z. With Kota Bharu aerodrome in their possession, the aviators of the Imperial Japanese Army and Navy turned their attention to Kuantan, which like the northern Malayan airfields lacked both anti-aircraft guns and radar. About midday, with little prior warning, nine Japanese Nells plastered the aerodrome from 5000 feet. The Nells completed their bombing runs, then came down to strafe the aerodrome from a lower altitude. Another group of raiders soon arrived to force the ground staff to scatter and seek shelter again. A number of aircraft were destroyed or damaged on the ground. A Hudson returning from a reconnaissance flight hit back at the first group of attackers. One Japanese bomber was seen from the ground to catch fire, and two parachutists jumped out. It was a rare aerial combat success for the RAF.

As Kuantan aerodrome was under heavy attack, Air Headquarters Singapore decided to withdraw all aircraft at Kuantan to Singapore. The Blenheims of No. 60 Squadron had already been transferred back to Singapore earlier that morning. The remaining Hudsons and Vildebeests had left by 4 p.m., and their departure sparked rumours that the evacuation of all personnel had been ordered, though this was not the case. In the panic that followed the mostly Australian ground staff seized any transport they could lay their hands on and fled inland to the nearest railway station. It was later alleged that trucks were requisitioned at gunpoint. Even a vehicle as inappropriate as a petrol tanker was pressed into service as a getaway car. Only a handful of men remained at the aerodrome, including Wing Commander R. C. Councell, the bewildered station commander. The evacuation of Kuantan was later the subject of a RAF court of inquiry.[14]

Elsewhere in Malaya that day three of six Blenheims sent to bomb Singora aerodrome failed to return. Japanese bombers raided Butterworth during the afternoon, and all four No. 21 Squadron Buffaloes in the air at the time were forced down by Japanese fighters. A group of Blenheims had been in the process of taking off for another attack on Singora when the Japanese raid began. Only two of the Blenheims readying to depart managed to get airborne. One aircraft returned to the aerodrome, but No. 62 Squadron's Squadron Leader Arthur Scarf and his crew took their Blenheim all the way to Singora and dropped their bombs over Singora airfield. The bomber was jumped by Japanese fighters on the return journey, and Scarf was badly wounded in the back and left arm. Propped up on either side by his gunner and navigator, Scarf flew the Blenheim back to Malaya, crash landing in a paddy field near Alor Star aerodrome. Scarf died soon after landing. In 1946, after the full tale of his exploit became known, Scarf was given a posthumous award of the Victoria Cross.

With the buildings of Butterworth aerodrome reduced to smouldering ruins, and the fields littered with broken aircraft, the commander of the RAF's group in northern Malaya, Wing Commander R. G. Forbes, ordered those aircraft still flyable to evacuate southwards to Ipoh, Taiping or Singapore. By the end of 9 December on the whole of the Malayan mainland the RAF had been reduced to a handful of aircraft. Most Japanese aircraft losses so far had been due to accidents caused by flying in the monsoonal conditions prevailing over the Gulf of Siam and the South China Sea. An estimated 150 Japanese aircraft had already been relocated to the Singora-Patani area. Four Dutch squadrons (three bomber and one fighter) arrived at Singapore during 9 December, the last reinforcement likely to reach the RAF in Malaya for some time to come.[15]

As Force Z steamed back towards Singapore through the darkness of the night of 9/10 December, the closest friendly army formation was stationed at the east coast town of Kuantan. Some troops of Brigadier G. W. A. Painter's 22nd Indian Brigade had been unsettled by rumours that a debacle had taken place at Kuantan aerodrome that day. To add to the uncertainty, late in the afternoon the crew of a Hudson on a reconnaissance flight had reported sighting a 3000-ton ship travelling south, seventy-five miles north of Kuantan. Some barges had also allegedly been spotted a similar distance south of Kuantan.

Soon after dark an observation post of the 21st Mountain Battery, at the northern end of the brigade's beach defences, reported that the Japanese were landing near Pelingdong in five boats. The gunners opened fire, and reported to their headquarters that the Japanese had got back into their boats and headed off to the north. More than one infantry post corroborated the gunners' report. Other guns opened fire on previously arranged targets in the area. The infantry fired Verey lights and anxiously searched their sections of the beach. Machine gun fire could be heard in the distance, and gradually became intense across the beaches held by the 2/18th Garhwal Rifles.

A stream of messages flowed inland from Kuantan to the 9th Division's headquarters. From General Heath's III Corps headquarters the news of a reported landing had by 10 p.m. reached Malaya Command at Singapore. Senior commanders had no choice but to regard the information as true. Surely a report that the enemy had landed on the 22nd Brigade's beaches could not be imagined!

The alarm and firing at Kuantan continued into the early hours of the morning. At one stage infantry posts on the beach reported that they were being heavily sniped at from the flanks. At Kuantan's artillery headquarters Major G. W. P. Fennell recorded that, 'at this point Colonel Jephson (5th Field Regiment) smelt a rat, for how could there be sniping from the flanks if the enemy had not yet landed'. Jephson got in touch with the Garhwal Rifles' Lieutenant-Colonel Hartigan 'to call the party off'. But according to Fennell:

> The excitements of the night were not yet over. A report had been received that boats were to be seen at the mouth of the Kuantan River ... Hogshaw started to let drive from Tembeling Point and had a grand time shooting up boats. The OP line went through RHQ [Regimental Headquarters] and such remarks as 'Good shot', 'got the sods', 'keep at it' came floating through at intervals.

Next morning, rumours of piles of bodies went round, but no one could say definitely where the bodies were and how many. One small boat was found on the beach with four dead Malays near it, and at the mouth of the Kuantan River, a number of logs were seen floating about. Can it have been that the logs were the invading fleet? At any rate, logs or no logs, a very happy evening was spent by all.[16]

This brought to a close 'Blitzkrieg Night', as it was labelled by certain local humourists.

There were many theories as to what had happened at Kuantan on the night of 9/10 December. Some days later two bullet-ridden lifeboats were allegedly found ashore on a beach near Kuantan with Japanese equipment in them.[17] Some officers of the brigade have always held to the story that the Japanese had been probing the east coast with reconnaissance parties. Others present that night believed that a high tide or other natural agent had set off mines on the beach, as happened on other occasions, thereby causing troops to panic and fire at shadows. Certainly no trace of a Japanese landing was ever found at the beaches on which it was supposed to have happened. Not a footprint, cartridge case or scrap of uniform could be produced as evidence. Possibly some returning fishermen had been shot up by the defenders, but that is the most favourable interpretation that can be put on events.

The farcical situation that developed at Kuantan was to have wide-ranging consequences. Air Headquarters Singapore dispatched six Vildebeests and three Hudsons to investigate the reported landing on the east coast. Taking off at 2 a.m. on 10 December one Vildebeest collided head on with another on the blacked out Seletar aerodrome. Bombs being carried by the aircraft exploded in a huge flash. Squadron Leader G. Witney and his No. 36 Squadron crew were killed, as was the pilot of the other torpedo-bomber. The remaining Vildebeests and Hudsons found no sign of an invasion fleet. Two Buffaloes, dispatched from Singapore at dawn to search the Kuantan area, confirmed that all was quiet in that part of the world.[18]

Force Z's return journey to Singapore proved to be eventful. At 9.45 p.m. on 9 December Palliser in Singapore had reported to Admiral Phillips on the RAF's disastrous day. He signalled that Kota Bharu aerodrome was now in Japanese hands:

All our northern aerodromes are becoming untenable due to enemy air action. C.-in-C. Far East hints he is considering concentrating all air efforts on defence of Singapore area.[19]

About midnight another report was received by Phillips's staff stating that a Japanese landing at Kuantan was believed to be underway. As Kuantan was not far from Force Z's route back to Singapore, Captain Bell had Phillips roused from his cabin and suggested a change of course, to which the admiral agreed. The report of a landing at Kuantan was quite untrue, but no signal was ever sent to Phillips either doubting or denying the report.

As noted earlier, Phillips was a great believer in radio silence at sea. He therefore did not signal Palliser his change in plan. This was another symptom of the fact that Phillips had not been to sea since the war began. The admiral did not fully understand the capabilities and limitations of some pieces of modern equipment. Indeed the Japanese had no particular capacity for the direction-finding of radio signals. The Imperial Japanese Navy's shortcomings in the realm of electronic warfare was in fact its one clear-cut technological failing. Commander M. Goodenough, Phillips's chief operations staff officer, assumed that Palliser would guess that Force Z was heading for Kuantan, and Phillips may have thought that too.[20] But Palliser had no idea where Force Z was located, and had little solid information upon which to base any assumption.

By 8 a.m. Force Z was off Kuantan. The destroyer *Express* was sent close to shore to reconnoitre. It reported back: 'All is as quiet as a wet Sunday afternoon.' The *Express* rejoined the battleships at 8.45 a.m. Now, instead of continuing onwards towards Singapore, Phillips decided to turn north on Captain Tennant's suggestion to investigate a fishing boat and barges seen nearby earlier in the morning. Force Z was now 450 miles from Japanese aerodromes in Indo-China, and both Bell and Goodenough later agreed that Phillips probably believed he was well beyond the effective range of torpedo-bombers. But this calculation was based on the relatively short range of antiquated British torpedo-bombers.[21]

The tug and barges proved to be civilian, and the search of them wasted an hour and a half. As the search neared completion a Japanese scout plane was seen in the distance. A Japanese submarine had sighted Force Z's battleships heading towards Singapore during the night. Eighty-five twin-engine medium bombers – Nells and Bettys – preceded by reconnaissance aircraft, had taken off in Indo-China earlier that morning to intercept Force Z on its homeward journey. The Genzan, Mihoro and Kanoya groups comprised ten squadrons, six carrying torpedoes and four bombs. The bombers cruised across the South China Sea southwards of the Anambas Islands. A Genzan squadron found the destroyer *Tenedos*, already well on her way to Singapore. The bombers' thousand pound bombs missed the little ship. With fuel running low the group leaders were relieved finally to get news that Force Z had been located.

The first bombers arrived within sight of Force Z at 11 a.m. The *Prince of Wales*'s anti-aircraft armament comprised sixteen 5.25 inch guns which could be used against either surface or high-level targets. Against low-flying aircraft there were several eight-barrelled two-pounder pom-poms, and a number of 40 mm Bofors and 20 mm Oerlikon guns. The elderly *Repulse* had a secondary armament of twelve four-inch guns, but these were by design purely anti-surface weapons. The *Repulse* had only a handful of anti-aircraft guns: six old four-inch weapons, three pom-poms, and some cannons and machine guns.[22]

In a steady line abreast a squadron of Mihoro group flew over the *Repulse* at 10,000 feet. The high level anti-aircraft guns hammered away at this excellent target. The gunners crouched beneath tin helmets, clad in anti-flash hoods and gloves. Five of the eight aircraft were slightly damaged, but none was shot down. The bombers released the bombs together and they fell either side of the *Repulse*. Tall water spouts leapt skywards. One bomb fell through the port hanger and burst on the armoured deck. There were a number of casualties, and a damaged Walrus seaplane was tipped overboard.

Two Genzan group torpedo squadrons prepared for the next series of attacks. An officer on the *Repulse* noted that 'they seemed to circle our ships like Red Indians about to attack wagons'. On the *Prince of Wales*'s bridge, Lieutenant-Commander R. F. Harland, the torpedo officer, commented aloud that the circling aircraft seemed to be carrying torpedoes. Phillips overheard the remark and replied that there were no such aircraft about. The admiral was not alone in his opinion. Officers much younger than Phillips were surprised that twin-engine bombers could carry torpedoes.[23]

The aircraft swept down towards the big ships in waves of two or three. The pom-poms and machine guns joined the flak barrage. A flimsy curtain of bursting shells and arching tracers leapt upwards. The anti-aircraft gunners were unprepared, however, for the sheer speed of the Japanese bombers, and the great bulk of the shells burst well behind them.

Captain Tennant turned the *Repulse* towards the aircraft diving at his ship to comb the torpedoes they were going to drop. No hits were scored on the *Repulse*, but the *Prince of Wales* was not so fortunate. One aircraft was shot down on its attack run but the torpedo-bombers scored two hits. One torpedo holed the outer hull, but merely caused the flooding of compartments between the outer and inner hull. The other torpedo struck the port outer propeller shaft under the stern. The ship was rent by a tremendous vibration as the buckled propeller shaft continued to work at full power, breaking down bulkheads within the ship until the machinery driving it was shut down. Water flooded down the shaft opening into the bowels of the ship. The *Prince of Wales*'s speed dropped, and a list quickly developed. A power failure shut off lighting and ventilation in a large part of the battleship's rear section. Damaged steering gear meant that the *Prince of Wales* was no longer under the control of the helm.

With the flagship badly damaged, Captain Tennant took it upon himself to radio Singapore at 11.58 a.m. for help. The signal reached Singapore at 12.04 p.m. This was the first information received of Force Z's exact location. If Phillips had signalled Singapore when the first Japanese reconnaissance aircraft was sighted, fighters could have arrived minutes before the first attack. Early in the afternoon all four of Pulford's Buffalo squadrons were still at Singapore, but only eleven Buffaloes of No. 453 Squadron were ordered to take off. There had not been any serious air attack on the island over the previous two days, nor were any of the squadrons on the immediate verge of being transferred northwards. Apart from patrolling around Singapore, the pilots of the forty to fifty Buffaloes stationed on the island had had little to do since the outbreak of war.

In the meantime Kanoya group, the third of the 22nd Air Flotilla's three groups, had arrived over Force Z. Six torpedo-bombers of the group scored four hits on the stricken *Prince of Wales*, now moving at less than ten knots. The twenty remaining torpedo-bombers of Kanoya group attacked the *Repulse* from different directions. The first eight aircraft dropped their torpedoes on the starboard side. Tennant turned the *Repulse* to comb them, but three more aircraft attacked on the port side. A torpedo holed the outer hull doing little damage, but another torpedo hit jammed the ship's rudder. Immediately afterwards Kanoya group's 3rd Squadron swooped down to attack. Lieutenant Iki's and two other aircraft dropped their torpedoes only 600 yards from the target. Another two hits were scored. The aircraft pulled up over the *Repulse*, and Iki could see sailors running to cover to avoid his machine gunners' fire. The other two aircraft though were hit by pom-pom shells and brought down into the sea, one of them in a ball of fire. The final six torpedo bombers managed another hit. The time was now 12.25 p.m.[24]

As her rudder was jammed, the listing *Repulse* was reduced to sailing in a wide circle. Tennant ordered all hands to the main deck to abandon ship. The life rafts made of cork and canvas were released, and men jumped over the side into a vast pool of spreading oil. One officer was seen to mistime his leap and plunged back into the ship through a torpedo hole in the side. A group of marines jumped off the stern into the still turning blades of the propellers. Tennant was swept off the tilting deck by the sea and surfaced alongside a raft. The cries of those still trapped in the darkness below could be heard up the ventilation shafts. The *Repulse* soon rolled over and sank stern first, her bow hanging in the air.

The last two Mihoro group bomber squadrons dropped their bombs on

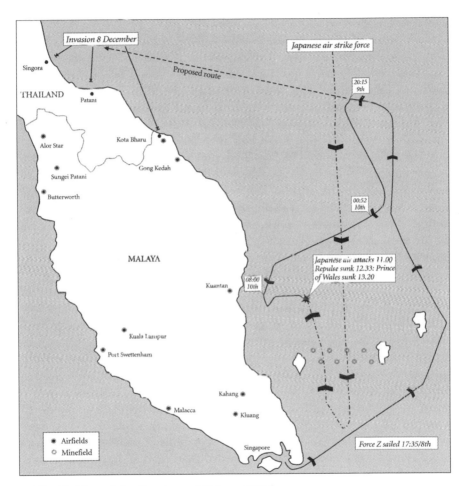

Invasion 8 December

Japanese air strike force

Singora

THAILAND

Patani

Proposed route

20:15
9th

Alor Star

Kota Bharu

Sungei Patani

Gong Kedah

Butterworth

MALAYA

00:52
10th

Japanese air attacks 11.00
Repulse sunk 12.33: Prince
of Wales sunk 13.20

Kuantan

08:00
10th

Kuala Lumpur

Port Swettenham

Kahang

Malacca

Kluang

Singapore

⦿ Airfields
◎ Minefield

Force Z sailed 17:35/8th

4. The Sinking of the *Repulse* and *Prince of Wales*.

the destroyers and the *Prince of Wales*. One bomb hit the flagship, exploding on the main armoured deck. No structural damage was done to the ship, but the compartment in which the bomb burst was being used as a dressing station for wounded and heat exhaustion cases. By this stage Phillips had finally broken radio silence to give Singapore his location. The admiral asked for more destroyers, but did not ask for air cover. At 12.52 p.m. Phillips signalled Singapore again to ask for 'tugs'.[25]

Time was running out. The crew of the sinking *Prince of Wales* was ordered to abandon ship. The destroyer *Express* was brought alongside by Lieutenant-Commander F. J. Cartwright. Hundreds of men crossed over on makeshift lines and gang planks. The destroyer had to pull away as the battleship's list worsened, leaving the remaining crew to queue at the rails, and slide or leap into the oil-slicked ocean. The *Prince of Wales* capsized and sank about 1.20 p.m., roughly an hour and a half after the first torpedo hit.

A despondent Admiral Phillips had remained on the captain's bridge almost till the end. He had waved away those on the admiral's bridge below, and ordered those still around him to put on and inflate their life-saving belts. Bell and Leach advised Phillips to go to the upper deck but he refused, though there was ample opportunity to do so. Phillips was last seen alive on the horizontal side of the bridge as the *Prince of Wales* rolled over. The bodies of Phillips and Leach were later found floating in the water, having been dragged under by the sinking ship.[26]

Among the first RAF aircraft to arrive on the scene had been a pair of Buffaloes of No. 243 Squadron. Flight Lieutenant M. Garden saw a badly listing battleship drifting in a great slick of oil. The *Prince of Wales*'s anti-aircraft guns had opened fire but Garden had used a Verey pistol to give the recognition signal. Before long Flight Lieutenant T. A. Vigors arrived with the Buffaloes of No. 453 Squadron, just in time to see Phillips's flagship sink on the horizon. By the time Vigors was overhead there was not a Japanese aircraft in sight. Hundreds of men were helplessly clinging to wreckage or life rafts in the oily water. Vigors later wrote that they were 'waving, cheering and joking as if they were holiday makers at Brighton'. More cynical commentators have suggested that the men in the water were waving their fists in fury at the late arriving RAF fighters.[27]

The battleships had sunk in under two hundred feet of water, less than the length of the ships. The weather was fine. The seas were calm and warm, and there were several hours of daylight left. The conditions were ideal for rescuing the surviving crew. Over the course of three hours the destroyers plucked 2081 officers and ratings out of the water. 840 men had lost their lives, 513 of the *Repulse*'s crew and 327 from the *Prince of Wales*. The Japanese had lost eighteen dead in the three aircraft shot down.

The destroyers brought the survivors back to Singapore with the Buffaloes flying overhead as escort. At Singapore Air Vice-Marshal Pulford said to Captain Tennant: 'My God I hope you don't blame me for this. I had no idea where you were.'[28] The destroyer *Stronghold* and four United States Navy destroyers steamed north from Singapore to re-search the area in which the battleships had sunk, but they found no more survivors.

News of the battleships' sinking was dispatched to London. On the morning of 10 December Admiral Pound rang Churchill with the bad news. Churchill was still in bed. He wrote in his memoirs: 'I put the telephone down. I was thankful to be alone. In all the war I never received a more direct shock ... As I turned over and twisted in bed the full horror of the news sank in upon me.' Churchill had worked with Phillips over a long period, and he had sailed on the *Prince of Wales* during his Atlantic crossing to meet with Roosevelt in the late summer of 1941. Churchill had also been personally responsible for sending the *Prince of Wales* to the Far East.

Reaction from other senior naval figures was scathing. With Phillips dead, Layton regained his command at Singapore. He told his secretary soon after hearing news of Force Z's demise: 'I don't know exactly what's happened. But I always said he would make a balls of it, and he has.' At Gibraltar Admiral Somerville remarked: 'thoroughly bad show ... Why the hell don't they send someone out there who has been through the mill and knows his stuff?'[29] The Admiralty responded to the sinking of the two great ships by falling back upon a scheme to build up a fleet in the Indian Ocean by April 1942 at the earliest. In practice (after the sinking of Force Z), the Admiralty did not dispatch a single ship to aid in the local defence of either Singapore or the Malay Barrier.[30]

Amongst Malaya's military and civilian population the loss of the two great warships so soon after their arrival, and so soon after the outbreak of war with Japan, was a terrible blow. Major F. Spencer Chapman later wrote:

> I shall never forget the sense of utter calamity with which we heard the news. Until this disaster neither I nor any of those with whom I discussed the war situation had any real doubt that we should be able to hold the Japs, even if it meant giving ground until we had regained the initiative.
>
> Now our sense of security and faith in the future vanished completely. For the first time I began to consider the possibility of losing Malaya.[31]

Duff Cooper, the Resident Minister for Far Eastern Affairs, felt that the sinking of the battleships

> was the worst single piece of news I have ever received. More disastrous things,

such as the Fall of France have happened, but the news of them arrived gradually
and the mind had time to prepare itself for the catastrophe.[32]

A sense of forboding filled the hearts and minds of all those in Malaya who
had reason to fear a Japanese victory in the war.

After the Royal Navy had suffered catastrophic losses during the evacuation of Crete, Admiral Cunningham was said to have asserted that it takes
the Navy three years to build a ship, but it would take three hundred to
rebuild a tradition. Apologists for Phillips have claimed that the admiral
was upholding the fighting traditions of the Royal Navy by taking Force
Z into the South China Sea to look for Japanese shipping. If Phillips's
foray had been well timed and executed that line of argument might have
had some validity. But Force Z's final cruise was launched too late to be
effective and was riddled with operational mistakes. Two capital ships and
many lives were wasted. If Force Z had retired to the Dutch East Indies,
Phillips might still have been able to influence events by deterring the
Japanese from sending seaborne expeditions directly against Singapore and
southern Malaya. The *Repulse* and the *Prince of Wales* at the bottom of
the sea helped nobody but Imperial Japan.

# 6

## *Jitra*

As disaster had overtaken the Royal Navy and RAF in Malaya, the army was left to shoulder the bulk of the burden of fighting the Japanese invaders. In north-west Malaya the right flank of the 11th Indian Division's main position at Jitra was to be protected by a two battalion force advancing into Thailand from Kroh. Kroh Column's objective was a defile known as the Ledge, roughly midway between the Thai-Malayan frontier near Kroh and the Thai coast at Patani. The Ledge was a six mile stretch of road cut out of the hillside high above the Patani River. The British hoped to demolish stretches of the road – blowing it off the hillside in places – to render the route impassable to vehicles for weeks to come. If the position at Jitra was to be held for any length of time, the road south from Patani leading towards Kroh and the Trunk Road on the west coast of Malaya, well to the south of Jitra, had to be firmly blocked. But due to a bad organizational oversight, on 8 December the 5/14th Punjabis and a mountain battery, both based at Penang, had yet to reach their war stations at Kroh. Lieutenant-Colonel H. D. Moorhead's 3/16th Punjabis, only half Krohcol's allocated strength, had to commence the advance alone.

At the Thai-Malayan frontier the first sepoy to cross the customs barrier was shot dead by armed Thai constabulary. Though Thai resistance abruptly ceased during the afternoon of the following day, 9 December, the town of Betong, only five miles over the frontier, was not reached till that evening. A Thai official at Betong apologized for the constabulary's mistaken defiance.[1] At dawn on 10 December, the campaign's third day, the 3/16th Punjabis embussed in lorries. Rapid progress was made, and the troops disembussed six miles south of the Ledge. But the Japanese 42nd Regiment and two companies of light tanks had been landed at Patani at 3 a.m. on 8 December. By the afternoon of 10 December they had already reached the Ledge and Krohcol had lost the race.

After leaving their transport, Moorhead's Punjabis advanced on foot for another mile towards the Ledge, only to be attacked and roughly handled by a Japanese force supported by tanks. The seriously wounded Subedar Sher Khan was crushed beneath a tank's wheels. Two Punjabi companies were cut off from the rest of the battalion. The following day, 11 December, one company rejoined, but most of the other company remained missing. That afternoon the Punjabis defended the bank of a small stream twenty-five miles north of Betong. Moorhead feared that the Japanese force opposing him was the advance guard of a whole regiment, and that evening he rang the 11th Division's headquarters to request permission to withdraw. 'There are too many slit eyes round here', Moorhead told the divisional GSO 1, Lieutenant-Colonel A. M. L. Harrison. Permission was granted for a retreat to Kroh, on the Malayan side of the frontier, but even Kroh was dangerously close to the Trunk Road, the force at Jitra's only line of communication southwards.[2]

Moorhead planned to withdraw the Punjabis towards Kroh at 9 a.m. on 12 December, but half an hour before the retreat was due to begin the enterprising Japanese attacked in strength, having moved around the Punjabis' flanks during the night. C Company was surrounded and only ten men fought their way clear. Both of C Company's British officers were killed and B Company was also mauled. The carrier platoon's four remaining vehicles covered the withdrawal but only two got clear. Moorhead himself departed in one of the carriers, having carried to safety a wounded lance-naik lying by the roadside. The retreating Punjabis, now reduced to 350 officers and men, blew bridges behind them to delay the Japanese. Passing back through the 5/14th Punjabis, Moorhead told their commander that his sepoys had 'fought well, but I think I hung on too long'.[3] The slowly but steadily deteriorating situation on the Kroh-Patani road was always at the back of the 11th Division's commander's mind during this period.

Though the Japanese were already cutting behind the right flank of Jitra, the troops of the 11th Division set about putting the Jitra position in order, somewhat down at heart over the cancellation of the general advance into Thailand. In the meantime small advance guards were sent forward to delay the Japanese. An armoured train steamed up the railway through Perlis state into Thailand, almost halfway to Singora. Sappers blew an important rail bridge and the train withdrew, the sappers blowing other demolitions en route.

A motorised detachment under the command of Major Andrews advanced up the Trunk Road to Sadao, ten miles over the frontier. About 9 p.m. on 9 December a Japanese column of vehicles, headlamps blazing, approached Sadao. The Japanese 5th Division's advance guard was Saeki Detachment, so-called as its commander was Lieutenant-Colonel Saeki. Saeki was a relatively old man for his rank. He had been at the Military College the same time as the XXV Army's Chief of Staff, Lieutenant-General Suzuki. Saeki Detachment comprised only five hundred men, and its principal units

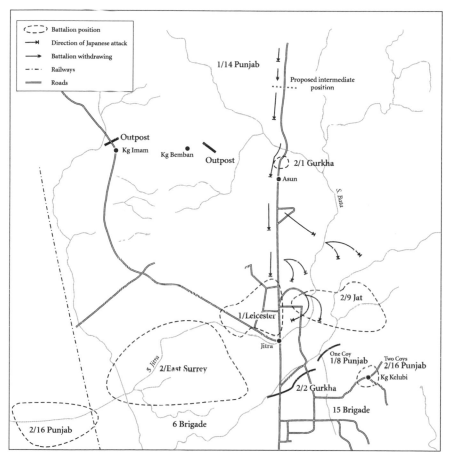

Legend:
- Battalion position
- Direction of Japanese attack
- Battalion withdrawing
- Railways
- Roads

1/14 Punjab

Proposed intermediate position

Outpost
Kg Imam
Kg Bemban
Outpost

2/1 Gurkha

Asun

S. Bata

2/9 Jat

1/Leicester

Jitra

S. Jitra

2/East Surrey

One Coy
1/8 Punjab

Two Coys
2/16 Punjab
Kg Kelubi

2/2 Gurkha

15 Brigade

2/16 Punjab

6 Brigade

5. Jitra.

were the 5th Division's Reconnaissance Regiment (less its 3rd Company), and one company of the 1st Tank Regiment.[4]

A section of anti-tank guns with Andrews's detachment halted the Japanese column by scoring hits on two or three tanks. As Japanese infantry tumbled out of their lorries to attack, the detachment withdrew southwards back across the frontier. The British had received clear warning that the Japanese had quickly got tanks ashore to lead their advance. Lieutenant-Colonel Tsuji, XXV Army's Chief of Planning and Operations, later claimed that Japanese troops found a blood-stained map in an abandoned vehicle, complete with pencilled unit positions marked around Changlun and Jitra. This was particularly significant as the Japanese advance guard did not possess a single detailed map of the ground that lay ahead.[5]

Well aware that work at Jitra was far from complete, the 11th Division's commander, Major-General Murray-Lyon, decided that he wanted the Japanese held north of Jitra until 12 December, so as to give his troops extra time in which to finish their preparations. Murray-Lyon had been an enthusiastic supporter of Operation Matador, and he had devoted more attention to the possibilities of advancing into Thailand than the problems of defending Jitra.

Brigadier K. A. Garrett, the 15th Indian Brigade's commander, was given the 2/1st Gurkhas and the 1/14th Punjabis, and ordered to delay the advancing Japanese north of Jitra. The Gurkhas occupied a position forward of Asun behind a stream, the best defensive locality between the frontier and Jitra. The Punjabis, with a mountain battery and a section of anti-tank guns, were posted further north astride the Trunk Road. The Punjabis had taken up position at Changlun, six miles south of the frontier, by the evening of 10 December. The Japanese had spent the day repairing bridges and damage to the Trunk Road, surprised to have met no opposition at the actual frontier.

On 10 December the aerodrome at Alor Star, the main reason the 11th Division was at Jitra, was hurriedly abandoned by RAF ground staff. The sight of billowing smoke, and the sound of explosions coming from the aerodrome, was bad for troop morale. The division's headquarters was not given prior warning of the RAF's departure, and armed guards had to be posted to stop the destruction of stores useful to the army. Murray-Lyon later claimed that knowledge that demolitions were taking place caused troops to think a withdrawal was imminent. Another consequence of Japanese aerial superiority was the commencement of a string of false and distracting reports about alleged Japanese parachute landings behind British lines. It was later concluded that puffs of bursting anti-aircraft fire were probably mistaken for parachutists.[6]

1. Lieutenant-General A. E. Percival, GOC Malaya from May 1941. (*IWM*)

2. Left to right: Sir Robert Brooke-Popham, Duff Cooper, Sir Earl Page, Sir Archibald Clark-Kerr, Sir Shenton Thomas, Sir Geoffrey Layton. (*IWM*)

3. General Sir Archibald Wavell and Lieutenant-General Percival. (*IWM*)

4. Lieutenant-General Percival and Major-General H. G. Bennett, the commander of the 8th Australian Division. (*IWM*)

5. Lieutenant General Sir Lionel Bond inspects Australian troops. Behind him is Major-General Bennett. (*IWM*)

6. General Wavell inspecting the trench mortar section of an Indian regiment. (*IWM*)

7. An Indian regiment in column in typical Malayan countryside. (*IWM*)

8. The Governor of Malaya, Sir Shenton Thomas (in topee) and senior officers meet the *Queen Mary,* carrying 5750 Australian troops, 18 February 1941. (*AWM*)

9. The 22nd Australian Brigade disembarks at Singapore, 18 February 1941. (*AWM*)

10. Prime Minister Hideki Tojo with the Japanese War Cabinet. (*IWM*)

11. Japanese troops enter Hong Kong, led by Lieutenant-General Sakai, December 1941. (*IWM*)

12. Lieutenant-General Tomoyuki Yamashita, commander of the Japanese XXV Army, inspecting a scene of recent fighting. (*AWM*)

13. Japanese troops landing equipment at Singora.

14. Admiral Sir Tom Phillips, the commander of Force Z, inspecting an Australian soldier. (*IWM*)

15. HMS *Prince of Wales*. (*IWM*)

Yet another thing taking off in Malaya was spy mania. A Malay overseer was arrested at Alor Star with plans of the aerodrome in his possession. As the overseer was working at the aerodrome, it was actually quite proper that he should have had the plans. Seven more Malays were arrested at Alor Star for allegedly making an arrow with a goalpost and a palm tree pointing towards a gun position. In an area full of troops and installations, building materials, cut down trees, even washing on a line often pointed towards something if an observer had enough imagination to establish a connection. Many ground observers, most of whom had never been in an aircraft in their lives, seldom understood that a pilot travelling at high speed could never have seen the signs that they believed they had detected. III Corps headquarters gave directions that fifth columnists were to be 'disposed of as expeditiously as possible'.[7]

At Changlun on the morning of 11 December the 1/14th Punjabis were dug in behind the Sungei Laka. A patrol of two platoons was sent out at dawn under Captain Mohammed Akhram but was never seen again. A Japanese spotter plane was soon buzzing overhead and the Punjabis were under attack by 8 a.m. The first Japanese assault on the bridge over the stream was stopped. The demolition charge on the bridge was blown as a precaution, but the explosives were either poorly placed, insufficiently strong or damaged by the rain. The bridge was damaged but remained passable. Mortar bombs landing near the Punjabis' headquarters wounded Brigadier Garrett in the neck. By early afternoon Japanese troops had captured the damaged bridge.

The 1/14th Punjabis were ordered to disengage and withdrew towards the 2/1st Gurkhas at Asun, eight miles south of Changlun. But at 3 p.m. Murray-Lyon visited Lieutenant-Colonel Fitzpatrick, the Punjabis' commander, accompanied by Brigadier Garrett and Lieutenant-Colonel Fulton, the Gurkhas' commander. Garrett and Fitzpatrick were keen to complete a retirement behind the stream at Asun, after which the causeway across the stream could be blown to form an anti-tank barrier. This manoeuvre had been practised prior to the outbreak of war. However Murray-Lyon, still worried about the state of preparations at Jitra, wanted the Punjabis to make another stand two miles in front of Asun so as to impose an additional delay upon the Japanese advance. Captain Mohan Singh, the commander of the Punjabis' headquarters company, was called over by Fitzpatrick and told of the change in plan. Mohan Singh was surprised, and 'I noticed the same disbelief in the eyes of the Commanding Officer'. Murray-Lyon assured them that the Japanese had no tanks and could easily be held in front of Asun till the next morning.[8] Fitzpatrick and his unit's senior officers went to reconnoitre the terrain north of the Asun causeway.

Meanwhile the Japanese had managed to repair the road bridge at Chang-lun to bear the weight of armoured vehicles. Amid heavy rain, Saeki Detachment resumed the advance with Saeki, a one-time instructor at the Cavalry School, and Lieutenant-Colonel Tsuji riding in a captured black motor car at the rear of the column. The armoured column could boast ten medium tanks and the reconnaissance regiment's two dozen light tanks and armoured cars.

As the Punjabis approached their designated position, two miles north of Asun, all was quiet but for the sound of rain. About 4.30 p.m. the downpour became torrential and visibility was cut to twenty yards. Suddenly out of the gloom a column of tanks and lorries came down the jungle- and rubber-lined road. The Punjabis, taken completely by surprise, were scattered, some in shock at their first sight of tanks spitting gunfire at such close quarters. A Japanese account of the action later claimed:

> Because of the heavy squall, the enemy had left the tanks, trucks and guns on the road and had taken shelter from the rain in the rubber plantations. With the fierce advancing attack of the Japanese Army, the enemy started to fire in con-sternation but, fearing danger, they started to scatter in a disorderly fashion in tanks and trucks. Our tanks rushed fiercely into this panic-stricken array sand-wiching the enemy tanks among our own tanks. While the enemy were fumbling around not being able to fire for fear of hitting their own tanks, our tank turret covers were lifted and our courageous soldiers started to attack with hand grenades and bayonets to annihilate the enemy. The enemy fled, without orders, leaving approximately twenty tanks [bren-gun carriers] stranded on the road side.[9]

Two anti-tank guns and two mountain guns were overrun. The anti-tank guns had been caught still limbered up. Lieutenant-Colonel Fitzpatrick was wounded trying to improvise a road-block with the battalion's vehicles.

Captain Mohan Singh had been looking for a new site for the battalion's headquarters when the Japanese tanks swept through. He was driving back up the Trunk Road when a tank coming down the road forced him to abandon the lorry he was travelling in. From behind a rubber tree Mohan Singh watched the first tank pass, the turret open and the gunner standing up and looking around. 'Then came the second one. Its gunner saw me peeping from the side of the tree and fired a long burst from his machine gun and laughed heartily.'[10] The Punjabis had ceased to be an organized unit.

Japanese tanks and motorized infantry rapidly 'blitzed' their way to Asun. The leading Gurkha company was scattered to the immediate north of its battalion's main position. As tanks neared the Asun causeway the sapper Viceroy's Commissioned Officer in charge of the demolition party was hit by Japanese fire. The commander of the 23rd Field Company, Major Bate, dashed forward to take his place. Bate was mortally wounded after pressing the demolition plunger, but the water-logged charge failed to explode. The leading tank was stopped by Company Havildar Manbahadur Gurung, armed with an anti-tank rifle. The tank column ground to a halt. The havildar then ran out and dragged to cover the dying Major Bate. Damaged tanks formed a makeshift road-block, but Japanese infantry waded across the waist deep stream and swamp to drive off the Indians who had stopped the tanks.

Further to the rear, at the Gurkhas' headquarters, the first indication that something was amiss was when a long column of Punjabi transport roared down the road without stopping. An officer on a motor cycle gave Lieutenant-Colonel Fulton the unwelcome news that Japanese tanks had reached the Asun causeway. Fulton commented: 'Wind up. Why I only left the 1/14th [Punjabis] an hour or two ago and they were right as rain.' [11]

The tank column swept onward to bypass the Gurkhas in position behind the swamp. By 6.45 p.m. the Japanese had reached the battalion's head-quarters area, which was subdued after a half hour fight. Of 550 Gurkhas to go into action, only two hundred made their way back to British lines. Of the 350 missing, perhaps twenty to thirty were killed in the fighting and the rest were eventually rounded up and taken prisoner. Of the Punjabis, around 270 were led southwards by Garrett and other officers to escape capture. [12]

By the afternoon of 11 December it was clear that the Jitra Line – the Maginot Line of Malaya – would soon be under attack. The troops of the 6th and the 15th Brigades had spent the previous three days digging weapon pits, clearing fields of fire, wiring, mining, laying field telephone cable and building obstacles. Intermittent torrential rain showers had interfered with the work, and had slowly but surely turned unmetalled tracks into quag-mires. Troops had to haul ammunition and stores by hand once tracks became impassable for vehicles. No wire had been put up prior to the outbreak of hostilities for fear of positions being mapped by spies. In fact a lot of wire and signal cable had been reserved for Operation Matador, and had had to be unloaded again from train wagons. The bottom of trenches kept filling with water, causing the sides to crumble, and the wheels of guns sank into the mud at the bottom of gun-pits. In some places open topped breast-works had had to be built instead of trenches, and some sections of the front remained unwired as supplies had run out.

The creatures of the wild were disturbed by these activities. Centipedes, leeches, scorpions, spiders, and the occasional menacing hooded black cobra, put in appearances to alarm and harass the labouring soldiers.

Animals and insects such as these were hardly edible, but some ducks unwisely lingering in the neighbourhood supplemented the rations of the sub-unit that was lucky enough to catch them. At night the men had no shelter as tents had been struck, so they tried to sleep rolled in their gas capes with sodden feet. The rest of one unit was disturbed by a water buffalo blowing up on an anti-tank mine. To add insult to discomfort Japanese aircraft dropped propaganda leaflets in three languages across the Jitra area. Rumours circulated as to the strength of the Japanese force known to be approaching.[13]

Each night sentries were posted and patrols sent out into the rainy night. The nerves of tired men became frayed. On the night of 10/11 December, on the front of the 2nd East Surreys, the noise of the rain had been broken from 10 p.m. onwards by sounds of firing. Lieutenant S. Abbott recorded:

> A particularly disturbing LMG [light machine gun] is potting away at frequent intervals from one of our forward platoon posts. I go out there and am informed that the Section Commander is absolutely certain that there are Japs about one hundred yards away! We find, on closer investigation, that it is one of our own patrols trying to find a way in!! Poor devils! They have had a foul time lying in a three-foot-deep paddy.[14]

The division's preparations were incomplete, but they still enjoyed the considerable advantage of fighting on ground with which they were familiar. On the right flank, Garrett's 15th Brigade was allocated a 6000 yard sector that included both the roads approaching Jitra from the north. On the left flank, Brigadier W. O. Lay's 6th Brigade held 18,000 yards of marshy country between Garrett's brigade and the coast. Brigadier W. St J. Carpendale's 28th Brigade was in reserve, and the Lanarkshire Yeomanry's 155th Field Regiment (sixteen 4.5 inch howitzers), two batteries and a section of a mountain regiment, and an anti-tank regiment (less one battery) were available to support the infantry. Other artillery units were due to join the division in the next few days. Given the length of the Jitra front, the existence of a reserve brigade was vital, as otherwise the Japanese might concentrate their strength against a narrow portion of the line and punch right through. Unfortunately for Murray-Lyon, the strength of the division's reserve had been eaten into as two battalions had already been scattered by the approaching Japanese at Asun.

The battalion of the division on the extreme right flank at Jitra was the 2/9th Jats (Lieutenant-Colonel C. K. Tester). The Jats' sector was 3000 yards wide and was of particular importance as it was just east of the vital Trunk Road. On the Jats' right Captain Hislop's B Company occupied a position among rubber trees, with jungle-covered hills beyond their right flank. To the left of B Company stretched 1300 yards of knee-deep paddy fields and mud, bisected by the thirty foot-wide Sungei Bata stream, swollen by monsoon rains and unfordable. The Bata and another stream were bordered by jungle. The Jats' C Company was deployed along the rear edge of the paddy. On the Jats' left flank Captain C. B. V. Holden's D Company held ground that was mostly under rubber. D Company's front was protected by an anti-tank ditch, but the Jats' barbed wire entanglement was only partly complete. Tester's battalion headquarters and A Company (less a platoon still at Tanjong Pau camp) were in reserve five hundred yards behind D Company's right flank.[15]

To the left of the Jats the 1st Leicesters held a comparatively strong position. Many of the Leicesters forward posts were located along the edge of a rubber plantation, overlooking paddy that stretched for four or five hundred yards. A partly completed anti-tank ditch had been dug across the paddy, and the machine used to dig the ditch lay abandoned by its human operators in the middle of the fields. However the Leicesters were also charged with the vital responsibility of blocking both the roads heading into the Jitra position from the north. Two anti-tank guns were sited near the Trunk Road to cover a bridge which crossed a small stream running in front of the Leicesters. The Leicesters had a partly obscured view of both roads from their main line of weapon pits.

The chief problem with the Leicesters' position were two patches of vegetation given the names 'copse' and 'market garden', in the far right-hand corner of their sector. The market garden was mined, and the copse provided useful cover for the anti-tank gun detachment covering the bridge, but otherwise the area contained no infantry. It was hoped that this locality would be covered by fire from nearby Leicester and Jat platoon posts, and a Leicester platoon half a mile to the south of the copse. This clumsy defensive arrangement so close to the Trunk Road, the most likely Japanese line of advance, was a prime example of the way in which preparations for Operation Matador had been allowed to distract attention from quite basic safeguards at Jitra. The 15th Brigade's original reserve battalion, the now crippled 1/14th Punjabis, was replaced by the 2/2nd Gurkhas from the 28th Brigade.

In the 6th Brigade's sector, the 2nd East Surreys prolonged the line from the left of the Leicesters towards the railway. On the brigade's left flank, the 2/16th Punjabis held a long front with one company dug in at the railway and another near the coast. Much of the intervening swamp was watched only by patrols. The large marsh between the railway and the coast was thought to be tactically impassable even in the dry season. The 1/8th Punjabis was the brigade's reserve battalion.

Of the 28th Brigade's two remaining battalions, the 2/1st Gurkhas had been shattered at Asun, and the 2/9th Gurkhas were deployed to the division's rear to guard the abandoned Alor Star and Sungei Patani aerodromes from Japanese paratroopers. There was thus no divisional reserve worthy of the name. Also, because Brigadier Garrett was missing after the fiasco at Asun, the 28th Brigade's Brigadier Carpendale had had to take over command of the 15th Brigade at a crucial moment. Until a few days previously, Carpendale had been based at Ipoh far to the south. His experience of the Jitra position was confined to 'one flight over it and one superficial drive and walk round it'.

The brigade's headquarters was located at the northern edge of Tanjong Pau camp, just behind the Trunk Road's iron bridge over the Sungei Bata. Carpendale arrived at Tanjong Pau after nightfall on 11 December. A truck was being used as an office as there was no hut available. Carpendale later recalled that 'the ground was soaking wet and covered with pools of water; most of the trenches were waterlogged as high as the fire-step, and it was pitch dark'. Carpendale was not the only late arrival at Jitra. A month previously the Leicesters' commanding officer had left the battalion for a staff appointment. His replacement, Lieutenant-Colonel C. E. Morrison, only appeared at 5 p.m. that afternoon.[16]

At 8.30 p.m. on 11 December Japanese tanks on the Trunk Road finally reached the Jitra Line. Clanking vehicles with lights showing were seen looming forward out of the darkness. The officer with a patrol on the road fired a white flare as a warning signal. The flare climbed into the warm night air, floating momentarily at the top of its arc. The lights of the Japanese tanks went out and British and Indian troops opened fire. The rain-sodden charge on the road bridge over the stream in front of the Leicesters' right flank company failed to detonate, just like the demolition at Asun earlier in the day. But the nearby anti-tank gunners were equal to the challenge, and two tanks were hit to form an effective road block on a narrow embankment. The tank column closed up behind but soon withdrew harassed by British field artillery fire.

On the 6th Brigade's front, on the road that ran south from Perlis state, outpost troops withdrawing towards Jitra were mistaken for Japanese. A demolition over a stream at Manggoi was successfully blown in front of the outpost troops. A number of vehicles, carriers, seven anti-tank guns and a mountain battery's four 3.7 inch howitzers had to be abandoned, equipment the brigade could not afford to give away without a fight. There had been no sign of Japanese activity on the road to Perlis.

With their column halted on the Trunk Road, Lieutenant-Colonels Saeki and Tsuji left their car to stretch their legs amid the rubber trees. Saeki was keen to try an immediate attack and Tsuji was in agreement. Japanese patrols pressed forward intrepidly during the night to look for gaps between defended localities. Though telephone contact with the Jats' right-hand B Company had failed, reports from that quarter were received at the 15th Brigade's headquarters. The reports vaguely claimed that the Japanese were pushing past the exposed right flank of the Jats. An alarmed Carpendale appealed to the 6th Brigade for reinforcements, though little effort was made to keep divisional headquarters and Murray-Lyon informed of these developments. Brigadier Lay sent two companies of the 2/16th Punjabis and two companies of the 1/8th Punjabis across to Carpendale, who deployed them well to the rear of the Jats' right flank to counter a wide turning movement. The 6th Brigade had now lost most of its reserve. Carpendale also ordered the 2/2nd Gurkhas to dig in along the south bank of the Sungei Bata, east of the iron bridge.

Meanwhile a young Japanese officer, Second Lieutenant Oto, had returned from a patrol to report to Saeki and Tsuji. By the light of an electric torch Tsuji could see that Oto's coat was stained with blood. Oto said that he had crept into enemy lines and killed a sentry at the far end of the bridge. He claimed that the line of advance into the British position was not difficult. 'There are wire entanglements, but there are gaps between them, and enemy troops are not yet in position. It seems as if a night attack would be possible.' [17] Saeki issued orders for an immediate attack.

Lieutenant Oto's No. 1 Company of the 5th Reconnaissance Regiment set off down the road around 3 a.m. to set in motion another audacious and opportunistic assault. The road-block that had been hastily thrown across the Trunk Road by the Leicesters the previous evening was rushed by the Japanese, and some further penetration was made until halted by a Leicesters' counter-attack at dawn. By 6 a.m., amid heavy rain, another Japanese company had been thrown into the attack, and not surprisingly it had found and moved into the unoccupied gap dominated by the market garden and copse. A badly wounded messenger returned to Saeki Detachment's headquarters to report this success, but Tsuji had been hoping for more rapid progress.

Aided by tank gunfire, Japanese troops in the copse soon rushed towards the left-hand platoon of the Jats' D Company. A section covering a pillbox artillery observation post was bundled aside. An artillery forward observation officer was killed, and for the rest of the day a small Japanese flag fluttered from the pillbox. A counter-attack by D Company's reserve platoon failed to retake the pillbox. The section of anti-tank guns that had been covering the road bridge attempted to relocate to another position but was badly shot up whilst on the move. One gun was overturned by a direct hit from a tank shell and the survivors scattered to cover. The detachment's commander, Lieutenant Hare, quickly brought another gun into action to keep the tanks at bay.[18]

As the morning progressed Tsuji was increasingly worried about the situation. Nearby tanks and vehicles on the road were under heavy British artillery fire. Lieutenant Oto reported to Tsuji again covered in more blood and mud, and apologized with tears in his eyes for having underestimated the strength of the enemy the previous night. Oto had been wounded in the shoulder. The torn flesh was red and swollen, and his face was drained of colour. Tsuji told the young officer not to worry, gave him some chocolate, and had him carried off on a stretcher. (Oto later died of gangrene at Saigon.) By now Saeki Detachment had committed all its infantry. Tsuji borrowed a car and drove through shellfire towards the rear to summon forward troops that were trailing behind the Japanese advance guard. Tsuji met Major-General Kawamura, the commander of the 9th Infantry Brigade, and the 41st Regiment's Colonel Okabe. He urged them both to march their men towards the sound of the guns with all haste.[19]

Major-General Murray-Lyon had arrived at the 15th Brigade's headquarters at 9 a.m. As the Japanese were reported to be making alarming progress towards Kroh and the division's rear, and given the number of troops already lost around Asun, Murray-Lyon soon decided to request Heath's permission to immediately withdraw from Jitra. Heath, however, was away from his headquarters and travelling to Singapore on an overnight train. (Heath wanted to see Percival to insist that Brigadier Key be allowed to withdraw his brigade from Kelantan state.) Murray-Lyon's brief request was referred from the headquarters of III Corps directly to Percival but was not granted. The next position at which the division could make a stand was Gurun, thirty miles to the rear of Jitra. To pull back that far without a major battle was contrary to Percival's conception of a fighting retreat.

After reaching Singapore during the day a dismayed Heath heard of Percival's refusal to back Murray-Lyon's judgement. Heath has been criticised for not being present at his headquarters at such a vital moment, but any withdrawal from Jitra would always have required Percival's consent.

As the morning of 12 December wore on, amid the rain and mud of Jitra, Brigadier Carpendale again asked Lay for reinforcements. Lay generously agreed to give the 15th Brigade the 1/8th Punjabis' two remaining rifle companies. By now Lay had given half of his brigade's infantry to Carpendale, though the latter had already sent back one of the Punjabi companies given him during the night, as he believed it was too unsteady to be of any use.

The fresh 1/8th Punjabi companies were sent forward to counter-attack Japanese troops holding the wedge of ground between the Leicesters and Jats. Murray-Lyon saw the Punjabis filing forward near the iron bridge and he tried to encourage them without much obvious success. He turned to his attendant GSO 1, Lieutenant-Colonel Harrison, and told him, 'I haven't seen that look on men's faces since March 1918' (the time of one of the worst British defeats of the First World War).[20]

As the Punjabis began to pass Jitra village a battery commenced a fifteen minute bombardment of the Japanese they were to attack. At about the same time the Jats' Lieutenant-Colonel Tester ordered another platoon from his battalion's reserve to sweep the same area the Punjabis were heading towards. Moving through rubber trees and patches of jungle, the Jats believed they had encountered the enemy and opened fire. The mistake soon became apparent, but the two Punjabi companies had been reduced in strength by panic and casualties. The Punjabis' commander, Lieutenant-Colonel L. V. Bates, rang Tester from the headquarters of the Jats' D Company to say that his carriers had become bogged and that little could be seen to the front. Tester rang brigade headquarters to pass on this information, but he was told that the attack had to go ahead.

About 10 a.m. the remaining Punjabis finally set out on their attack. The pillbox observation post was retaken, but advancing onwards towards the copse the Punjabis were met by a hail of fire. Bates, two other officers and a number of men were killed. Those who reached the copse were swiftly dispatched by the Japanese, and more than one sepoy died trying to drag in the body of their commanding officer.[21]

By midday Major-General Kawamura had arrived to take charge of the Japanese side of the battle. Kawamura sent the 41st Regiment to reinforce Saeki Detachment east of the Trunk Road. The 11th Regiment was instructed to deploy west of the road when it arrived, and both regiments were ordered to prepare to attack that night. The 41st Regiment's 2nd Battalion was the first fresh Japanese unit to reach the front. It began to work its way forward against the left flank of the Jats, into the wedge still held by Saeki's troops.[22]

The commander of the Jats' D Company, Captain Holden, was able to direct artillery fire using the telephone line back to battalion and brigade headquarters. The artillery fire helped to keep the Japanese in check for a time. The shells whining overhead split rubber trees with a fearful crack and sent showers of soil and mud skyward. However the artillery support gradually waned as ammunition ran low. Holden reported on the telephone that the Japanese were massing in the anti-tank ditch covering his front, uncomfortably close to the company's weapon pits. Lieutenant-Colonel

Tester told him that they would have to hang on as best they could. With their rifles and machine guns beginning to jam in the mud and rain, the Japanese eventually ran over the top of the company. Holden was killed and the rest of his men with few exceptions either shared that fate or were taken prisoner.[23]

Within the hour Japanese troops had pressed south to come into contact with the 2/2nd Gurkhas behind the Sungei Bata. The Leicesters' and the Surreys' carrier platoons helped to repel Japanese troops pushing against the Leicesters' exposed right flank. Troops of the Leicesters' headquarters company were used to form a defensive flank.

About 3 p.m. Murray-Lyon left divisional headquarters to visit the 15th Brigade's headquarters again. Carpendale told him that the Japanese had 'shot their bolt for the day'. Carpendale was even thinking of counter-attacking the following morning. Murray-Lyon then headed off to visit Lay's headquarters. The day so far had been quiet on Lay's front. A Japanese patrol had been driven off by the East Surreys and little else of note had occurred. Thinking to secure the division's line of retreat, Murray-Lyon ordered two of the Surreys' companies to the rear to guard the Trunk Road bridges over the Sungei Kedah at Kepala Batas. The rest of the battalion was to move to Alor Star aerodrome once the situation in the 15th Brigade's area had been stabilized.

In Murray-Lyon's absence Carpendale's optimism had begun to wane. He ordered the Leicesters to pivot backwards so that their right flank might link up with the Gurkhas near the iron bridge over the Sungei Bata. The Leicesters had felt relatively secure in their original position and had lost only thirty casualties in the previous twenty-four hours. In Lieutenant-Colonel Morrison's temporary absence, Major Harvey strongly protested against the proposed move without success. At 4 p.m. the Leicesters began a complicated partial retirement, which was only completed after nightfall amid considerable confusion. Carriers dragged most of the bogged anti-tank guns back to the new line. The Leicesters' left flank company maintained its position, and the rest of the battalion pulled back to a narrow ridge with deep paddy in front and behind. Digging was impossible and troops had to stand up in a pool of water to see over the crops around them.

To conform with the Leicesters' retirement, the Jats were ordered to pull back to a line between Tanjong Pau and Kelubi. Contact had long since been lost with the Jats' right-hand company, and the company was incorrectly reported to have been captured during the afternoon.[24]

Units behind the Sungei Bata were under sporadic artillery and mortar fire. As the afternoon drew to a close a steady stream of troops and transport moved back along the Trunk Road over the Sungei Bata's iron bridge, the division's principal line of retreat. The Leicesters' war diarist recorded:

> The scene at the Bata Bridge and for two hundred yards south of it from 5 p.m. onwards, was one of indescribable confusion. Indians and Gurkhas were firing in most directions, but chiefly to the north east, from both sides of the main road and, as far as could be seen, into the backs of elements of the 2/9th Jats and one of the Gurkha battalions. Several men were seen to be shot dead by their comrades at a range of less than the road's breadth.
>
> A Royal Engineer havildar, in the temporary absence of his British officer, was asking officers for authority to blow the Bata Bridge, with all our transport and some anti-tank guns still north of it. Japanese mortar bombs were falling in Jitra village and on the Jat and British battalions and our artillery were frequently falling short and hitting the Bata Bridge.[25]

When the Japanese neared the north bank of the Bata crossing the Leicesters were effectively cut off on the wrong side of the river. The Leicesters had been unable to make contact with the Gurkhas near the iron bridge, not least because 'heavy rifle and light automatic fire was opened on anyone approaching their [the Gurkhas'] position'.[26]

Murray-Lyon and Harrison arrived at the Trunk Road about 6 p.m., and saw for themselves the panic and indiscriminate firing. Upon returning to divisional headquarters, Murray-Lyon was greeted by false reports that the Leicesters were under renewed attack, and that the Jats had been overrun. There was also news waiting of further Japanese progress down the Kroh road that was only too true. At 7.30 p.m. Murray-Lyon again asked Malaya Command at Singapore for permission to withdraw from Jitra. Percival gave his approval on this occasion and Heath sent a message back to Murray-Lyon via his corps headquarters an hour later. Murray-Lyon was also given the welcome news that Krohcol would be transferred back to the control of III Corps. At 10 p.m. divisional headquarters issued orders for a general withdraw to begin at midnight.

The Japanese were caught off guard by the British retreat. At 2 a.m. the demolitions under the iron bridge were blown, and the Gurkhas and other units in the vicinity retired southwards. Those units still under the command of the 6th Brigade made a reasonably clean break from the battlefield, but for most units of the 15th Brigade the disengagement at Jitra was a disastrous affair.

From the north side of the fast-flowing Sungei Bata, the Leicesters' Major Kennedy swam across the river after dark to visit brigade headquarters. Kennedy returned to his now isolated unit in the early hours of the morning with news of the retreat. A rickety wooden bridge downstream of the iron bridge had been swept away, and a sampan rigged to a cable was used to ferry men across. By 5 a.m. only Kennedy and forty-three others had passed over the turbulent river. Lieutenant-Colonel Morrison ordered them to head south independently, which they did through rain and swamp, whilst Morrison led a party westwards, still north of the Sungei Bata, to the railway bridge. Morrison had lost contact with two of his companies and they were left behind.[27]

Out on the right flank at Kelubi, the Jats and Major Emsden-Lambert's two 2/16th Punjab companies were having problems of their own. Earlier in the evening the Punjabis had been fired on whilst moving into a night perimeter, and one of their companies had scattered into the darkness in panic. When the time came to pull out, the Jats' Lieutenant-Colonel Tester was still unable to contact Captain Hislop's company on the extreme right flank. But a retreat could not be delayed any longer. The Jats disabled all of their carriers but one, in which Lieutenant Hibbert of the Punjabis led the column back towards Tanjong Pau and the Trunk Road. Tester's small force was ambushed amid the buildings and huts of Tanjong Pau camp, and, as the Jats' war diarist chose to describe the situation, 'a *sauve qui peut* ensued'. The Jats and Punjabis broke up into small groups, some of which regained friendly lines. Hibbert was wounded in the clash, but he survived to spend several weeks at large prior to capture.[28]

The battle at Jitra had been a calamity for the British-led force. Apart from the killed, wounded, and missing, a great deal of precious equipment was lost, and a cruel blow dealt to the collective morale of the 11th Division. In total two 4.5 inch howitzers, six 3.7 inch howitzers, thirteen two-pounder anti-tank guns, and a number of Bredas and 18-pounder field guns had been lost between Changlun and Jitra. A series of poor decisions by the division's commanders, and the offhand way in which the so-called Jitra Line had been prepared, had given inexperienced soldiers little opportunity to learn on their feet.

British commanders at Jitra never realised how small the force opposed to them had been. Murray-Lyon was later to claim that the 15th Brigade had been subjected to four heavy attacks on 12 December. 'Each of these attacks appeared to be carried out by fresh troops, a battalion in each of the first two attacks and two battalions in the case of the third and fourth.'[29] The attacking Japanese force had actually been only two battalions strong, and it was later asserted in a Japanese source that their losses had been a mere twenty-seven killed and eighty-three wounded.

Saeki Detachment's assault had been opportunistic, not the result of meticulous planning. The probing of the Indian division's positions either side of the Trunk Road was an obvious course of action. Both Murray-Lyon and Heath believed that the battle would have been a good deal less ill-starred if Percival had been willing to trust the judgement of his subordinates, and had permitted the retirement to begin during the day. Murray-Lyon was later to write that 'the reluctance to face facts which caused the delay in granting permission to withdraw, was undoubtedly an important contributory cause of the difficulty and costliness of the withdrawal'.[30]

The Japanese were surprised at the extent of their success. For Tsuji the battle was 'a glorious exploit' by soldiers who had been living on dry bread and salt, a victory that had not been founded on 'common sense'. Tsuji asked a captured British officer how long the British had hoped to retain Jitra. Tsuji was told that, as the Japanese had failed to beat the Chinese army in four years, Jitra had been expected to hold out for a long period. When asked why the defenders had collapsed so quickly, the officer could only say, 'God alone knows'.[31]

Over the next few days hundreds of prisoners were rounded up wandering in the jungle. One of those prisoners was Captain Mohan Singh. Mohan Singh met the exiled nationalist Pritam Singh, and Major Fujiwara, the Japanese officer responsible for organizing subversive activities among Indians in Malaya. Fujiwara and Pritam Singh explained to the captured Indian officer the aims of the Indian Independence League, and avowed Japanese plans to liberate Asia from colonial rule. Mohan Singh was asked to join their organization and to take charge of his fellow Indian prisoners. Opportunistically Mohan Singh quickly put his existing allegiances aside to seize the chance offered him.

# 7

# *Retreat*

In the rain and darkness of the night of 12/13 December the 11th Division's units headed southwards from Jitra as best they could. Some troops found their unit transport, others marched or hitched a ride. Tired, hungry, burdened by heavy equipment made heavier when soaked by the rain, the long trek after a lost battle was a demoralizing conclusion to the day. The 16th Punjab Regiment's historian noted that 'for the troops a worse baptism of fire would be difficult to imagine'.[1] The division's first aim was to get behind the Sungei Kedah, ten to fifteen miles to the rear, depending on a unit's exact starting point. The Trunk Road's bridge over the Kedah was at Alor Star, and through this bottle-neck most of the force would have to pass.

A rearguard comprising two 2/9th Gurkha companies took up a position to cover the retreat. An overturned bullock cart, some furniture and a few strands of wire were jumbled together to orchestrate a makeshift road-block. At 3 a.m. the last formed unit from Jitra passed through. Half an hour later the first Japanese arrived. The rain beating on the rubber trees and the darkness cloaked the initial Japanese rush. In the commotion that followed Gurkhas were physically bundled away from the road-block in a surging press of bodies. A succession of assaults by men screaming 'Banzai!' were beaten back. The Gurkhas' adjutant, Captain G. C. Graham-Hogg, was mortally wounded, and their commander, Major Allesbrook, was also injured. At 4.30 a.m. the rearguard disengaged and withdrew southwards. The Japanese did not catch up with retreating British-Indian troops again that night.

The main threat henceforward to the division's cohesion was dismay and exhaustion. At the Kepala Batas bridge, roughly halfway to Alor Star, Brigadiers Lay and Carpendale met amid the darkness of the night. Occasional bursts of indiscriminate firing could be heard in the distance. Lay waited at the bridge for a couple of hours after Carpendale had departed, at the end of which there was no sound of firing anywhere, and only stragglers were coming through.[2] A sleepless night's retreat was particularly hard on middle-aged senior officers, who had to cope with the responsibilities of their positions without the physical stamina of youth.[3]

Some troops at Jitra had never received the order to withdraw. Two companies of the Leicesters still north of the Sungei Bata moved off towards the coast once they realised they had been forgotten. Many of these men failed to evade capture as the balance headed south to safety in the days ahead.

B Company of the Jats, the far right-hand sub-unit in the Jitra Line, also found the dawn of 13 December strangely quiet. Sounds of battle could be heard far to the south. A patrol could not find the rest of their battalion, but a good deal of equipment was strewn about deserted positions. A party was sent over to pick up some abandoned rations for the hungry company. Captain Hislop ordered a withdrawal in the late afternoon, and the Jats were joined by one hundred newly arrived stragglers from the Changlun and Asun debacle. The group broke up during the night and only began to trickle back into British lines days later. Hislop reached Sumatra later in the month with a handful of men.

Lieutenant-Colonel Fulton and ninety men of the 2/1st Gurkhas, resting in the rear of the Jitra position after their ordeal at Asun, had also been left behind. Fulton and his Gurkhas, their party swollen to two hundred by stragglers from a number of units, made their way south independently to rejoin their division at Gurun.[4]

At the Alor Star bridge stragglers and transport continued to slowly hobble or drive through in the hours after dawn on 13 December. Lieutenant-Colonel Harrison later wrote: 'those stragglers ... in small parties, in ones and twos, [were] dazed with exhaustion, ready prey to panic; many of them frightened, most of them without arms, and many without their boots'.[5] By 9 a.m. the rearguard had withdrawn across the Sungei Kedah. Troops of the 2/9th and 2/1st Gurkhas and the 2nd East Surreys took up station along the Sungei Kedah's south bank. Four miles to the east a subsidiary bridge at Langgar was defended by the 2/2nd Gurkhas. Further south, officers of the 6th and 15th Brigades tried to reassemble their units.

That morning Murray-Lyon had fainted from tiredness by the roadside. The general had recovered quickly, and at 9.30 a.m. he was near the Alor Star bridge with a party of senior officers. Onlookers watched as motor cycle dispatch riders emerged from the town, on the north bank of the river, and roared across the bridge in front of a staff car and a couple of lorries. As the lead cyclist drew level with Murray-Lyon's party at the south end of the bridge the cyclist grimaced and waved. Murray-Lyon gasped 'My God, that's a Jap!' The recklessness of the Japanese cyclists took the troops in the vicinity completely by surprise. The leading cyclist rode clear to safety as Murray-Lyon and his colleagues drew their revolvers, and with help from nearby troops, shot down the next two riders.[6]

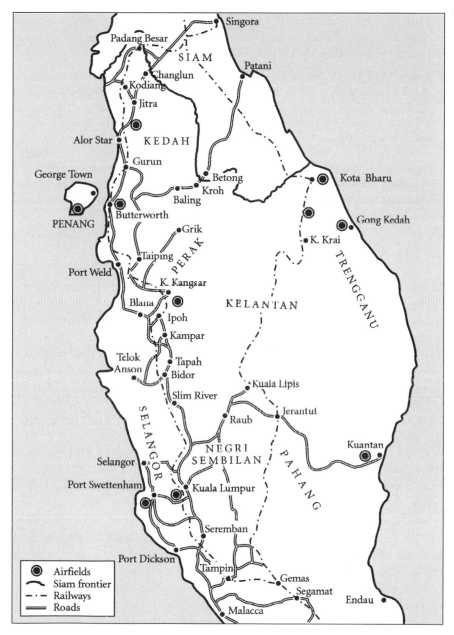

6. Northern and Central Malaya.

Murray-Lyon immediately ordered the wide Victorian bridge, already prepared for demolition, to be blown for fear of another 'tank blitz'. What happened next is best told by Murray-Lyon.

> Now a most regrettable incident took place, but one which illustrates the state of the morale of some of the units of the Division at this stage. When the bridge went up, although there had been no firing except for a few revolver shots against the motor cyclists and one burst of LMG fire, the 1/8th Punjab which was sitting down in a palm grove about six hundred yards from the bridge rose as one man and started to run down the road in panic. Two Companies of 2/16th Punjab did the same. [Both these units were greatly under strength by this stage.] It was only by getting into my car and getting ahead of them that I managed to stop them and turn them back. In the case of the 2/16th Punjab Companies I actually had to threaten some men with my pistol before they would stop.[7]

That a general was required to intervene personally in such a fashion did not bode well for the future of the division.

Soon after the road bridge was blown the demolitions on the rail bridge to the east were also set off. The charges failed to do their task and the bridge was left sagging, the rails broken, but still standing. An armoured train had been cut off north of the river by the attempt to demolish the bridge. Somebody decided to drive the train over the bridge in a final 'Hollywood-style' bid to collapse the damaged structure. The train was slowly rolled towards the bridge. The crew leapt off, but, with its whistle jammed and shrieking loudly, the train jumped the broken rails and steamed off southwards. An attempt was made to lay mines on the bridge, but a Gurkha officer was killed when a mine exploded in his hand. Before long the advance guard of the Japanese 11th Infantry Regiment arrived at Alor Star. The Japanese attacked the rail bridge but the vigilant Gurkhas held their ground.

At 6 p.m. British forces began to withdraw from Alor Star. The troops spent another exhausting night (13/14 December) amid rain and traffic congestion, traversing the twenty miles of road to Gurun, later described by Percival as one of the best natural defensive positions in Malaya. The Surreys' war diary noted that, 'again down this road came troops of all units, some not knowing what was happening or where they were going'.

Transport, troops and refugees had been moving slowly south towards Gurun all day. During daylight machine gunners had managed to bring down a low-flying Japanese aircraft strafing a convoy, but it had crashed onto a lorry killing three of its occupants. A frustrated Brigadier Carpendale drove down a long line of transport backed up for several miles to find the wrecked aircraft and a blazing truck surrounded by a crowd of onlookers. Japanese aircraft high in the sky were flying back to their bases after bombing

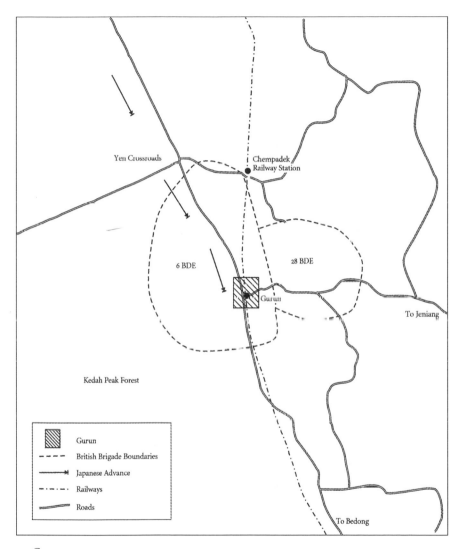

Yen Crossroads

Chempadek
Railway Station

6 BDE

28 BDE

Gurun

To Jeniang

Kedah Peak Forest

Gurun

British Brigade Boundaries

Japanese Advance

Railways

Roads

To Bedong

7. Gurun.

Penang. The occasional aircraft ducked down to have a closer look at the column.[8]

The Indian division was not directly pressed by Japanese ground forces as they retreated south from Alor Star. But during the night this was no guarantee of an uneventful journey. Lieutenant Abbott's company of the Surreys took a path through swampy rice fields and soon became lost. The company trudged on in exhaustion only to be brought to their senses by a hail of machine gun fire. 'Five of our company' wrote Abbott, 'were killed in that short battle with Indian troops of our own Brigade, guarding the next road bridge.'[9] The company was scattered by the incident.

Not all British parties even made it south of Alor Star. 110 officers and men of the Leicesters had arrived at Alor Star town, on the north bank of the Sungei Kedah, after the road bridge had been blown. The Leicesters were fired on in the back streets of Alor Star, and split into two groups in the resulting commotion. A party that included Lieutenant-Colonel Morrison passed through Japanese lines and across the river to safety, thanks to local Chinese boatmen. But another seventy Leicesters were cornered in the town. Three officers and forty men were killed in a disastrous fight and the survivors taken prisoner. At Alor Star aerodrome the Japanese found a large stock of fuel, and, as the runways had not been damaged, aircraft began landing almost immediately. During the afternoon British stragglers saw Japanese aircraft already sitting on the aerodrome.[10]

The last formed British-Indian units did not reach Gurun until midday on 14 December. Many men were very tired and hungry, some had leeches burrowing into their skin, and others were getting close to their last reserves of willpower. The Gurun position had been surveyed prior to the outbreak of war but had not been fortified. North of Gurun village there was a gap of less than four miles between Kedah Peak and the jungle-clad foothills of Malaya's central ranges to the east. Kedah Peak was an isolated and thickly wooded 4000 foot feature that rose abruptly from the plain near the coast. The Trunk Road and railway ran down through the gap less than a mile from the shoulder of Kedah Peak. A road from the coast at Yen ran westwards just north of Kedah Peak, across the Trunk Road and onwards to the railway at Chempedak station.

North of the Yen-Chempedak road, which was flanked by plantations, the countryside consisted mainly of rice paddy. From Kedah Peak there was a splendidly picturesque view across this fairly open stretch. But, further south, Gurun village was sited amid a network of dense rubber estates. Visibility within the rubber estates was, as always, poor, and gave an enemy a choice of covered lines of approach. Lieutenant-Colonel Selby of the 2/9th

Gurkhas had been sent to reconnoitre the Gurun area a few days previously. Selby had recommended that a defensive line be formed north of the Yen-Chempedak road. Islands in the paddy could have been converted into strong-points, and there were good fields of fire across the marshy ground to the north. Murray-Lyon, however, was of the view that positions in the paddy area would be vulnerable to air attack, and too exposed if it was necessary to withdraw during daylight hours. So a defensive line was dug just north of milestone twenty on the Trunk Road, three miles north of Gurun village, and well within the rubber estate zone.[11]

The most likely Japanese axis of approach was down the Trunk Road. On 14 December the 6th Brigade took up positions on a front of two miles in the left half of the Gurun gap. The 28th Brigade, under Carpendale's command again, was placed amid rubber to the right of the 6th Brigade on a front of less than three miles. The shattered 15th Brigade was in reserve south of Gurun village. The boundary line between the two forward brigades was just east of the railway. The Gurun gap did not have any sort of natural anti-tank barrier, and last-ditch attempts to organize civilian labour to help fortify the line failed. Given the nature of the terrain, the divisional front was very thinly held, particularly in the vital Trunk Road sector.

After the debacle at Jitra the division at Gurun was seriously under strength. The 15th Brigade, with Brigadier Garrett returned to duty, had been reduced to around six hundred men. The Leicesters had ten officers and 130 other ranks present on the morning of 14 December. The Jats comprised four officers and 187 men, and the 1/14th Punjabis had just two weak companies available. Only the Leicesters had any carriers or mortars left, and the bulk of the brigade's anti-tank rifles, signalling equipment, and machine guns had been lost.

Of the 28th Brigade, the 2/2nd and 2/9th Gurkhas had lost only seventy men each, but the 2/1st Gurkhas had been decimated at Asun. Even the 6th Brigade, whose positions on the Trunk Road and railway were most likely to be attacked, was well short of full strength. Most of the 2/16th Punjabis were still missing. The Surreys had lost the equivalent of a company of men in the retreat, and the 1/8th Punjabis had been reduced to three rifle companies.[12]

The exhausted troops of the division had to start digging in all over again. In the 6th Brigade's sector a small headquarters and a reinforced company of the 2/16th Punjabis held a position on the right flank astride the railway, in front of Chempedak station. The mile gap between the rail and road was filled by two companies of the Surreys. The 1/8th Punjabis held the Trunk Road itself with a composite company made up of the survivors of the two companies battered in the counter-attack at Jitra. To the left of the road the rest of the Punjabis held some rising ground in front of a side road that climbed up towards Kedah Peak. Over a mile behind the Punjabis' composite company astride the Trunk Road was the Surreys' depleted A Company. The Surreys' battalion headquarters was another few hundred yards to the south. The unit was under the command of Major Dowling, as their previous commander had broken a leg in a traffic accident during the retreat from Jitra.

The 6th Brigade's headquarters was sited in a hut in Gurun village, and the 28th Brigade's headquarters was near Gurun station. The 80th Anti-Tank Regiment's three batteries had guns left for only two batteries. These guns were scattered about the Gurun area in penny packets.[13]

By dawn on 14 December Japanese troops had begun to cross the Sungei Kedah at Alor Star. Decking was placed on the frame of the railway bridge so that heavy vehicles could cross. Again the British paid a high price for poor demolition work. By noon Japanese patrols were in contact with troops at the intersection of the Yen-Chempedak and Trunk Roads. A single anti-tank gun and a section of Surreys were covering a demolished culvert just north of the cross-roads. Two hours later three Japanese tanks and troops of the 11th Regiment's 3rd Battalion in a dozen lorries approached the cross-roads. Artillery observation posts high on Kedah Peak and its spurs could see the Japanese down through the rubber. The artillery was soon hammering away as the solitary anti-tank gun fired over open sights. One tank seemed to be hit and the column backed away.

Japanese infantry disembussed, and within an hour they had driven the small detachment at the cross-roads back into the division's main position. By 4 p.m. the Japanese were in a rubber plantation only one hundred yards ahead of the 1/8th Punjabis' composite company astride the Trunk Road, who now came under mortar and small arms fire. The Japanese began to infiltrate between the posts of the Punjabis. Brigadier Lay sent forward a squadron of the 3rd Cavalry to push the Japanese back towards the cross-roads. The cavalry were shot up by infiltrators and retired in disorder.

Further south along the Trunk Road, at the Surreys' A Company position, Lieutenant Abbott was horrified to see Indian troops

> running back towards us. [Captain] John Kerrich and I leapt into the road and make endeavours to send them back again, but it is useless ... We go back to our positions and prepare for the worst.

Then from behind up the road came Brigadier Lay, leading a mixed bag of fifty men from a number of units. According to Abbott

> The Brigade Commander has his pipe in his mouth, a cheery grin on his face,

and he is waving his walking-stick at us. He even has his battered old red hat on! As he goes by, he calls out to us: 'Come along, you fellows, we've got to push them back, they say there're hundreds of the blighters, all the more to kill!' [14]

The 2/16th Punjabis' carrier platoon led the attack.

We pass the Royal Artillery Observation Post, and the Brigadier shouts out to the gunner officer there: 'Lob over a few in ten minutes time just north of the cross-roads, will you?' As we go on, one or two Indian sections join us and the Brigadier pushes odd groups of men here and there into the jungle and rubber on either side of the road. Their orders are brief, to 'Get round the B ... s and push 'em out.'

Lieutenant Meston was in command of the carriers. He was badly wounded when his vehicle met a Japanese tank.[15]

The shambles soon resolved itself, and with dusk falling the Japanese who had infiltrated the 1/8th Punjabis' position were driven out. The line was restored north of milestone 20. The men of Kerrich's and Abbott's Surrey company returned to their posts and soon fell asleep.

General Murray-Lyon's headquarters was several miles south of Gurun. At 11 a.m. that day (14 December) Murray-Lyon had been on the point of going to visit his brigadiers when he received word that General Heath would be visiting him at 1 p.m., having returned from his trip to Singapore. An anxious Heath, still somewhat mystified as to why so much had gone wrong at Jitra, was delayed for a further two hours. When Heath arrived, Murray-Lyon told him that his troops were dangerously tired, and that there was a grave risk that the Japanese force advancing down the inland road from Patani would cut them off miles to the south, near the River Perak. Murray-Lyon saw no point standing to fight unless they could hold their ground.[16]

Heath told Murray-Lyon that he would have to make the best of a difficult situation and fight a battle at Gurun. That evening Heath rang Percival to tell him of Murray-Lyon's 'gloomy' views. Heath agreed with much of Murray-Lyon's appreciation, and could see that the troops of the division, with at least half the infantry still missing, were far from ready for another battle. Heath advised Percival that it was wrong to stand at Gurun, and that Murray-Lyon's division should be withdrawn behind the River Perak, with a brief halt at the Sungei Muda in the interim to permit the evacuation of Penang Island.[17]

Later that night Percival rang back to say that, if III Indian Corps could not hold the Japanese at Gurun, they had his permission to withdraw behind the River Muda but no further. Heath's advocacy of an early withdrawal all the way to the River Perak was not in accordance with Percival's view that the retreat should be as gradual as possible. Though worried by events in northern Malaya, Percival was just as concerned at the possibility of Japanese landings on the south-east coast of Malaya, or a *coup de main* on Singapore itself. On 13 December Malaya Command sent a warning to the 8th Australian Division in Johore that a Japanese convoy was sailing from Indo-China in the direction of south-east Malaya. The following day Percival saw Bennett and asked him if the AIF could assist the garrison at Singapore Island if it was attacked.[18]

Back at Gurun the situation had quietened down after an eventful day. That evening Brigadier Lay told Murray-Lyon that he planned to use the Surreys to recapture the cross-roads before dawn the following morning. The Japanese, however, had plans of their own. From 1 a.m. on 15 December intense mortar fire fell on the 1/8th Punjabi company astride the Trunk Road. Half an hour later troops of Kobayashi Battalion attacked straight down the road. SOS flares calling for artillery support were fired from the company's position, but by 3 a.m., after an hour-long fire fight, the Punjabis' right flank had collapsed. Soon a strong column of Japanese troops was seen marching southwards down the road, and the company's commander, Lieutenant Ghulam Akhbar, was carried into the main Punjabi position seriously wounded. Akhbar said that his company had been badly knocked about by the preliminary bombardment, and had then been gradually mopped up.[19]

Japanese troops advancing down the Trunk Road ran into the grossly under strength A Company of the Surreys. Captain Kerrich was killed by a sniper, and after several more men were killed the remnants of the company withdrew. By 5.30 a.m. the Surreys' battalion headquarters to the rear had also been overrun. A number of officers present were killed.[20]

To make matters worse the commanding officer of the 1/8th Punjabis, Major Anderson, decided about this time to retire his unit from the field of battle. Since 5 a.m. British shells had been falling on the rear of the Punjabis' area west of the road. With the sounds of battle moving southwards, Anderson, who had been wounded in the face in a prior engagement, decided that the situation had deteriorated beyond redemption. Anderson ordered his unit to withdraw westwards, through thick jungle skirting the northern fringe of Kedah Peak. Anderson's intention was to rejoin his division as it retreated southwards.[21] The Japanese had no doubt already penetrated to Gurun village before the departure of Anderson's battalion.

Prior to the Japanese reaching his headquarters, the Surreys' Major Dowling had reported in person at the 6th Brigade's headquarters in Gurun to say that the situation was desperate. Lay sent a message to Brigadier Garrett requesting that he send up a company from the 15th Brigade as soon as possible. Lay, accompanied by his brigade intelligence officer, Captain Sharpe, then left his headquarters to make the short trip to Carpendale's headquarters near Gurun station. As they left the building figures could be seen flitting about amid the rubber in the half light of dawn. Sharpe told Lay to go on ahead, and said that he would investigate the unidentified troops.

Events now moved swiftly. Around 6.30 a.m. proceedings at the 6th Brigade's headquarters were interrupted by the arrival of a wounded officer with the news that the Japanese were close at hand. Then a rifle was poked through the window to fire at the brigade-major talking on the telephone. A machine gun opened up to rake the flimsy wooden building at point blank range. Japanese soldiers charged indoors to finish the occupants off with the bayonet. Dowling was among the dead, and only a few survivors escaped to tell the tale. Lay, having already left his headquarters, stumbled the few hundred yards down the road to the 28th Brigade's headquarters and informed Carpendale that his staff had been wiped out.[22]

A rag-tag assortment of British-Indian units were scattered among the buildings and patches of cultivation in Gurun. A few guns fired at Japanese vehicles over open sights from the southern end of the village. Lieutenant Abbott and the remnants of his company were attacked by three tanks with guns blazing. 'I chuck a grenade at one of them, which makes no impression whatsoever, and then we just put our heads down and hope for the best.' An ad hoc company of the Leicesters who had been coming forward arrived to find their commander already dead, and the Gurun village area strangely deserted. The company was met by Lay, and directed onward with a few words of encouragement. Though pinned down amid huts and scrub, and roughly handled, particularly when they came up against tracer-spitting tanks, the poorly equipped Leicester company did at least provide the Japanese with some opposition. Lieutenant Chippington watched in horror when a vehicle towing a gun drove up from the railway crossing into Gurun, only to be blasted by a tank hidden amongst nearby buildings. A passenger was blown clean out of the cabin and staggered away, but the driver was not so lucky.[23]

At 8 a.m. mortar fire was falling on British positions around the Gurun level crossing. Several vehicles were hit, and Carpendale and Lay took shelter behind a tin shed as bombs burst on the wet ground as little as thirty yards away. Carpendale's brigade-major was killed organizing troops near the level crossing. A rather shaky Punjabi scratch company arrived from the 15th Brigade, one of the last cohesive sub-units Brigadier Garrett could put together from the remnants of his battered brigade. Five carriers of a Gurkha unit were sent to probe Gurun village. With his brigade ruined, Lay headed rearwards to report to General Murray-Lyon. On the way Lay met Lieutenant-Colonel Morrison of the Leicesters, who enquired as to the situation. Lay told him, 'I've just lost my Brigade', to which Morrison replied, 'And I, Sir, have lost my Battalion'.[24]

To the rear, at divisional headquarters, the night of 14/15 December had been the first quiet night for a week. A message arrived in the morning, however, with the news that the 6th Brigade was in grave trouble. Murray-Lyon and his GSO 1, Lieutenant-Colonel Harrison, set out to visit the front. Upon being informed of the situation at the 28th Brigade's headquarters Murray-Lyon ordered a retreat. Later in the day he realised that only a retirement behind the Muda River, twenty miles south of Gurun, would suffice to restore the situation.

As the division began its withdrawal from Gurun by day it was a rather more orderly affair than the retreat from Jitra. Nonetheless, where bridges had been prematurely blown, the rearguard had to abandon its transport and cross over the wreckage on foot. Detached parties pushed southwards through jungle and swamp on a compass bearing, trudging through heavy afternoon and evening rain. The rearguard was only picked up by divisional transport three miles north of Sungei Patani.[25]

The Japanese advance guard did not follow up the British retirement. In fact the Japanese had been strangely quiet from the time they overran Lay's headquarters. The battlefield had seemed almost empty of Japanese at times. This was because the force that had penetrated the Gurun position had been small in numbers. The Japanese had again achieved a great deal against heavy odds at little cost. Whereas two Japanese battalions with tanks had won the Jitra battle, it had only taken one battalion and tanks to complete the task at Gurun.

Major-General Kawamura's headquarters entered Gurun early in the afternoon. Lieutenant-Colonel Tsuji saw a number of abandoned trucks by the roadside loaded with 'Churchill supplies'. In the first vehicle a British soldier still sat behind the steering wheel, but the top of his head had been carved off by shrapnel. Forty to fifty Indian prisoners were sitting down nearby. To Tsuji the Indians seemed relieved, and they sprang quickly to attention when a captured British officer was led past. Tsuji wished to congratulate Major Kobayashi on his battalion's success. Kobayashi was discovered sound asleep on a bench. Tsuji did not wake him, and instead left a present of tobacco as a sign of his appreciation. Early next morning, after the bridges south of Gurun had been repaired, the advance was resumed.[26]

By the morning of 16 December the 11th Indian Division had crossed the Muda River amid more traffic jams, having abandoned stores and a big

fuel dump at Sungei Patani. The division was more exhausted and demoralized than ever. The East Surreys had been temporarily reduced to ten
officers and 260 men. Major Fujiwara later noted that the Japanese had
rounded up only three hundred Indian prisoners by 14 December, but
within three days the total had grown to a thousand.[27] The 6th Brigade
emerged from the Gurun battle as shattered as the 15th Brigade after the
retreat from Jitra.

The next problem that III Indian Corps had to face was the evacuation
of the garrison of Penang Island before they were cut off by the Japanese
advance. At Penang, in addition to a large multi-racial civilian population,
there was a small military garrison.[28] Penang had been under heavy air attack
since 11 December. The Japanese air force's concentration on the island had
been the main reason why Murray-Lyon's vulnerable division had seldom
been attacked from the air.

On the morning of 11 December eighty Japanese fighters and bombers
had flown over Georgetown unopposed, the bombers in neat V-formations.
Thousands of people had filled the streets to watch the spectacle, which
turned to tragedy when the bombs began to fall. Aircraft had then wheeled
down to dive-bomb and strafe. Mass panic was the result of the bombing,
and Penang had no anti-aircraft guns and few air-raid shelters. Most of the
bombs fell by design on Georgetown's densely populated Chinatown. The
fire station received a direct hit. Many people fled Georgetown for the safety
of Penang's interior. Shops were boarded up. The auxiliary services nearly
collapsed, and looting and the sight of abandoned corpses on the streets
were commonplace.[29]

There was another unopposed raid the following day, and only on 13 December did the Japanese face opposition from fighters of No. 453 Squadron
RAAF, which had flown up from Singapore that morning to reinforce the
RAF's shattered northern group. Sixteen Buffaloes left Singapore in four
flights. After refuelling at either Ipoh or Butterworth, they took off again
to engage far larger formations of superior Japanese aircraft. A number of
aircraft were lost by both sides in the dog-fights that followed, including
the Buffalo of Flight Lieutenant (and acting Squadron Leader) Tim Vigors,
a decorated Battle of Britain pilot credited with several confirmed kills. As
his aircraft's petrol tank was on fire, Vigors baled out over Penang. Japanese
attempts to machine gun him as he floated down failed, and Vigors was
rescued badly injured. The last three Buffaloes to leave Singapore became
lost in thick monsoons cloud and electrical storms. The pilots attempted to
crash land near the Sumatran coast. What seemed to be a field turned out
to be a paddy swamp. The first pilot survived a somersault landing, but the
other two were killed, including Wing Commander L. J. Neale, who was

flying up to become Ipoh station commander. In total five Buffaloes were destroyed that day and others damaged.[30]

The fires in Georgetown burnt for days. The 1st Independent Company's war diarist recorded on 14 December: 'Georgetown was an awe-inspiring sight never to be forgotten. Great fires raged throughout the length and breadth of the Chinese quarter right down to the jetties.'[31] The evacuation of European women and children from Penang had begun on 13 December, and by the morning of 17 December all Europeans and military personnel had left. Five hundred Volunteer Force Asians elected to stay behind with their families rather than be evacuated. It was estimated that six hundred civilians had been killed and another 1100 wounded in the air attacks. In the rush to evacuate, much useful military equipment was left behind to fall into Japanese hands, including twenty-four motor boats and many barges, and an undamaged broadcasting station. Before long the Japanese had the station back on the air to transmit propaganda. A Japanese battalion and a battery of artillery made an unopposed landing at Penang 'Fortress' on 19 December.[32]

There was a brief delay before the fall of Penang was officially announced at Singapore. Disturbing rumours circulated in the meantime. Later in the month Duff Cooper, the Resident Minister for Far Eastern Affairs, made a public radio broadcast intended to boost morale. In the course of the broadcast he spoke of the successful evacuation of Penang's population. As few Asians had been evacuated, the Minister's words caused a great deal of disquiet amongst Malaya's Asian communities. Governor Thomas had to meet delegations of Chinese, Malays and Indians to reassure them of the government's intention to respect their interests as the crisis unfolded. Local people were beginning to question British authority. But, in spite of growing public uncertainty, the dance halls and other civic entertainments at Singapore continued to do a brisk trade. Civilians could follow the progress of the Japanese down the peninsula by perusing the Hong Kong and Shanghai Bank's sequence of advertisements listing their branches 'closed until further notice'.[33]

# 8

# *Perak and Pahang*

As the 11th Division retreated south of Penang, Krohcol withdrew from its isolated inland position towards the coastal plain. The retreat from Kroh laid open the narrow, jungle-lined road plunging south towards Grik and the Perak River beyond. General Heath sent a company of the 12th Indian Brigade's 2nd Argyll and Sutherland Highlanders and some armoured cars to Grik as a first step towards blocking that route. Brigadier A. C. M. Paris's 12th Brigade had come forward from reserve south of Kuala Lumpur to shore up Murray-Lyon's division. The brigade was nominally part of Malaya Command's reserve, but was in practice Heath's III Corps reserve.

The crippled 6th and 15th Brigades were sent well to the rear to rest, whilst troops of the 28th Brigade and the 12th Brigade watched the line of the Muda River. The 12th Brigade's fresh 5/2nd Punjabis were in position behind a bridge over the Muda at Batu Pakaka when, at 2 p.m. on 16 December, a small party led by a European approached the bridge. The European was ordered to cross to identify himself, but was shot dead after he leapt upon a havildar covering him with a tommy-gun. Japanese troops promptly proceeded to attack the bridge but were driven off.

At 6 p.m. that evening another attack sent the Punjabis' forward companies tumbling back in disorder. Lieutenant-Colonel C. C. Deakin was furious with the panicky behaviour of his troops. The enemy was falsely rumoured to be advancing with armoured vehicles. The rearward drift was halted by Deakin, 'in some cases at the point of the revolver', and the companies were reorganized and sent back up the road to retake the partly demolished bridge.[1]

Meanwhile Generals Heath and Percival had spoken on the telephone about future strategy. Heath told Percival:

> The 6/15th Brigades will not be of the slightest fighting value for a matter of many days. It is therefore for consideration for the whole Command to assist in this very delicate situation ... It seems to need two forces – at least one fresh Australian Brigade – to be formed at once at Ipoh and for the 11th Division and 12th Brigade to go back to the Perak line. Perhaps it will be necessary to go back to the Slim [River].

Heath was clearly asking for reinforcements. But, despite the obvious extent of the 11th Division's defeat in Kedah state, and Malaya Command's estimate that the Japanese had two divisions and a tank regiment on the west coast (twice their actual strength), Percival did not agree with Heath's assessment of the situation.

From Singapore Percival told Heath:

> We don't want to dissipate forces from down here. I think the right course is to try if you can to get back behind the Perak line at least for the first step. This is my feeling, and also for the Slim River line to be reconnoitred.[2]

Percival was loath to transfer the 8th Australian Division northwards for fear of leaving southern Malaya and Singapore denuded of troops in the face of the threat of new Japanese landings in Johore. Forty-one Japanese transports carrying the second flight of Yamashita's XXV Army had arrived at Singora and Patani on 16 December, but Percival could not predict the destination of the next convoy. As he later explained,

> Until the Japanese had definitely shown their hand there was always a possibility that the threat against Thailand and Northern Malaya was intended to draw off our forces to that area with a view to facilitating sea-borne operation against Johore.[3]

Yet Percival did not want to withdraw from northern Malaya too rapidly for fear that the Japanese air force would obtain bases from which they might attack reinforcement convoys bound for Singapore. Percival had already asked the War Office for a fresh infantry brigade group, anti-tank weaponry, and four hundred replacements for each of III Corps's Indian battalions.[4]

Percival travelled up to Ipoh during the night of 17–18 December, and the next day he gave Heath permission to withdraw behind the Perak River after imposing the maximum delay on the Japanese further north. Defensive positions were to be prepared south of Ipoh. The two generals toured the line of the Perak and Percival left for his headquarters the next morning. Heath travelled with Percival part of the way south. Together they provisionally selected some places at which III Corps might make a stand. On the return journey to Singapore Percival also visited General Barstow, the 9th Division's commander, and confirmed that the latter's principal tasks were to cover Kuantan and the 11th Division's communications.

The immediate threat facing the 11th Division was the fact that the Japanese 42nd Regiment at Kroh had swung south onto the difficult route leading to Grik. The 42nd Regiment was not supported by tanks as the track between Kroh and Grik was too difficult for armoured vehicles to traverse during the wet season. A Japanese force moving down this route could cut off all

British forces north of the Perak River. Heath was forced to transfer the main body of the 12th Brigade to the Grik road to contest the Japanese advance. The agility the Argylls had acquired through energetic pre-war training served them well in the several days fighting that lay ahead.

On the coastal plain, by 21 December the division had retreated behind the swampy Krian River, the last major natural obstacle before the Perak River. There was the occasional skirmish with Japanese troops, but to some extent the invaders were struggling to keep up with the fully motorized British-Indian force. Critics of the British Army described its troops as walking Christmas trees, equipped as they were with heavy boots, blankets, weaponry, ammunition, packs and pouches, ground sheets and great coats. Soldiers, though, soon learned to leave unnecessary items of equipment with their transport, and there was little to gain from going underequipped.

Retreating with the army was the European administrative, business and planting community. Rubber estate and tin mining managers endeavoured to set fire to stocks of rubber, destroyed machinery, and flooded the mines before leaving. The work-force was paid off with whatever dollars and provisions were available, but faced destitution in the months and years ahead.

Fifth columnist stories were becoming increasingly rife as the rumour spread that Japanese troops were dressing in native costume. Some European troops came to suspect all Asians. *The Times* correspondent, Ian Morrison, saw a Chinese man brought to the Argylls' headquarters accused of placing a large arrow of banana leaves outside a hut pointing towards the head-quarters. The Chinese was summarily shot. On the east coast it was claimed that a signal had been laid out pointing at a gun position. One Malay and two Tamils detained on the spot were also eventually shot. Elsewhere in Malaya another Tamil was shot merely for putting a red sari out to dry.

Officials familiar with Malaya were sceptical of the spy rumours. An intelligence officer noted that wood placed alongside many bridges, which was claimed by some to be the work of fifth columnists, had actually been placed there by the Public Works Department in case the bridges were damaged by Japanese bombing. Allegations that there had been fifth columnist sponsored attempts to bomb General Heath, on 20–22 December, could be explained by the fact that he was near railway stations in an operational area on each occasion. Lieutenant E. L. Randle recorded that the authorities had been told that a Malay spy ring wore black sarongs to identify themselves to each other, and that people had been arrested on the strength of that information. Another officer noted that natives had been shot without further enquiry if found too close to the front line in an area banned to civilians. An incredulous gunner officer even saw his troops open fire on fireflies, as they believed them to be fifth columnists flashing torches out to sea. Investigating officers found that troops strongly believed in the fifth column menace, but could only repeat general rumours when pressed to be specific.[5]

For the Japanese XXV Army the campaign thus far had been a triumph. Morale among Japanese troops could hardly have been higher. The invaders made full use of the lorries and cars they had captured to help transport heavy equipment. But the infantry rode ahead on bicycles down Malaya's excellent roads. General equipment, weapons, simple cooking gear, and rations of rice and tinned fish were strapped to a bicycle's frame. Hard-working engineers laboured quickly to repair damaged bridges and gaps blown in the road.

The roads heading south were choked with British transport. The Japanese air force did not take full advantage of the situation, but low-flying aircraft managed to bomb Brigadier Carpendale's 28th Brigade headquarters in a town near the Krian River whilst a conference was underway. According to an officer present:

> It was a fair shaker; one or two were knocked arseways by the blast as dust and plaster rained on us. After we'd recovered we counted heads. We were all present and correct, not even a scratch among us to show for it.

Outside the rest of the stick of bombs had fallen amongst resting Gurkhas. Twelve Gurkhas were killed and another twenty-six seriously wounded.[6] The bombing prompted the usual rumours and gossip about fifth columnists passing on the location of headquarters to the Japanese. The bombing of a large building surrounded by troops, however, in a village virtually in the front line, was just the sort of target Japanese aviators should have been attacking. An exhausted Carpendale went on sick leave and returned to India shortly after this incident.

By 23 December the division had retired behind the eight hundred yards wide Perak, the broadest river in Malaya. But the Perak was not a very useful defensive barrier as it ran largely north to south: the Japanese force coming down the Grik road could only too easily slip behind troops deployed along its bank.

Nonetheless the retirement behind the river provided a good opportunity to dismiss General Murray-Lyon. There was no denying the fact that Murray-Lyon's period of command had been an unmitigated disaster. Despite the shortcomings in pre-war defence preparations in northern Malaya, operational command error had played a major role in the division's defeat. The comparative skill of Brigadier Key's handling of the fighting on the east coast highlighted that point.[7]

The finding of a replacement for Murray-Lyon became another field of disagreement for Generals Percival and Heath. Heath wanted to put an Indian Army officer in command of the 11th Indian Division. As Key had been the outstanding brigadier in the campaign to date, Key was Heath's nominee. But Percival decided to make the 12th Brigade's Brigadier Paris, a British service officer, the division's new commander. Paris was senior to Key. The division's poor showing at Jitra was in Percival's eyes a black mark against the Indian Army and its leaders.

Brigadier Paris, a man of confident and cheerful temperament, had spent most of his career with British troops, but he had been in charge of an Indian formation for three years. Paris had been longer in Malaya than any other senior officer, and was believed to have acquitted himself well during the 12th Brigade's difficult operations along the Kroh and Grik roads. Paris told Lieutenant-Colonel Harrison, the division's principal staff officer, 'take not counsel of your fears' when he arrived at his new headquarters. The Argylls' Sergeant W. Gibson later wrote that Paris was

> a powerfully built, handsome officer, his face deep tanned through his years of service, his iron-grey moustache always neatly clipped, his eyes shrewd and quizzical. Always a great all-round athlete, of exceptional strength, he took tremendous pride in his physical fitness, and on many an occasion was able to outmarch men many years his junior.[8]

The promotion of Paris meant that somebody had to take over command of the 12th Brigade. Lieutenant-Colonel Stewart of the Argylls, the brigade's senior battalion commander, became the new brigadier, thus putting another British service officer in command of an Indian formation.

The army was not the only British contingent pulling out of northern Malaya. The Royal Air Force was evacuating all stations north of Kuala Lumpur. On the morning of 22 December the largest air battle of the campaign took place. A dozen Buffaloes of the RAAF's No. 453 Squadron, still the only fighter unit based outside Singapore, took off from Kuala Lumpur to intercept a Japanese force approaching from the north. The squadron met up to twenty Japanese fighters, mostly Navy Zeros.

The fighting that followed was fast and furious. One Buffalo pilot crash-landed on the aerodrome without an undercarriage. Sergeant M. N. Read was killed after ramming a Zero. Another pilot limped back to Singapore with seventy bullet holes in his aircraft. Two pilots baled out of stricken machines. Another pilot died in hospital after crashing, and yet another pilot landed with a hand wound and his windscreen shot away. Seven Buffaloes were destroyed or damaged in the morning's dog-fights. That afternoon low-flying Zeros attacked Kuala Lumpur aerodrome and caught a Buffalo just after it had taken off. The pilot was killed when his aircraft spun into the ground. Japanese aviators did not escape unscathed, though not nearly as many Japanese aircraft were shot down as claimed by the Buffaloes' pilots. By evening only three Buffaloes were still fit for service. For ground observers the day's aerial combat had been a riveting spectacle.[9]

The following day it was decided to evacuate Kuala Lumpur aerodrome. By 24 December the RAF in Malaya had only thirty-eight British and Dutch Buffaloes left, in addition to the rest of its motley collection of mostly obsolete aircraft.[10] The authorities at Singapore decided that the protection of convoys carrying reinforcements to the island from the south should become the RAF's principal task.

As the RAF's aerodromes were abandoned, the anti-aircraft guns that had been deployed for their protection were also withdrawn. The inexperience of the gunners had been a problem at times. The 14th Battery Hong Kong and Singapore Royal Artillery managed to bag a No. 62 Squadron Blenheim bomber at Port Swettenham, and damaged another friendly bomber into the bargain. It was, reported an officer, 'the best shot we had and the only plane which crashed in full view of the gun site'.[11] About this time Brooke-Popham publicly lambasted those ground staff reputed to have left their aerodromes up-country in a state of wild panic. The Commander-in-Chief stated in a communique to all RAF units:

> in the majority of cases the bombing of aerodromes has been on a far smaller scale than that suffered calmly by women and children in London and other towns in England, and aerodromes have usually been vacated whilst still well out of range of enemy land forces.[12]

As northern Malaya was being overrun by invading Japanese, thousands of miles away in London the British Empire's war leaders hurriedly framed a response to the Far East crisis. On the evening of 11 December Churchill and the Chiefs of Staff met to discuss the situation in the wake of the sinking of the *Prince of Wales* and the *Repulse*. There was little collective desire to dispatch major reinforcements to Singapore from either the United Kingdom or the Middle East. This viewpoint was consistent with decisions made over the previous eighteen months. Instead it was agreed to divert to India the 18th British Division, currently in transports off the coast of Africa and bound for the Middle East. The 17th Indian Division, due to sail for the Middle East from India, was also to remain in India in case it was needed in the Far East. Responsibility for the defence of Burma was transferred from Far East Command to New Delhi.

With these preliminary decisions made, Churchill left Britain on 12 December in the battleship *Duke of York* to meet President Roosevelt and members of his administration in the United States. Now that the United States was formally at war with the Axis, there was a great deal that needed to be hammered out before a fully working Anglo-American alliance could proceed harmoniously. Admiral Pound, Air Chief Marshal Portal (Chief of the Air Staff) and General Dill sailed with Churchill, leaving General Alan Brooke, the new Chief of the Imperial General Staff, behind in London as the senior service officer.

The Admiralty took little further interest in the Far East. The loss of Force Z, coupled with the recent sinkings of the carrier *Ark Royal* and battleship *Barham* in the Mediterranean, and the mining of the battleships *Queen Elizabeth* and *Valiant* in Alexandria harbour on 19 December, had left the Royal Navy vulnerable on a number of fronts. The damaged aircraft carrier *Indomitable* was the only modern capital ship likely to become available for Far East service in the near future.

As the Air Ministry was obsessed with the strategic bombing of Germany, and the maintenance of air supremacy over the coast of northern France, by default Brooke's War Office became chiefly responsible for the Far East.[13] Yet, as commander of Home Forces, Brooke had paid a crucial role in withholding British troops and equipment from overseas commands. On 15 December Brooke wrote in his diary: 'Far East situation far from rosy! I doubt whether Hong Kong will hold out a fortnight and Malaya two months!' Two days later Brooke wrote after a Chiefs of Staff meeting:

> A very difficult problem trying to patch holes out there without interfering with the Middle East offensive. Personally I do not feel that there is much hope of saving Singapore, but feel that we ought to try and make certain of Burma.[14]

On 27 December Brooke repeated in a memorandum for the Defence Committee the old platitude that Singapore and the Indian Ocean were second in importance to the United Kingdom. He added, however, that Germany was the main enemy and 'consequently for the present we should not divert more of our resources than are necessary to hold the Japanese'. The oft-cited official claim that Singapore was a high priority had never carried much weight in London with the men who really mattered. Brooke had scant intention of launching any new initiatives in the Far East whilst Churchill was absent in America.

At sea in the Atlantic Churchill was busy drafting memoranda. Churchill put on paper for the Chiefs of Staff the way in which he thought the campaign in the Far East might develop.

> The Japanese must be expected to establish themselves on both sides of the Straits of Malacca and in the Straits of Sunda [at Java and Sumatra] ... We expect,

however, that Singapore island and fortress will stand an attack for at least six months, although meanwhile the naval base will not be usable by either side. A large Japanese army with its siege train and ample supplies of ammunition and engineering stores will be required for their attack upon Singapore.[15]

Churchill was fully aware that heavy losses in the Far East were inevitable before the Japanese whirlwind was spent, but he had high hopes that Singapore would delay the Japanese for a considerable period.

The primary aim of Churchill's mission to America was to persuade America's politicians and service chiefs to follow a 'Germany first' grand strategy. The bombing of Germany, the Battle of the Atlantic, the campaign in North Africa and aid to the USSR were at the forefront of British strategic priorities. Churchill's entourage wanted to guide the Americans in those directions rather than see them throw their full weight against Japan. Roosevelt's administration was already inclined to focus on Germany, and the advisability of a 'Germany first' grand strategy was not a fundamental issue of dispute between Britain and the United States. In the Far East the Americans were keen to establish a unified command structure, preferably under a British general. The British delegation in Washington agreed to this with considerable reluctance, as a good deal of blame was likely to be heaped on the shoulders of that new commander. In the meantime Churchill suffered a mild heart attack in his bedroom at the White House in the evening of 26 December.

Roosevelt suggested that General Sir Archibald Wavell, Commander-in-Chief of the Indian Army, should be made the chief of a new ABDA (American-British-Dutch-Australian) Command stretching across South-East Asia and the western Pacific. Wavell was the logical man for the job, given that he had until six months previously been in charge of Middle East Command. The son of a major-general, Wavell possessed an intellect well above that of the typical senior British officer, and his passage up the army's promotion ladder had owed much to that fact. Wavell's genuine interest in poetry and military history set him well apart from other generals, such as Percival, who have sometimes been labelled 'intellectual'. At Winchester school young Wavell had studied the classics, and at one time the headmaster had written to his father: 'There is no need for your son to go into the Army: he is really quite intelligent.'[16] But Wavell had followed in his father's footsteps. He lost an eye to a shell splinter in 1915, and finished the First World War in Palestine as a senior staff officer at General Allenby's headquarters. By 1939 Wavell had risen to be Commander-in-Chief Middle East.

Conscientious and even-tempered, Wavell was not without his faults. He was dangerously taciturn for a man whose business was the command and inspiration of other men. Wavell was at heart a staff officer and strategist, without the complementing interest in battlefield tactics and weaponry that a truly first-rate general possesses.

Wavell's relationship with the naturally boisterous Churchill had been difficult from the start of the latter's premiership in May 1940. But Wavell's command had soon achieved great success against the Italians in Egypt and Cyrenaica, and the Italian empire in Abyssinia had been overrun early in 1941. Wavell had supported Churchill's desire to send an expedition to Greece, but during that campaign the bulk of the force in Libya had been besieged at Tobruk by the newly arrived General Rommel and his Africa Corps. This had been the last straw for Churchill, who swapped Wavell with General Sir Claude Auchinleck, the Indian Army's Commander-in-Chief. Churchill told Dill that Wavell should enjoy 'sitting under a pagoda tree'.[17] Indeed Wavell had found life at New Delhi pleasant prior to the outbreak of war in the Pacific. He was cabled news of his unpromising new appointment on 29 December, and commented privately that he had been handed not just a baby but twins.

Meanwhile at Singapore General Pownall had finally arrived to replace Brooke-Popham as commander-in-chief. Brooke-Popham departed on 31 December. The reinforcement situation continued to take shape. On Christmas day the War Office ordered that the 18th Division's 53rd Brigade sail directly to Singapore, and by 1 January the War Cabinet had decided to send the whole division to the Far East. (By this time the rest of the 18th Division had landed at Bombay, and had been packed off to camps inland.) The Australian government also agreed to send a machine-gun battalion and reinforcements for the 8th Division, and by early January they had consented to the transfer of the 6th and 7th Australian Divisions from the Middle East to the Far East.

Elsewhere in the Far East, in the early hours of 26 December, the last British troops at Hong Kong surrendered. Resistance had lasted only eighteen days, despite an order from London instructing the garrison to fight to the finish. 11,848 combatants were lost at Hong Kong. Japanese casualties were 675 killed and 2079 wounded. Japan's conquest of the colony was accompanied by an orgy of looting, torture and rape. In the Philippines, converging columns of Japanese were pushing the Filipino-American army into the confined space of the Bataan peninsula, not far from Manila. The pre-war plan had been to hold out at Bataan until relief arrived from America.[18]

In northern Malaya the Japanese quickly organised themselves to cross the Perak River. General Yamashita concentrated his 5th Division and the newly arrived 4th Guards Regiment at Blanja and Kuala Kangsar respectively. These two places were the better part of twenty miles apart. General Heath decided that the front was too wide for the 11th Division to defend. Instead of lining the banks of the Perak River, the 12th and 28th Brigades were deployed further south to cover Ipoh whilst the 15th Brigade dug in at Kampar, twenty miles south of Ipoh, in preparation for the division's next major stand. The Japanese were both surprised and delighted to make an unopposed crossing of the river.

Brigadier Stewart's 12th Brigade faced the advancing Imperial Guards north of Ipoh. The Japanese attacked on the afternoon of 26 December in front of Chemor, and were held by the 5/2nd Punjabis in reasonably open tin-mining country. That evening Stewart concocted a complex scheme to trap the Japanese the following morning. The Punjabis were to hold their positions until 9 a.m., after which they would retire. The advancing Japanese were then to be caught by an artillery barrage, and taken in the flank from the east by a hitherto hidden company of the 4/19th Hyderabads. At divisional headquarters Lieutenant-Colonel Harrison told General Paris that Stewart's plan 'ought to work well, Sir, provided Stewart has taken the Japanese into his confidence and obtained confirmation that they'll play their part'.[19]

On the morning of 27 December, however, the Japanese attacked first and pushed back the Punjabis before the time of the latter's scheduled withdrawal. Captain Harris's Hyderabad company was taken by surprise moving towards their start line. Few men of the company escaped and Harris and his senior VCO were both killed. The brigade lost two hundred casualties in this local engagement, and the troops' spirits took a battering.[20]

Ipoh was abandoned during the night of 27/28 December. The tired 12th Brigade retreated to take up positions on the Trunk Road south of Ipoh at Gopeng. During the morning of 29 December the brigade withdrew again under aerial bombardment. The three battalions of the brigade were deployed one behind the other. That afternoon a Japanese attack led by eight tanks caught the Argylls without any anti-tank support. The Argylls were bundled clear of the road and fell back in disorder. The Argylls' armoured cars and carriers tried to cover the retreat. Several vehicles were hit by tank shells or sprayed with armour-piercing machine gun fire. The Argylls fell back onto the 5/2nd Punjabis, the forward companies of whom also commenced a panicky movement rearwards. Eventually anti-tank gunners managed to hit the leading tank to bring the Japanese advance to a halt three-quarters of a mile north of Dipang. An exhausted brigade crossed the Sungei Kampar at Dipang in the rain that evening. At the bridge a relieved Stewart handed over the front to Brigadier Selby's 28th Brigade. Stewart told Selby that the situation 'was a running concern'.[21]

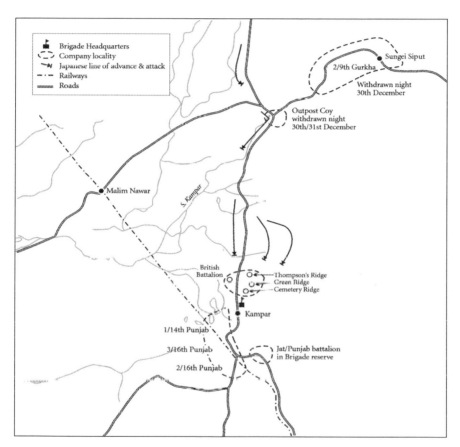

8. Kampar.

Dipang was only a short distance north of the position the 15th Brigade had been digging astride the Trunk Road near Kampar in central Malaya. At Kampar the 4070 foot mountain of Bujang Melaka rose up sharply to the immediate east of the Trunk Road. Thickly covered with jungle, the precipitous mountain overlooked an open tin-mining district. Of the division's other brigades, the 28th Brigade was deployed to block a loop road skirting the eastern side of Bujang Melaka some distance further inland. The 12th Brigade was resting to the rear at Bidor, and was available if necessary to contest the advance of any Japanese force landed on the coast near Telok Anson. General Paris had already sent a small force to screen Telok Anson. (General Percival visited Paris's headquarters on 31 December and also met Stewart).

The 15th Brigade had absorbed the remnants of the 6th Brigade after the Gurun battle, and Brigadier Lay had been dispatched to hospital. Four units from the brigades were amalgamated to form two battalions. The Jats and the 1/8th Punjabis had become the 'Jat/Punjab Battalion', and the Leicesters and the Surreys had joined forces to form the 'British Battalion'. Assailed by heat and rain, the brigade had spent a week digging, clearing, mining and wiring its position at Kampar. On 26 December the 3/16th Punjabis' Lieutenant-Colonel Moorhead had taken over command of the brigade after Brigadier Garrett was ordered to the rear and sent on sick leave.

The British Battalion held the brigade's most northern position on the Trunk Road, about a mile from Kampar. The Jat/Punjab Battalion formed the brigade's reserve, and the battered 1/14th, 2/16th and 3/16th Punjabis formed a ring to guard the approaches to Kampar down the railway and across tin-mining estates to the west. On 30 and 31 December Japanese aircraft dropped propaganda leaflets over Kampar. An aircraft was brought down by small arms fire and promptly claimed by all units.

The next move was for General Yamashita to make and it was not long in coming. On 31 December a convoy of small boats was spotted moving down the coast, presumably with the intention of making a landing somewhere near the mouth of the Perak River. Lieutenant-Colonel Tsuji recorded that twenty small boats had been captured at Penang. Another forty motor launches landed at Singora had been moved overland to complete the formation of a flotilla to operate down the west coast of Malaya whenever opportunity allowed.[22]

At Kampar Japanese troops squared up to the British Battalion's position astride the Trunk Road, and patrols felt for the brigade's flanks. To the immediate east of the Trunk Road the British Battalion held three successive parallel ridges named 'Thompson's', 'Green', and 'Cemetery'. The ridges were spurs running off the jungle-clad mountain looming above the right flank of the British Battalion. Captain Thompson's A Company held the first ridge. The several hundred yard long ridge was covered with long grass, scrub and rubber. The ridge overlooked a small stream in a steep valley leading towards a spur held by the Japanese. Five hundred yards behind Thompson's ridge, across a scrub covered valley, was Cemetery ridge. The British Battalion's B Company occupied Cemetery ridge, as well as holding a short spur between the two main ridges named Green ridge. C Company extended the battalion's front across flat ground to the west of the Trunk Road, and D Company was held in reserve. The bridge over the stream just north of the British Battalion had been thoroughly demolished. The approaches to the British Battalion's position were open to the north west, but on the unit's right flank the jungle of the lower slopes of Bujang Melaka was dangerously close. There was less than fifty yards of open ground between the jungle and the right-hand posts on Thompson's ridge and Green ridge.

The Japanese plan was to land Colonel Watanabe's 11th Regiment at the mouth of the Bernam River. From there the regiment was to advance to Telok Anson and cut inland to the Trunk Road south of Kampar. Major-General Kawamura's 9th Brigade was in charge of the local battle around Kampar. Kawamura's 41st Regiment was to attack down the Trunk Road, and the 42nd Regiment was to advance around the left flank of Moorhead's brigade, through the swamps of the Sungei Kampar.[23] Demonstrations were also to be made along the road leading around the eastern side of Bujang Melaka.

About 7 a.m. on New Year's Day 1942 the Japanese attack on Thompson's ridge began after half an hour's bombardment. The Japanese ran into a heavy artillery barrage and made little headway, but the assaulting troops were able to make a small lodgement on the right flank overlooking much of the battalion's position. The Japanese foothold was a precarious one, and the situation was soon restored by a counter-attack led by Captain W. G. Vickers. There was no further attack that day but a lot of mortar fire fell on the forward slope of Thompson's ridge. Captain Thompson was seriously wounded in the jaw. Overnight the defenders searched for infiltrators with the aid of flares, but only corpses were seen.[24]

Late on 1 January one and a half battalions of the Japanese 11th Regiment landed on the coast amid a tangle of mangrove swamps and streams. Churchill was later to write that the 'command of the western shores of Malaya by the Japanese without the possession of a single ship of war must be reckoned as one of the most astonishing British lapses in naval history'.[25] General Paris sent the weary 12th Brigade back into action to assist those troops already posted to defend the routes leading inland from Telok Anson.

Early the next day a battalion of the 4th Guards Regiment arrived at Telok Anson, having sailed down the Perak River in boats. Japanese plans had, however, come a little unstuck as Colonel Ando's 42nd Regiment was still ensnared in the wilderness of the valley of the Sungei Kampar, and had made scant progress towards turning the left flank of Moorhead's brigade.

At dawn on 2 January the 41st Regiment again attacked the British Battalion. The attack was halted with the assistance of heavy artillery fire. 'Contrary to expectation hostile resistance was firm and strong', wrote a Japanese war diarist. But by 7.30 a.m. the Japanese had overrun the right-hand platoon position on Thompson's ridge, close to the jungle fringe of the mountain. At 11 a.m. Lieutenant-Colonel Morrison requested that a brigade counter-attack be mounted to restore the situation.[26] The Jat/Punjab Battalion sent forward a company that had originally belonged to the Jats. After some delay the attack went ahead, only to be halted by machine gun fire.

C Company of the Jat/Punjab Battalion, comprising Sikhs and Gujars from the 1/8th Punjabis, was brought up for another attempt. The company set out for its objective at 5 p.m. Prior to the assault the company was addressed by Captain John Graham, the battalion's second-in-command. Graham told them that the situation was critical. Though few would witness their actions, the honour of the regiment depended on their success. For extra encouragement every man was served with two drams of rum. The company set out toward their objective, hugging the relative shelter of the reverse slope of Thompson's ridge where they could. The company's commander, Second Lieutenant Charles Lamb, was among the first to fall. A foothold was secured on the lost position in the opening rush, and the company regrouped and pushed on again under Graham to drive the last Japanese off Thompson's ridge. The assault had been expensive, and there were only thirty unwounded men in the company. Captain Graham lost both legs when a mortar bomb was lobbed at his feet. He died on a stretcher as he was being carried to the rear.[27]

Towards the coast the 12th Brigade gradually conceded ground to the advancing Japanese. General Paris decided to abandon Kampar and the 15th Brigade withdrew that evening. The British Battalion and the Jat/Punjab Battalion had each lost around a hundred casualties during the battle.[28] The Japanese were estimated to have lost four to five hundred dead, but that figure was a considerable exaggeration. The 12th Brigade continued to block the route from the coast, whilst the 15th and 28th Brigades retired southwards.

As the 11th Indian Division was retiring down the west coast of Malaya, the 9th Indian Division fought a relatively separate battle in eastern Malaya. Brigadier Key's 8th Brigade had withdrawn down the railway from

Kelantan state into central Malaya. By 27 December Key's men had reached the Kuala Lipis-Jerantut area.[29] The Japanese were not closely following the brigade. The force that had landed at Kota Bharu had their eyes firmly fixed on Kuantan, a small, isolated coastal town in Pahang state, connected with the railway at Jerantut by a single road running through a hundred miles of jungle. Brigadier Painter's 22nd Indian Brigade held Kuantan town and aerodrome. General Percival wanted to retain Kuantan for as long as possible in order to prevent the aerodrome falling into Japanese hands.

The Japanese 56th Regiment advanced south along the coast from Kota Bharu using horse and sea transport. There was no metalled road down the east coast of Malaya either north or south of Kuantan. Plans to land the 55th Regiment at Kuantan had been abandoned, and instead the regiment landed at Kota Bharu on 30 December. At Kuantan the 22nd Indian Brigade was deployed to oppose a landing from the sea. The 2/18th Garhwal Rifles held eleven miles of coast north of Kuantan River. The 5/11th Sikhs were posted along the south bank of the Kuantan River, and the 2/12th Frontier Force Regiment was in reserve south of the river, though one of its companies was operating with the Garhwalis. For artillery support the brigade had three batteries. There was no bridge across the Kuantan River. Instead a ferry was used to shift men, vehicles, and equipment laboriously from one bank to the other.

As the Japanese neared Kuantan tensions mounted amongst the officers and men of the Indian brigade. Track watchers in the jungle under a local forestry officer kept an irregular eye on the route leading northwards towards Kota Bharu. On Christmas Eve the brigade was ordered to stand-to as a Japanese invasion fleet was reported to be approaching Kuantan. The cause of the report was probably a stray fishing boat, and later in the night overenthusiastic gunners fired on imagined enemy shipping.[30]

On 27 December General Heath advised the 9th Division's Major-General Barstow to withdraw all of the 22nd Brigade's units south of Kuantan River, so as to face the attack that was obviously developing from the north. The following day Barstow visited Brigadier Painter at Kuantan. Painter was emphatic that a battle must be fought north of the river, as the river line was vulnerable to infiltration and impossible to defend.[31] He insisted that he had spent months studying the problem. Barstow relented, but the following day, 29 December, Heath, with Percival's approval, overruled Barstow. Heath sent Barstow his orders in writing this time to prevent any further prevarication. Painter was instructed to withdraw his vehicles south of the river, and to be ready to withdraw all his troops south of the river at short notice.

Indian troops had made solid contact with the approaching Japanese on

29 December, and the following day an estimated two hundred Japanese were discovered advancing down the Jabor valley, to the left rear of the Garhwalis. Troops sent to deal with the intruders did not fare well in the confused and scattered fighting that followed. In the meantime vehicles piled up on the road leading to the ferry. The ferry had recently been split in two. One half was damaged in an afternoon bombing raid, but the other half continued to operate. That afternoon (30 December) Painter belatedly ordered a general retirement to a bridgehead covering the ferry.

Just before first light on 31 December Japanese troops attempted to rush the ferry, not long after the last vehicles and guns had been brought across. The Japanese advanced at the outset with their hands above their heads to allay suspicion. The attackers were halted by a shower of grenades. At noon a strong Japanese force was reported to be advancing down the beach. Contact was lost with two companies of the Garhwalis, and the rest of the battalion retired to the south bank of the river that evening without them. A company of Frontier Force was also missing. Small parties from the companies left behind rejoined their units over the next few days. Two Garhwalis claimed that the rest of their platoon had been executed.[32]

From the south side of the river British artillery shelled Japanese-occupied Kuantan town on New Year's Day. Kuantan aerodrome was nine miles inland, south of Kuantan River. The 5/11th Sikhs still held the south bank of the river, while the other two battalions were concentrated near the aerodrome. The river was easily fordable upstream, however, and Painter was worried that the Japanese might move inland around his left flank to cut the road leading to Jerantut. He suggested to Barstow that the brigade should withdraw to Maran, halfway to Jerantut. But at Singapore General Percival was adamant that Kuantan aerodrome had to be held for a few more days.

The brigade was eventually given permission to retire to Maran on the night of 3/4 January. By this time Japanese troops had moved inland to outflank the Sikhs, and were infiltrating south of the river towards the aerodrome. During 3 January the Sikhs, and the bulk of the artillery, transport and sappers, withdrew without incident, but after dark Japanese mortar fire came down on the north-west corner of the aerodrome as the Garhwalis were departing.

The brigade's rearguard, the Frontier Force (less two companies), was due to pull out at 9 p.m. Lieutenant-Colonel A. E. Cumming's headquarters was situated in a glade of scattered rubber trees, surrounded by jungle. About 8 p.m., with the moon risen, a burst of firing from a nearby piquet caused Cumming and his adjutant, Captain Ian Grimwood, to creep out with drawn pistols to investigate. The two officers were barely fifteen yards from their headquarters when a body of Japanese rushed towards them out of the gloom. Cumming and Grimwood blazed away as the surge of men ran over the top of them. Cumming was bayoneted twice in the stomach, and hit on the head and knocked unconscious. He was dragged out of the melée by his havildar-major.[33] A hand-to-hand fight swirled on for some time before the Japanese tide receded.

A revived Cumming ordered the rearguard to retire. He later passed out from blood loss. When Cumming came round he was told by his carrier's driver, Sepoy Albel Chani, that the Japanese had blocked the road that was their principal line of retreat. Cumming told the sepoy to charge through the road block. The carrier set off a mine but was not seriously damaged. Grenades bounced off the frame of fine wire erected over the carrier for just that purpose. Machine gun and rifle fire struck the vehicle, hitting Cumming in the right arm, and passing through both thighs of Sepoy Albel Chani. The sepoy drove on through to brigade headquarters, after which both he and Cumming were evacuated to hospital at Singapore. For his conduct at Kuantan, Cumming was awarded the Victoria Cross.[34]

The 22nd Indian Brigade withdrew along the jungle road to the railway at Jerantut. The fighting had reduced the Frontier Force to 220 officers and men, and the Garhwalis had lost over 250 officers and men killed, wounded and missing. Sixty Frontier Force sepoys rejoined during the following night, and thirty more later reached an Australian unit many miles to the south, after an adventurous three week trek. In total the brigade had lost a third of its infantry without inflicting comparable losses on the Japanese.[35] III Corps's grip on central Malaya was beginning to slip.

# 9

# Slim River

As III Indian Corps retreated through central Malaya, a reinforcement convoy sailed into Singapore. On 3 January the 45th Indian Brigade, which had been detached from its parent division, arrived. The RAF's remaining Buffaloes covered the convoy from above without interference.

At a senior commanders' conference convened by General Percival on 5 January it was decided to evacuate Kuala Lumpur, and to form a new defence line at the northern border of Johore state. Percival ordered Heath to deny the Japanese the aerodromes of Kuala Lumpur and Port Swettenham until at least 14 January in order to shield the arrival of another reinforcement convoy expected at Singapore about that date. Percival urged Heath to delay the Japanese and to accept casualties up to a reasonable limit.[1]

North of Kuala Lumpur the 11th Division prepared for the next battle. The 12th and 28th Brigades occupied delaying positions in the Trolak-Slim River area, whilst other troops prepared a position near Tanjong Malim ten miles to the rear. The area the 11th Division was falling back into was some of the best defensive terrain in Malaya. Heath was concerned though that the Japanese would again hook around his left flank from the sea. South of Telok Anson and the mouth of the Perak River a forty mile stretch of swampy jungle effectively covered the coastal flank of the division, but further south at Kuala Selangor and Port Swettenham troops landed on the coast could cut inland to reach the Trunk Road and Kuala Lumpur far behind Slim River and Tanjong Malim.

Heath dispatched an ad hoc force of Indian and Volunteer troops to guard the coast around Kuala Selangor. This was just as well as the wily Yamashita, never one to miss an opportunity, was planning to send a battalion of the Japanese 11th Regiment and the 4th Guards Regiment down the coast by land and sea to Kuala Selangor. On the Trunk Road front the XXV Army's 42nd Regiment led the pursuit south from Kampar, with the remainder of the 11th Regiment to the rear. The 41st Regiment rested in reserve after its exertions at Kampar. The four regiments mentioned above comprised the entire force at Yamashita's disposal in western Malaya.[2]

Thanks to Heath's prescience, when Japanese landing craft approached Kuala Selangor in the afternoon of 2 January they received a hot reception

from British and Volunteer gunners. An old cargo steamer towing and
accompanied by a dozen sampans and motor launches arrived several
thousand yards out to sea. The small craft headed towards the shore and
were fired upon at less than a thousand yards' range. Two sampans were
promptly sunk, others were damaged, and the rest scuttled back to their
parent ship, which was also set on fire by a couple of accurate shots.[3]

Japanese craft approached the shore again in the early hours of 3 January,
but they soon withdrew once they had ascertained that the shore was still
occupied. The plan to land from the sea had not succeeded, but by 4 January
the Japanese had managed to advance on Kuala Selangor down the coastal
track. At the Sungei Selangor a battalion of the 4th Guards Regiment turned
inland, and moved along the Sungei Selangor's north bank to the bridges
at Batang Berjuntai that were only eleven miles from Rawang on the Trunk
Road and over thirty miles south of Slim River.

Heath sent a battalion and other detachments to parry this Japanese
move. He then hastily shifted Brigadier Moorhead's 15th Brigade to Rawang.
The bridges over the Sungei Selangor at Batang Berjuntai were blown by
the defenders on the morning of 6 January, and the front in that quarter
was stabilised after several anxious days.

The 12th Brigade had withdrawn southwards to settle into a position at
Trolak, north of Slim River. Slim River itself was an excellent anti-tank
obstacle, but the Trunk Road and railway crossed the river five miles apart,
and did not rejoin until Tanjong Malim was reached further to the south.
It would have required two separate forces to defend Slim River. North of
Slim River at Trolak the road and railway ran close together to form a single
corridor. General Paris's 11th Division headquarters was located at Tanjong
Malim, ten miles to the rear of Slim, where the bulk of the 80th Anti-Tank
Regiment was also bivouacked. Paris had one eye on Slim River and the
other on Kuala Selangor, forty miles apart.

After three weeks continually in action the 12th Brigade was very tired.
The troops were 'asleep on their feet'. Japanese aerial activity forced the
brigade's battalions to dig and wire their new positions at night. By day
the roar of aircraft cruising down the Trunk Road kept men under cover.
The Japanese air force had missed many opportunities to interfere with
III Corps troops during the campaign, but they partly made up for their
neglect by dive-bombing and strafing the brigade at Trolak with considerable
enthusiasm. There were no anti-aircraft guns sited in the immediate area.
The 5/2nd Punjabis lost at least twenty casualties during this period,
including their adjutant.[4] In total the Punjabis had lost 250 casualties in the
previous few weeks, the majority killed and wounded. The Argylls had lost

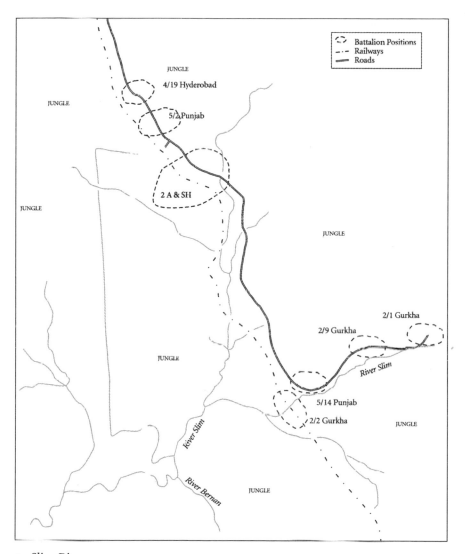

9. Slim River.

thirteen officers and two hundred men, and the 4/19th Hyderabads almost as many.

In theory the 12th Brigade's new position was not difficult to defend. North of Trolak the jungle and vegetation in overgrown plantations was very dense, and was pierced only by the road and railway running parallel a few hundred yards apart. Though the Japanese had already made landings to the south, locally the Trolak sector's seaward flank was guarded by miles of marshy jungle. East of Trolak lay more jungle leading towards mountainous country. The brigade's three battalions were deployed in a line down the Trunk Road, one behind the other. The rear units were placed to counter wide encircling movements through the jungle.

The 4/19th Hyderabads were the brigade's lead battalion at milestone 60, with the 5/2nd Punjabis behind them between milestones 61 and 62. The 2nd Argylls were deployed to the rear along an estate road running at right angles to the Trunk Road, less than a mile north of Trolak village. From Trolak large rubber estates stretched southwards to Slim River. The 5/14th Punjabis were due to come up from divisional reserve and move into a supporting position south of Trolak. Due to a lack of radio sets and a shortage of telephone cable, communications within the division were primitive. Even though 1400 anti-tank mines were in stock, only twenty-four had been released and given to the 5/2nd Punjabis.

In the Hyderabads' sector A Company was deployed astride the railway and C Company astride the road. B Company was to the rear on a track between the railway and road. The unit had been reduced to three rifle companies by earlier fighting. The Hyderabads' commanding officer, Lieutenant-Colonel Wilson Haffenden, had also been wounded in an air attack on 3 January. The troops were young, undertrained, and had been further unsettled by the long retreat. Apart from an anti-tank gun, and some concrete blocks in tar barrels, the Hyderabads had no other prepared defences except for barbed wire and trenches.

The 5/2nd Punjabis manned the brigade's principal defence line. The Hyderabads were only meant to fight a delaying action in front of them.[5] But there was no natural tank obstacle in the Punjabis' area. To make matters worse Brigadier Stewart had ordered that the roadway be kept undamaged so that carriers and armoured cars could work with the Hyderabads further forward. The brigade had a single troop of anti-tank guns under command, and one battery of the 137th Field Regiment in support. The rest of the field regiment was parked in the Cluny rubber estate, between Slim River station and Slim River bridge. Paris and Stewart both felt that artillery had only a limited role to play in the dense country north of Trolak. The 28th Brigade had reconnoitred positions near Kampong Slim and the Cluny estate, and was resting around Kampong Slim. Stewart considered his troops to be in good heart, and he believed that the threat of tank attack was exaggerated. Stewart's Argylls and the 12th Brigade had fared well against the Japanese astride the Grik road, and the brigadier was optimistic that they could repeat that success.[6]

The bridges leading south towards Trolak had been blown by retreating Indian sappers, but the Japanese kept advancing on bicycles. Troops could carry the bicycles on their shoulders when they waded across streams or clambered over ruined bridges. Engineers were then set to work to repair the route. With their usual speed the engineers rebuilt the bridges to carry heavy vehicles.

Late in the afternoon of 5 January one or two Japanese companies advanced down the railway behind a mortar barrage. The Hyderabads' A Company opened fire when the Japanese were almost at their wire. The attack was swiftly broken up, and a sheaf of bodies was left lying beside the rails. The Hyderabads lost very few casualties in the engagement. Nonetheless the Hyderabads' senior officer, Major Brown, rang brigade headquarters to say that the commander of his A Company had reported that Japanese were gathering around his flank. Brown doubted whether his battalion could maintain its position overnight, and requested permission to withdraw. As Stewart was absent from brigade headquarters, his brigade-major granted Brown's request. The brigadier cancelled this order half an hour later.

Stewart's habitually positive view of events was well founded on this occasion. There was minor skirmishing along the railway the following day, but nothing untoward occurred. Lieutenant-Colonel Deakin of the 5/2nd Punjabis later commented: 'this episode clearly demonstrated, if any proof was necessary, the low morale of at least one of the Battalions in the Brigade'. Deakin was also having a few problems of his own. When a havildar in command of a platoon kept complaining about Japanese in the jungle around his position, Deakin told him that he was 'well on the way to getting shot for spreading undue alarm and despondency'.[7] In private, however, Deakin advised Stewart to withdraw the brigade to a more secure position when he saw him during the day.

With the Trunk Road front strangely quiet during 6 January General Paris suspected that the Japanese were working around the 12th Brigade through the jungle, so he decided to withdraw that formation behind the 28th Brigade during the night of 7/8 January. In the meantime the 28th Brigade would have another night's rest, before taking up positions just north of Slim River at midday on 7 January. Lieutenant-Colonel Harrison drove up from divisional headquarters to convey Paris's instructions to the brigades. Distracted by a menacing Japanese aircraft overhead, Harrison missed the turning to the 12th Brigade's headquarters, and drove right up into the Hyderabads' area before noticing his mistake. After seeing Stewart, Harrison visited Brigadier Selby at the 28th Brigade's headquarters. Selby wanted to know why his brigade had not received any replacement anti-tank rifles. Harrison suggested that Malaya Command had probably run out. After returning to divisional headquarters Harrison found a message from the 12th Brigade requesting a supply of luminous paint to be used by patrols to rattle the supposedly superstitious Japanese.[8]

Late on 6 January an Asian refugee came into British lines with information. He was brought to the 12th Brigade's headquarters for questioning. The Asian claimed that he had seen a column of 'iron land-ships' at Sungkai, eight miles north of Trolak. He also said that the bridge at Sungkai had been repaired. Stewart concluded that the vehicles were only lorries. As Stewart would not permit Deakin's Punjabis to damage the road in their area, Deakin ordered his sepoys to lay anti-tank mines on the Trunk Road in a narrow cutting. Old loop roads in the Punjabis' sector were left open for the Hyderabads' vehicles.[9]

After the failed probe down the railway on 5 January, the 42nd Regiment's commander, Colonel Ando, had decided to prepare a more deliberate assault. During the afternoon of 6 January Ando told his battalion commanders that next day part of their force would advance through the jungle around the enemy's flank to reach Trolak village. The rest of the regiment would attack down the road with tanks moving in support. Major Shimada, a tank company commander, persuaded a doubtful Ando to change his plans and launch a tank attack that night. If the tanks' assault failed, the infantry could still attack as originally intended.[10]

That evening a battalion of the 42nd Regiment prepared to advance in close support of a tank regiment. The 42nd Regiment's other two battalions were to undertake flanking movements through the thick jungle. Soon the forward posts of the Hyderabads could hear the roar of tracked vehicles in the distance. Major Shimada's tank company led the advance with an infantry company and some engineers close behind. In support stretched a long surging column of armoured vehicles and lorries.

About 3.30 a.m. on 7 January, in bright moonlight, the Japanese column moved down the road behind a mortar and artillery barrage. Each of the Hyderabads' forward companies had an attached artillery observation officer. Lieutenant Moss was in the observation post near the road. Through the moonlight Moss could see tanks halted two hundred yards down the hill. Japanese soldiers were removing the cylinders that formed an ad hoc road block. There was no sign of opposition from a patrol that was supposed to cover the block. A column of tanks then drove down the road followed by jogging infantry. The tanks ran over any wire in their path, and tracer was soon flickering over the heads of the defenders crouched in their trenches. The tank gunners peering through their fire slits could see little in the darkness, and they were further blinded by the flashes of explosions and weapon discharges. The tanks blazed away at random and the Hyderabads' single anti-tank gun was soon put out of action. There was nothing to stop them. Some Japanese tanks used an abandoned section of an old road to make further progress into the rear of the Hyderabads' area. (Some bends in the Trunk Road had been recently straightened, but the old overgrown sections were still passable.) The remainder of the Hyderabads withdrew down the railway.[11]

Sepoys of the Hyderabads began streaming back into the 5/2nd Punjabis' area, and firing could be heard up the road. It was clear that something had gone amiss further forward. The onward rush of the Japanese armoured column, a column that contained the better part of thirty light and medium tanks, was brought to a halt at 4.30 a.m. when it ran into a small minefield in a cutting in front of the Punjabis' D Company. Two tanks blew up on mines and the rest jammed the road behind. They would have been a superb target if anti-tank artillery had been available. Another tank was put out of action. It was probably hit by an anti-tank round. Punjabis lined the high banks on either side of the cutting and hurled grenades onto the tanks below. Some men tried in vain to set fire to the tanks with Molotov cocktails. The tanks used an unblocked loop road to advance around this defensive position.

Japanese tanks and accompanying infantry quickly overran the Punjabis' next rifle company as it had no anti-tank defences. By now men from the forward Punjabi companies were falling back towards the rear of the battalion's area. Lieutenant-Colonel Deakin had rung brigade headquarters to report that the Japanese had penetrated the Hyderabads, and had pushed back his leading company. But shortly after all line communications between brigade headquarters and its units went dead, except for the line to a nearby Argyll company.

At 5.30 a.m. Japanese tanks ran onto more mines in front of the Punjabis' rear B Company, just north of milestone 62. The fighting was drawing close to Deakin's headquarters, and 'the din which followed defies description. The tanks behind were nose to tail – their engines roaring, their crews yelling, their machine guns spitting tracer, and their mortars and cannon firing all out'.[12] The leading tank blew up on a mine. Another tank had its track smashed by a round from an anti-tank rifle. Two anti-tank guns each fired twice, and another tank was put out of action. Despite this, Japanese tanks found yet another loop road to by-pass B Company. By 6.30 a.m. the

Punjabis had been overrun. Deakin and a headquarters party of about thirty men headed rearwards to make their escape, as did many other groups.[13] The Punjabis had delayed the Japanese for two hours, but communications had broken down so badly that news of the battle's progress was still to reach units further south.

It was only at 6.30 a.m. that a first vague message reached divisional headquarters on the 12th Brigade's unreliable wireless. 'There has been some sort of break-through. Send staff officer immediately.' Lieutenant-Colonel Harrison set out with his orderly to investigate. Before leaving, Harrison had a junior staff officer send off a message ordering the 28th Brigade to deploy immediately. About this time an officer from the 12th Brigade arrived at the 28th Brigade's headquarters to say that things were going badly. Upon hearing the news Brigadier Selby ordered his brigade to deploy on his own initiative.[14] The units of the 28th Brigade had received orders to march by 7 a.m.

Upon getting Deakin's message that the Japanese were breaking through his unit, Stewart had had a message carried to the Argylls, to the rear of the Punjabis, ordering them to build road-blocks. The Argylls were deployed with a company each on the road and railway, and their other two rifle companies further out on the flanks. The Argylls had received a hundred reinforcements overnight, including a new commanding officer, Lieutenant-Colonel L. B. Robertson, who had come from a staff appointment at short notice. The new men had not been allocated to their companies yet and were still at rear battalion headquarters at Trolak. Stragglers from units up the road had already alerted the Argylls to the fact that something was wrong.

Up to this time the 350th Field Battery, which had one troop in the Argylls' area and another three miles to the south, was still putting harassing fire in front of the original front line. The battery's commander was told by an Argyll officer that it might soon be necessary to blow the Trolak bridge. The forward troop was thus withdrawn south of the Trolak bridge, along with some carriers and armoured cars and a stray anti-tank gun.[15]

The Argylls' intelligence officer, Lieutenant Tom Slessor, set out up the road on a motor cycle to visit the Punjabis' headquarters. The darkness of the night was turning to the greyish half-light of dawn. Turning a corner Slessor saw something on the road fifty yards ahead. 'I wasn't sure what it was ... until it opened fire.' Having sought refuge in the jungle Slessor watched tanks move slowly down the road in small groups. About 6.30 a.m. four Japanese medium tanks arrived in front of the Argylls' position. Two improvised road-blocks had been hastily established, one a hundred yards from the bridge and the other further forward. The first block was quickly brushed aside. The Argylls had no anti-tank guns, but one of the guns that had come back from the Punjabis' area was manned and fired until overrun. An officer said later: 'our chaps could do nothing. They just looked helplessly at the passing tanks which were firing hard; a few threw grenades'.[16]

At the second block, one tank was set on fire externally by Molotovs, but there were no sappers on hand to blow the demolitions on the bridge which might have halted the Japanese column in its tracks. The Trolak stream was fordable, but not for wheeled traffic. A knocked out armoured car was pushed onto the bridge but the tanks shoved it aside. Second Lieutenant Sadanobu Watanabe, the commander of the leading tank platoon and a recent graduate from the Military Academy, dismounted from his tank, and cut the demolition wire with his sabre. Another Japanese officer, Second Lieutenant Morokuma, chimed in to kill a soldier running forward to throw a grenade at Watanabe.[17]

News that the Argylls were being overrun had been passed back to the 350th Field Battery. As the 12th Brigade had virtually collapsed, the battery commander ordered his unit to pack up. The battery drove back through the 28th Brigade's sector to Slim River road bridge and southwards towards Tanjong Malim.[18]

By 8.30 a.m. the Argylls' B and C Companies and headquarters had begun to reassemble near Trolak village. But within half an hour more tanks and cyclists were seen coming down the road. The Argylls disabled their transport and carriers and established a perimeter two hundred yards south of Trolak. Later in the morning Lieutenant-Colonel Robertson ordered his men to push south into the jungle towards Slim River. Few men of B or C Company would ever rejoin their unit. They lost their way in the jungle and a sizeable number died of disease and exposure. The rest were captured in dribs and drabs. Robertson travelled south with a small party and was ambushed and killed six weeks later. Several Argylls remained at large behind Japanese lines with Chinese guerillas.

West of Trolak the Argylls' A Company skirmished with Japanese infantry advancing down the railway, and later withdrew down the railway to Slim River station. Out on the left flank the Argylls' D Company was posted on an estate road a mile ahead of the 12th Brigade's headquarters. At 9 a.m. Stewart told the company's commander to delay the enemy's advance down the estate road to cover his headquarters' retirement. In confused fighting D Company was destroyed. Several days later the remnants were captured by a Japanese patrol. The wounded who could not walk were shot and the rest made prisoner.[19]

As the Argylls were fighting their doomed battle, Brigadier Selby had made his way forward to the 12th Brigade's headquarters. Stewart told Selby that there had been heavy fighting on his front and some enemy penetration, but the isolated location of Stewart's headquarters had made it difficult to stay in touch with events. The logical site for the 12th Brigade's headquarters was Trolak, but, as Stewart later explained, Trolak had been occupied by divisional headquarters when his brigade had first arrived in the area. After the divisional headquarters had retired to Tanjong Malim, Stewart had decided against another move as his staff were tired.[20] If the 12th Brigade's headquarters had been located near Trolak, Stewart and his staff would have had a far better picture of events taking place up the road, and would also have been in a good position to dispatch timely information to units further south.

As the eight guns of the 350th Field Battery were no longer in position, there was nothing to stop the tank column making further progress after it crossed the bridge at Trolak. Lieutenant-Colonel Collins of the 36th Field Ambulance, travelling on a motor cycle half a mile south of Trolak, was the next man to encounter the tanks. Collins dived off his motor cycle into a ditch and watched two groups of six or seven tanks each advance slowly down the road at walking pace.[21]

Worse was to come for the division. Pursuant to an order received from the 12th Brigade earlier that morning, the 5/14th Punjabis were marching up from their bivouac to a position south of Trolak. The Punjabis were not aware that they were marching towards a battle, and their anti-tank rifles were stowed in transport trucks. At 7.30 a.m the Punjabis were a mile north of Kampong Slim, alongside a cemetery, when they were surprised by fifteen tanks and some lorried infantry. The two leading companies were caught on the road and destroyed in minutes. The first company scattered, and the second had only twenty unwounded men. The Punjabis' Lieutenant-Colonel Stokes had been riding in a car. He later died of wounds incurred when a tank shell hit the vehicle.

The Punjabis' rear companies suffered fewer casualties as the tanks passed by. They had time to find refuge amid vegetation bordering the road. Attempts to re-form the battalion were disrupted by the appearance of more tanks, which paused to pour fire into the rubber plantations on either side of the road. Behind the Punjabis were the 28th Brigade's troop of anti-tank guns. The first two guns were quickly overrun, and the third suffered the same fate as its crew was trying to unlimber it from a tractor.[22]

As recounted earlier, Selby's 28th Brigade headquarters had ordered its units to deploy to their prearranged battle positions north of Slim River. The 2/2nd Gurkhas took up their post on the railway around Slim River station. The 2/9th Gurkhas were to deploy near Kampong Slim, and were lucky that an officer was able to warn them that tanks were approaching. At 8 a.m. a Japanese tank column drove by. Rifle fire and grenades bounced off the tanks harmlessly. A second group of tanks came down the road and passed through, to be followed by a third group which halted to fire into the rubber and jungle. The 28th Brigade's headquarters was also in Kampong Slim. It was later claimed, perhaps apocryphally, that the first news they had of the tanks' approach was when Major Stephens, the brigade-major, saw tanks behind his shoulder in the reflection of his shaving mirror.[23]

Further down the road the 2/1st Gurkhas were marching eastwards, away from the battle, towards Cluny estate, midway between Kampong Slim and Slim River bridge. The road was narrow, twisting, and lined by dense rubber and jungle. The atmosphere was oppressive. Insects and birds threw up a chorus of noise, and visibility was limited. The Gurkhas had passed the 5/14th Punjabis heading in the opposite direction earlier in the morning. The battalion had been rebuilt after its shattering experience at Asun, during the opening days of the campaign, and was now able to field over five hundred officers and men. The Gurkhas had no anti-tank rifles.

The Gurkhas' commanding officer had gone on ahead, so the marching column was under the immediate command of Major W. J. Winkfield. The battalion was moving in open file on either side of the road. Winkfield felt a sense of unease amongst the troops behind him, and the noise of battle seemed to be getting closer.

> The next thing I knew was a gun and machine gun blazing in my ear, a bullet grazed my leg, and I dived into the ditch as a tank bore down on me. It had passed through half of my battalion without my realising anything was amiss.

About a dozen tanks stopped for ten minutes to fire into the rubber plantations bordering the road. Winkfield emerged from cover to find that his battalion had 'vanished'.[24] He waited further down the road for some time hoping to contact survivors but none appeared. The Gurkhas' Lieutenant-Colonel Fulton was later found lying by the roadside with a shattered thigh and a wound to the stomach. Fulton's badly wounded orderly had borrowed his officer's revolver and shot himself in the head.[25] Fulton later died in Japanese hands at Taiping.

Soon after passing through the Gurkhas, Japanese tanks raked the 36th Field Ambulance between milestones 71 and 72. The tanks rolled on, and the two remaining batteries of the 137th Field Regiment were parked nearby in Cluny estate. Rubber plantations were airless and gloomy. The fronds of trees often blocked out the sky. But it was not difficult to move men or vehicles under a high canopy of mature trees in a well-tended estate. A large estate was riddled with the kind of lanes on which 25-pounder guns and tractors could be secreted.

The marauding tanks chanced upon the gunners whilst they were breakfasting, and paused to shoot them up with cannon and machine gun fire.
A few guns and some vehicles were hit, and the tanks rolled on again. The
tanks had not been accompanied by Japanese infantry, nor is there any
evidence to suggest that infantry penetrated beyond Kampong Slim for a
number of hours to come. In the absence of the regiment's commanding
officer, second-in-command, and headquarters, which were in the 2/2nd
Gurkhas' area, the battery commanders present at Cluny estate assumed
that the day was lost. The officers collected enough men together to spike
the guns. The unit then dispersed into the jungle. Meantime the commander
of the field regiment, Lieutenant-Colonel Holme, had set out from his
headquarters on a motor cycle after being told that tanks had driven through
the Gurkhas towards Cluny estate. Holme was killed en route, another one
of a number of commanding officers to die that day.

Lieutenant-Colonel Harrison had left divisional headquarters earlier in
the day to investigate the situation north of Slim River. He passed the 350th
Field Battery on the south side of Slim River bridge heading in the opposite
direction. He stopped an officer to ask where they were going. Harrison was
told there had been a minor breakthrough. In consequence the battery had
been ordered back to Tanjong Malim.

Harrison crossed the bridge, and a couple of miles further on

> I rounded a sharp bend near the Cluny Estate, and thirty yards ahead of me I
> saw what I took to be one of our armoured cars bearing down on me. The next
> thing I knew a deafening volley of machine gun bullets shattered my windscreen.
> I wrenched the wheel hard to starboard, crashed into the ditch, opened the door,
> leapt out and ran like hell over fifty yards of open ground to the flimsy security
> of some scattered rubber. Then I flopped down into a foot of muddy water at
> the bottom of a far too shallow irrigation ditch.

Harrison was soon joined by his Indian orderly, 'with his shoulder shot to
bits. He lay down beside me, and said in a hurt voice: "Were those our
armoured cars, Sahib?"' [26]

Harrison pushed on. Hearing sounds of firing, and seeing figures moving
about in the distance, he assumed that a battle was underway. A dispatch
rider however informed him that it was British artillerymen burning their
ammunition trucks. Harrison briefly sought cover again as five more tanks
cruised down the road. He then walked on to see the chaos in Cluny estate
for himself.

> The ammunition trucks and limbers were burning hard, and shells were exploding
> and bullets cracking all round the place. I saw an ambulance bumping drunkenly
> over the broken ground till it hit a tree and overturned.[27]

Harrison headed back to his wrecked staff car to recover some maps, only to be forced to hide in the ditch again as another five Japanese tanks went by. Harrison returned to Cluny estate, now almost empty of British troops. He walked up the road and soon came upon the 36th Field Ambulance. Medical Corps personnel had been shot up by each of the three groups of tanks to drive past, but they had re-emerged from their hiding places in the undergrowth and carried on with their duties. Harrison continued onwards, and after passing some dead Gurkhas he finally reached the 28th Brigade's headquarters on a bicycle.[28]

At 8.40 a.m. the tanks reached the Slim River's road bridge, and a nearby troop of four guns of the 16th Light Anti-Aircraft Battery Hong Kong and Singapore Royal Artillery and some sappers. Two of the guns depressed their barrels to fire at the tanks at one hundred yards' range. The guns had no armour-piercing rounds. The shells ricocheted away harmlessly, and the gunners beat a retreat into the jungle. After the tanks had passed, the battery's commander, Captain Newington, found that most of his men had disappeared. The sappers did not have time to fire the demolition charges already placed under the bridge. Second Lieutenant Watanabe, still with the leading Japanese tank troop, fired a machine gun from inside his tank to sever the electric wires leading to the charges.[29]

One Japanese tank was left to guard the bridge over the Slim River. A dozen tanks trundled southwards until they ran into the 155th Field Regiment two miles down the road, driving up to join the troops north of the river. The artillery column had received a warning that Japanese tanks were nearing the headquarters of the 28th Brigade but that news was badly out of date. The regiment's headquarters was travelling ahead of the column and was quickly overrun, Lieutenant-Colonel Murdoch being among those killed.

The regiment's adjutant, Captain Gordon Brown, was still with the main body of the column, and he heard from a dispatch rider that tanks were approaching. The adjutant got on a motor cycle, caught up with the leading guns, and ordered them into action on the road. The first gun was knocked out, but the next howitzer's crew waited until the tanks were only twenty-five yards away before opening fire. The gun's second round set the leading tank on fire, and the tank crew was shot down by small arms fire as they tried to escape. The gun's tractor was hit by a shell and Brown was severely wounded. (Captain Brown lost a leg but survived the war.) The leading tank had been commanded by First Lieutenant Sato. Tsuji later recorded:

> He [Sato] remained sitting upright among the ruins still grasping his sword. Hasi, a 1st-class private, was dead at his machine-gun and Sergeant Totu had collapsed beside his gun like a dish of *ame* [soft jelly].[30]

A hastily arranged defence was able to stop the tanks making any further progress. The Japanese tanks withdrew back to the bridge during the afternoon, and were subjected to harassing gun fire. The 155th Field Regiment had lost three officers and seventeen men killed, and three officers and two men wounded. The regiment's next commanding officer described 7 January as 'a very costly if glorious day' for the unit.

It had taken Japanese tanks only six hours to wreak havoc throughout the 11th Division's two northernmost brigades. As the 9th Gurkha Rifle's regimental historian sagely commented: 'The single gun which stopped the Japanese tanks after a rush of nineteen miles might have accomplished as much in the first hundred yards of the onset.'[31] After General Paris heard that Japanese tanks had crossed Slim River, he ordered the underemployed 80th Anti-Tank Regiment north from Tanjong Malim to help block the road. General Heath hastily sent an Indian reserve battalion to assist them.

As the tanks were rampaging southwards, Brigadiers Selby and Stewart had re-established their headquarters on a hill near Kampong Slim. Tanks shot them up around midday, accounting for the 28th Brigade's wireless. Selby, after consulting with Stewart and Harrison, decided to hold out till nightfall. The brigades would then withdraw across Slim River and down the railway to Tanjong Malim.

The 2/2nd and 2/9th Gurkha Rifles were still in position near the Trunk Road and relatively intact. Japanese lorried infantry and armoured vehicles gathered opposite them during the early afternoon. From 4 p.m. the Gurkhas began falling back towards the rail bridge over Slim River. By this stage the Japanese had begun working into the gaps between the Gurkha companies and breaking contact was difficult.

The railway bridge over the swampy river, swollen by flood, had already been partly demolished. Sappers laid a plank walkway on the wreckage of the bridge so that troops could cross the river in single file. Crowds of troops at the approaches to the river, and growing Japanese pressure, encouraged others to ford the Slim elsewhere. Some Gurkhas crossed at the bridge, but several companies were diverted to a footbridge thought to exist downstream. No footbridge was found in the darkness. The Gurkhas forded the river across a submerged log, or by swimming and using lifelines. Most of these Gurkhas lost their way in the tangled jungle as they tried to cut their way south.[32]

The remnants of the 12th and 28th Brigades had crossed the river by 7.30 p.m. The rearguard had not been heavily engaged, and a few Japanese shells fired at the bridge had fallen wide of the mark. The troops made their way twelve miles down the railway to Tanjong Malim as best they could. The head of the tired, hungry and bedraggled column had arrived by midnight, and the rest of the troops slowly staggered in over the next few hours of darkness. At Tanjong Malim transport was waiting to drive them further south. A battalion from the 15th Brigade, some anti-tank guns, the 350th Field Battery, and the 155th Field Regiment were all that remained to face the XXV Army's next push down the Trunk Road.[33]

The battle was far from over for some men of the 11th Division. Groups of men drawn from a variety of units tried to make their way south to regain British lines in the days and weeks ahead. The swamps, jungle and lack of roads that had made the Slim River area such good defensive terrain did not aid the flight of escapees. Those men who did succeed in remaining at large for a time did so often because of the aid they received from friendly civilians. As one officer later put it:

> If any memorials are erected in Malaya after it again becomes British, the first should be one to the Unknown Chinese Villager who from his poor resources and at the risk of everything he had gave food, shelter and succour to fugitive troops and set them further on their way.[34]

During an eventful five or six days on the run prior to capture, Lieutenant-Colonel Deakin and his companions came across a hut in which lived an old Sikh, and his wife and son. The Sikh fed them, but

> was extremely agitated. He told me [Deakin] a harrowing tale of how the Japanese were shooting all families for giving even the slightest assistance to any Britisher, even shooting them if a bunch of escapees had passed and they had not reported it. He implored me to go away.[35]

A number of groups of men shifted in and out of Deakin's party as it retreated. At one stage Deakin met up with the commander of one of his companies, Subedar Saut Ram, and a few of that company's Dogras.

> I unmercifully cursed him for having failed to stop the enemy and for having let the battalion down. Even now I can see him looking at me and saying, 'Sahib, we destroyed three tanks almost with our bare hands and this is all that remains alive of my company'.

Deakin roundly abused the subedar again, but later in the day 'I realised my abuse had been completely unjustified'. Deakin sent for his subordinate, to be told that Saut Ram had dropped out of the ragged column and could not be found.[36] Inevitably, rightly or wrongly, there was a great deal of soul-searching after a debacle such as that at Slim.

The battle at Slim River had been a truly extraordinary encounter. The spearhead of the attacking Japanese force had comprised only a tank regiment and a motorized infantry battalion. Lieutenant-Colonel Tsuji claimed that, 'the Jitra Battle dealt a crushing blow to the morale of the enemy, and the Slim Battle completely choked the breath out of them'.[37] The Anglo-Indian defenders of Malaya seemed to have learnt nothing since the opening of the campaign. Of course neither General Paris nor Brigadier Stewart had been present at Jitra, and the fighting along the rugged Grik road which had earned them promotion had not involved tanks.

According to a refreshingly candid Stewart, 'the moral effect of meeting tanks for the first time was too much for the anti-tank gunners and some infantry'.[38] After the war, Stewart wrote to the official historian:

> I am rightly criticised for the location of Brigade Headquarters, and for not using the Field Artillery in an anti-tank role ... It is no excuse, but I had never taken part in an exercise embodying a coordinated anti-tank defence or this type of attack. The use of tanks on a road at night [was] a surprise.[39]

But Stewart could hardly be blamed for the fact that the twenty-four guns of his supporting field regiment did not fire a single shot at the tanks over open sights. And the sappers at Trolak and Slim River again failed to blow mined bridges at short notice. After a month in action without relief, the officers and men of the 11th Indian Division were both physically and mentally fatigued. The battle at Slim was more, however, than just another defeat. The destruction of the division undermined the whole defence of Malaya. Neither Heath nor Percival could fathom how Paris and Stewart had managed to suffer such a crushing rout.[40] Percival had paid a heavy price for refusing to swap the exhausted division with fresh troops sitting idle at Singapore and Johore.

The Japanese were left in possession of the battlefield at Slim River. According to one estimate, they counted five hundred British-Indian dead.[41] Days after the battle a captured Gurkha officer, Captain G. C. Wylie, was driven through the area. 'The bodies of Battalion dead were still where they had fallen – many mere smudges on the road where they had been run over by tanks and motor transport.'[42] The Japanese claimed to have captured 1200 prisoners in the vicinity of the fighting. Several hundred seriously wounded men were recovered, and another 2000 prisoners were taken over the following week as bewildered and hungry men emerged voluntarily, or were caught wandering in the jungle. With hindsight these figures seem only too reasonable. (One Gurkha non-commissioned officer, Naik Nakam Gurung, lived in the jungle until he was found during the Malayan Emergency in October 1949.) Indian prisoners enrolled in Major Fujiwara's organization helped to round up new prisoners.[43]

The grateful Japanese captured supplies for two brigades for a month and much weaponry. The haul included fifty light armoured cars (bren gun carriers), and many vehicles, of enormous value to the transport-starved Japanese. A Japanese communique listed their casualties at Trolak as seventeen killed and sixty wounded. This figure may only have referred to one particular unit, but total Japanese casualties on 7 January were but a fraction of British-Indian losses. Tsuji paid tribute to the skill and fighting spirit of the front-line Japanese soldier. Second Lieutenant Watanabe was described as having carried out his duties like a 'war god'.[44]

When the remnants of the 12th and 28th Brigades assembled on 8 January they presented a sorry sight. The 12th Brigade (including the 5/14th Punjabis) comprised fourteen officers and 409 men, only half of whom were armed. The Argylls and the 5/2nd Punjabis each fielded fewer than a hundred men. The 28th Brigade was not in much better shape and had just 750 officers and men present. The 2/1st Gurkhas had almost ceased to exist. Only Major Winkfield, four VCOs and twenty Gurkha other ranks had escaped. The 2/2nd and 2/9th Gurkhas, however, with four hundred and over three hundred respectively, were relatively intact. (The above figures excluded a unit's B echelon in some cases.) In addition to the losses amongst the infantry, large parties of sappers, gunners and medical personnel had also gone into the bag. Sixteen 25-pounders and seven anti-tank guns had been lost.[45] It was going to take a great deal of time and work to reforge some of the units shredded at Slim River into reliable fighting forces.

# 10

# The Road to Johore

On the day of the Slim River battle General Wavell flew into Singapore to begin his assignment in the Far East. ABDA (American-British-Dutch-Australian) Command headquarters was due to open at Batavia, Java, on 15 January. Wavell's instructions were to hold the 'Malay barrier' of Malaya, Sumatra, Java and northern Australia, and to operate as far forward as possible to link back up with cut off forces.

On 7 January Wavell met Duff Cooper, the Resident Minister for Far Eastern Affairs, and General Pownall, the newly arrived chief of Far East Command. As Far East Command was closing down, Pownall was to become Wavell's chief of staff. Duff Cooper had been ordered back to the United Kingdom. Pownall noted that Wavell had doubts about General Heath, and 'he's not at all happy about Percival, who has the knowledge but not the personality to carry through a tough fight'. Pownall had already reached his own conclusions about Percival, writing in his diary:

> he is an uninspiring leader, and rather gloomy (as he was in France when Brigadier General Staff to I Corps). I hope it won't mean that I have to relieve Percival, pro tem., until someone tougher than he can come from elsewhere. But it might so happen.[1]

Wavell may have considered swapping Percival with Pownall, but Pownall was an archetypal staff officer, not an obvious candidate as a field commander. There was no other British officer in the Far East senior enough to replace Percival. Given the enormous scope of Wavell's responsibility as ABDA Supreme Commander, he did not feel able to take over local command at Singapore himself. From Percival's viewpoint, Wavell's arrival meant that he had had three different commanders in less than three weeks.

The following day, 8 January, Wavell flew up from Singapore to Kuala Lumpur aerodrome, escorted by almost every available RAF fighter in Malaya. Wavell knew little of the region, his new subordinates or the Japanese. The best way to correct that was to see things for himself. After arriving at Kuala Lumpur Wavell met Heath, and he then saw Paris, Selby and Stewart, and the wreckage of the 11th Indian Division. After discussions with Stewart, Wavell commented to another officer, 'Well, I have never listened to a more garbled account of an operation'.

Wavell flew back to Singapore late on 8 January. That evening General Percival was summoned into Wavell's presence, and issued with a set of instructions for the defence of southern Malaya. A few days previously Percival had decided that the 8th Australian Division's commander, Major-General Bennett, would be responsible for the eastern half of Johore state, and Heath's III Indian Corps, with an Australian brigade under command, responsible for western Johore. In fact, on the day of the battle at Slim River, Percival had been optimistically speculating that it might be possible to take the offensive in Johore by the middle of February, after reinforcements had arrived.

Wavell, however, was not overly interested in Percival's views. Not surprisingly, the new Supreme Commander suspected that the British generals on the spot, Percival and Heath in particular, were in some way responsible for the disasters that had happened in northern and central Malaya. Wavell decided to put Bennett in charge of the front in north-west Johore, with the 9th Indian Division under his command. Heath's headquarters and his battered 11th Division were to rest in southern Johore, and Heath was to assume responsibility for eastern Johore and the state's south-west coast. Bennett was to have the 27th Australian Brigade under his command immediately, and the 22nd Australian Brigade was to be sent across from the east coast town of Mersing as soon as it could be relieved. Wavell's decision to elevate Bennett was an important step. Wavell hardly knew Bennett, but there were few other untried generals available in Malaya. On 10 January Wavell flew off to Java to establish ABDA Command headquarters.

The 11th Division's ordeal was by no means over. General Heath ordered the division to cover Kuala Lumpur until the night of 10/11 January. General Paris, optimistic as ever, felt that his troops could carry out one more task, but Lieutenant-Colonel Harrison believed that one or two units would collapse as soon as the Japanese lent upon them.[2] Demolitions at Kuala Lumpur's aerodrome and wireless station had begun. The back-loading of supplies, and the evacuation of European civilians and a tiny minority of Asian civilians, was also well underway. Pillars of smoke stained the skyline of the capital of the Federated Malay States.

Two under strength 9th Division battalions had been sent across to the west coast, but otherwise the 11th Division's battered 15th and 28th Brigades had to front up again for another round of fighting. The 28th Brigade was positioned astride the Trunk Road. The 15th Brigade blocked the route leading from the coast to Rawang. An ad hoc force watched the coast southwards from Kuala Selangor. Mountain gunners had driven off another Japanese attempt to land at the mouth of the Sungei Selangor on 8 January, an otherwise mercifully quiet day for the division.

The next Japanese move fell upon the 15th Brigade. The four battalions of the brigade were deployed on the south bank of the Sungei Selangor, with wide gaps between each unit. The 4th Guards Regiment had been relatively inactive on the north bank for the previous two to three days. But during the night of 8/9 January a Japanese force crossed the river and fell upon the 1/14th Punjabis from the rear. Amid the half light of dawn, in a gloomy rubber estate, the battalion's headquarters was rushed, and its commanding officer, Lieutenant-Colonel Anderson, killed. Punjabi stragglers drifted across to a neighbouring unit. However the rest of the brigade had an undisturbed day.[3]

In the Trunk Road sector the 28th Brigade had retired to take up a position near Serendah, twenty-five miles south of Tanjong Malim. The troops spent the wet night of 9/10 January trying to dig in with hoes and bayonets. The following morning Japanese infantry and aircraft attacked. Hand-to-hand fighting ensued, and the brigade began a controlled withdrawal. Two miles south of Serendah was the village of Choh. The retreating troops found Choh full of Japanese, and three of the brigade's four battalions were cut off. The 3/17th Dogras tried to force their way through but were badly cut up within the village. In the absence of wireless communication, Brigadier Selby, at brigade headquarters further south, was unsure what had happened to his troops.

Captain North of the Dogras offered to try regain contact with the units cut off by the Japanese in Choh. Two Gurkhas, Naik Berman and Rifleman Lalbahadur, volunteered to go with North. They set out in a carrier but the vehicle was shot up in Choh. Naik Berman was killed and North and Lalbahadur spent the day hiding in a wet ditch under the overturned carrier. North and his companion made their escape that night, but they were captured five days later and shot. They awoke the next morning to find they were still alive, and after being hidden and fed by workers at a nearby rubber estate, North headed south alone. He was only recaptured after travelling over a hundred miles.[4]

Meanwhile at Choh, during the afternoon North was taking cover under his vehicle, carriers of the troops cut off burst through the village and reported to Selby that the forward battalions were dispersing to head south through the jungle. For the rest of the day and night remnants of the units cut off trickled in, but hundreds of men were lost.[5] But the time had come to abandon Kuala Lumpur and transport drove the 28th Brigade southwards during the night. Likewise the 15th Brigade motored back through Kuala Lumpur on the evening of 10 January.

On the west coast troops were still in position to stop the Japanese heading inland south of Kuala Lumpur to cut off the 15th and 28th Brigades. On 10 January Indian troops were covering Klang. The main body of the Japanese 4th Guards Regiment advanced down the coast to make contact during the morning. By noon the Indian forward companies had been pushed back, and one company was compelled to surrender as it had been surrounded. The officers of the artillery observation post with this company called down fire upon themselves to cover their escape when the infantry around them began laying down their arms.[6]

At 6.30 p.m. the British-Indian force withdrew from Klang as planned and headed east along the road to Kuala Lumpur. About 10 p.m., amid a rain shower, the 3rd Cavalry and the Jat/Punjab Battalion were ambushed and disintegrated. Only two hundred survivors were gathered together at Batu Tiga to continue the retreat southwards.

Complaints made by surviving British gunners about the performance of an Indian battalion were passed up the chain of command. Two days later Percival signalled to Wavell at Batavia that the morale of some Indian troops was reaching crisis point. As an example, he stated that on 10 January two companies of the 2/9th Jat Regiment had 'surrendered without fighting'. Such specific information would never have been passed around at such a high level if the alleged culprits had been British service troops.[7]

In a further bid to encircle Kuala Lumpur, a Japanese Guards battalion had landed at Port Swettenham during the afternoon of 10 January. The Guards bypassed Klang to reach the Trunk Road south of Kuala Lumpur on the evening of 11 January. They only missed the last retreating motor convoys of the 11th Division by a few hours. Japanese forces entered Kuala Lumpur at 8 p.m., whilst the weary British-Indian division drove on south to the presumed sanctuary of Johore. Kuala Lumpur was relatively undamaged, and the Chinese merchants' shops reminded Lieutenant-Colonel Tsuji of the central provinces of China. There were more of the large stockpiles of provisions and munitions that the Japanese had become accustomed to capturing in Malaya. The aerodrome was quickly brought into operation. XXV Army headquarters moved into a large barracks on the outskirts of Kuala Lumpur. Before long Japanese military police had mounted the severed heads of looters, and others suspected of anti-Japanese activities, on poles in public places as a warning to the populace.

The fall of Kuala Lumpur so early in the campaign was a blow to Percival's Malaya Command. On a brighter note for the British, on 13 January a major reinforcement convoy sailed into Singapore. The convoy included several

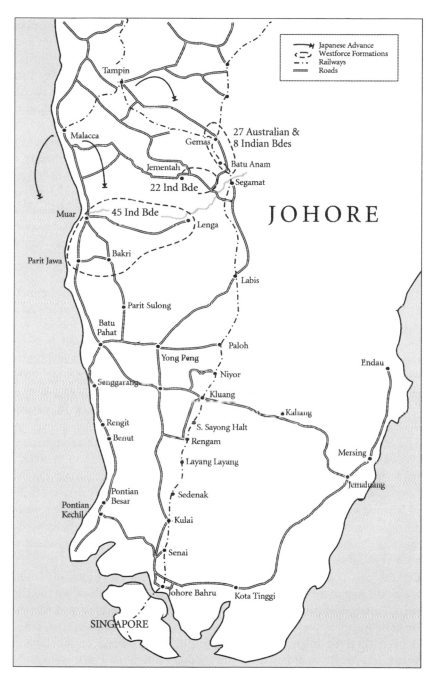

Japanese Advance
Westforce Formations
Railways
Roads

Tampin

Malacca

Gemas

27 Australian &
8 Indian Bdes

Jementah

Batu Anam

22 Ind Bde

Segamat

JOHORE

Muar

45 Ind Bde

Lenga

Bakri

Parit Jawa

Labis

Parit Sulong

Batu
Pahat

Paloh

Yong Peng

Endau

Niyor

Senggarang

Kluang

Kahang

Rengit

S. Sayong Halt

Benut

Rengam

Mersing

Layang Layang

Pontian
Besar

Sedenak

Jemaluang

Pontian
Kechil

Kulai

Senai

Johore Bahru

Kota Tinggi

SINGAPORE

10.  Johore.

large ships. Low cloud, mist and heavy rain squalls masked their approach. Eighty Japanese bombers with a fighter escort were over Singapore at the time, but they could see nothing and dropped their bombs blindly through the clouds. The ships disgorged the 18th Division's 53rd Brigade, some anti-aircraft and anti-tank units, and fifty-one crated Hurricanes and twenty-four pilots. RAF ground crews began the complex task of assembling the aircraft.

The victorious Japanese were also in the process of organizing reinforcements. Until now XXV Army had used only four infantry regiments on the west coast, but the 21st Regiment (5th Division) had landed at Singora on 8 January, and the 5th Guards Regiment was moving south through Malaya from Thailand. Part of the Japanese 18th Division was at Kuantan, and to make matters worse for General Percival's army, the Japanese were making plans to land the balance of the 18th Division at Endau, near Mersing, towards the end of January.

In light of General Wavell's instructions to Percival, Major-General Bennett's 8th Australian Divisional headquarters (relabelled as 'Westforce' headquarters) took over command of British forces in north-west Johore. With the army in Johore split into two groups, Percival was compelled to take personal control of the tactical battle for the first time. As Percival had no advance headquarters on the mainland, he had to make a tiring journey from Singapore whenever he wished to meet Generals Heath and Bennett, in addition to being somewhat out of touch with events in between visits.[8]

The 8th Division was temporarily split in two by the new arrangements, and Bennett badgered Percival for the transfer of the 22nd Australian Brigade from Mersing to north-west Johore on several occasions. Percival, however, refused to relieve the 22nd Brigade until the newly arrived British 53rd Brigade was ready to undertake the relief. Percival might have replaced the brigade with troops of Singapore's garrison as an interim measure, but as always he was unable to countenance running a risk in any sector for even a few days.

On the east coast of the peninsula, two Japanese battalions of Colonel Koba's 55th Regiment were laboriously marching southwards down the coast from Kuantan, towards the 22nd Australian Brigade at Endau and Mersing. (The 56th Regiment, which had landed at Kota Bharu and seized Kuantan, had been diverted inland to Kuala Lumpur). The speed of the Japanese advance was greatly hampered by the roadless jungle of Pahang state.

At Mersing the population had been evacuated and the beaches were heavily defended. One night dark objects had been seen moving on the beach. The ensuing water buffalo massacre had been one of the few note-worthy military incidents to date, as had been the capture of two shot down Japanese airmen. Australian troops in the area had also been puzzled as to why the Japanese-operated transmitter at Penang had been able to broadcast their passwords. It was rumoured among senior ranks that an officer of the Johore Military Force was trafficking information to the enemy. Unlike the troops at Kuantan, Brigadier Taylor's Australian force was actively patrolling the approaches to Mersing, and a watchful eye was kept on the slowly advancing Japanese. So long as the Japanese did not attempt a fresh assault landing from the sea, the front on the east coast was reasonably secure.[9]

In north-west Johore General Bennett deployed the bulk of his strength down the Trunk Road, which had until now been the main Japanese axis of advance. The 27th Australian Brigade was the leading formation astride the Trunk Road. The brigade's forward battalion took up a position three miles west of the Sungei Gemas. Gemas town was important as it was the junction at which the rail from eastern Malaya met the west coast railway and Trunk Road. The brigade's other two battalions were strung out along the road to the rear with those of the 8th Indian Brigade. The six battalions of the two brigades held roughly twenty miles of road leading north west from Segamat. The 9th Division's other brigade, Painter's 22nd, was deployed along the road leading westwards from Segamat towards Jementah to parry any Japanese attempt to outflank the troops on the Trunk Road by that route.[10] The 9th Division comprised barely three thousand infantrymen. The 2nd Loyal North Lancashire had come forward from Singapore, and was in reserve at Segamat. The bulk of the guns of the AIF's 2/4th Anti-Tank Regiment's two batteries, and the 80th Anti-Tank Regiment's remaining guns, were distributed among the infantry battalions, together with four field regiments (less a battery).

The three brigades guarding the Trunk Road looked relatively secure on paper, but this was not the case on the coastal flank of north-west Johore. The 45th Indian Brigade, and a battery borrowed from the 2/15th Field Regiment, held a twenty-five mile front behind the unbridged Muar River. (The 45th Brigade had only arrived at Singapore early in January.) Bennett had visited the brigade, and he had told sceptical senior officers to conduct a mobile defence. Percival approved Bennett's decision to post the Indians at Muar, as up to that time Japanese coastal landings had involved only small forces without tanks. The Muar River was quite wide at its mouth, and Percival believed that 'if all small craft were taken across to the south bank, it would be difficult for the Japanese to cross in strength'.[11] The two wings of Westforce, at Gemas and behind the Muar River respectively, were separated by the mist-clad Mount Ophir. Road communication between the two areas ran through Yong Peng miles to the rear.

General Yamashita and his XXV Army staff had been surprised and delighted by their troops' progress down Malaya, but they expected to encounter more formal and effective defences in Johore, which was the natural outer bastion of Singapore. As the Japanese 5th Division was becoming increasingly tired, a new detachment was formed under the control of XXV Army headquarters to spearhead the advance into Johore. The rest of the division took a long overdue two day's rest at Kuala Lumpur. Mukaide Detachment comprised part of the 1st Tank Regiment, one battalion, and some artillery and engineers.[12] When the Imperial Guards Division had assembled that formation was to support the 5th Division by pushing down the west coast.

Before going into action Westforce's Australians had to witness the retreat of the soundly beaten 11th Division. The motor convoy carrying the division took hours to drive slowly southwards through the bottlenecks of Gemas and Segamat. The column received little attention from the Japanese air force. Civilian transport carrying last minute evacuees was mixed with military vehicles, and included a convoy of ponderous Public Works Department steam-rollers. A British staff officer reported:

> Rain, darkness, inexperienced and weary drivers, congestion, delays and lack of control, all contributed to a state of affairs which still lives as a nightmare in the minds of many who experienced it. Frayed and tired tempers were not improved by the unfortunate attitude of a minority of the Australian troops moving up, who were at no pains to conceal their opinion of the retiring troops whom, in their ignorance, they blamed for the failure in the North. But the efforts of officers managed in most cases to avert actual blows, and the troops of the 11th Division were too tired to feel resentment for long.[13]

Lieutenant-Colonel Galleghan of the 2/30th Battalion later commented that 'a retreating army is a horrible sight'. A British general noted that on some lorries the chalked slogan 'Tokyo or bust' had been amended to 'Singapore or bust'.[14]

As the 11th Division passed into reserve to rest and rebuild, at General Heath's request Paris was demoted back to the command of the 12th Indian Brigade. Key of the 8th Brigade, the best-performing senior officer in Malaya and Heath's original nominee to replace Murray-Lyon, was belatedly made the division's new commander. The always considerate Percival 'took pains to explain to Paris that the change by no means indicated loss of confidence in him'.[15]

The 2/30th Battalion, three miles west of Gemas, was Bennett's foremost

unit astride the Trunk Road. Bennett had long been thinking about am-
bushes as a way to counter-attack the advancing Japanese. Early thoughts
of a battalion-sized ambush had been discarded as the most appropriate
location could only play host to an ambushing force a company strong. The
ambush was laid three miles west of the battalion's main position. This
ambush near Gemas has a disputed parentage. Even General Percival was
later to claim a hand in its design. Brigadier Maxwell of the 27th Brigade
and the 2/30th Battalion's Lieutenant-Colonel Galleghan also claimed to
have played important roles in the ambush's planning. Australians had been
in the area for some time, where coincidentally Maxwell's brother, another
decorated First World War veteran, managed a local rubber estate.[16]

The rapidly retreating 11th Division had broken contact with the Japanese
south of Kuala Lumpur. The Japanese advance was unopposed for over
thirty miles, and some of the bridges leading towards Gemas had been left
undamaged to disguise the fact that the ambush site was also located beyond
an unbroken bridge. The 2/30th Battalion's ambush site was on the Singapore side of the Sungei Gemencheh. On the Australians' side of the
stream the Trunk Road was winding and bordered by thick jungle. A twelve
foot high cutting forty yards long began sixty yards beyond the bridge.
The ambush zone stretched for several hundred yards. Lots were drawn to
decide which company would be responsible for the ambush, and Captain
D. J. Duffy's B Company was awarded the task. The Australians took up
their positions on 13 January and began to wait amid pouring rain. After
the ambush was sprung Duffy's company was to withdraw back to the
main battalion position along a subsidiary track. Duffy did not have a
wireless set, and signal lines running back to battalion headquarters were
laid beside the road.

By the morning of 14 January there were no other troops between the
Australians and the Japanese. Just before 4 p.m. a column of two to three
hundred Japanese cyclists crossed the Gemencheh bridge, and rode through
the ambush position unaware of the tense, watching troops in the jungle.
The Japanese seemed relaxed and chattered to each other. Some bicycles
had no tyres and their rims made a grinding noise as they rolled. One
observer compared the sound of the approaching cyclists to that of a swarm
of bees. The first group of cyclists was followed by three motor cyclists, and
several hundred more cyclists riding up to five or six abreast.

The first group of cyclists was allowed to pass through the ambush.
When Captain Duffy adjudged that the second main group of Japanese
was neatly within the ambush site he gave the order for the bridge to be
blown. Those Japanese cyclists on the bridge were tossed like rag dolls into
the air by the blast. The Australians poured grenades, machine gun and

rifle fire into the mass of cyclists, whose weapons were strapped impotently to their machines, or slung across their backs. Duffy reported that 'the entire 300 yards of road was thickly covered with dead and dying men'.[17] Bren guns firing from the knoll above the cutting were able to rake the road on the Japanese side of the stream. The signal wires, which had been left exposed beside the road, were cut in the first phase of the ambush.

Duffy ordered his company to withdraw as planned after it had dealt with all targets on offer. There were several sharp clashes with Japanese who had struggled clear of the ambush. The company broke into groups during a confused retirement through the jungle. After further encounters with Japanese across their path, the Australians regained friendly lines over the next two days.

The 2/30th Battalion claimed that six hundred Japanese had been killed in the ambush. The 27th Brigade's war diary recorded that 750 casualties had been inflicted. Did all those broken bicycles help boost the estimate? Officers at the ambush scene claimed that seven or eight hundred cyclists were in the group of Japanese directly ambushed. But this can never be proved in the absence of a 'body count'.[18] Lieutenant-Colonel Tsuji later noted that there were only two infantry companies in the van when contact was made ten kilometres west of Gemas. The war diary of the Japanese 9th Infantry Brigade recorded for 14 January that Mukaide Detachment had

> suffered seventy dead and fifty-seven wounded. Details and reports are still lacking, but I fear that while pushing on precipitously through the jungle they may have been ambushed.[19]

The main body of the 2/30th Battalion waited for the Japanese to square up to their position in front of Gemas. Galleghan had sent most of his battalion's transport and carriers well to the rear to reduce the likelihood of detection from the air. He had even told his men that Japanese aviators could see upturned faces. Three to four miles west of Gemas, at a point where the rail and Trunk Road ran close together, the battalion held a half mile front with all three remaining rifle companies in line abreast. One company was on either side of the Trunk Road, and out on the left another company continued the line to the railway. The population of Gemas village had been forcibly evacuated.

Two Australian anti-tank guns were in position with Galleghan's infantry, one either side of the Trunk Road, the forward gun about fifty feet ahead of the other. The gun commanders, Sergeants Ken Harrison and Charlie Parsons, had reported to Galleghan. They had been abruptly told that the Japanese would not use tanks, and that anti-tank guns were a nuisance. Harrison later heard that his officer had received similar treatment from

Galleghan the previous day, and that a third gun sent forward had been promptly sent to the rear again.

There was a bend in the Trunk Road in a cutting two hundred yards ahead of the anti-tank guns. A road-block made of concrete pylons was between the guns and the cutting. The road was bordered by undergrowth and rubber trees in neat rows, with lush, green jungle beyond. The anti-tank gunners were visited by a brigadier who

> impressed on us what an honour it was to open the batting and strike the first blow for Australia. 'Hit them out of the ground for six', he suggested. He then completely spoilt the effect on leaving by bidding us 'goodbye' in a tone of deepest gloom and melancholy.

Sergeant Harrison spent a restless night. The weather was as humid as ever.[20]

Overnight Galleghan sent patrols up the road to try and discover what exactly had happened to Duffy's company. Early next morning a patrol spied a view of the previous day's ambush site. The bodies and bicycles had been pushed to the side of the road. Japanese troops were assembling to resume the advance. It had taken the Japanese only six hours to repair the Gemencheh bridge. Another patrol led by Sergeant S. F. Arneil shot up a small group of Japanese and retrieved maps from a young officer's body.[21]

Soon after 9 a.m. on 15 January Japanese tanks began to approach the road-block in front of the Australian battalion. The anti-tank gunners had been warned of the approach of tanks by an infantry patrol, and they could hear the rumble of armoured vehicles beyond the cutting. The first two tanks nosed their way around the bend of the road, but reversed back to cover again. Three more tanks soon approached. The guns fired as they neared the road-block. One tank was struck by a shell and another tank was set on fire, its hatches flying open as the surviving crew tried to scramble for safety. Harrison's gun switched from armour-piercing to high explosive shells. The flash of the shells could now be seen as they burst on the tanks. Ammunition exploded in the burning tank. To Harrison 'judging by the dense black smoke drifting out of the side ventilators, a few bodies were being incinerated too. The memory of this sight was often to be a grim consolation in the bitter years to come.'[22] The disabled tank was towed away by the third tank behind a smoke pall drifting in the cutting.

During the brief interval that followed Harrison ran from the rear gun to the forward gun. Soon another four tanks came down the road, using the still smouldering tank for cover. The guns opened fire again and a light armoured vehicle toppled over onto its side. The rearmost tank suffered the fatal indignity of a mortar bomb falling through its open turret. The tanks returned fire and Harrison's loader was wounded in the head by shrapnel and struck on the shoulder by the recoiling breech as he fell. Another shell came skidding under the gun shield and exploded to throw Harrison onto his back, and mortally wound another crewman. The cutting had been turned into 'a spectacular mass of smoke and flame'. The anti-tank guns could only fire blindly into the pall. Gun flashes amid the smoke indicated that at least one tank was still shooting back, as did the sound of shells thundering past down the road. A rubber tree oozing white latex was brought down by a Japanese round in front of the leading gun. In the furious exchange of fire all four tanks were disabled or damaged. The surviving Japanese tank crewmen retreated on foot and their tanks fell silent. The whole action had taken less than an hour. The leading anti-tank gun had only four shells left, and was surrounded by brass shell cases twinkling in the bright sunlight. The gunners received cheers and congratulations from grateful nearby infantrymen emerging from cover.[23]

The Australians' position at Gemas was bombed and strafed as the morning wore on. A signal truck was destroyed at battalion headquarters, and Galleghan, probably incorrectly, suspected that it was the wireless transmissions that had given the position away. Galleghan decided that the battalion should withdraw behind the Sungei Gemas that evening, but, buoyed by news that part of Duffy's company had returned, he ordered Captain W. S. Melville's D Company to advance from its left flank position to keep the Japanese off balance. The troops bounded forward but encountered Japanese amid thick vegetation only three hundred yards from their start line. Two crew-served weapons were captured, but a hasty retreat became necessary when tanks began working through the rubber against their flank. Early in the afternoon tanks also began moving towards the company north of the Trunk Road. After a confused clash the tanks temporarily withdrew.[24]

Midway through the afternoon Galleghan ordered his battalion to retire. Sergeant Harrison could distinctly see six armoured vehicles still smouldering on the road. Another column of smoke around the bend beyond the cutting suggested that other vehicles had also been damaged. The Australians' left behind three 25-pounders bogged in the mud. A carrier drove up to tow away one of the anti-tank guns, but with bullets flying about and retreating infantry dashing by, the driver panicked and drove off down the road leaving the gun behind. The driver demanded that the crew get in immediately or stay behind as well. Later that evening Harrison told the story of the day to the brigadier and his staff. The brigadier was not too concerned at the loss of the anti-tank guns, and said that up to 14 January British anti-tank gunners had lost twenty-three guns for the destruction of only a handful of tanks. Two new guns soon arrived from Singapore, and Harrison and Parsons were back in business.[25] (The extent of the anti-tank gun crews' success at Gemas does not say much for the performance of the large force of artillery at Slim River.)

On the evening of 15 January the now battered Mukaide Detachment came back under the command of the Japanese 5th Division's 9th Brigade. The next day the 9th Brigade followed up the Australian withdrawal towards the 27th Brigade's main position astride the Trunk Road around Batu Anam, some ten miles in front of Segamat. Meanwhile the 5th Division's 21st Brigade began a wide detour down side roads leading to Jementah and Segamat.

The 2/30th Battalion's engagement near Gemas was undoubtedly a success. It was later claimed by General Bennett, based on the battalion's estimates, that a thousand Japanese had been killed and wounded on 14–15 January. Needless to say this was a gross exaggeration, 'absurdly over-sanguine' according to one official commentator. But even if the Australians had managed to inflict only a few hundred casualties, in return for less than a hundred of their own, this was a most creditable performance. The battalion's reported losses were one officer and sixteen men killed, nine men missing, and four officers and fifty-one men wounded.[26]

Lieutenant-Colonel Tsuji wrote of the fighting at Gemas:

> The 8th Australian Division, which had newly arrived on the battlefield, relying on the advantage of its position, fought with a bravery we had not previously seen.[27]

The AIF was given a great deal of flattering publicity in the *Straits Times* in the immediate aftermath of the fighting around Gemas. However, though the action at Gemas was a considerable local victory against the tide of events, in reality it was little more than a pinprick to XXV Army. Bennett's Westforce had had ten battalions in the Trunk Road sector, yet only a single battalion had been deployed to strike the first blow against the Japanese in Johore. As the Gemas battle was taking place, the position of the main body of Bennett's Westforce had been gravely jeopardized by events unfolding on the coast at Muar.

Whilst the Japanese 5th Division's advance guard had been pushing down the Trunk Road, the Imperial Guards Division had moved southwards in support close to the west coast. The Imperial Guards had entered unoccupied Malacca on 14 January. Further south Japanese aircraft had been bombing Muar town and the 45th Indian Brigade since 11 January. This novice brigade's situation was not rosy. Visibility in local plantations and scrub was often under one hundred yards. And the monsoonal rains had ensured that weapon pits were flooded and vehicles bogged. The AIF's 65th Battery was the Indians only artillery support, rather than the usual three batteries.

The 65th Battery's commander was Major W. W. Julius. The most famous member of the unit, Gunner Russell Braddon (the future author of *The Naked Island*), later wrote that Julius was a bad-tempered man with a dark complexion, known 'respectfully' to his men as 'the Black Bastard'.[28]

The 45th Brigade had only embarked from India late in 1941 with a newly acquired and conspicuously desert-camouflaged complement of vehicles. The troops thought they were heading for Iraq and a further long spell of training. Newer officers still lacked fluency in Indian languages, and the men were far from fully proficient at basic musketry. Upon arriving in the unfamiliar environment of Malaya, one unit had practised movement in the jungle. When set a two mile march, some groups had finished a full mile from their objective.

The units of the brigade had been raised within the previous eighteen months. The 7/6th Rajputana Rifles had only 170 men with more than a year's service, and over six hundred with less than a year. Three of the battalion's rifle companies were commanded by European second lieutenants, and the other was commanded by a first lieutenant. By comparison British or Australian rifle companies would have been led by a major or captain in most cases.

The Indians first encounter with what they believed to be the enemy had occurred on 11 January. Brigade personnel had been told many stories about native fifth columnists, and Japanese in civilian clothes carrying concealed weapons. A chevrolet staff car with military markings had arrived at a company headquarters of the 4/9th Jats. The car's occupants had asked to see Major White, the battalion's second-in-command. Lieutenant-Colonel John Williams was suspicious as the men claimed a connection with the Australians without having the right accents or complexions. The men were taken to brigade headquarters, where, as they were clearly Eurasians, they were declared to be 'bogus' and locked up. A battle-hardened formation might well have shot them out of hand.[29]

Behind the twisting Muar River the brigade's 7/6th Rajputana Rifles held nine miles of front stretching inland from the coast. The 4/9th Jats prolonged the line for another fifteen miles, and the 5/18th Garhwal Rifles were in reserve near brigade headquarters at Bakri. General Bennett had expressly told Brigadier Duncan to position two companies from each forward battalion on the north bank of the Muar River. This idea of Bennett's mirrored the plan of the ambush near Gemas but was quite inappropriate given the 45th Brigade's very different situation. Percival was later to comment that if Bennett had placed all of the Indians south of the Muar River, 'instead of wasting four companies north of it, he would have had quite a good chance of stopping the enemy crossings'.[30]

On the morning of 15 January, the day of the main Gemas battle, the Japanese Imperial Guards advanced boldly southwards. The 4th Guards Regiment (less a battalion) was to head down the coast towards Muar town, whilst the 5th Guards Regiment crossed the river upstream and cut down onto the town from the flank and rear. After seizing Muar town (which was on the south bank of the river), the 4th Regiment was to carry on down the coast to Batu Pahat. The 5th Regiment's next objective was Yong Peng on the Trunk Road behind the main body of Westforce.

The Guards rapidly deployed to infiltrate and overrun the Rajputana Rifles' companies on the north side of the river.[31] That night (15/16 January), a Guards battalion crossed the Muar River unopposed in Malay boats found hidden or tied up to the river bank. The Japanese moved into the large gap between the Rajputanas and the Jats further inland astride the jungle bordered river. Hooking back towards Muar, the Guards surprised a Rajputana company amid dense scrub south of the river.

By late morning other Japanese troops had advanced from their bridgehead to threaten the road between Muar and brigade headquarters at Bakri. The company of the 5/18th Garhwal Rifles at Simpang Jeram had been joined by the battalion's advance headquarters the previous evening. About 6.30 a.m. on 16 January the Garhwalis' Lieutenant-Colonel James Wooldridge had visited Muar. He was killed when his party was ambushed on the return journey to Simpang Jeram. A Garhwali patrol was also ambushed forward of the village. The company's commander was among the dead.

The Garhwalis' adjutant, Captain Rodgers, was now in command at Simpang Jeram, and he decided to form a close perimeter in a rubber estate. The estate was overlooked from higher ground but it was the best position available. The Japanese attacked the perimeter from the shelter of the village. The young riflemen were bewildered and they fired wildly. As the situation worsened, Rodgers and Lieutenant Robson, the battalion's motor transport officer, each manned a bren gun at the forward corners of the perimeter, an indication of the low state of the sepoys' training. Robson was shot in the chest crawling out to retrieve ammunition from a casualty. Early in the afternoon, Rodgers ordered a retreat shortly before he was killed.[32] In the meantime a counter-attack towards Simpang Jeram by another Garhwali company had ground to a halt. By evening the battalion had been bundled back to Bakri.

That afternoon the Japanese Imperial Guards made an attempt to cross the four hundred yards wide Muar River directly, close to the town. A group of motor barges entered the mouth of the river but were driven back by Australian gunners firing over open sights. But Japanese troops already across the river gradually boxed the remainder of the Rajputana Rifles into

Muar town. Just before 2 p.m. news reached battalion headquarters that Japanese south of the town were poised to cut the main line of retreat. Lieutenant-Colonel J. A. Lewis and Captain R. H. R. Alderman led a scratch party of thirty men to deal with the intruders, but both officers were killed in a fire-fight in a patch of rubber. Later in the afternoon the adjutant, Captain S. Watt, ordered the remnants of the Rajputana Rifles to pull out of Muar. The battalion retreated eight miles down the coast road to Parit Jawa without interference. The guns of the Australian battery withdrew with the Indians.

With the Muar battle only thirty-six hours old, the Rajputanas had been reduced to two officers (Watt and the medical officer) and 120 men.[33] Of the officers to start the battle with the Rajputanas, eight were already dead and another evacuated wounded. A disaster of the first magnitude was rapidly unfolding at Muar. If the Japanese could reach the Trunk Road at Yong Peng, behind the main body of Westforce, a decisive defeat might soon be inflicted on General Bennett's command.

# 11

# The Road from Bakri

With the battle rapidly slipping through his fingers, General Bennett sent an Australian battalion to the Muar front to restore the situation. On the morning of 17 January Bennett told the commanding officer of the 2/29th Battalion, the 27th Brigade's reserve battalion, that the enemy force near Muar was only two hundred strong. A counter-attack should regain the initiative. Of course, by that stage the bulk of the Imperial Guards Division had passed across the Muar River.

Meanwhile the newly arrived British 53rd Brigade was given by Percival to III Corps to help guard Westforce's communications. Since arriving at Singapore on 13 January the brigade, whilst wilting under the humidity and rain of the tropics, had hastily assembled the transport and equipment needed for battle. As part of General Key's 11th Division, the brigade's 2nd Cambridgeshires were dispatched to Batu Pahat, south of which Malaya Command had received a report of a Japanese landing. The 6th Norfolks were sent to a defile between milestones 78 and 79 on the Yong Peng-Muar road, and the 5th Norfolks were transferred to the 22nd Australian Brigade at Mersing, which in exchange released the 2/19th Battalion to Westforce and the Muar front.

After eleven weeks at sea the men of the 53rd Brigade were no longer in peak condition. A British officer observed of one battalion:

> The jungle was a completely strange and seemingly hostile environment to most officers and men of the Norfolks, the majority of whom had never moved far from their homes. The enervating heat, the mosquitoes and strange jungle noises at night deprived them of sleep and aggravated the softening effects of their long sea journey.[1]

It would have been preferable to send the brigade to Mersing to relieve the 22nd Brigade, the best jungle-trained formation in Malaya. But Percival did not think there was time for the exchange. By the standards of the First World War that was true, but the 2/19th Battalion, once it had packed up, traversed the lateral road that ran direct from Mersing to the west coast in a matter of hours.

On the Muar front, the 45th Indian Brigade's headquarters was at Bakri, eight miles behind the river, and thirty miles from the Trunk Road at Yong Peng. The 2/29th Battalion (less a company and a platoon) took up position one and half miles forward of Bakri late on 17 January. The battalion was ordered by Brigadier Duncan, acting on General Bennett's instructions, to prepare for an attack towards the Muar River planned for the following day. The reorganized 5/18th Garhwal Rifles was sent from Bakri to the coastal village of Parit Jawa that night, also in readiness for an attack the next morning. The Japanese, however, were already at Parit Jawa. The Garhwalis were badly ambushed as they approached the village. Duncan cancelled the Australians' planned attack when he heard of the Garhwalis' rout.[2]

After such a favourable start to the battle, the Imperial Guards Division's commander, Lieutenant-General Nishimura, prepared to finish off his opponents. The Guards had spent 17 January ferrying more troops over the Muar River. That evening the 5th Guards Regiment was ordered to attack and encircle Bakri, whilst the 4th Guards Regiment undertook a deep encircling movement to reach the road between Bakri and the Trunk Road at Yong Peng.

The 2/29th Battalion had been given a composite troop of four anti-tank guns. The troop's commander was Lieutenant R. M. McCure, and included the gun crews of Sergeants Harrison and Parsons. The battalion's Lieutenant-Colonel J. C. Robertson did not expect the Japanese to use tanks, and he told McCure when asked where he wanted the guns: 'For all I care, Mr McCure, you can take them back to base!' Harrison later speculated that Robertson's attitude stemmed from an ongoing general ignorance of what had transpired at Slim River.

Lieutenant McCure left a pair of two-pounders at Bakri. The other two guns joined the battalion on the road leading towards the Muar River. Sergeant C. W. Thornton's gun was sited to cover a slight bend in the road leading towards the Australians' perimeter. Sergeant Parsons's gun was placed four hundred yards to the rear. Thornton was a farmer from Berrigan in New South Wales who had been in the militia prior to the war.[2]

During the night there were clashes with Japanese patrols around the Australians' perimeter, but most of the handful of wounded were hit by Lee-Enfield bullets. Henceforward the order was given that only grenades and bayonets were to be used at night. After dawn, at 6.45 a.m. on 18 January, Japanese tanks advanced along the jungle-lined road leading from the Muar River direct to Bakri. From behind a mound, about a hundred yards from the road, Thornton's crew watched five tanks trundling along the road at fifteen miles an hour. The first two tanks were hit as they drew abreast. The Japanese had probably not spotted the gun. The armour-piercing shells seemed to pass through the tanks. The tanks were hit again, and they rolled

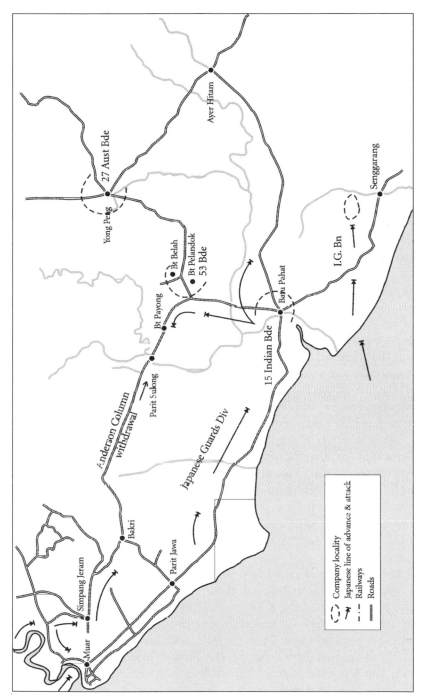

11. The Retreat from Bakri.

on at walking pace to be finally brought to a halt only yards from the muzzle of Parsons's backstop gun. The following three tanks were soon knocked out as well. Nearby infantry cut down the escaping crews, and an officer clambered onto the tanks to drop grenades into the turrets.

Three more Japanese tanks came down the road. They had by this stage located the guns that had destroyed the first five tanks. But they too were destroyed in a brutal duel. By the end of the action Thornton had been wounded in the hip and his gun had fired seventy rounds. The gun crews achieved enduring fame as a war photographer was on hand to photograph both them and the burning tanks. Lieutenant Ben Hackney compared the sound of ammunition exploding in the tanks to an Empire Day celebration. Sergeant Harrison later came forward from Bakri to inspect the derelict tanks. The officer in the first tank had taken a direct hit, and a driver in another tank was still at the controls but without his head.[3]

Lieutenant McCure's men had been fortunate that the tanks had chosen to advance without infantry support, but the Japanese had advanced with reckless speed throughout the campaign. The chief difference on this occasion was that a small group of men had the skill and morale to take advantage of habitual Japanese overconfidence. A history of the Japanese Imperial Guards noted that the spirits of the men of Gotanda tank company were high, but that they were 'careless and mistaken' in their attack. 'The British had dexterously camouflaged anti-tank weapons in the proper locations.'[4]

After warding off this latest Japanese thrust, Lieutenant-Colonel Robertson left for a conference at brigade headquarters at Bakri. On the return journey Robertson was riding pillion on a motorcycle. Japanese waiting in the jungle shot up the motorcycle, and both Robertson and the rider were sent crashing to the ground. The driver struggled on down the road to the 2/29th Battalion's perimeter. A carrier went out to pick up Robertson, who died half an hour later. Shortly before his death, whilst lying on a stretcher, Robertson apologised to McCure for his earlier scepticism, and acknowledged that the anti-tank guns had been of tremendous help to his battalion. Command of the unit devolved to Major S. F. Olliff, formerly a reserve officer in a British regiment.[5]

That same morning of 18 January, the 2/19th Battalion (less two platoons of D Company) arrived at Bakri at about 10 a.m. to join the remnants of the 45th Brigade gathered there. The battalion's commander was Lieutenant-Colonel Charles Anderson. Anderson was not a native-born Australian. He had been born at Cape Town in 1897, and had served in the King's African Rifles in East Africa during the First World War. In the 1920s Anderson had led game-hunting expeditions in Africa. After marrying an Australian, he emigrated to Australia in 1934, and bought a grazing property

in rural New South Wales. Anderson joined the militia in 1939, and transferred to the AIF in 1940. He was sturdily built, mild-mannered, and quick
on his feet.[6]

At Bakri Anderson estimated that the Rajputana Rifles and the Garhwal
Rifles had only a few officers and four to five hundred other ranks between
them. The Indians were tired, stressed and hungry, and some were unarmed.
Anderson later wrote:

> I saw Indian troops in action in the German East Africa campaign 1914–18 war
> and have the highest regard for their fighting qualities, and have no doubt in my
> mind that the 45th Brigade had the same fighting material, but, in common with
> my officers, I felt extremely disturbed that it was necessary to have had to employ
> such immature and partly trained troops ...
>
> Most of the troops were I should say about seventeen years old and had
> adolescent fluff on their cheeks; six months formed, and it takes four months to
> teach them to wear boots!!![7]

Brigadier Duncan ordered Anderson's men to form a perimeter with the
Indians around Bakri. He had sent out patrols that morning to order the Jats,
who were still posted along an inland stretch of the Muar River, to rejoin
the rest of the brigade.

During 18 January Percival reacted to events on the Muar front by
transferring that part of the battlefield from Bennett's command to Heath's
III Corps. As Heath could only contact the 45th Brigade on the wireless at
Bennett's Westforce headquarters, that was not a particularly helpful
development. By this time Malaya Command's Intelligence branch had
belatedly realised that the Imperial Guards Division was deployed at Muar.
Percival now believed the Japanese to have five divisions in Malaya. (They
actually had elements of three.)[8]

General Bennett remained in command of Westforce troops in the vicinity
of the Trunk Road, where the situation was still relatively secure. On 16 and
17 January a lot of artillery fire had been exchanged as the 27th Brigade
slowly withdrew towards Batu Anam, six miles behind Gemas. On 18 January
the 1/13th Frontier Force Rifles was strongly attacked near Batu Anam.
A number of posts were overrun. Most of a company and five anti-tank
guns were left behind when the rest of the unit retired.

Near Bakri the 2/29th Battalion maintained its position during 18 January.
There was skirmishing during the day with infiltrating Japanese infantry,
and after nightfall the battalion perimeter was probed for an hour. The
Australians held their ground without any great difficulty. Foreign voices
cried ominously out of the darkness, 'Yoh die, yoh die tommorroh'.

During the night of 18/19 January the Japanese worked around the flanks of both the 2/29th Battalion and the force behind them at Bakri. Around Bakri troops of the 2/19th Battalion held a perimeter of posts astride the three roads that led into the village, and on intervening patches of rising ground. The 350th Field Battery had reported at Bakri overnight to support the Australians. Anderson had sent the battery back again as he did not want to detach infantry to protect the guns.[9]

After daylight on 19 January a section of carriers had been posted on a low, rubber-planted ridge five hundred yards to the south and south east of the Bakri crossroads. The 2/19th Battalion's A Company had held the ridge overnight, but had been withdrawn to the crossroads for redeployment elsewhere. But at 8 a.m. the Japanese attacked the ridge, having crept eastwards past Captain R. W. Keegan's B Company astride the road to the coast. The carriers were swiftly bundled off the rising ground.

From Anderson's nearby headquarters it was possible to ascertain what was happening. Anderson ordered Lieutenant F. G. Beverley's A Company, which was still at the crossroads, southwards to attack the intruders' front and flanks. Meanwhile Keegan's company swung back off the coast road to take the Japanese from the rear. After almost a year's training in Malaya, the battalion was particularly adept at moving through rubber and clumps of jungle, and could manoeuvre in a fashion forbidden to a less well-trained unit. The Japanese force was caught neatly between the two companies and destroyed in the melee that followed. 140 Japanese bodies were counted on the ridge. Ten Australians were killed and fifteen wounded. A small cannon and seventeen light machine guns were among the weapons captured. This was the first time in Malaya that a British Empire force had overrun a Japanese contingent and maintained control of the battlefield long enough to count the bodies of the fallen. The Japanese custom of refusing to surrender made itself apparent. Bloody corpses that miraculously sprang to life, and badly wounded Japanese who continued to struggle to fire weapons or detonate grenades, had had to be slain one by one.[10]

As this fight had been taking place, news arrived that the battalion's transport harbour was under attack on the road leading to Parit Sulong, two miles east of the Bakri crossroads, and only half a mile to the rear of brigade headquarters. The Japanese pincer movement against Bakri was rather more developed than British commanders realised. Whilst one Guards battalion had squared up against the 2/29th Battalion's perimeter, another had advanced up the coast road from Parit Jawa to attack Bakri from the south, and a third had hooked south around both the 2/29th Battalion and Bakri to reach the transport lines beyond Bakri. Two other Guards battalions were heading across country to threaten Yong Peng.

The gloss of the morning's success was further tarnished when at 10 a.m.

on 19 January brigade headquarters, which was located in a lone white house near the Bakri-Parit Sulong road, was hit by an aerial bomb. The conspicuous collection of motor vehicles outside the building had made it an obvious target. According to Sergeant Thornton:

> The devastation was shocking ... [an officer] was running around with one arm blown off. One Indian soldier lay in the wreckage weirdly distorted; his uniform, shorts, shirt, and boots were all intact on his bones – all his flesh had been blown off by the blast. All around us lay a mass of parts of bodies blown to bits, some hanging overhead on the broken branches of the rubber trees.[11]

The wounded were left writhing on the ground. Panic reigned among the survivors.

The bomb had scored a direct hit on the wireless room, and all personnel of the signal section were killed. In an adjoining room seven suspected fifth columnists were killed. Brigadier Duncan had been stunned by the blast and all his staff officers but one were killed or wounded. The 65th Battery's Major Julius had also been seriously wounded. The brigade-major, Major R. Anderson, asked Lieutenant-Colonel C. Anderson of the 2/19th Battalion to take command of the brigade as Duncan was in no condition to carry on. Lieutenant-Colonel Anderson later said that Duncan was brave and popular, but 'out of his depth owing to lack of experience'.[12]

At this time the 2/29th Battalion was still positioned over a mile from Bakri, but Anderson refrained from ordering it back to the brigade perimeter so long as the whereabouts of the 4/9th Jats remained uncertain.[13] As the morning wore on the Japanese again attacked the perimeter around Bakri from the south and north west. The assaults were repulsed with rifle and automatic fire and fighting continued well into the afternoon. In consequence the transport personnel under attack to the rear of Bakri had to be left to fend for themselves, and they dispersed into the jungle late in the afternoon after an engagement lasting some hours.

Earlier in the afternoon of 19 January the missing Jats finally reached the 2/29th Battalion along a side track. The Jats had known that something had gone wrong towards the coast, but had received little reliable information until they were contacted by an Australian patrol. From the 2/29th Battalion's perimeter the Jats marched down the road to Bakri. It was upon this stretch of jungle lined road that Robertson had been ambushed earlier in the day.

The leading pair of Jat companies were fired at from the jungle but lost only a few casualties. Battalion headquarters was the next sub-unit in the column. The other two rifle companies and the transport brought up the rear. As the Jats' headquarters passed into the zone of the earlier skirmish the firing intensified. According to the Jat Regiment's history:

Colonel [John] Williams, who was following with headquarters behind C Company, moved forward to take in the situation but, when attempting to peer over a mud bank, his head was severed by a Japanese sword; the adjutant, Captain Brian Lee, rushed to his assistance but was cut down in a similar manner.[14]

The battalion was split in two by the Japanese ambush. Major White and two hundred Jats of the first two companies managed to reach the Bakri perimeter. Another three hundred Jats from the rear half of the column made their way back to the 2/29th Battalion's perimeter. The rest of the Jats either became casualties or scattered into the swamps.

The 13th Field Company Madras Sappers and Miners was in the perimeter, and the returning Jats were herded towards the sappers' position. Japanese watching from the jungle directed mortar fire onto the Indians. Aircraft used the hulks of the tanks as an aiming point, and their bombs added to the confusion. The sappers' commanding officer, Major B. E. Whitman, estimated that a quarter of the Jats and his men received some sort of injury from bursting shells and bombs.[15]

At 6.30 p.m. on 19 January Anderson used the wireless to order the 2/29th Battalion to fall back to Bakri. The Australian and Indian troops present formed a column for the short march. But by this stage the Japanese had firmly blocked the route. A number of Japanese machine gun posts had been dug in either side of the road. Attacking Australian infantry could get no closer than sixty yards of the Japanese, and the rest of the column banked up on the road behind.

Major Olliff, the battalion's new commander, decided to work around the flank of the road-block. Sergeant Harrison was with Olliff's headquarters party. Olliff was killed within yards of Harrison. 'He was almost in cover when a bullet shot off four fingers from his left hand. He stopped, completely shocked, looked at his bloody hand in astonishment and said, "God", in an incredulous tone. As he spoke, a burst of fire ripped into his back.' The column broke up in the growing darkness. The walking wounded stumbled off into the jungle with the medical officer. A private soldier later recalled:

> As the Japs were not taking prisoners, the ones we were unable to help asked to be shot, they would have been bayoneted. We used a revolver through the heart. Hard, as some had enlisted at the same time.[16]

Part of the column made their way laboriously across country to Yong Peng; part reached Anderson's force at Bakri; and others lost their way in swamps and jungle to be eventually rounded up as prisoners. Of the Indians, only Major Whitman and a few of his sappers reached Bakri the next day.

That afternoon the Japanese Imperial Guards' plan to cut off the force at

Bakri had taken further major strides forward. Miles inland of Bakri lead elements of a Guards battalion had emerged from the jungle to surprise a company of the 53rd Brigade's 6th Norfolks on Bukit Pelandok, south of the defile through which the road ran from Bakri to Yong Peng on the Trunk Road. The Japanese soon crossed the road to take the lower slopes of Bukit Belah on the north side of the defile.[17] Another Norfolks company was still on the summit of Bukit Belah, but the Japanese had effectively blocked the roads between Yong Peng and Bakri, and Yong Peng and Batu Pahat. Later in the afternoon a detached company of the 2nd Loyals, newly arrived from Singapore, was sent into the jungle to retake Bukit Pelandok. The going was extremely tough, and the next day the exhausted company withdrew back to its starting point.

South of the Muar front on 19 January other III Corps formations did what they could to keep open communications with British forces in action with the Imperial Guards Division. The 11th Indian Division's Major-General Key sent the 15th Brigade's headquarters and the British Battalion to the west coast town of Batu Pahat. The brigade was now under the command of Brigadier B. S. Challen, an Indian Army staff officer. Moorhead had reverted to the command of his 3/16th Punjabis at his own request. The 2/16th and 3/16th Punjabis had by now completed an amalgamation (though the resulting unit has always been known as the 3/16th Punjabis). General Key directed the Punjabis to join Brigadier C. L. B. Duke's 53rd Brigade, which at the time had only the battered 6th Norfolks under command in front of the recently lost defile on the Bakri-Yong Peng road. Key also asked Percival to send the 53rd Brigade's 5th Norfolks over from Brigadier Taylor's force at Mersing. (The 5th Norfolks had gone to Mersing to release the 2/19th Battalion to come to Westforce. The 2nd Cambridgeshire, the brigade's other battalion, was still at Batu Pahat and was now under the command of the 15th Brigade.)

Yet because Percival had transferred the 45th Brigade to the grossly over-stretched III Corps, the reinforcement of the brigade depended on Percival's own willingness to send units from Westforce or Singapore to its aid. At a conference at Yong Peng on 19 January, whilst Jats, Australians and Norfolks were being scuppered elsewhere, Percival decided merely to transfer the main body of the Loyals from Westforce's Trunk Road sector to the 53rd Brigade on the Bakri-Yong Peng road. The 45th Brigade was then ordered to withdraw through the 53rd Brigade, whilst Westforce stepped back to Labis on the Trunk Road, over fifteen miles south of Segamat. But the Loyals were one of nine battalions still in position on the Trunk Road, of which only two had been seriously engaged over the previous week. In addition to this, half a dozen battalions continued to sit comparatively idle either at

Singapore or on Johore's east coast. Percival's inability to concentrate his forces at a point of crisis, even with the location of the point of crisis clearly identified, was one of the enduring themes of the Malayan campaign.

That evening of 19 January Westforce withdrew down the Trunk Road through Segamat whilst the buildings along its narrow main street blazed with fire. Fifth columnists? No. A senior liaison officer had fired stores of rice to prevent them falling into enemy hands. In his enthusiasm he had set the town ablaze.[18]

Lieutenant-Colonel Anderson had decided independently to withdraw the 45th Brigade from Bakri on 20 January. Anderson's column was organized into five Australian companies, including seven officers and 190 men of the 2/29th Battalion, and two Indian detachments. Fifty vehicles carried the force's wounded, ammunition, and meagre remaining supplies of food. Anderson's aim for that day was to traverse five miles of jungle and rubber lined road to the edge of a stretch of swampland that was too open to be crossed during daylight.

The column moved out at 7 a.m., and an hour later it reached a road-block in a swamp defile. A Japanese force was dug in south of the road to cover the block. The advance guard, Captain Keegan's B Company, attacked and was pinned down by machine gun fire. Lieutenant Beverley's A Company came up and moved around the flank of the Japanese to take them from the rear. Led by Anderson, B Company advanced again to finish off the force blocking the column's passage. Anderson himself lobbed grenades into machine gun posts and shot a pair of Japanese with his revolver. B Company lost fifteen killed and twenty wounded in the brisk engagement. Lieutenant-Colonel Tsuji later recorded that more than half of Ogaki Battalion was killed, including its commander, during the fighting around Bakri. Like Gotanda Tank Company, Ogaki Battalion received a unit citation.[19]

The British column continued forward at walking pace in a tight box formation. The transport was nose to tail, three wide on the road in places. Deep drainage ditches either side of the road made it difficult for vehicles to drive off the road into cover when aircraft attacked, but though Japanese aircraft were often circling in the sky strafing was infrequent. The airmen may have been unable to distinguish friend from foe on a shifting battlefield. Before long the column passed through the scene of the previous day's battle around the transport harbour. Soldiers searched for food and water among the wrecked trucks and blackening corpses.

Soon after midday a set of three strong road-blocks made of vehicles and tree trunks were encountered. The defending Japanese garrison was estimated to be two companies strong. Beverley's company was now the advance guard, and was pinned down by a half dozen machine guns covering the road. To the rear of the column the jammed transport was coming under artillery fire. In the rearguard part of one of the Jats' companies was driven back in disorder by a sudden Japanese thrust, but the Jats were rallied by Brigadier Duncan who led a counter-attack to retake several vehicles. Duncan lost his life in the process and Captain Frank Cope was also killed trying to drag the mortally wounded Duncan to cover.

As the afternoon of 20 January wore on, at the head of the column Captain K. L. Westbrook's composite company attacked to the left of the pinned down advance guard but also ground to a halt. Amid swampy country the watery flanks of the Japanese position were too difficult to turn, and there was little alternative to variations of frontal assault. In Anderson's absence at the rear of the column, Major T. G. Vincent organised mortars to fire on the blocks. When Anderson returned he decided to throw in his reserve, C Company. Anderson considered leading the company himself. However Vincent persuaded him against the idea and Anderson gave the troops a pre-assault address instead. A 25-pounder gun was pushed around a slight bend to fire directly on the road-blocks at seventy-five yards range. The vehicles were blown to wreckage and the road was filled with torn timber, dust, and smoke. With the aid of machine gun fire from carriers, C Company rushed the road-blocks and chased the Japanese off at bayonet point. The corpses of guardsmen left behind were fine physical specimens. The Japanese force may have been under instructions only to fight a delaying action.[20]

Night fell abruptly, and the column was able to cross open country ahead unseen by Japanese aviators. The column edged forward at walking pace, the trucks in low gear, along a flooded causeway. With crickets chirping, and fireflies dancing around them, tired and hungry men manhandled trucks over craters and breaches in the roadway. The brigade halted for the night of 20/21 January amid the relative safety of jungle. Bad news was received later that night. The bridge ahead at Parit Sulong village was no longer in friendly hands. A British detachment that had been posted at the bridge had taken to the jungle and headed south the previous morning. Given the strength of the Japanese force now at Parit Sulong they would have been swept aside anyway. Dispatch riders sent from the column towards Parit Sulong confirmed that the village was in hostile hands. Two Japanese Guards Battalions had taken up positions between the defile at Bukit Pelandok and Parit Sulong.

As Anderson's force fought its way towards Parit Sulong, an increasingly gloomy General Percival sent a letter to Generals Heath and Bennett with instructions that their next task was to hold a line across central Johore, running from Mersing on the east coast to Batu Pahat on the west coast.

On that line 'are situated three important aerodromes and ... the air observation system'.[21] Percival also attached an outline plan for operations should the army be forced to withdraw from Johore to Singapore Island. At 8 p.m. that evening of 20 January Percival ordered Westforce to retire south of Labis, the point at which the Trunk Road and railway diverged. Percival also directed Westforce to send a brigade (the 27th Brigade) to defend Yong Peng.

Elsewhere on 20 January an effort was made by the 53rd Brigade to clear the Japanese force from the road between Yong Peng and Anderson's column. In the early hours of the morning two companies of the 3/16th Punjabis had set out to recapture Bukit Belah, and join up with the 6th Norfolk company still on its higher slopes. Another Norfolk company was poised to attack Bukit Pelandok south of the road after dawn to complete the reopening of the defile.

On Bukit Belah the advancing Punjabis were fired on by Norfolks in the dark as they neared their objective, losing several casualties. Once the mistake was realised, Lieutenant-Colonel Moorhead set about reorganizing the leading Punjabi company. When a shower of grenades burst further along the ridge Moorhead assumed it was another friendly fire incident, and rushed off to halt the firing. But it was a Japanese attack. Moorhead was soon mortally wounded. Two other British Punjabi officers became casualties as well, and many Punjabis failed to regain British lines. By the end of the day there were few Punjabis or Norfolks left on Bukit Belah. Moorhead's sepoys were much affected by the death of their commanding officer. A Punjabi havildar was recorded as saying, 'My heart is broken. There will never be a man more brave than he'.[22]

South of the road defile and Bukit Belah a 6th Norfolks company had been held-up by machine gun fire during their advance on Bukit Pelandok. An angry Brigadier Duke sacked the company commander and dispatched him to a reinforcement camp at Singapore. After the full extent of the 53rd Brigade's failure that day became apparent, Duke ordered his units, including the newly arrived Loyals, to take up defensive positions facing the hills flanking the road defile. Later in the afternoon the 11th Division's commander, General Key, ordered another assault at dawn next morning. Duke protested that his men were exhausted, and Key relented – provided that the brigade attacked at the first reasonable opportunity.

The following morning, 21 January, Anderson's brigade was transferred by General Percival from III Corps to Westforce at Bennett's request, cancelling the transfer of the brigade out of Westforce made three days previously. Bennett believed that he needed personal control of operations on the Yong Peng-Muar road given their crucial relevance to the rest of Westforce's communications. Percival's bouncing of the 45th Brigade between his two senior generals had only made an awkward situation worse.

Percival ordered a commanders' conference to assemble at Yong Peng at 12.30 p.m. on 21 January. On his way to the conference, General Key called at the 53rd Brigade's headquarters to find that his order from the previous day regarding the mounting of a fresh attack on the road defile had been garbled in transmission. Brigadier Duke was not planning another assault. Key told Duke's brigade-major that the brigade would come under Bennett's command from midday, and ordered an attack at 2 p.m., subject to Bennett's confirmation. At noon a staff officer arrived at brigade headquarters from Westforce to confirm Key's order, but the day was already half over.

At Percival's Yong Peng conference he broke his troops on the mainland into three forces – Brigadier Taylor's Eastforce, Bennett's Westforce and Key's 11th Indian Division – all to be coordinated by Heath's III Corps headquarters. Percival's decision to anchor his new line on the west coast town of Batu Pahat was to have important ramifications in the future. Already Brigadier Challen could see that his 15th Brigade at Batu Pahat was being bypassed. Challen told Generals Heath and Key of his fears when they visited him later that day.[23]

Lieutenant-Colonel Anderson's column had reached the outskirts of Parit Sulong village by 9.30 a.m. on 21 January. The bridge over the river at Parit Sulong lay on the Japanese side of the village. Japanese troops had had ample time to prepare for the column's arrival. By now the Australians and Indians were almost out of mortar ammunition and very short of water and food. Major Anderson led an Indian detachment in an attack on the village at 11 a.m., passing through the pinned-down Australian advance guard. The Indians swung wide to reach the river. During the early afternoon Beverley and Keegan's companies also forced their way through the village to reach the river in places. But pressure was mounting on the rear of the column's perimeter, and the Japanese still held the immediate approaches to the bridge.

At 5 p.m. the medical officers asked Lieutenant-Colonel Anderson if they could send two ambulances to the bridge loaded with dying men, and request of the Japanese that they be allowed to pass. A sceptical Anderson agreed but not surprisingly the Japanese officer at the bridge refused to let the vehicles through, and demanded that they remain at the point to which they had been driven. After dark the brakes on the ambulances were released. They rolled backwards, and were then reversed into the perimeter.

During the night of 21/22 January Japanese tanks on the road behind the column menaced the perimeter. Japanese voices could be heard out in the surrounding jungle. An ammunition limber was hit and exploded in a ball of fire. A gun was set up on the road, one of the column's four remaining 25-pounders. At one stage the crew fired into the darkness at a target they could hear rather than see. A tank was knocked out, and the flames coming from the wreck provided light by which other tanks could be seen and fired at. Later, amid the darkness, Gunner Braddon had the satisfaction of impaling a running Japanese on his rifle and bayonet, 'just like a stop volley at tennis'.[24]

At dawn on 22 January the Japanese grip on the bridge was as firm as ever. Two antiquated aircraft from Singapore dropped medical supplies and food to Anderson's force, and made a speculative attempt to bomb the Japanese at the far end of the bridge. The shelling of the shrinking perimeter was getting heavier. About 9 a.m., after another probe towards the bridge had failed, Lieutenant-Colonel Anderson ordered the remainder of his column to abandon the road and their vehicles, and take to the jungle in a bid to get around the Japanese. Major Anderson, the brigade-major, had been killed by shell fire only an hour previously. Over the space of an hour Australians and Indians stole away northwards from their perimeter, and the volume of firing gradually fell away. The walking wounded hobbled off with the able bodied.

Later in the morning Japanese slowly emerged from the surrounding jungle. The wounded who remained behind were herded into a group with angry kicks and prods of the bayonet. 110 Australian and forty Indian wounded were rounded up as prisoners. As the day wore on, passing Japanese troops took pleasure in taunting the prisoners and kicking their open wounds. The Australians and Indians were forced into a shed, and later crammed into a small bungalow. Badly injured men were in agony and some were delirious. Those unable to move as the Japanese wished were bayoneted or clubbed where they lay. The officers were separated from their men, but the two groups would later share the same fate.

During the afternoon Lieutenant Hackney saw a pair of staff cars pull up on the scene, preceded and followed by tanks and motor cycles. An officer alighted and was treated with great deference. In Hackney's opinion the newly arrived senior officer gave quite specific orders to the junior officer in charge of the prisoners, before departing again with his attendant escort.

At dusk the prisoners were roped or wired together, and led away to meet a variety of grisly fates. Anderson's force had taken no Japanese prisoners, nor had cornered Japanese soldiers permitted themselves to be taken prisoner. Some Australian and Indian prisoners were machine gunned or bayoneted. Others were set on fire with petrol. A barely conscious Hackney had been left behind when the Japanese led the prisoners away. He crawled off into the undergrowth and heard machine gun fire in the distance. Later he came upon two Australians who had managed to escape from a group of men who had been dowsed in petrol and set alight. Other prisoners were taken down to the river bank for beheading. Lance-Havildar John Benedict (an Indian sapper) escaped by swimming the river as the Japanese fired over his head. From the jungle on the far side Benedict watched the massacre continue. He later swam back across the river to rescue two sappers still alive. The head of one of the sappers was partly severed. After nightfall wild pigs and dogs emerged from the jungle to feast upon the carnage.[25]

Most of the men who broke out from the perimeter at Parit Sulong made the fifteen mile march through rubber, swamp and jungle back to the safety of friendly lines at Yong Peng. General Bennett met Anderson at Yong Peng:

> The colonel immediately called on me and then, before he had washed or had a meal, gave a full report on the whole situation, talking it over as coolly and calmly as if it had been no more than a training exercise.[26]

(Anderson was later awarded the Victoria Cross.) Only four hundred Indian troops and five hundred Australians escaped. Small groups of stragglers and individuals arrived to add to that total in the days ahead. Some men cut off during the battle eventually made their way in small boats to Sumatra. The dead of the 45th Brigade's Indians and Australians ran into the hundreds. In B Company of the 2/19th Battalion two officers and forty-eight men were killed or died of wounds, and all but Major Keegan and about ten others received some sort of wound or minor injury.[27]

Anderson's force between Bakri and Parit Sulong had kept the Imperial Guards engaged for four days. They had ensured that those Westforce units posted along the Trunk Road could withdraw southwards in an orderly manner. But the strategic achievements of the Bakri-Parit Sulong battle can perhaps be exaggerated. With the 53rd Brigade opposite the Bukit Pelandok-Bukit Belah defile, and another Westforce brigade a short distance from the Yong Peng junction, the safety of Westforce had not depended on exactly how long Anderson's force could block the direct route between Muar and Yong Peng. On a tactical level though the story was different. General Yamashita later described the fighting south of the Muar River as the most 'savage encounter' of the campaign. Between 16 and 22 January the Imperial Guards lost a company of tanks, and a battalion's worth of infantry casualties.[28] There were many engagements in Malaya where British led forces suffered crippling losses whilst hardly seeming to lay a glove on their Japanese assailants. The significance of the fighting between Bakri and Parit Sulong is that it was one of the few occasions where the Japanese received as good as they gave.

During the early afternoon of 21 January, whilst the 45th Brigade was still bogged down at Parit Sulong, the 53rd Brigade's Brigadier Duke began planning for another assault on the defile. As little time remained in which to complete arrangements, General Key's proposed 2 p.m. starting time soon passed and a new zero hour was fixed. But by late afternoon the artillery had not registered the range of the hills flanking the defile, and the Loyals had not arrived at their allotted position. An increasingly frustrated Duke decided to postpone the attack until the next morning. That evening West-force's chief artillery officer visited brigade headquarters, and was told by Duke's brigade-major that no further artillery support was needed. The 350th Battery would be sufficient.

The next morning, 22 January, once it was light enough to spot the fall of bursting shells, the guns fired from extreme range, whilst the Loyals anxiously lay out in the open below the defile. The rather unrealistic plan was to send a handful of carriers up the road to Parit Sulong after the hills overlooking the defile had been seized. However the gunners still could not fire accurately onto the infantry's objective due to faulty ammunition, the climate and the range. Meanwhile the Loyals and a Punjabi company had been discovered by eagle-eyed Japanese aviators. Dive-bombing quickly inflicted thirty casualties on the exposed infantry.

Midway through the morning Duke cancelled the attack. All hope of surprise had been lost, and there was no point sending the infantry forward without effective artillery support. Indeed, even if the Loyals could have taken the defile, seven miles of jungle-lined road lay between the defile and Parit Sulong. Ultimately the brigade had not been given enough troops to capture the defile. Neither Generals Percival nor Bennett had sent any reinforcement to the brigade apart from the Loyals. In fact, the 27th Brigade had been resting at Yong Peng since the morning of the previous day, a little over five miles behind the 53rd Brigade.[29]

On 23 January, as the last men of Anderson's column trickled into British lines, the 53rd Brigade prepared to withdraw to Yong Peng and the Trunk Road. The Punjabis were holding exposed ground at the foot of the defile, and began to pull out according to plan at midday. From the hills above the Japanese enthusiastically fired mortar bombs at the Punjabis, and circling aircraft made a couple of bombing runs. The Punjabis, along with an attached pair of anti-tank guns, had passed through the Loyals by 2 p.m. But as the Loyals were on the verge of departing a Japanese tank force followed by infantry emerged from the defile to decimate the Loyals' forward companies. The Loyals had no anti-tank guns. The tanks shot up infantry in their pits and blasted vehicles off the roadway. The Loyals had been holding ground in front of a causeway across a patch of swamp. The Loyals'

Lieutenant-Colonel M. Elrington later commented that his battalion had been planted in

> a happy hunting ground for tanks ... on the wrong side of a tank-proof locality ... All control was lost and it became a case of *sauve qui peut*, those that were able to do so taking to the *ulu* [swamp grass].[30]

The battered 6th Norfolks were responsible for defending the causeway, and an anti-tank gun sited in their area set on fire the leading tank. Advancing Japanese infantry were halted by small arms fire and Duke ordered sappers to blow demolitions on the causeway. The brigade's retreat back to Yong Peng was a less chaotic affair from that point onwards, bringing to an end the Muar phase of the campaign.

Far from Malaya, Churchill and the Chiefs of Staff were beset by Far Eastern problems. On 15 January Churchill had sent General Wavell, ABDA Supreme Commander, a signal asking how long an isolated Singapore Island could hold out.

> What are defences and obstructions on landward side? Are you sure that you can dominate with fortress cannon any attempt to plant siege batteries?

Wavell promptly cabled back:

> Until quite recently all plans based on repulsing seaborne attack on Island and holding land attack in Johore or further north, and little or nothing was done to construct defences on north side of island to prevent crossing of Johore Strait.

On 19 January Wavell hammered home his point to London.

> I must warn you, however, that I doubt whether Island can be held for long once Johore lost ... many troops remaining are of doubtful value. I am sorry to give you a depressing picture but I do not want you to have false picture of Island Fortress.[31]

Over the years Churchill had come to believe the propaganda that described Singapore as one of the world's great fortresses. Now that Wavell had torn the wool from his eyes, a furious Churchill, recently returned to London from America, complained to the Chiefs of Staff:

> It never occurred to me for a moment ... that the gorge of the fortress of Singapore with its splendid moat half a mile to a mile wide was not entirely fortified against an attack from the northward.

Churchill had hoped that Singapore might hold out for months and prove to be another Verdun, though he was in no doubt as to its likely ultimate fate. But now, wrote Churchill, 'I saw before me the hideous spectacle of the almost naked island and of the wearied, if not exhausted, troops retreating upon it'.[32] Nonetheless, Churchill sent Wavell on 20 January the fiery instruction that he was to fight for every inch of ground in Malaya, and that 'no question of surrender [was] to be entertained until after protracted fighting among the ruins of Singapore City'.[33]

Singapore's true status as a pretend fortress, 'a battleship ... without a bottom', and Wavell's doubts as to whether resistance could last more than several weeks, raised the awkward question of whether Malaya should be reinforced, whilst Burma, the only land route to Nationalist China and the eastern doorway to India, cried out for men and material. General Brooke, Chief of the Imperial General Staff, wasted no time in drawing Churchill's attention to the gravity of the Japanese threat to Rangoon.

The Prime Minister responded to the crisis by preparing a memorandum for the Chiefs of Staff Committee canvassing the option of evacuating Singapore and diverting reinforcements to Rangoon otherwise bound for Singapore. Churchill wrote:

> We may, by muddling things and hesitating to take an ugly decision, lose both Singapore and the Burma Road. Obviously the decision depends upon how long the defence of Singapore Island can be maintained. If it is only for a few weeks, it is certainly not worth losing all our reinforcements and aircraft.[34]

On the morning of 21 January the Chiefs of Staff discussed the memorandum. That evening the Defence Committee held a meeting, followed by the War Cabinet. (The Defence Committee comprised Churchill, the service chiefs and ministers, the diplomatic ministers, and other interested parties.) At the Defence Committee meeting General Brooke stated his opinion that Wavell should be given discretion to deploy the forces under his command as he thought best. After these meetings, however, there was no change to the instructions Churchill had previously sent Wavell. The battle underway in Johore and the defence of Singapore remained the highest war priority in the Far East.[35]

Sir Earle Page, a former conservative Australian Prime Minister, and the current Australian Labor Party government's envoy in London, had opposed Churchill's hypothetical suggestion at the War Cabinet meeting. He had told the assembled company that

> Australia would never stand our men being deserted ... the course proposed would be more fatal and injurious to the lives and fortunes of the army and the war than standing and fighting at Johore on the line that was there.

On 23 January Page cabled Australia that the British government had considered the evacuation of Singapore.[36]

Whereas British-protected Asian subjects in Hong Kong, Borneo, Malaya and Burma were represented in London by the Colonial Office, the Australian government could speak with a stronger voice. After Page's report had been received in Australia, the Minister for External Affairs, Dr H. V. Evatt, amended a message to London decided upon by the Australian War Cabinet in Prime Minister John Curtin's absence. (Curtin was in West Australia, and the War Cabinet meeting in Melbourne on 23 January was chaired by the Deputy Prime Minister.) Evatt inserted the famous paragraph:

> Page has reported the Defence Committee has been considering evacuation of Malaya and Singapore. After all the assurances we have been given, the evacuation of Singapore would be regarded here and elsewhere as an inexcusable betrayal. Singapore is a central fortress in the system of Empire and local defence ... we understood that it was to be made impregnable and in any event it was to be capable of holding out for a prolonged period until arrival of the main fleet.[37]

Churchill was far from pleased with the Australian government's cable. Churchill was angry that such a vigorous exchange of panicky telegrams could be caused by general discussions. He was also angry that Page had not informed his government that the current instructions to Wavell were that the defence of Johore and Singapore remained the highest British priority in the Far East.

Churchill later claimed that the views of the Australian government had no impact on the decision to keep reinforcing Singapore. Churchill did though concede that 'there is no doubt what a purely military decision should have been'. But if the British government was forced resolutely to defend Singapore for reasons of politics and prestige, it was the British themselves who had invested the island with so much significance over many years. Additionally, the now all-important Americans were likely to react badly if Britain scuttled from the Far East whilst fighting in the Philippines was still underway. Churchill and a number of his senior military and political colleagues had just returned to London from a lengthy trip to Washington to hammer out a grand strategy for the western Allies. The importance of American opinion to Britain's leaders at this point in time should not be underestimated.[38]

# 12

# The Loss of the Mainland

Upon withdrawing from Yong Peng, Westforce came under the command of III Indian Corps, and the 53rd Brigade reverted to the command of the 11th Division. All troops on the mainland were now controlled by Heath's III Corps headquarters. After being pushed out of northern Johore, General Percival's army had one more realistic chance to build a stable front on the Malayan mainland. Percival chose to try and hold a line between Mersing on the east coast and Batu Pahat on the west coast. On 24 January Brigadier Taylor's Eastforce held Mersing, Westforce's 9th Indian Division and the 27th Australian Brigade were at Kluang and Ayer Hitam respectively, and the 11th Division was endeavouring to cover Batu Pahat.

But Percival did not choose his next line of resistance for local tactical reasons. Rather he wanted to hang onto the aerodromes of central and southern Johore, thus keeping the Japanese air force as far away from Singapore's reinforcement convoys as possible. This sort of reasoning soon led to problems at Batu Pahat, around which there had been skirmishing for several days. General Nishimura had sent his Imperial Guards reconnaissance battalion to deal with British troops in the area, whilst the rest of the division completed the 45th Brigade's rout. The relatively passable rubber plantations and mines in the vicinity of Batu Pahat rendered the town's garrison vulnerable to encirclement. But further south, particularly near Rengit, encroaching jungle narrowed the coastal strip to a defendable width. The 15th Brigade's Brigadier Challen understood the local geography. He was keen to withdraw from Batu Pahat. Percival blocked a request to withdraw from Batu Pahat on 23 January. (On that day the 5th Norfolks arrived at Batu Pahat from Mersing.)

There was more skirmishing around Batu Pahat the next day, and on 25 January Challen again sought permission to withdraw before the coastal road was cut behind his brigade. A sympathetic Key rang Heath to pass on the request. Heath told Key that a decision would be made by Percival at a command conference to be held during the afternoon. Key later received information that an enemy battalion had been sighted in a rubber plantation near Sengarrang, well to the south of Batu Pahat.

Meantime the 53rd Brigade had arrived at Benut, over twenty miles south of Batu Pahat on the west coast road. The battered 6th Norfolks and the 3/16th Punjabis could field only two rifle companies each. Brigadier Duke sent the Norfolks and some armoured cars and artillery up the coast road with a convoy to Batu Pahat. But during 25 January the Japanese established a series of road-blocks between Sengarrang and Rengit. The bulk of the Japanese Imperial Guards had swung south from Bakri and Parit Sulong, and were now in the process of bypassing Batu Pahat.

At a conference in the afternoon of 25 January General Percival, with Generals Heath, Bennett and Key present, finally agreed that the 15th Brigade should pull back to the Sengarrang area, and that in consequence the other forces on the mainland should also make further withdrawals. The situation was already unravelling thanks to Percival's continual unwillingness to let his subordinates take up positions that were locally tenable. Heath was to coordinate the next round of retirements. He gave Key and Bennett maps marked with provisional positions and timings for a staged withdrawal due to reach Singapore by the night of 31 January.

In the interim heavy fighting had developed astride the Trunk Road. On 24 January the 27th Brigade had occupied a line of hills either side of the Trunk Road, three miles north of the Ayer Hitam road junction. There was a swampy stream running less than half a mile behind the forward defensive positions. Lieutenant-Colonel Galleghan's 2/30th Battalion had a company and a platoon on the feature to the right of the Trunk Road, and the Loyals, temporarily reduced to 240 officers and men, held station to the left of the road. The rest of the Australian battalion was located to the immediate north of Ayer Hitam.[1]

Overnight the soldiers were pestered by mosquitoes, and next morning, 25 January, there was heavy rain. The long grass on the hills was fine cover from aerial observation. The hills also offered good fields of fire, though the Loyals' position left of the Trunk Road was subject to jungle encroachment. Patrol skirmishing in the morning preceded a Japanese mortar barrage about midday, and a series of attacks in the afternoon. An officer carrying a large Japanese flag was shot down, but some attackers got to within eighty yards of the defenders. The Japanese were estimated to have used two companies in the assault and their casualties littered the hillside. As the survivors fell back they were accurately mortared.

The Loyals played their part in repelling Japanese attempts to advance down the Trunk Road. But towards evening, as darkness fell, the Japanese pounced upon the Loyals' left flank from the cover of a marsh in which they had stealthily gathered. The night was made hideous with the sound of machine gun fire, bursting grenades and yelling Japanese. The Loyals were bumped off part of their ridge after hand to hand fighting.

Due to the decisions made by Percival and his senior commanders that afternoon of 25 January, the 27th Brigade was due to retire that night. Lieutenant-Colonel Galleghan sent an officer across the stream to order a withdrawal to Ayer Hitam. The Australians and Loyals had to wade through the high reeds and mud of swamps to avoid Japanese machine guns sited to cover the Trunk Road. The brigade began its retreat that night to a new position at Simpang Jeram. The 2/30th Battalion had lost a mere four killed, and twelve wounded and missing during the day's fighting, and were quite pleased with their work.[2] The exhausted Loyals were sent back to Singapore to rest and re-form.

Astride the railway the 9th Indian Division, the other half of Bennett's Westforce, covered Kluang whilst the 27th Brigade was at Ayer Hitam. On 24 January two battalions of the 22nd Indian Brigade moved forward from Kluang to counter-attack up the railway towards Niyor. To the west of the railway the 5/11th Sikhs advanced along a track. The main body of the brigade was soon held up by the Japanese, and Brigadier Painter ordered the Sikhs to cut back towards the railway onto the flank of those Japanese barring the progress of the rest of his force.

The commander of the Sikhs was Lieutenant-Colonel John Parkin, a short, white-haired bachelor, who had won the Distinguished Service Order in an earlier campaign on India's North-West Frontier. As the terrain between Parkin's column and the railway was full of unmapped jungle, and was too difficult for artillery to traverse, Parkin decided to continue the advance towards Niyor and then swing back to take the Japanese in the rear. The Sikhs halted for the night two miles short of Niyor. The next morning the Sikhs fought a brisk action against a Japanese force assembling to their front, before withdrawing to rejoin the rest of their brigade.

During the night of 25/26 January, the 15th Brigade, comprising the British Battalion, the 2nd Cambridgeshire, and the 5th and a detachment of the 6th Norfolks finally retired from Batu Pahat on the west coast. The brigade's passage southwards on 26 January was blocked by the Japanese at Sengar-rang, three to four miles inland amid coconut plantations and swampy jungle. Japanese troops had blocked the road south of the village with wire and logs as it ran along an embankment through scrub, swamp and chest high grass. Attacks by the column's advance guard, the 2nd Cambridgeshire, failed to clear the road block during the morning. As the day wore on the Cambridgeshires made slow progress through swamps around the flanks of the Japanese defending the road. Some men reached the road-block, but suffered heavily to unseen machine guns as they tried to dismantle the tangle of wire and tree trunks. Early in the afternoon two 25-pounders were pushed to within three hundred yards of the block, but the shells could not hit entrenched troops at such close range.

By 11.00 a.m. Lieutenant-Colonel Morrison of the British Battalion had reported to Brigadier Challen that his unit had reached the outskirts of Sengarrang, with the Norfolks bringing up the rear of the column. However Challen did not deploy the rest of his brigade to help the Cambridgeshires. When Morrison offered to send his men into action, Challen told him he wanted to save the British Battalion and the Norfolks for the clearance of other blocks he expected the column to encounter further down the road.[3]

That morning General Key had ordered Brigadier Duke's 53rd Brigade to force a passage northwards up the coastal road to Challen's brigade. A small relieving column comprising some armoured cars, carriers, artillery and over one hundred 6th Norfolk first-line reinforcements left Benut at 12.30 p.m. Key instructed Duke that the column should advance on foot beyond Rengit, and Duke passed on the message to the column's commander, a gunner named Major C. F. W. Banham. At Rengit, Banham ordered his troops to disembus after they were fired upon, but after brushing aside a Japanese patrol, the column drove on in close formation. Banham's force soon ran into an ambush and was shot to pieces in minutes. Most of the vehicles were wrecked or ditched and the survivors fled into the jungle. (Months later thirty to forty abandoned and derelict lorries and carriers still lay beside the road near Rengit.) A majority of the Norfolks' reinforcements were killed.[4]

At the head of the column, Major Banham's carrier drove clear of the ambush, and after bypassing several road blocks reached Sengarrang at 2 p.m., dramatically toppling over the final barricade that had caused the Cambridgeshires so many problems. An increasingly anxious Challen had been on the verge of launching a coordinated brigade attack southwards when Banham arrived. Banham took the brigadier aside and warned that it would be difficult to force a passage to Rengit. He added that a withdrawal to Singapore was rumoured to be imminent. The Causeway to the island might be blown in as little as two or three days. Influenced by Banham's advice, Challen ordered a break-out through the jungle.[5]

By this stage the Cambridgeshires had worked past the road-block on both flanks. Some men had even managed to reach a second block on the road to the rear of the Japanese force which, in so far as it had been enveloped by a single battalion, may not have been much more than one or two companies strong. Runners were sent out to recall the Cambridgeshires, and a fleet of vehicles, and seven field and eight anti-tank guns were disabled and abandoned. Around a hundred sick and wounded unable to march were left behind under the care of a chaplain, the Reverend Duck-worth, and medical personnel.[6]

Not long after 6 p.m. the 15th Brigade took to the jungle. One party of 1200 successfully traversed an inland route to bypass the Japanese, and reached Benut during the afternoon of 27 January in a state of exhaustion. The party Challen was leading was not so fortunate. After crossing several fast-flowing streams, an impassable mangrove swamp was encountered. Challen and his orderly became lost moving between sections of the column, and the brigadier was later taken prisoner.

The remaining senior officers of the scattered column took parties under their control to the coast, six miles from their starting point at Sengarrang. The troops lay low amid coconut trees and mangrove swamp. The sound of Japanese motor vehicles could be heard on the road only a mile away. The previous day a RAF pilot had reported to Singapore that he could find no sign of friendly troops at Sengarrang. But after Lieutenant-Colonel Morrison sent an officer down the coast in a sampan, firm news was received at Singapore of the location and plight of the force stranded near Ponggor. A naval evacuation was arranged by Rear-Admiral Spooner. The gunboats *Dragonfly* and *Scorpion*, and other smaller craft, successfully picked up Morrison's force without interference. The evacuation took three nights and was not completed until 30/31 January. 1500 officers and men of the brigade were ferried to Singapore by sea.[7]

After the 15th Brigade's collapse the British position along the west coast became dangerously weak. On 26 January a detachment at Rengit was strongly attacked and forced to escape through the jungle by night. The Imperial Guards Division had won another victory. Japanese losses in the fighting south of Batu Pahat had been light.

Unlike at Parit Sulong, the wounded left behind by the 15th Brigade were not slaughtered. Indeed Japanese advancing from Batu Pahat only reached the Reverend Duckworth's party on the morning of 27 January, the day after the brigade took to the jungle. A Japanese guard put over the dressing station was removed after only twenty-four hours, and British medical personnel and wounded were left to fend for themselves. There was little military movement on the coast road, and with food and other supplies running very short a medical officer eventually had to walk into Batu Pahat to remind the local Japanese commander of their presence.[8]

On the east coast of Johore a separate battle was developing. The Japanese had emerged from the jungle to enter the town of Endau on 21 January. On 25 January General Heath had ordered Brigadier Taylor's Eastforce to abandon Mersing, which lay to the south of Endau. The Australians had to vacate carefully prepared defences on the beaches of Mersing that had taken months to complete. The Japanese had been planning to land part of their 18th Division on the east coast of Johore, but in Saigon Field Marshal Terauchi's headquarters had decided that the risk was too great, and the balance of the division had been sent to Singora. However the Japanese decided to sail a small convoy to Endau. The convoy carried air force personnel and stores to help bring the aerodromes of Kahang and Kluang rapidly into operation.

At 7.45 a.m. on 26 January the crew of a Hudson bomber flying out to sea on reconnaissance saw the Japanese convoy twenty miles north east of Endau. Air Headquarters Singapore decided to attack the convoy with all available aircraft. The antiquated Vildebeeste torpedo-bombers of No. 36 and No. 100 Squadrons, aircraft that had hitherto been confined to the relative safety of night sorties, were ordered to lead the strike. The Vildebeeste biplane's design dated from 1928. The bomber struggled to cruise above 100 m.p.h., was festooned with rigging wire, and had fixed landing gear and open cockpits for its three man crew. The RAF had intended to replace the Vildebeeste with modern Beauforts but, whilst this had taken place elsewhere, the Vildebeeste was still a front line aircraft at Singapore. *The Times* correspondent Ian Morrison wrote of the Vildebeeste: 'These biplanes flew so slowly that they gave the impression of being suspended motionless in mid-air.' Amongst RAF aircrew it had been joked that the only chance a Vildebeeste had of causing an enemy casualty was for a Japanese pilot to see one and laugh himself to death.[9]

The decision to use the Vildebeestes on a daylight operation was a shock to the aircrew of No. 36 and No. 100 Squadrons, some of whom had been on a tiring bombing mission the previous night. But early in the afternoon twelve Vildebeestes and nine Hudsons, escorted by Buffaloes and Hurricanes, set out for Endau, flying at low altitude through broken cloud. As Air Headquarters Singapore believed that the Japanese convoy was nearing shallow water, the Vildebeestes were armed with bombs instead of torpedoes.

At 3 p.m. the bombers reached Endau. Two transports and two warships lay off shore, and more warships were visible in the distance. The Vildebeestes began their bombing runs, but Japanese fighters dived down to attack both them and their escorting fighters. The leading section of three Vildebeestes were all shot down. The Vildebeeste of No. 100 Squadron's Squadron Leader I. T. B. Rowlands exploded after probably receiving a direct hit from an anti-aircraft shell. The Vildebeestes and Hudsons bombed the ships, and strafed barges ferrying men and equipment between ship and shore. Hits were scored on the convoy, but five Vildebeestes were shot down. Only one Japanese fighter involved in the air battle was destroyed.

At 5.30 p.m. another wave of nine Vildebeestes and three Fairy Albacores arrived over the target. (The Albacore was another slow biplane.) By now there was not a cloud in the sky and the sun shone brightly. The Hurricanes and Buffaloes of the escort lagged well behind the bombers as they had had to refuel and rearm after the earlier mission. Seven bombers and a Hurricane were lost when Japanese fighters pounced. The bombers had hastily to unload their bombs under heavy attack.

Of the seventy-two RAF, RAAF and RNZAF Vildebeeste and Albacore aircrew who took part in the two raids, twenty-seven died, seven returned wounded and two were made prisoner. Surviving aircrew from downed aircraft were left stranded in the jungle, or paddling in the sea. None of the convoy's ships had been sunk. The way in which Air Headquarters Singapore had planned the raids on Endau was strongly criticised. Air Vice-Marshal Maltby visited the survivors of the torpedo bomber squadrons to congratulate them on their gallantry, and to promise that further daylight operations would not be necessary.[10]

At 4.30 p.m. that afternoon of 26 January two destroyers had left Singapore to have another crack at the Japanese shipping at Endau. The old destroyers HMS *Thanet* and HMAS *Vampire* carried only three torpedoes each. They ran into modern Japanese destroyers in the early hours of the following morning. The Japanese ships were soon joined by a light cruiser. The *Thanet* was quickly sunk by the guns of the cruiser, with much loss of life, but the *Vampire*, with the help of a smoke-screen and the darkness of the night, slipped away back to Singapore.[11] By this stage of the campaign both the RAF and Royal Navy were struggling to make an impact on Japanese forces even when they were almost at Singapore's doorstep.

On dry land, after abandoning Endau and Mersing, Brigadier Taylor's Eastforce fell back to Jemaluang, just south of which the lateral road from Kluang met the east coast road. As Eastforce retired southwards, Lieutenant-Colonel A. L. Varley's 2/18th Battalion laid an ambush amid the Nithsdale and Joo Lye estates bordering the road between Mersing and Jemaluang. Taylor had agreed to Varley's plan, but he warned Varley to be ready quickly to disengage as further retirements towards Singapore were likely. There was also a danger that Eastforce might be attacked in the flank by forces advancing from the direction of Japanese occupied Kluang.

The battalion's companies were deployed along the rubber and jungle-lined road. At the northern end of a four thousand yard ambush zone, D Company was positioned almost a mile ahead of B Company. Both companies bivouacked for the night in readiness for the next day's expected battle. Another half a mile further south the rest of the battalion firmly blocked the road. When the Japanese collided with the force astride the road, the guns of two batteries would open fire into the ambush zone, and D and B Companies, placed wide of the road to avoid the initial barrage, would fall upon their startled victims.

A force of a thousand Japanese had been sighted by RAF aircrew heading south from Endau towards Mersing. This force was not expected to reach the ambush till the morning of 27 January.[12] But, unbeknownst to the Australians, there was another body of Japanese troops already south of Mersing, and Japanese began to march into the ambush zone during the night of 26/27 January. A column of troops a battalion strong passed down the road, and confused fighting began about 2 a.m. after Japanese ran into the force blocking the road. Lieutenant-Colonel Varley's headquarters ordered the artillery to open fire when they realised what had happened. Captain J. L. Edgley's D Company advanced down onto the road after the barrage had passed, but the only Japanese they found was a small party working on a nearby wooden bridge. Major C. B. O'Brien's B Company also moved towards the road. According to O'Brien:

> The night was pitch black. We 'B Company' moved forward by each man holding the bayonet scabbard of the man in front and so dark was it that most of the time I was unable to see any sign of the man whose bayonet I was holding.[13]

Only a handful of Japanese were encountered by the company and the roadway was soon secured.

What had happened to those Japanese sighted entering the ambush zone? It later became apparent that, after reaching the main Australian position, the Japanese had pulled back onto some rising ground, right in the middle of the thousand yard gap between the points at which D and B Companies later reached the road. The Japanese had hastily scraped out small pits for themselves. As the artillery barrage walked over them rubber trees were split and stripped, but the Japanese hugging the earth had emerged shaken and thoroughly alert. Japanese machine guns were sited to command the road. When Edgley's D Company tried to force a passage southwards the leading platoon was badly shot up as it attacked the feature upon which the Japanese were entrenched. Edgley sent a second platoon to work around the flank of the Japanese barring their path, provoking another round of chaotic skirmishes in the darkness. Fighting lasted into the following morning, and the rest of company was overwhelmed.

The situation was still unclear to Varley as day broke, but artillery fire was reopened on the Japanese after firm news of their location reached battalion headquarters. A Company was ordered to concentrate and move forward to join B Company for a counter-attack, but this plan was abandoned at

9.30 a.m. Brigadier Taylor told Varley not to commit any more troops to the battle.[14] The battalion withdrew to Jemaluang at noon.

In total the 2/18th Battalion lost six officers and seventy-seven other ranks killed and twelve other ranks wounded in the action in Nithsdale and Joo Lye estates. Some D Company stragglers rejoined their unit during 28 and 29 January. Not a single man was taken prisoner. The Japanese left the Australian dead unburied. Weeks later 'clotted along the roadside were little heaps of clothing, gleaming bones, respirators and tin hats'.[15] The site was later visited by a burial party of Australian POWs. The consensus of opinion, based on the positions of the remains and spent cartridge cases, was that the dead had died fighting, and had not been executed after capture.

The ambush had certainly been a disappointment for Varley. Despite months of training in the jungle, the battalion had been taken by surprise in dispositions quite inappropriate for a night battle. There was a good deal of ill-feeling within the battalion over the perceived abandonment of D Company. The battalion's war diary claimed that the unit had inflicted six hundred casualties on the Japanese.[16] This was a considerable exaggeration, though a later inspection of Japanese graves near the battlefield suggested that the Australians had given at least as good as they got. A Japanese account referred to the fighting near Jemaluang as 'an appalling hand-to-hand battle'.

Those troops of the Japanese 55th Regiment involved in the fighting with the 2/18th Battalion withdrew back towards Mersing after the engagement. XXV Army headquarters was alarmed by a report of the action, and reinforcements were sent across from Kluang to assist with the eventual occupation of Jemaluang at dusk on 28 July. The Japanese seldom regained contact with troops retreating down the east coast road to Singapore in the days ahead.

If General Percival's army was to regain the sanctuary of Singapore Island, Bennett's Westforce had to hold the Japanese 5th Division astride both the Trunk Road and the railway. The 5th Division's 21st Brigade was advancing southwards down the Trunk Road, and the 9th Brigade was advancing down the railway line.

After pulling out of Ayer Hitam on 25 January, the 27th Australian Brigade had withdrawn almost ten miles down the Trunk Road to road mile 50. The 2nd Gordon Highlanders had come forward from Singapore to replace the Loyals, and on 26 January they were the brigade's leading battalion. During the afternoon the Gordons skirmished with Japanese infantry. They lost fifty-eight casualties and retired after dark, dangerously short of food, water and ammunition.[17] For the Indian units astride the railway, less than ten miles away from the 27th Brigade, 26 January had been a quiet day.[18]

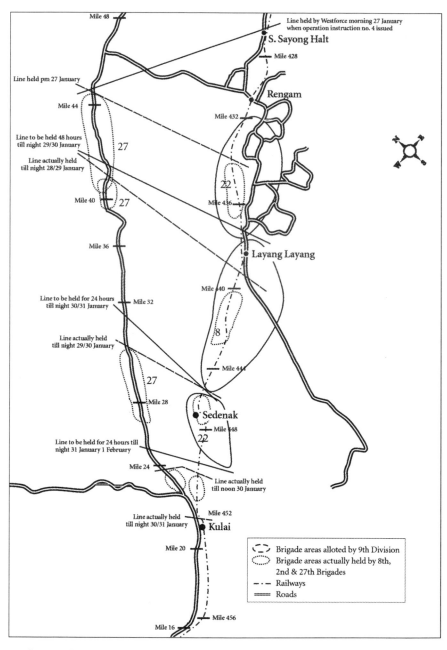

Mile 48

Line held by Westforce morning 27 January
when operation instruction no. 4 issued

S. Sayong Halt

Mile 428

Line held pm 27 January

Rengam

Mile 44

Mile 432

Line to be held 48 hours
till night 29/30 January

27

Line actually held
till night 28/29 January

22

Mile 40

27

Mile 436

Mile 36

Layang Layang

Mile 440

Line to be held for 24 hours
till night 30/31 January

Mile 32

8

Line actually held
till night 29/30 January

Mile 444

27

Mile 28

Sedenak

Mile 448

Line to be held for 24 hours till
night 31 January 1 February

22

Mile 24

Line actually held
till noon 30 January

1

Mile 452

Line actually held
till night 30/31 January

Kulai

Mile 20

Brigade areas alloted by 9th Division
Brigade areas actually held by 8th,
2nd & 27th Brigades
— · — Railways
═══ Roads

Mile 456

Mile 16

12. Layang Layang.

However, to the rear at 27th Brigade headquarters, Brigadier Maxwell had had an anxious time during 26 January. Maxwell wrongly believed that the Gordons had suffered crippling losses, and he had pestered General Bennett for permission to withdraw earlier than planned without success. The following day Bennett, having ascertained that only a small number of Gordons had received medical treatment over the previous twenty-four hours, gave Maxwell a pep talk to bolster the latter's spirits. Bennett commented in his diary that the morale of the men seemed to be better than that of some fatigued and depressed senior officers.[19]

That afternoon of 26 January Heath had held a conference at III Corps headquarters to discuss further a general timetable for the withdrawal towards Singapore. As a result of those deliberations, shortly after midnight in the early hours of 27 January Bennett's Australian staff drew up a schedule of the 27th Brigade's and the 9th Indian Division's planned future movements, and issued it as Westforce Operation Instruction No. 4. There was never any doubt in the mind of Lieutenant-Colonel J. H. Thyer, Bennett's GSO 1, as to where the 9th Division's defence line should be the following night of 27/28 January. From Rengam at rail mile 430 southwards for ten miles to rail mile 440 the railway was bordered by rubber estates stretching for several miles eastwards. The tracks in the estates would make troops on the adjacent railway easy to outflank. According to Thyer the orders issued by Westforce were framed so as 'to bring the Indian Division out of the maze of tracks forward of Layang Layang [at rail mile 438½] and reduce the risk of outflanking movements'.[20] The staff, however, showed their fatigue by giving the 9th Division different locations for the night of 27/28 January in the main body and appendix of the operation instruction: rail mile 440 in the main body, and rail mile 437 in the appendix. But the drafting of the instruction was not the only cause of the confusion that followed.

General Barstow, the 9th Division's commander, visited Westforce headquarters during the morning of 27 January. Upon his return to Rengam he called his brigadiers together and gave Painter and Lay verbal orders. (Brigadier Lay had returned to duty as the commander of the 8th Brigade after Key was promoted to command a division.) Barstow chose to interpret Westforce's instruction to the disadvantage of his division. He ordered the 22nd Brigade to hold a very vulnerable sector from rail mile 437 to rail mile 432, further north than Westforce headquarters had intended. The 8th Brigade was to leapfrog south of the 22nd Brigade and defend a block of rail leading to Sedenak.[21] Brigadier Painter protested to General Barstow that his 22nd Brigade's prospective position was too easy to outflank, but Barstow told him that Westforce's instructions were specific. In order to cover the flank of the 27th Brigade, the cross-track leading to the Trunk

Road at milestone 40½ had to be denied until at least the following
afternoon.

Why Barstow chose to interpret his orders in such a fashion is unclear.
It has been suggested by the British official historian of the Malayan campaign, Major-General S. Woodburn Kirby, that Barstow, given his closeness
to the Australian camp – 'he was always eager to cooperate' recalled Thyer
– was particularly aware of Australian criticism of Indian troops. Barstow
was thus, in Kirby's view, desperate for his formation fully to support the
troops on the Trunk Road 'and show that the Indian Army was not as effete
as Bennett thought'.[22] During the fighting in north-west Johore a week
previously, the 9th Division had been shielded behind the 27th Brigade, so
strong was Bennett's belief that the Indians would fall apart if given a more
exposed role. Barstow may also have been aware of Maxwell's fears for his
brigade, and have received an exaggerated sense of the dangers facing troops
astride the Trunk Road. Barstow, after all, had six battalions under his
command, whereas Maxwell only had three.

The plot thickens as Barstow had spoken with Bennett when he had visited
Westforce headquarters that morning of 27 January. Bennett may have told
Barstow to stand in front of rail mile 437, or have approved a suggestion
by Barstow to do so, but Barstow was never to invoke Bennett's authority
for his deviation from the written instructions issued by Westforce's
staff.[23] We do not know what Bennett and Barstow discussed, though
Bennett later recorded in his diary that Barstow had told him that he would
like to replace both his brigadiers when they reached Singapore.[24]

Brigadier Painter's subsequent actions did not help matters, as he chose
to deploy the three battalions of his brigade one behind the other astride
the railway. The previous day Lieutenant-Colonel Parkin of the Sikhs had
discovered that there were even more tracks stretching to the east between
rail miles 430 and 440 than indicated by the map. Parkin asked Painter if
his battalion could sidestep to the right to block the tracks, but Painter
refused permission.[25] The problem from Painter's viewpoint was that his
other two battalions, the 2/18th Garhwal Rifles and the 2/12th Frontier Force
Regiment, had been mauled at Kuantan and he wanted to use Parkin's Sikhs
to defend the railway. To make matters even more complex there was no
road next to the railway between Layang Layang and Sedenak. The division
was forced to send all vehicles and heavy equipment, including artillery and
wireless, along the cross-track to the Trunk Road behind the 27th Brigade
during the day. The officers and men of the division loaded up with as
much ammunition as they could carry.

During the afternoon of 27 January Barstow came forward again from his
headquarters at Sedenak. He told Brigadier Lay to occupy a small hill at

rail mile 439½ that evening, a mile south of Layang Layang village. The 8th Brigade passed back through the 22nd Brigade about 4 p.m., and the Sikhs became the division's leading unit. Parkin was aware that there was no tenable defensive position north of Layang Layang. He requested Painter that they start to withdraw back to Layang Layang after dark. This request was refused, as was a later request by Parkin to send at least a company to Layang Layang to act as a link between the two brigades of the division. Painter knew that his brigade was in danger of being outflanked, but he was neither prepared to deploy troops in the path of that predicted move, nor send any troops south of rail mile 437 to guard the gap to his rear. The Japanese made contact with the Sikhs late in the afternoon, and Parkin had withdrawn his battalion to a night position at rail mile 434 by 7.30 p.m.[26]

On the Trunk Road on 27 January the 2/26th Battalion was the leading unit of the 27th Brigade. The battalion was shelled and probed during the afternoon. The Australians repelled the Japanese forward movement and retired after dark to road mile 42. Sometime that evening Brigadier Maxwell secured General Bennett's permission to withdraw his brigade the following night of 28/29 January if its flanks were threatened.[27]

By evening of 27 January Barstow had departed for his headquarters at Sedenak, having told his brigadiers to coordinate their movements together in the absence of wireless communication with divisional headquarters. At 10 p.m. Brigadier Lay used the railway telephone to tell the 22nd Brigade's headquarters that his formation was moving south of Layang Layang. Lay said that he would call again. But the telephone line was severed when a demolition on a railway bridge over a stream south of Layang Layang was accidentally blown. The stream was not deep, and the 22nd Brigade no longer had any wheeled transport, but the loss of telephone communication would prove critical. Moreover the 8th Brigade did not occupy the hill just south of the stream as General Barstow had ordered during the day, and its forward posts finished up a mile further south towards Sedenak.

Brigadier Lay did not send a messenger up the railway to inform Brigadier Painter of his new location. It is not clear why Lay placed his brigade in the position he chose. The most likely explanation is that during the evening the Japanese began to shell the area around Layang Layang station, and Lay did not want his troops to bivouac amid bursting shells.[28]

During the night of 27/28 January the Japanese 41st Regiment passed through the 11th Regiment at Rengam to take over the advance southwards astride the railway. At 1.30 a.m. those Sikhs still awake after another exhausting and famishing day could hear Japanese troops and transport rumbling around their right flank down the unguarded estate roads. The irrepressible Parkin contacted brigade headquarters again to urge a withdrawal to

Layang Layang. But Painter was still not prepared to disobey General Barstow's specific orders.[29] By daylight the Japanese had got behind the 22nd Brigade to cut it off from the rest of the division. Once Painter realised his brigade had been cut off, he finally felt able to disobey his original instructions and issued orders for a retirement southwards.

At midday of 28 January, the Sikhs, still the leading battalion of the brigade, encountered Japanese north of Layang Layang village amid rubber, jungle and swamp. Advancing west of the railway the Sikhs avoided walking into an ambush, but it took an hour and a half of bitter fighting to prise the Japanese out of their immediate path. The Sikhs lost ten killed and another thirty-five wounded in the engagement.

The brigade could have continued moving down the railway towards Layang Layang. But there were probably more Japanese lying in wait, and with further casualties likely Painter did not want to encumber his force with more wounded, each wounded man requiring another four men to carry him. Painter decided to leave the line of the railway in a bid to get around the Japanese blocking the route. British columns, large and small, had frequently set off into the jungle to bypass Japanese concentrations during the campaign.[30] The brigade entered the jungle along a track marked on Painter's map, but the track ended unexpectedly and the whole brigade became lost in dense vegetation somewhere west of the railway.

Meantime, after daylight on 28 January, General Barstow had set out from his headquarters at Sedenak on a railway trolley car to see how his brigades had fared overnight. Arriving at the 8th Brigade's headquarters, Barstow heard that contact with the 22nd Brigade had been lost, and that Brigadier Lay had not occupied the ridge just south of the stream as he had been instructed. An alarmed Barstow ordered Lay to send troops up to the ridge, and set out to visit the 22nd Brigade accompanied by Lieutenant-Colonel W. A. Trott, a divisional staff officer, and Major Charles Moses, a liaison officer from Bennett's headquarters, both of them Australians. The three men went further up the railway on the trolley and reached the 8th Brigade's lead unit, the 2/10th Baluchis. The Baluchis' adjutant, Captain P. E. Campbell, spoke with Barstow and warned him of the dangers that lay ahead. Barstow brushed the information aside, and recklessly pushed on, the red staff band on his hat plain for all to see.[31]

By this stage General Barstow must have been very worried about the 22nd Brigade. At the stream Barstow, Trott, and Moses clambered across the broken railway bridge on foot, and walked on along a high railway embankment towards Layang Layang village. When they were 150 yards beyond the stream unseen Japanese opened fire. Barstow, in the lead, dived or toppled down the right side of the embankment, and Moses and Trott, well to the rear, dived down the left side. With fire sweeping over the embankment at any sign of movement, Moses and Trott prudently decided there was no chance of rescuing the general and headed back to the 8th Brigade.[32] Barstow had been killed in the ambush.

That morning, an attempt by the Baluchis to capture the ridge just south of the stream, as ordered by Barstow, ground to a halt in the face of heavy fire, and no further attack was made by the 8th Brigade that day. Back at divisional headquarters the situation was unclear, and the fact that Barstow was missing added to the confusion. At 10 a.m. a staff officer rang Westforce to tell them: 'Undoubtedly bit of a shimozzle going on in difficult palm oil area north of Layang Layang.'[33]

Brigadier Lay would be heavily criticised for his failure to obey General Barstow's order to occupy the ridge just south of the railway bridge. As Lieutenant-Colonel Trott later wrote, 'Lay was useless as a brigadier. He was washed up'.[34] However it needs to be remembered that if troops had been on the hill feature nominated by Barstow they would still have been a little over a mile south of Layang Layang village. Given the intervening trees and scrub, small arms fire from the feature, even by day, could have done little to prevent the Japanese from occupying the village in strength. Indeed Painter decided to take the 22nd Brigade into the jungle after fighting with Japanese to the north of Layang Layang. The occupation of the ridge south of Layang Layang would have given the 8th Brigade a better jumping off point for a counter-attack towards Painter's brigade, but by this stage of the campaign the 8th Brigade, having lost nearly half its infantry, and without artillery and few mortars, had little offensive value.

The fate of the 22nd Brigade had been determined in no small part by the actions of Barstow and Painter. Barstow's and Painter's tactical mistakes mirrored their poor handling of the battle around Kuantan earlier in the campaign. Once Barstow was dead it became difficult for his contemporaries to criticise his conduct. After the war the official historian, General Kirby, interviewed Lay about the events of 27/28 January, only to scissor Lay's comments out of the transcript records in a rare act of explicit censorship. And of course the Japanese had, yet again, aggressively seized an opportunity presented to them by endemic British blundering.[35]

Whilst so much drama was unfolding on the railway front, less than ten miles away astride the Trunk Road another battle was fought on 28 January. The 27th Brigade's position at road mile 41½ was reasonably secure to the left, thanks to thick encroaching jungle. But to the right flank the hilly, track-ridden Namazie estate stretched for a considerable distance eastwards. The Gordons were posted on the Trunk Road, with the 2/26th Battalion to their right. The battle hardened 2/30th Battalion was in reserve and poised to swing into action should the Japanese attempt a fairly predictable hook through the Namazie estate. The dense rubber of the plantation was only broken by drainage ditches and estate roads. The Trunk Road became a jungle defile to the rear of the brigade, and if the Japanese could block this route the Australians might be forced to take to the jungle in disarray.

During the morning of 28 January the Japanese probed the Gordons and the 2/26th Battalion. By midday the Japanese were beginning to work around the 2/26th Battalion into the gloomy Namazie estate. Vigilant patrols monitored Japanese infiltration, and were not fooled by Japanese wearing British helmets, one of whom replied to a challenge in English. Lieutenant-Colonel Galleghan fed the equivalent of two 2/30th Battalion companies into the rubber estate to block the Japanese movement, and borrowed another company from the 2/26th Battalion. Under the direction of Captain Duffy, at 4.40 p.m. an attack was launched against some high ground in the estate occupied by the Japanese. With visibility reduced to fifty yards the troops bounded up the shadowy, tree-covered slope. There was hand-to-hand fighting in places and the Japanese retreated. The Australian advance pulled up sharply when canisters emitting stinging yellow smoke exploded amongst them. The smoke was not poison gas, as first feared, but the Australians were not carrying respirators and the smoke caused a good deal of alarm.[36]

The Japanese were obviously feeling for the rear of the brigade. Brigadier Maxwell's headquarters was twelve miles behind the forward units, and he had sent forward a staff officer, Captain J. W. C. Wyett, with authority, if necessary, to issue orders for a withdrawal. That day Bennett wrote in his diary that a very tired Maxwell was 'again full of flap messages. Fearful of his men's comfort. Makes wild statements.' With Maxwell so far to the rear, Lieutenant-Colonel Galleghan had been in de facto control of the brigade, and he did not take the authority Maxwell had delegated to Wyett seriously.[37] Galleghan was later to comment of Maxwell:

> How do you make a commander of a man who in 1940 was a Regimental Medical Officer? He had had no experience of issuing orders. He had never been told that a commander should go forward.

As night fell Galleghan called the brigade's battalion commanders together and organized a retirement. The troops had to march twelve miles into the darkness to reach their transport, but casualties had been light. Galleghan stood by the road and encouraged particularly tired men with a swig from a bottle of brandy.[38]

At a conference arranged by General Percival on the morning of 28 January the decision to evacuate the Malayan mainland was confirmed. As the 11th

Division was crumbling on the west coast it was decided to bring forward the final evacuation to the night of 30/31 January. Bennett, after attending Percival's conference at Johore Bharu, made a farewell visit to his friend the Sultan of Johore. Bennett recorded: 'Tears rolled down his rugged cheeks as this rough but big-hearted ruler of Johore discussed the capture of his country by the Japanese.' Rather more controversially Bennett confided to the Sultan that he had no intention of being captured should Singapore capitulate, and that he might need assistance to secure a boat when the time came. (The following evening Bennett told his divisional signals officer they would be 'caught like rats in a trap' once they reached Singapore Island. 'But they won't get me').[39]

Upon returning to his headquarters after dark, having been unnecessarily absent for several hours, Bennett gave Lieutenant-Colonel Thyer the accelerated withdrawal timetable. The 27th Brigade had already inadvertently conformed to the new timetable by retiring from Namazie estate at dusk. During the night of 28/29 January Westforce ordered the 9th Division to withdraw. It looked as though Painter's brigade, which was still lost in the jungle, was going to get left behind.

It was business as usual for the 27th Brigade on 29 January, this time at road mile 31 to the north of Ayer Bemban. Surrounded by rubber and swampy jungle the 2/26th Battalion blocked the Trunk Road. By mid-morning the battalion was engaged across its front. The fighting became hand to hand when Japanese gathering in dead ground close to the Australians were counter-attacked. With the aid of two field batteries, the battalion was still holding its ground at dusk. In a battle lasting most of the day the battalion lost only six killed and twenty-five wounded. This marked another successful fight for the 27th Brigade, which had enjoyed unbroken success over the previous fortnight defending the most important route to Singapore. But Brigadier Maxwell was as worried as ever, and again Bennett had to speak to him 'roundly and frankly', pointing out that he had no right to complain that his formation was fatigued when some Indian units had been in action for a far longer period. Maxwell's pessimistic perception of events was becoming increasingly detached from the true tactical situation of his brigade.[40]

Astride the railway, the 8th Brigade fell back from Sedenak during the evening of 29 January, and suffered some losses breaking clear of pursuing Japanese troops. On the west coast road the Japanese had finally regained contact with Indian troops north of Pontian Kechil. On the east coast road there was little sign of the Japanese.

During 30 January there was no fighting on the front of the 27th Brigade, and that formation joined forces with the 9th Division when the railway and Trunk Road came together just north of Kulai. That afternoon General Bennett passed through the deserted and cratered streets of Johore Bharu on the way to his new headquarters at Singapore. 'The whole operation', wrote Bennett, 'seems incredible: 550 miles in 55 days, forced back by a small Japanese army of only two divisions, riding stolen bicycles and without artillery support'.[41]

The final withdrawal to Singapore during the night of 30/31 January went quite smoothly. Making good use of their abundant motor transport, Indian, Australian and British troops converging on Johore Bharu sprang back distances of over twenty miles in a single bound. The Japanese had little chance of keeping pace. There was a degree of confusion of course, not least because a key road bridge was blown too soon. Neither the 11th Division, nor Westforce, nor Eastforce were under any significant enemy pressure during their final twenty-four hours on the mainland. The Japanese air force neglected to bomb the Causeway, thus missing a vital opportunity to disrupt the retreat.

At 7 a.m. on 31 January the last Australians on the mainland and the Gordon Highlanders retired over the Causeway. They were later followed by 250 men of the Argylls, the last unit to leave Johore. With an eye to history Lieutenant-Colonel Stewart had two pipers march at the head of the Argylls. Soon after 8.00 a.m. naval depth charges planted in the Causeway were detonated. The explosion could be clearly heard on the south side of the island. A seventy foot gap was successfully created. The gap was only four feet deep at low tide, but it was still an effective barrier.[42]

But what had happened to Brigadier Painter's 22nd Indian Brigade? It was as if the jungle had swallowed them up. After leaving the railway in the afternoon of 27 January, and heading off westwards along a track that abruptly ended in thick jungle, the troops had continued marching on a compass bearing. The following day the brigade had carried on through thick, swampy jungle, across hills and deep ravines. They had only reached open country at daylight on 30 January. All ranks were now exhausted. The wounded were in great difficulty and several had died. Painter collapsed with heat exhaustion when climbing a hill to reconnoitre, but he recovered after a short rest.

During the night of 30/31 January, the column crossed the railway from west to east two miles north of Sedenak, over forty-eight hours after they had originally taken to the jungle. The rest of Westforce had long since left the vicinity of Sedenak, and was at that time completing its final retreat across the Causeway. The following day, 31 January, after more meandering under the directions of a bad guide, the wounded were left behind at a rubber plantation dispensary.

The brigade's agony finally came to an end on 1 February, more than twenty-four hours after the Causeway was blown, by which time there were only four hundred men left with the column. Painter authorized a surrender that morning. Only seventy to eighty men from the brigade made their way back to Singapore, and the majority of those were from the Sikhs, including Lieutenant-Colonel Parkin. Lieutenant-Colonel G. J. Hawkins of the Frontier Force and a few of his officers also made a successful escape.[43] The almost complete destruction of the brigade was a high price to pay for the mix-ups around Layang Layang, but was typical of so much that had happened in Malaya over the previous several weeks.

# 13

# Singapore Island

The general strategic situation was getting steadily worse for the Allies in the Far East, quite apart from the misfortunes that had driven Percival's army back to Singapore. American and Philippine forces had been boxed into the Bataan peninsula. The Japanese were beginning a serious thrust into Burma from occupied Thailand, and they already had control of large parts of the Dutch East Indies lying north of Java. At Ambon and Rabaul units of the 8th Australian Division's absent brigade had been captured or dispersed into the jungle.[1]

The shooting war came to Singapore well in advance of the troops of the Imperial Japanese Army. After the initial air raid on the night war began in the Far East, Singapore had been bothered only by occasional hit and run night attacks during the rest of December. But on 12 January the Japanese Army and Navy Air Forces, now well established in northern Malaya, began a daylight blitz on the island that was only interrupted when monsoon storms and heavy cloud ruined flying conditions.

Two or three times a day Japanese bombers, usually in groups of twenty-seven or fifty-four, floated over Singapore in precise formations. With only about forty 3.7 inch heavy anti-aircraft guns at Singapore capable of firing over 20,000 feet, the bombers had little to fear from ground fire. There were radar stations in Johore and Singapore, but these seldom gave sufficient warning for defending fighters to climb high enough to meet the bombers. When bomber formations were intercepted there were too few RAF fighters to both ward off the bombers' escort and attack the bombers. On a daily basis the RAF at Singapore had only two to three dozen fighters available, whereas the Japanese had four hundred fighters and bombers based in southern Thailand and Malaya. Fortunately for embattled RAF pilots the outclassed Buffalo, thanks to its weight and solid construction, could outdive the lightly built Zero. Experienced Buffalo pilots, provided their nerves continued to hold up, could avoid disaster by hurtling earthwards to escape from dog-fights they had little chance of winning.[2]

British commanders had hoped that RAF reinforcements would reach Singapore to turn the tables on the Japanese. The crated Hurricanes that had arrived with a convoy about the middle of January were turned over

to ground staff to assemble hurriedly. But the heavy dust filters designed
for service in the Middle East and the weight of twelve guns and ammunition
in the wings, instead of the usual eight, took at least 30 m.p.h. off the Hurricane's predicted performance. The Hurricanes were a match for Japanese
fighters over 20,000 feet but proved disappointing at lower altitudes.

Mid-morning on 20 January eighty Japanese bombers swanned over
Singapore, one of the biggest raids yet. A dozen newly assembled Hurricanes
dived on the bombers from 28,000 feet, only to be attacked themselves by
escorting Japanese fighters. Three Hurricanes were lost that day. Squadron
Leader L. N. Landels of No. 232 Squadron was killed when his damaged
Hurricane crashed into the sea after striking the mast of a fishing boat.
According to Japanese records, they also lost three aircraft in the dog-fights.
The Hurricane, unlike the Buffalo, could at least give as good as it got, even
when faced by great odds. There were, however, too few Hurricanes to make
an impact on the daily armada of Japanese aircraft.[3]

The next day, 21 January, bombers returned to raid Keppel Harbour. One
bomber was hit by a RAF fighter and exploded in a ball of black smoke and
flame. As both Keppel Harbour and Kallang aerodrome lay on the fringe
of Singapore town, bombs falling wide of the mark caused heavy casualties
in crowded Chinese districts. Almost a thousand civilian killed and injured
had been reported by the following morning.[4] Known civilian air raid
casualties during January were estimated as 600 killed and 1500 wounded,
but the true figure was certainly higher.

Also on 21 January a damaged Hurricane flown by Pilot Officer John
Gorton, a future Australian Prime Minister, crash landed on a Dutch island
south of Singapore. The Hurricane hit a low wall between oil storage tanks
and flipped over. Gorton's face was rammed against the instrument panel
causing extensive injuries. Gorton clambered out and Dutch native soldiers
fired at him before realising he was not Japanese. A launch was sent out
from Singapore to pick Gorton up. Two airmen from the launch took one
look at the prostrate pilot and decided that he was at death's door. They
returned to Singapore with his wallet, watch and pay book to send to his
next of kin. Nine days later a No. 453 Squadron Buffalo piloted by Sergeant
Matt O'Mara crash-landed in a swamp on the island, and came to rest a
few hundred yards from where the recovering Gorton was staying. O'Mara
was dragged out of the wreckage unconscious, and when the launch next
came out from Singapore both pilots got a ride back to base.[5] (When Gorton
was evacuated from Singapore the ship on which he was sailing was sunk
to round off an eventful sojourn in the Far East.)

During January all RAF bombers had been withdrawn from Singapore.
The ground staff were sent out by sea to join the aircraft at new destinations,

mostly in the Dutch East Indies. By 28 January, of the fifty-one Hurricanes that had arrived at Singapore a fortnight previously, only twenty-one were available for operations. Seventeen had been destroyed, and others were in need of repair. More Hurricanes of No. 258 Squadron were beginning to arrive in the Far East on the aircraft carrier *Indomitable*, but when the army withdrew from the mainland Air Headquarters decided to keep only eight Hurricanes and six of the last surviving Buffaloes at Singapore. Once Japanese artillery was established across the Johore Strait, Tengah, Semba-wang and Seletar aerodromes had to be evacuated. The last RAF aircraft at Singapore were forced to fly out of the badly cratered Kallang aerodrome on the south-east coast. On 4 February Group Captain F. G. Watts, the station commander at Tengah for the previous two years, shot himself. He had been behaving oddly for some time, and the never-ending train of setbacks had finally become too much.[6]

After the armies of the British Empire had finished filing back to Singapore, it was time to count the costs of the campaign on the mainland. A week after a gap was blown in the Causeway, Malaya Command's casualty returns revealed that 19,123 men had been lost to date killed and wounded – but mostly missing. Vast quantities of equipment had also been left behind. Japanese losses on the mainland had been relatively low, a mere 1793 dead and 2772 wounded.[7]

In the last days of January and the first week of February, with only minor interference from Japanese aviators, the main body of the 18th British Division, the 44th Indian Brigade, 7000 Indian replacements, the 2/4th Machine Gun Battalion AIF, and 1900 Australian replacements sailed into Singapore from India and Australia. The convoys passed through the Sunda Strait between Sumatra and Java accompanied by small escorts. A Japanese submarine lurking on the sea bed of the Sunda Strait had been sunk on 17 January.[8]

The only significant success scored by Japanese bombers against convoys sailing to and from Singapore was the sinking of the *Empress of Asia*. On 5 February convoy BM 12 was attacked in fine weather as it neared Singapore. In the course of an hour long attack the *Empress of Asia* attracted most of the bombers' attention. At least three direct hits were scored amidships, and fires soon spread out of control as the water pipes to the fire hydrants had been damaged. The *Empress of Asia* was deliberately run aground on a shoal, and smaller ships came alongside to take off the crew and passengers. The *Empress of Asia* later sank, but the tops of her three funnels remained visible above the water. Almost the entire ship's crew and troops of the 18th Reconnaissance Battalion (5th Loyals), the 125th Anti-Tank Regiment,

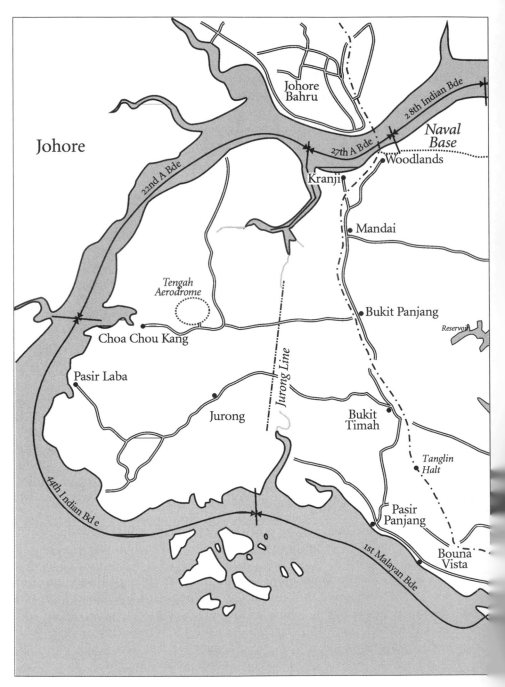

13. Singapore Island.

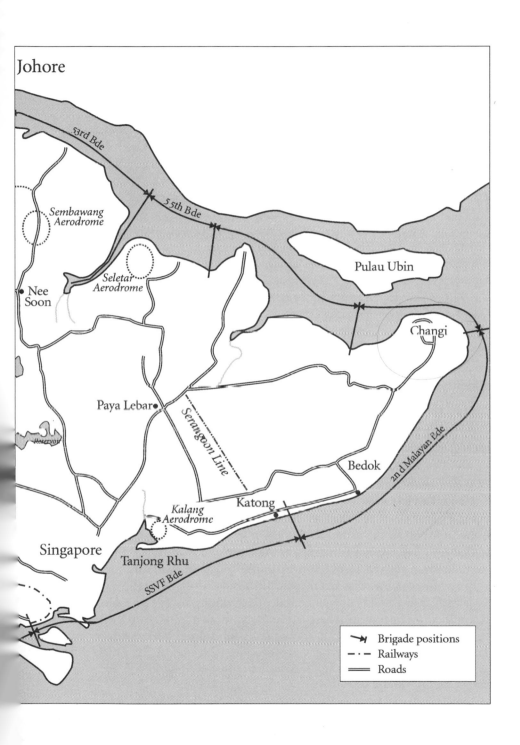

Johore

53rd Bde

Sembawang
Aerodrome

5 5th Bde

Pulau Ubin

Seletar
Aerodrome

Nee
Soon

Changi

Paya Lebar

Serangoon Line

2nd Malayan Bde

Bedok

Reservoir

Katong

Kalang
Aerodrome

Singapore

Tanjong Rhu

SSVF Bde

⌐➤ Brigade positions
─ · ─ Railways
═══ Roads

and other 18th Division units were rescued. Relatively few had been killed by the bombs, but many men had been burnt to varying degrees in the fires that had followed. A great deal of equipment was lost, including the weapons of the anti-tank gunners, most of which was not replaceable given Singapore's depleted stocks.[9]

After the convoys arrived at Singapore the ships were used to evacuate European women and children, and RAF personnel. Convoy BM 11 had arrived on 29 January, and by the night of 30/31 January four of its large transports had left carrying over 5000 evacuees and servicemen. On 6 February three transports from convoy BM 12 also left Singapore carrying 4100 people. The ships could have carried more passengers, and the government was willing to pay the fares of European civilians, but this was not widely advertised for fear of alienating Asian opinion.

The belatedly arriving reinforcements brought Singapore's garrison to over 100,000 men, the majority of whom were Indians. The 44th Indian Brigade was a sister formation of the ill-fated 45th Brigade, and had also been scheduled to sail for the Middle East for a long period of much needed training before it was hastily dispatched to Malaya. Like the 45th Brigade, the 44th Brigade's battalions had only three regular British officers on average, and the majority of sepoys in the rifle companies were young, undertrained recruits.[10]

The 7000 Indian replacements who had been packed off to Singapore, many without rifles, were in a particularly sorry state. Too many of the sepoys had been plucked straight from a training depot. There were very few non-commissioned officers or trained specialists among the reinforcements. Regular officers at Singapore released drafts of these men to units of their parent regiment with considerable reluctance.

The Indian battalion at Singapore in best condition was the 2/17th Dogras, but they had been banished to Pulau Tekong Besar, an island five miles from Singapore at the eastern end of the Johore Strait. Every other III Corps Indian unit had taken a battering on the mainland. A number of battalions were amalgamated to form stronger units, and then made up to strength with reinforcements. The 2/10th Baluch, 2/2nd Gurkhas, 4/19th Hyderabad and 1/8th Punjab were the only Indian battalions from the mainland to retain their original form. These last four mentioned units, with the possible exception of the 2/2nd Gurkhas, were dangerously top heavy with recruits. The 3rd Cavalry had arrived back at Singapore with only eight of their thirty armoured cars. The Indian States Force battalions were sent to guard mostly empty aerodromes.[11]

The III Indian Corps' artillery had returned to Singapore in better shape than the infantry. The surviving battery of the 137th Field Regiment had been placed under the command of the 155th Field Regiment, but otherwise most units were substantially intact. III Corps' three British battalions had not been quite so fortunate. The 2nd Argyll and Sutherland Highlanders could only scrape together 250 officers and men, and Royal Marines formerly of the *Prince of Wales* and *Repulse* were added to the unit to boost its strength above four hundred. The British Battalion was already an amalgamation of the 2nd East Surreys and the 1st Leicestershires.

The Volunteer Forces still had a presence at Singapore. The two Singapore battalions of the Straits Settlements Volunteer Force were at full strength, but the Penang and Malacca battalions had disbanded the majority of their personnel. The Volunteer units of the unfederated Malay States had also been mostly disbanded, except for the Johore Volunteer Engineers. The Federated Malay States Volunteer Force could field only a nine hundred to a thousand strong and mostly European depot battalion. No provision had been made for the evacuation of the families of Asian members of the Volunteer Forces from the mainland. In consequence most non-Europeans had elected to stay behind when the rest of their unit was withdrawn to Singapore.[12]

At the last minute a fresh local irregular formation was raised from all factions of Singapore's Chinese community. These irregulars were organized by police officers and became known as 'Dalforce', as their commander was Lieutenant-Colonel J. D. Daley of the Federated Malay States Police. Dalforce was armed with an ad hoc assortment of weapons, ranging from sporting rifles to shotguns, and did not have a clear distinguishing uniform. A British brigadier to whose formation was allotted a company of irregulars commented:

> Actually they were City-bred folk, who had never been nearer swamps than a bus might take them. They proved very trigger-happy and [were] a constant source of alarm and unease.

The garrison was not lacking in numbers and already had too many undertrained men.[13]

The 53rd British Brigade had also taken a heavy knock in Johore, and had lost over five hundred killed, wounded and missing, along with a great deal of equipment. After absorbing their first-line reinforcements, the 53rd Brigade's battalions averaged a respectable seven hundred. They were able to re-equip at the expense of other newly arrived 18th Division units.[14]

The 18th Division's headquarters had arrived with Major-General M. B. Beckwith-Smith. The troops of the 54th and 55th Brigades, and the divisional machine gun battalion and reconnaissance regiment, were valuable eleventh-hour additions to the Singapore garrison, but like the 53rd Brigade they would not be given time to fully adjust to the oppressive humidity and stifling heat of their new environment.[15]

The 8th Australian Division, still only two brigades strong, was never quite the same again after the withdrawal from Johore. Of the seven Australian battalions, including the newly arrived 2/4th Machine Gun Battalion, five were in reasonable shape. But after the fighting near Muar the 2/29th Battalion, a Victorian unit, had taken in five hundred replacements from four different Australian states, including nineteen officers. Only one company commander from the Bakri-Parit Sulong battle was still with the unit. The battalion's new commander, Lieutenant-Colonel S. A. F. Pond, formerly the 27th Brigade's brigade-major, protested to General Bennett that the new battalion was not 'a fighting force at all'. The 2/19th Battalion had also required several hundred new men. Major R. F. Oakes described that unit as 'only a makeshift compared with its former efficiency and esprit de corps'. Other battalions took in smaller numbers of replacements, after which those men remaining in the reinforcement pool were distributed across all units to add an extra platoon to each rifle company. (Thus the 2/19th Battalion's new establishment was thirty-eight officers and 930 other ranks.) Spare Army Service Corps men and the 2/4th Machine Gun Battalion's first-line reinforcement company were used to form the Special Reserve Battalion.[16]

The newly arrived reinforcements who were used to fill the ranks of Australian units were a grave disappointment. Most had only been in the army for a matter of weeks, and some had yet to complete a course in musketry. Unacclimatized, with few specialists or NCOs, and unused to military discipline, it was extraordinary that such men could be sent to a desperately active theatre of war. Major O'Brien described the newly arrived reinforcements as 'not only almost useless but actually a positive menace to anyone near them and to any commander who expected his orders to be carried out'.[17] The 8th Division's new soldiers were, needless to say, more sinned against than sinners. After the start of the war in the Pacific, the military authorities in Australia had simply packed off to Singapore recent AIF recruits when it was belatedly realised that the 8th Division might need replacements in the near future.

In addition to the infantry formations and the field artillery, Singapore's garrison comprised a great array of support and base units. Medical, transport, army service corps, engineer, ordnance, signals, post office, laundry and other units all had valuable tasks to perform. Coastal gunners manned the big guns of Changi and Faber Fire Commands, and gunners of six heavy and light anti-aircraft regiments and a searchlight regiment served approximately 150 anti-aircraft guns. In theory servicemen no longer required for

16. Indian sappers preparing to blow up a bridge. (*AWM*)

17. Japanese troops crossing a demolished bridge. (*AWM*)

18. British troops crossing a pontoon. (*IWM*)

19. A two-pounder gun, of the 2/4th Anti-Tank Regiment, in action near Bakri. From this position two guns accounted for eight Japanese tanks. (*AWM*)

20. The British had far more motorised transport than their opponents. (*AWM*)

21. The Japanese troops advanced rapidly using bicycles.

22. The Johore Strait, with Johore Bahru behind it, showing the breach made in the Causeway. (*AWM*)

23. Japanese troops crossing the repaired Causeway.

24. Bombs falling on Singapore, February 1942. (*AWM*)

25. Smoke from the Naval Base casts a pall over Singapore, February 1942. (*AWM*)

26. Japanese troops attack on Singapore Island, February 1942.

27. The British surrender party, led by Lieutenant-General Percival (far right). (*IWM*)

28. Yamashita face to face with Percival in the Ford Factory, Bukit Timah, 15 February 1942. (*IWM*)

29. Percival signs the single copy of the surrender agreement. (*AWM*)

30. Yamashita (fifth from right) next to Percival after the surrender. On Yamashita's right is the XXV Army Chief of Staff, Lieutenant-General Suzuki.

31. Japanese soldiers rejoice at their victory.

rear echelon tasks could be redeployed to fighting units, but in practice men not schooled in the brutal craft of the infantry by months of training had little chance of performing to an acceptable standard.

Singapore Island was doomed to become another Second World War battle-field. Separated from Johore by a narrow strait, Singapore Island was only a maximum of thirteen miles from north to south, and twenty-seven miles from east to west; 220 square miles in all. On the south coast Singapore town stretched along the waterfront for six miles. The Chinese districts were very crowded. The town was fringed by spacious residential suburbs for wealthy European and Asian citizens. The peacetime population of Singapore was estimated to be 769,216, though after the population had been properly registered, preparatory to the issuing of food ration cards, the correct figure proved to be over 900,000. There had been no more than a slow trickle of refugees from the mainland to Singapore. One senior official noted that 'the average peasant from the north knows nothing of Singapore and would regard it as the last place in which to look for refuge'.[18]

Good roads radiated out from Singapore town across the island. The main road ran to the Causeway through Bukit Timah village. Much of the island was flat and covered by rubber, other plantation crops, and patches of secondary or primary jungle. In the centre of the island the highest point, at Bukit Timah (Silver Mountain), was only 581 feet high. Also in the centre of the island was a network of three reservoirs surrounded by a stretch of mainly primary jungle. Part of Singapore's water was pumped in a pipeline over the Causeway from Johore, but with rationing the island's reservoirs could supply all reasonable needs.

The northern and western coastline of Singapore was edged with man-grove swamp interrupted by small creeks. The immediate environs of the Naval Base was just about the only area from which the mangroves had been comprehensively cleared. Extensive drainage work carried out for agricultural and anti-malarial purposes had, however, done much to render the mangroves firm under foot. Most of the southern coast was lined with sandy beaches.

Upon General Wavell's arrival in the Far East there had been some discussion as to whether a military governor for Singapore should be ap-pointed. But both Wavell and the Colonial Office had turned down the suggestion as a window-dressing that would not help matters. Percival's chief Royal Engineer, Brigadier Simson, had been belatedly appointed Director-General of Civil Defence (and only after a heated dispute between the Governor and Duff Cooper). An air raid precautions, fire fighting and medical auxiliary service had long since been formed at Singapore, but the administration was criticised for not doing enough to build public air raid shelters or blast walls. Entire streets in Chinatown had been levelled to the ground by bombing. Key buildings were damaged and the wailing of air raid sirens had become part of everyday life. Corpses were buried in mass graves or left under the rubble. Labourers on the docks became increasingly reluctant to work. To add insult to injury, the Japanese also dropped leaflets depicting European planters and soldiers living a luxurious existence at the expense of the colony's Asian citizens.

By the end of January a rough and ready rationing system, a curfew and martial law had been instituted. Food supplies for the civilian population and military garrison were expected to last for at least several months. However, most of the stores were kept in warehouses in the dock area, and were suffering from a rising level of bomb damage. Refugees from mainland Malaya lived out of suitcases in temporary accommodation. And much to the shock of those directly affected, local traders stopped selling goods on credit. Nonetheless, during January the Raffles Hotel had still featured a blacked out dance room, with an orchestra from 8 p.m. till midnight. There was no good reason why cinemas and popular dance halls should close their doors.

In the *Straits Times* the editor ranted and raved against the administration, as if the Governor, Sir Shenton Thomas, and the Malayan Civil Service were substantially to blame for the defeats of the armed services. This was of course not the case, but the wartime writings of frustrated journalists tended to paint the civil authorities of Malaya in a very bad light. The civil officials were, moreover, a soft target. Similar and rather more justified criticism of the military would have been regarded not merely as unpatriotic, but as outright sedition.

On General Wavell's first visit to Singapore on 7–8 January he had asked to be shown the island's north coast defences. He was told there were no defences. That General Percival, despite the pleadings of his chief engineer, Brigadier Simson, did not do more to build defensive works on the north coast of Singapore has always been a matter of controversy. Simson had met Percival late at night towards the close of December to press his case. After two and a half hours discussion Simson would later claim that the general's only reason for not building defences was that they were bad for morale. However, Simson's version of events oversimplifies the issue. The origin of the problem was that little had been done to fortify Singapore Island before the war. The prepared fortifications that did exist had been designed to repel attack from the sea. Large naval guns only protected the approaches to the Naval Base and Keppel Harbour. Even the local defences of the Naval Base were little better than elsewhere on the north coast.

Thanks to Wavell's prodding and the approach of Yamashita's army, a limited amount of work was carried out on the north coast during the latter part of January. But labour, both civil and military, was in short supply in January 1942. What little labour was available was used to repair bombed aerodromes and work on the docks. At ABDA Command head-quarters at Java General Pownall noted in his diary that it was hardly surprising that the north coast of Singapore had been neglected with an army on the mainland and the Japanese hundreds of miles away; after all, work on the coast of Kent had only begun after the Dunkirk evacuation. Lieutenant-Colonel Tsuji wrote of the defenceless north shore: 'Whatever the period, whatever the country, there are always those who perpetrate such blunders.' [19]

The most pressing set of decisions facing General Percival and his staff involved the garrison's dispositions to face the expected Japanese assault. If Percival could predict from which direction Yamashita was going to attack, there was a lot to be said for massing troops along that stretch of coast. On 20 January, when General Wavell was again at Singapore, he told Percival that he should place the 18th Division, as the 'freshest and strongest forma-tion', in the most exposed sector of Singapore's defences. Wavell added that in his view the north west of the island was the place most likely to be attacked, and that the Australians should hold the north-east coast. Whereas the Johore Strait north east of Singapore was up to 5000 yards across, west of the Causeway the water was only 800 to 2000 yards wide. The main Japanese axis of advance thus far had also been down the western side of Malaya. According to Wavell:

> General Percival demurred to this and said that his opinion was that the main Japanese attack would be made down the Johore river and on the east of the Island. He therefore wished to place the 18th Division on the eastern portion of the Island and the Australians on the west. Since he had been studying the problem for so long and seemed quite convinced of the probable direction of the Japanese attack, I accepted his judgement and allowed him to dispose the troops as he wished.[20]

Wavell, though, was not satisfied with Percival as a commander. He later told General Brooke that he wanted 'to find some really vigorous, ruthless personality to organize the defence of the island ... I looked for one but could not see him'.[21]

General Percival put the 8th Australian Division on the north-west coast of Singapore Island, and sent the 18th Division and the best of the Indian formations to the north-east coast. Percival's explanation for his actions altered over the years ahead. Towards the end of 1945 Percival wrote,

> In point of fact I put the Australians in the north west chiefly because I thought it was the most vulnerable area and that as the Australians had had experience of fighting on the mainland and training in bush warfare, it would be better to put them there than the newly arrived 18th Division.

In his own despatch and book on the campaign Percival reproduced views similar to those expressed above.

Some years later Percival conceded to the official historian, General Kirby:

> I was probably wrong when I said in my despatch that I expected the attack to develop from the west and ... I probably had little preference between the two lines of advance i.e. from the west or down the river from Kota Tinggi [towards the north-east coast of Singapore] ... in all pre-war planning, a landing at Mersing followed by an advance to Kota Tinggi and thence down the river to Changi had always been thought possible.[22]

Percival's judgement that Singapore was faced by a multitude of threats was greatly influenced by the inflated estimates of Japanese strength in Malaya. Percival assessed Japanese strength at five or six divisions and two tank regiments, somewhere in the region of 150,000 men and three hundred tanks.[23] Local commanders and intelligence officers had made exaggerated estimates of Japanese strength and losses at every stage of the campaign. These often hopelessly wrong guesstimates had combined to build an extremely misleading picture at Malaya Command headquarters.

Thanks to the speed of the final retirement from Johore, the bulk of the 18th Division, arriving as it did on 29 January, barely reached Singapore in time for the next phase of the campaign. Percival put Heath's III Corps headquarters in command of 'Northern Area'. Heath's sector stretched along the north-east coast from the Causeway to Changi Point. Both the 18th British Division and the 11th Indian Division (which had absorbed much of the shattered 9th Indian Division) were placed under Heath's command. Twice as much artillery was deployed east of the Causeway as to the west.[24] General Bennett commanded 'Western Area'. Two Australian brigades and the 44th Indian Brigade were deployed to hold the north-west, west and part of the south-west coast.[25]

Unwilling to take a risk in any sector, Percival placed most of his remaining troops on the south and south-east coasts of the island (General Keith Simmons's 'Southern Area'). There was only a small central reserve. Percival had always feared a landing on the south coast of Singapore. On 4 February ABDA Command Intelligence learned that a Japanese convoy would soon arrive at the Anambas Islands off the east coast of Johore. This was later confirmed by aerial reconnaissance. ABDA Command Intelligence was correctly of the view that the convoy was bound for Sumatra, but Percival was unsure of the accuracy of their advice.[26]

With the garrison spread right around the entire seventy miles of Singapore's coast, and with no central reserve worthy of the name, Percival had no option other than to make the coast his principal line of defence. Malaya Command's defence policy was to defend the coast with posts prepared for prolonged resistance. If the posts were surrounded they were to hang on and wait for relief by a counter-attacking force. Where this counter-attacking force was to be conjured from troubled many local commanders.

Across the Johore Strait the Japanese were completing their own preparations. In terms of 'rifle strength', General Yamashita's XXV Army, as had so often been the case during the campaign, was numerically weaker than the British force it was preparing to attack. The Japanese, however, were not fully aware of that fact. According to Lieutenant-Colonel Tsuji, XXV Army estimated British fighting strength at Singapore to be 30,000 men.[27] In reality Yamashita had nine regiment-sized formations compared with Percival's thirteen brigades. Percival's numbers should have been stronger still, but three Indian brigades had been annihilated on the mainland and the majority of the Volunteers had been disbanded. Yamashita's troops were also running short of ammunition. The landing of essential supplies at Mersing late in January did much to relieve the crisis, but only by a small margin.

To his great credit Yamashita resolved to attack Singapore after only a week's pause. In an act of bravado he decided to establish forward XXV Army headquarters in the Sultan of Johore's Green Palace, the Istana Hijau. The picturesque red-bricked and green-tiled palace was situated in a large landscaped park, on high ground overlooking the Johore Strait, just west of the Causeway. The palace was within easy reach of British artillery fire. A nearby five-storey observation tower permitted a tremendous view. The glass enclosed room at the top was not unlike the conning tower of a warship, and was used as an operations room and observation post. Tsuji wrote that from the tower 'the naval port of Seletar lay beneath one's eyes, and Tengah Aerodrome appeared as if it could be grasped in the hand'. Yamashita sent a message to his divisional commanders telling them that he would directly observe their efforts from his new command post. General Yamashita's leadership was, as always, energetically driving his army forward.[28]

Given XXV Army's lack of numbers and shipping, a landing on the seaward coast of Singapore was never seriously considered. Japanese Southern Army headquarters at Saigon had at no stage been planning to send an expedition directly against Singapore. Indeed Southern Army was already well advanced in planning for seaborne expeditions to Sumatra and Java. Necessity dictated that Yamashita's assault on Singapore be launched across the Johore Strait. Japanese intelligence had concluded that, because the Naval Base was sited to the east of the Causeway, the north coast's defences would be strongest in that area. The Japanese were also aware of the naval batteries and barracks near Changi, which also helped to rule out a landing on the north-east coast of the island. Therefore the obvious thing to do was to attack the north-west coast, whilst a diversion was organized opposite Singapore's north-east coast to attract the attention of British commanders. Though Singapore had not been turned into a literal fortress, those defensive works that had been built greatly influenced the location of the Japanese assault.

Landing craft were assembled in Johore, mostly collapsable motor boats that carried a dozen men, and smaller numbers of barges and pontoons that could transport two or three dozen men or a tank or a motor vehicle. Japanese preparations were greatly aided by the fact that much of the road and railway network behind them had been swiftly repaired. All civilians were evacuated from a twenty kilometre strip north of the strait.

The 5th and 18th Divisions were to cross the Johore Strait onto the north-west corner of the island. The troops were concentrated for the assault well inland of the crossing points. They were not due to move down to the shore until the day of the attack. The night following the initial landing, the Imperial Guards Division, having conducted a diversion opposite the north-east coast, was to cross the strait behind the 5th Division, and move towards the eastern half of the island through the Mandai area. At the last minute Yamashita amended his plan to allow the Imperial Guards to attack between the Causeway and the Kranji River on the second night of the battle. The commander of the Guards, General Nishimura, had complained that his division did not have a distinctive assault role.

After subordinate formations were given the outline plan, senior officers and their staffs set out to reconnoitre British positions across the strait. The 9th Brigade's commander, Major-General Kawamura, wrote in his war diary:

> I feel relieved now [that I know] that the mangrove is not impassable. Besides, I learn that some of the defeated [enemy] remnants, not knowing our presence, have fled to the opposite bank, showing that the soil about here is not yielding.

Yamashita had been concerned that the oil in the tanks near Kranji and the Naval Base might be released into the Johore Strait, and set ablaze whilst an assault was in progress. But XXV Army staff concluded that the peculiarities of the tide and current made this impractical. They need not have worried. Malaya Command was not considering such a measure.[29]

The Japanese assembled their artillery opposite Singapore Island. Many of the heavier guns were sited on high ground behind Johore Bharu, from which they could fire at both sides of the north coast. In total XXV Army possessed 168 guns, plus other regimental and anti-aircraft guns, and some heavy mortars. This was considerably less that the ordnance at Percival's disposal. Likewise the Japanese supply of ammunition, a thousand rounds for each field gun, and five hundred rounds for each heavy gun, was less than that available to the British. From 1 February the Japanese commenced harassing and registration fire. On 5 February Japanese artillery fire increased, most of it falling behind the north-east coast and the Causeway. An observation balloon bobbed up behind Johore Bharu to correct the aim of the gunners.

During the first week of February Singapore's garrison began to settle into its new environment. The north-east monsoon was passing. Where once there had been violent storms, there were now only occasional showers. The tired troops that had arrived at Singapore from the mainland did not find the defenceless north coast of the 'naked island' encouraging. Captain F. Gaven of the 2/20th Battalion went down to the waterfront to view the position his unit's A Company was to hold.

> It was impenetrable, with all the streams coming in along the foreshore through the mangroves. I have never felt such a feeling of desperation in all my life. I then realised that forward defence in this situation was an impossible task.[30]

The drained mangrove swamps were for the most part no barrier to an attacker, but by cutting down or eliminating so many fields of fire they were a grave disadvantage to the defenders. Morale slumped as sub-units began to dig in on frontages that would be impossible to hold in the face of a heavy assault. The propaganda of Singapore fortress was still ringing in the ears of the infantry. Japanese shelling soon set the fuel dumps at the evacuated Naval Base ablaze, and a vast pillar of dark smoke billowed skywards.

Australian and British officers saw Japanese observers in the high tower of the Johore Municipal Building searching the foreshore with field glasses. A report even reached Bennett's Western Area headquarters that the Japanese were using the Sultan's Palace as an observation post. Bennett refused to permit the artillery to open fire, saying the post would only move somewhere else. Bennett believed 'that unnecessary shelling of Johore Bharu should be avoided'. This was presumedly a consequence of Bennett's friendship with the Sultan of Johore. There was not a lot of ammunition available for the artillery to fire anyway. Strict rationing designed to last a three-month siege had been introduced.[31]

In the cramped confines of Singapore Island there were few natural switch lines behind the north coast. The best option ran from north to south in the western third of the island, between the headwaters of the Sungei Kranji and Sungei Jurong. The gap covered by the so-called 'Jurong Line' was less than three miles, a vast improvement on the twenty miles of coast held by Western Area. When Brigadier Taylor met General Bennett in Singapore town on 2 February, after protesting about the frontage he had to hold and the absence of reserves, he requested that a reconnaissance of the Jurong Line be put in hand. Bennett's chief of staff, Lieutenant-Colonel Thyer, later put a map in front of Bennett, and also requested that a defensive plan be drawn up for a reserve line in the area. Bennett ignored Taylor's suggestion, and accused Thyer of having a 'withdrawal complex'. On 6 February Brigadier Maxwell asked Bennett how long the battle on the island would last. Bennett gave the garrison about ten days.[32]

On 5 February General Percival held a press conference to assure the public that Singapore would be stoutly defended. *The Times* correspondent Ian Morrison was not impressed by proceedings.

> Much of what the general said was sensible. But never have I heard a message put across with less conviction, with less force ... It was embarrassing as well as uninspiring.[33]

After listening to a question and answer session Morrison doubted whether Percival had the capacity to lead any group of men. But the die had been cast. Percival had arranged his forces, and the troops were preparing their posts.

By 5 February Japanese artillery fire over the strait was becoming noticeably heavier. A single shell fell through the door of a magazine at the Naval Base and killed ten men of the 2/1st Gurkhas and wounded thirteen others. A long-range gun shelled Government House in the centre of Singapore town. British gunners were eventually permitted to fire at the Johore Administration Building, and its imposing facade was scarred by bursting shells.

British boat patrols operated in front of parts of Northern Area. Parties from the 18th Division were sent across the strait regularly, though little was found on the other side. The Japanese were themselves sending patrols over the strait to probe Singapore's defences. Suspicious footprints in the mud and vague figures flitting through the undergrowth were sighted in the Australians' sector. On the night of 7/8 February a small Japanese boat approaching the 27th Brigade's front west of the Causeway was spotted amid the darkness and destroyed by machine gun fire.

The Japanese diversion plan was now in full swing. The Imperial Guards drove lorries eastwards from Johore Bharu towards dummy camps. On the evening of 7 February the Guards landed four hundred men in collapsible boats on Pulau Ubin Island between Johore and the north-east coast of Singapore. A British patrol on the island was forced to beat a hasty retreat.

Percival later said that the Japanese deception plan did not cause any alteration to his dispositions. The general's claim was correct. The Japanese feint was directed against an area that was already strongly held, and merely confirmed what Malaya Command was already inclined to believe. Early on 8 February Percival sent a message to Wavell at ABDA Command headquarters at Java: 'Present indications show main enemy strength north of Pulau Ubin.' Malaya Command's Lieutenant-Colonel B. H. Ashmore also noted that 'all intelligence indicated the massing of Japanese troops on the east of Johore Bharu opposite the Island of Pulau Ubin'. Yet Malaya Command's Intelligence branch was starting to wonder whether the Japanese attack might be directed against the north-west coast of Singapore. Movements detected east of the Causeway seemed too obvious, whilst in the western half of Johore all was quiet. But the Intelligence Branch had little evidence with which to make a case, and scant influence with Percival anyway.[34]

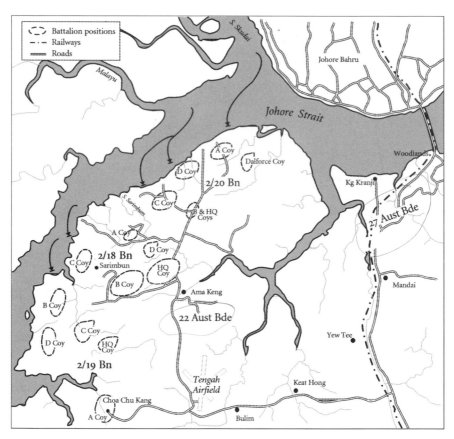

Battalion positions
Railways
Roads

*S. Skudai*

Johore Bahru

*Malayu*

*Johore Strait*

Woodlands

A Coy

Dalforce Coy

D Coy

2/20 Bn

Kg Kranji

*S. Sarimbun*

C Coy

B & HQ Coys

27 Aust Bde

A Coy

2/18 Bn

D Coy

Mandai

C Coy · Sarimbun

HQ Coy

B Coy

B Coy

Ama Keng

22 Aust Bde

C Coy

Yew Tee

D Coy

HQ Coy

2/19 Bn

*Tengah Airfield*

Keat Hong

Choa Chu Kang

A Coy

Bulim

14. The Japanese Landings on Singapore Island.

# Across the Johore Strait

With the initiative completely in the hands of General Yamashita's XXV Army, senior British officers at Singapore waited for the next blow to fall. They did not have long to wait. During 8 February the Japanese completed their final preparations. The artillery supporting the Imperial Guards east of Johore Bharu continued to fire towards Changi as part of their successful diversion. The guns were scattered about in groups of one or two to give the impression that each gun position might be a battery. Across the Johore Strait from the 11th Indian Division observers believed that there were six Japanese artillery regiments present. British artillery in Northern Area indulged in counter-battery work with enthusiasm, and Lieutenant-Colonel Tsuji, who was visiting the Imperial Guards, noted that by noon incoming British shelling was more intense than Japanese fire. British shells fell around the Sultan's palace and sprayed its walls with splinters.[1]

Japanese shell fire onto the north-west corner of Singapore, the true location of the impending assault, grew as the day progressed. All categories of guns, bar those still taking part in the Imperial Guards diversion, were concentrated for the bombardment.[2] The Japanese fired heavy barrages at suspected defensive posts, but casualties among Australian units in the area were not heavy. One company commander recounted that he only had about five men wounded, and that the shell bursts lost much of their force in the soft ground of the swamp. Mortar bombs exploding amid trees overhead were more dangerous than shelling.[3] The bombardment was the Australians' first experience of heavy shellfire, however, and the ordeal left some men in a state of shock. A pall of smoke thrown up by groups of shell bursts drifted across the rubber and mangrove to obscure the vision of Japanese artillery observers.

Well to the rear, General Bennett's Western Area headquarters was bombed and shelled for half an hour during the morning of 8 February. The shift of Japanese fire from the north-east to the north-west corner of the island was at first believed to be part of a general programme designed to soften up Singapore. Bennett went to visit Taylor's 22nd Brigade, and later wrote in his diary: 'Taylor's headquarters have been having a rough time for the past two days and the brigadier appears somewhat shaken.'

Meanwhile Taylor was having a frustrating day trying to organize artillery support for his brigade. Requests for counter-battery fire yielded no result thanks to the need to work through the division's artillery headquarters. The strict rationing of artillery ammunition was still in force, and woe betide the troop or battery commander who squandered scarce shells on his own initiative.[4]

Earlier that morning two Australian patrols had returned from the other side of the Johore Strait. The young lieutenants in command of the patrols reported that they had seen equipment and preparations that suggested the presence of large numbers of troops, but no tell-tale landing craft or assembled units. General Percival visited Bennett early in the afternoon. Neither man indicated to the other an awareness that large troop concentrations were massing opposite the 8th Division's front. The patrols' information reached Malaya Command about 3.30 p.m., but was not adjudged to be of any special significance. It was only when Japanese gunfire reached a crescendo in the early evening that senior Australian officers began to suspect that an assault might be imminent. But as Lieutenant-Colonel Thyer, the 8th Division's GSO 1, later related: 'It did not, however, enter anybody's head to order harassing fire.'[5]

The 22nd Brigade, upon which the Japanese assault was about to descend, had been given a particularly tough defensive task by Malaya Command and Western Area headquarters.[6] Brigadier Taylor and his men were required to hold an excessively long front, despite the fact that the Johore Strait opposite the north-west coast was significantly narrower than elsewhere. The brigade had to occupy an eight mile front with three battalions, whereas, in the right half of Northern Area, an eight mile front between Changi and the mouth of the Sungei Seletar was held with six battalions. No less than twelve battalions of four brigades from Northern and Western Areas either held or were in close reserve behind the eight and a half mile stretch between the Sungei Seletar and Sungei Kranji, the central zone of Singapore Island's north coast defences.

The reason the 22nd Brigade had such a long front to hold was that late in January, when the sector boundaries were drawn up, Malaya Command had carelessly approved a decision to extend Western Area's boundary eastwards to the Causeway. As the mouth of the Sungei Kranji stretched for almost half a mile, and was surrounded by mangrove swamps of great depth, the 8th Division's area was split into two very unequal halves, one eight miles long west of the Kranji, and the other only 4000 yards wide between the eastern fringe of the Kranji swamps and the Causeway. This fact, combined with the need to defend the broken Causeway, had made it necessary to put the 27th Brigade's headquarters in charge of the 4000 yard front between the Kranji and the Causeway. Taylor's brigade was left to deal with the rest of the division's frontage. General Bennett had initially wanted to send one of the 27th Brigade's battalions to the west of the Kranji to add a fourth battalion to that sector. But when Lieutenant-Colonel Thyer had pointed out that logically that unit should be placed under Taylor's command, Bennett had changed his mind. Bennett did not want to do anything to increase the importance of Taylor's role.[7] (The 22nd Brigade and each of the other two brigades in Western Area had a company of the 2/4th Machine Gun Battalion, a battery of the 2/4th Anti-Tank Regiment and a field artillery regiment in support.)

Taylor was well aware that an attack in strength would soon bypass the posts of his fewer than 3000 infantrymen, causing the brigade to disintegrate once cohesion was lost. It was hard to find decent fields of fire amid the mangroves and scrub anywhere along the north coast, and Taylor's battalions, due to the folly of senior commanders, had to tolerate gaps between posts two to three times wider than elsewhere on the northern coast of Singapore. In the event of an overwhelming attack, Taylor had given his battalion commanders verbal instructions. As Taylor later recalled:

> In the event of a strong enemy attack, the plan in outline was that any portion of the force being overwhelmed, the remaining elements would fight their way back to Company Headquarters, and as a last resort Battalions would form perimeters around the present site of Battalion Headquarters, the 2/20th Battalion perimeter then to fall back on 2/18th Battalion at Ama Keng village. The three Battalions would then hold the line Ama Keng-Sungei Berih, to allow reserves to come up behind that line and to operate after first light.[8]

The neck of land between the headwaters of the Kranji and Sungei Berih, to the immediate rear of the brigade's extended front, was less than 4000 yards across and far more defensible.

It is unlikely Taylor had mentioned his ideas about defending his brigade's front to his estranged commander. General Bennett would not have approved.[9] Percival was later to write that Taylor's scheme of retirements was too difficult to implement in thick country at night, and that the only way to fight the battle was for the forward posts to hang on and wait for reserves to counter-attack to their relief.[10] But, in Taylor's view, Percival failed to 'realise the difference between theory and practice'. Taylor's dilemma was that his superiors had done nothing either to assemble reserves behind his brigade or prepare a reserve line. Once the brigade's posts were bypassed they could either retire to try and form a new line between the enemy and downtown Singapore, or remain in position to achieve little and disappear en masse. Taylor was experienced enough to realise that once bypassed his forward posts would tend to retire anyway, and that it would be wise to attempt to build those movements into a rational plan.[11]

Both the 5th and 18th Japanese Divisions were preparing to pile onto the 22nd Brigade. The 5th Division alone was going to strike the 2/20th Battalion. The placid waters of the Johore Strait was not much of a military obstacle, but it did at least stop the infantry of XXV Army from simply rising to their feet and charging forward simultaneously to swamp the Australians. The small motorized boats and barges that were carried down to the water's edge on the shoulders of Japanese troops could lift only 4000 men at a time with their equipment. Fifty small motor launches and a hundred collapsable launches had been allocated to each assaulting division. The engineers crewing the barges had the awful task before them of having to steer their craft into the teeth of the defenders' fire. But, though the initial assault wave would not appreciably outnumber the thin line of defenders, and faced the likelihood of heavy losses and possibly outright defeat, each succeeding wave of attackers carried across during the night would double, triple, and if all went to plan, quadruple the size of the force initially landed by dawn. The invaders planned to reach their first objective at Tengah aerodrome by the following morning.

From nightfall of 8 February onwards some Australians near the water's edge had been able to see the muzzle flashes of Japanese artillery hammering away on the mainland. As the bombardment lifted, the shaken defenders rose from their muddy, waterlogged weapon pits and braced themselves for the assault. Soon after 10.30 p.m. dark shapes emerged from the gloom on the water, and began to close with the Australians' side of the strait.

The defenders had arranged to call down artillery fire with flares and telephone messages. The preliminary bombardment had, however, severed most of the telephone lines running to the 22nd Brigade's companies. Cables in general had not been buried in the swamps, and a shortage of cable had made it difficult to double or triple the laying of particularly vital telephone links. The brigade's wireless sets had only returned from servicing that morning, and the smaller, less powerful battalion sets proved of little use, as had been the case throughout the campaign.[12] With lines cut and flares hard to see at the guns' positions, little supporting artillery fire arrived when the infantry tried to raise the alarm. It was later found that, of the 2/15th Field Regiment's seven troops, only two fired heavily on the night of 8/9 February, and two hardly fired at all. With only thirty guns behind the brigade, the artillery would not have had much impact along an eight mile front anyway.[13]

A handful of beach lights in Taylor's area, manned by British searchlight personnel, were not switched on during the assault. When later questioned, crewmen said no order had arrived to switch the lights on. Communications from the beach light positions back to battalion headquarters had been broken. But the idea that a handful of searchlights could have been profitably exposed in the face of the automatic weapons of a two division assault was always fanciful. A good deal of controversy was caused by gossipy claims that Taylor had ordered the lights not to be shown that night. Taylor, though sceptical of the practical use of beach lights, had clearly stated that the lights were a battalion responsibility, and that no brigade order was required to switch them on.[14]

On the brigade's right flank the 2/20th Battalion awaited the leading boats of the Japanese 5th Division. The battalion had three companies deployed along the strait to cover a front of 5000 yards: from left to right, C, D and A Companies, with B Company in reserve. A Dalforce company armed with a variety of weapons, and wearing headbands for identification, was placed amid mangrove swamp in support of the battalion's right flank. Further to the right, the swamps leading to the Sungei Kranji were left undefended as they were considered to be almost impassable.[15] In places across the battalion's front the swampy ground had made it difficult to dig trenches, so above ground weapon pits, protected by timber beams, had been built. The most obvious landing site in the battalion's area was where the east and west branches of the Lim Chu Kang Road ran north almost to the shore of the Johore Strait.

The darkness of the night of 8/9 February was broken by light from installations burning to the east. Japanese craft pulling towards the 2/20th Battalion were met by small arms fire. By an early stroke of luck for the defenders, a barge loaded with explosives caught fire. With the surrounding water lit up as it burned, machine guns ashore blasted nearby small craft. Few Japanese struggled ashore at that point. In a pattern that was to be repeated time and again along the brigade's front that night, however, Japanese landing craft shied away from strongly defended points. The absence of firing from some sectors quickly revealed the gaps in the defences, and the weight of the attack was such that some part of the assault force was bound to hit the gaps anyway. Barges trying to avoid the withering fire of Vickers machine guns soon found that a healthy gap lay between the battalion's centre D Company and right flank A Company.[16]

Coloured flares flew skyward to signal successful landings, and Japanese infantry pressed through the mangroves into the rubber and jungle, sensibly bypassing defended posts as much as possible. Many men had small compasses strapped to their wrists to aid navigation through the darkness. Ama Keng village burning far to the south served as a beacon for the advancing

Japanese. 'By midnight', wrote D Company's Captain R. J. D. Richardson, 'it was obvious that the Japs were getting ashore through the undefended sectors between the companies, and were pressing on our flanks.' At 1 a.m. Richardson ordered his company's forward posts to retreat to his head-quarters perimeter. Within the next half hour a platoon of the 2/4th Machine Gun Battalion, deployed near the end of Lim Chu Kang Road, also retired, having fired 10,000 rounds per gun and with little ammunition left.[17]

On the 2/20th Battalion's left flank, C Company had to defend a 2000 yard front. The gaps between platoons stretched for hundreds of yards. A search flare over the company area preceded the distant sound and shadowy approach of assault barges. Japanese mortars lobbed bombs onto the Aus-tralians from the island of Sarimbun in the strait. The vegetation was too thick for men to see and shoot beyond their immediate front. The Japanese had little trouble infiltrating along the Sungei Sarimbun, the boundary line between the 2/20th Battalion and its neighbouring battalion.

A patrol from the 2/20th Battalion's reserve B Company was sent into the gap between C and D Companies. The sight that greeted them was not a happy one. A sergeant recorded: 'There must have been a couple of batta-lions, landing craft were locked together and the men were jumping from barge to barge and forming up in company groups on the shore.' During the early hours of the morning the Australian forward companies struggled back towards battalion headquarters, which was situated a mile inland astride Lim Chu Kang road. G Troop of the 2/15th Field Regiment abandoned one of its guns bogged in the mud, but five other guns were hauled back to Tengah aerodrome.

On the battalion's right flank, A Company and the Dalforce Company had not been heavily engaged. But with the other forward companies retiring, orders were dispatched directing Major R. O. Merrett also to bring his troops back towards the battalion's headquarters perimeter. Nasty friendly fire incidents took place in the darkness when Australian troops saw armed Asians and started shooting at Dalforce men.[18]

The unit holding the vital central sector of the brigade's area, the 2/18th Battalion, had its C and A Companies deployed along the strait covering a two mile front. B Company was posted inland to guard a road at the junction with the unit beyond the battalion's left flank. D Company was in reserve. As the two forward companies had only two platoons each in forward locations, the battalion had just four rifle platoons covering the vital Johore Strait. The strait was the place at which the defenders had their best opportunity to kill large numbers of Japanese. The battalion's area was partly under rubber, but consisted mostly of scrub and mangroves amid which another man could be spotted only at the closest of ranges.

A Company, the battalion's right forward company, had its platoons located on rising ground that became a set of islands as the tide rose. When Japanese assault craft nosed out of the darkness, one platoon drove off an attack on its island by eighty Japanese, but was almost overrun by a second attack. In another post, Lieutenant Gordon Richardson's platoon was by-passed, but remained in position till the next day. C Company, the left forward company, had a 'wild complex of hills and inlets' to guard, and had been relying on artillery and mortar fire to help defend the frontage. As communication lines were cut there was no artillery support, and the Japanese tumbled ashore and rapidly infiltrated between the scattered posts. A machine gun platoon fought a lonely battle near the water's edge on a peninsula jutting out north of the mouth of the Sungei Murai.

The battalion's forward companies pulled back towards battalion head-quarters during the night. But by dawn only eighty-eight men from A and C Companies had reached the headquarters perimeter near Ama Keng. Major O'Brien's B Company had also been scattered as it withdrew from its station on the left flank. Many parties missed their way in the darkness and headed to the rear. Lieutenant-Colonel Varley was fortunate to have two hundred engineers on hand to flesh out his battalion perimeter.[19]

Further south on the brigade's left flank was the 2/19th Battalion. 8 Feb-ruary had started inauspiciously for the unit as its commander, Lieutenant-Colonel Anderson, had left for hospital in the morning suffering from a bout of dysentery. The newly promoted Lieutenant-Colonel A. E. Robertson, formerly a major in the 2/20th Battalion, was appointed by General Bennett to replace Anderson. Robertson was not acquainted with the terrain, and the extended front of undulating rubber, swamp and tangled undergrowth, pierced by a handful of tracks, did not lend itself to easy familiarization. The 2/19th Battalion's second-in-command, Major Oakes, also departed to take command of another unit soon after Robertson had arrived. Major Vincent, a proven soldier from the Bakri-Parit Sulong fighting, and Anderson's choice as his successor, had been overlooked by Bennett for promotion.

One of Lieutenant-Colonel Robertson's first decisions was to relocate the battalion's headquarters as its present situation was subject to frequent bombing and shell fire. Major Vincent did not agree with the decision to relocate. The headquarters position was the likely site of the battalion's final perimeter. Whereas the original headquarters site was on a rise with some fields of fire to the west, the proposed new location was dominated by high ground, and was no longer astride the road that led to the rear.[20]

When the Japanese assault came that evening of 8/9 February the battalion had two companies deployed along the strait. The battalion's left flank

boundary was the Sungei Berih estuary, on the far side of which was the
44th Indian Brigade. The estuary was the most heavily defended sector on
the north-west coast. There was a machine gun platoon on either bank, and
A Company was near the head of the estuary at Choa Chu Kang village.
But the Sungei Berih was at the far southern limit of the Japanese landing
zone. Five or six barges which entered the estuary were driven off or sunk
by artillery, and a few Japanese who came ashore were mopped up.

Two or three dozen landing craft approached Major Keegan's B Company
on the battalion's right flank. Another ten dots emerged from the gloom
of the Johore side of the strait towards Major Vincent's left forward
D Company. As elsewhere on the brigade front, the red and white Verey
flares did not call down any defensive artillery fire, and the telephone lines
to the rear had been cut by Japanese shelling.[21] B Company, part of which
was entrenched in a grassed coconut plantation, held their ground, and
the first wave of barges was caught in a withering hail of fire. Likewise fire
from D Company to the left forced the first barges on their front to veer
away. But the Japanese overlapped Keegan's defenders. Barges motoring
into the Sungei Murai, a small inlet between the 2/19th Battalion and the
embattled 2/18th Battalion, found an undefended gap. Japanese troops
commenced landing beyond B Company's right flank, and later in the
night were seen heading inland towards Ama Keng.

By 3 a.m. Keegan had decided that his company should fall back to the
battalion perimeter. Part of Vincent's company was cut off by rapidly
infiltrating Japanese. All contact was lost with A Company at Choa Chu
Kang village. The battalion was full of new recruits after the heavy losses
on the mainland, and some sub-units lost all cohesion trying to manoeuvre
in the darkness. For troops caught behind advancing waves of Japanese a
frightening game of hide and seek ensued. Keegan reached the battalion
perimeter and the reserve company, but most of his men lost their way and
scattered rearwards.

South of Taylor's brigade, overnight the 44th Indian Brigade had suffered
light shelling into its right-hand battalion area. Two hours of furious firing
had been heard further north, but little useful information had been received
at brigade headquarters. After dawn a hundred or so bedraggled Australians,
some without arms or equipment, were collected and put in lorries. Later
Japanese dive-bombers struck the battery of naval guns at Pasir Laba on the
south-west coast and put them out of action.[22]

By daylight of 9 February the disorganized remnants of the 22nd Brigade
had been swept off the strait. Taylor had spoken to Bennett during the
night, and Bennett had agreed to send his divisional reserve to the brigade's

assistance. A company of the 2/4th Machine Gun Battalion, the 2/29th Battalion and the Special Reserve Battalion were transferred to Taylor's command. (The Special Reserve Battalion comprised two companies of Army Service Corps personnel, and a company of the 2/4th Machine Gun Battalion's reinforcements – 450 officers and men in total.) Taylor's plan to form a defensive line from the Sungei Berih to Ama Keng village had had to be shelved as few parties from his forward battalions had arrived there by dawn. Taylor moved his headquarters from near Ama Keng to Bulim, behind Tengah aerodrome, after firing was heard nearby. A patchy Australian front was gradually stitched together across the aerodrome.

Lieutenant-Colonel Varley's 2/18th Battalion perimeter was able to fight its way back from near Ama Keng to Tengah aerodrome during the morning. The 2/10th Field Company played an important rearguard role. At Tengah the battalion could only muster seventeen officers and 318 men, well down from the thirty-seven officers and 826 men present the previous day.[23]

Further north a steady stream of Japanese had been passing inland around the western side of the 2/20th Battalion's perimeter. The battalion's transport was loaded up with the wounded and sent down the road towards Ama Keng. Some vehicles burst through heavily manned Japanese road-blocks, but many did not. Wrecked lorries littered the roadside. Those who fell into Japanese hands alive were shot or hacked to death. At 9.15 a.m. Lieutenant-Colonel C. F. Assheton ordered a general retreat through the swamps of the Sungei Kranji, and its feeder tributaries, in a bid to regain friendly lines. Assheton was killed by a burst of machine gun fire in a clash with Japanese north of Tengah aerodrome. The nature of the terrain, and a series of violent encounters, broke the battalion into small groups.[24]

At the southern end of the brigade's sector, the 2/19th Battalion was no more fortunate. During the night, as had been fearfully foreseen by some members of the unit the previous day, Japanese troops had occupied a ridge across the line of retreat from the battalion's perimeter. An attack towards the ridge failed and several carriers were wrecked in an attempt to break out. Lieutenant-Colonel Robertson ordered his battalion to abandon their transport and heavy equipment, and disperse southwards into the swamps fringing the Sungei Berih. Parties headed off in all directions. Only A Company and an attached machine gun platoon were able to withdraw intact from Choa Chu Kang village to join Taylor at Tengah aerodrome.[25]

The Australians coming out of action on the morning of 9 February were not a pretty sight. Covered in soot hanging in the air from the burning oil, and mud from the swamps through which they had passed, many were only partly dressed, and some were without arms.[26] Given the Australians' reputation, and customary bravado, signs of panic and demoralization evident amongst small parties and individuals were noted by bystanders with dismay. As the 2/29th Battalion had moved up earlier that morning, Lieutenant-Colonel Pond had been 'embarrassed' by troops moving back in the other direction. 'These troops were quite out of control and leaderless and stated they had had enough.' [27]

In addition to Lieutenant-Colonel Varley's men, a number of groups of Australians were collected and reorganized at Tengah behind the new firing line, but most of the scattered remnants of the 22nd Brigade's units had to be rounded up all over Western Area. [28] In France in the First World War, the zone behind an active battlefield had been packed with military police to detain and redirect soldiers drifting away from the fight, but there was not that level of foresight at Singapore. 'It was subsequently learned from the Provost Marshal at Singapore', reported Lieutenant-Colonel Thyer, 'that although there were many troops seeking safety and means of escape, the bulk of the men were stragglers who had come back looking for food and rest.' [29] Australians were collected at Bukit Timah village and other places, and sent back to the AIF General Base Depot. By the end of the day seven hundred men of the brigade had been assembled at the base depot. But not all stragglers were collected. Hundreds of infantrymen who were not casualties remained missing. [30]

On the morning of 9 February, General Bennett did not come forward from Western Area headquarters to see for himself what had happened to the 22nd Brigade. Instead at 9.30 a.m. Bennett had sent Taylor an order to counter-attack and recapture Ama Keng. Taylor disregarded the instruction as it was obviously impractical. Taylor then decided to withdraw his line a short distance from Tengah aerodrome to a point in front of Bulim village.

There was not a lot of Japanese activity evident on the front of their bridgehead on north-west Singapore during the latter part of the morning of 9 February. A carrier platoon sprayed with machine gun fire a Japanese company at Tengah aerodrome, but in general the invaders were busy consolidating their bridgehead. General Percival later estimated that 13,000 Japanese troops had landed during the night, and that another 10,000 had landed just before dawn to bring the total to 23,000. The industrious Japanese engineers may have been able to ferry across half that number during the night, but it is likely that it took the whole of 9 February, and much of the following night, to complete the transfer of the 5th and 18th Divisions' infantry to Singapore Island. Hence there was a twenty-four hour pause in Japanese operations in the north-west corner of the island between the mornings of 9 and 10 February. This was a vital period during which Malaya Command needed to react decisively to the landings. The manner in which Percival and his operations staff chose to respond to Yamashita's bold stroke against the 22nd Brigade's sector would greatly affect the future course of the battle for Singapore.

At 8.30 a.m. on 9 February Percival, after he had received reports that all was quiet in Northern Area, released his reserve brigade to Bennett's command. However the 12th Indian Brigade was an under strength formation that had hardly begun to recover from the pummelling it had received up-country at Slim River. The brigade had been placed in Malaya Command reserve precisely as it was the formation least fit to defend a vital coastal sector. The 5/2nd Punjabis were still not ready for combat and had not rejoined the brigade. The Hyderabads and the Argylls comprised less than nine hundred officers and men. The brigade did not have a supporting artillery regiment.[31]

At this early stage of the battle for Singapore General Percival was not prepared to shift troops away from the north-east and southern coasts. He still believed that fresh landings on other parts of the island were imminent, and was quite unaware that the bulk of XXV Army was already at or about to step ashore on the north-west corner of Singapore. Troops that might have been used to counter-attack the Japanese bridgehead continued to stand idle. Percival's greatly exaggerated estimate of the size of Yamashita's force was the main reason why he believed the Japanese had the ability to make multiple landings.[32] Reports of Japanese shipping gathered at the Anambas Islands off Johore's east coast continued to prey on Percival's mind.[33]

At 1.30 p.m. on 9 February Brigadier Paris arrived at the 22nd Brigade's headquarters, 'with a fine Irish setter on leash', to see how his 12th Indian Brigade could be of assistance. Taylor asked Paris to take up a position astride Choa Chu Kang Road, in support of the northern flank of his brigade.[34] About mid-afternoon Taylor telephoned Bennett.

> I informed the GOC by phone of what I had done, and was told that I had acted without orders, that what I had done was quite wrong, and that all I could think of was withdrawing.[35]

During the afternoon Percival visited Bennett's Western Area headquarters and agreed to dispatch Northern Area's reserve, the 15th Indian Brigade, to help build up a force to hold the so-called Jurong Line, the gap between the headwaters of the Kranji and Jurong Rivers. The Jurong Line was the only defensible natural switch line in the western half of Singapore Island. Percival also ordered the demolition of the oil tanks near the Causeway that night. The 44th Brigade was instructed to withdraw immediately to the southern end of the Jurong Line. Brigadier Ballentine, with his brigade's right flank exposed by the 22nd Brigade's rout, had been anxiously awaiting orders since daylight. Four brigades – the 22nd Australian, and 12th, 15th and 44th Indian – seemed sufficient on paper to defend the three mile Jurong Line. Bennett ordered the 15th Brigade to move forward into the Jurong Line as a misleading report had implied that the 44th Brigade was in danger of being cut off. In consequence the 44th Brigade, which had reached the Jurong Line by 10 p.m., had to shuffle southwards in the dark to make way for the 15th Brigade. During the evening Brigadier Taylor received orders to deny Bulim until 6 a.m. on 10 February, and then retire to take over the central sector of the Jurong Line.

For General Yamashita the opening night and day of the assault on Singapore Island had been a great success. A lodgement had been made on the north-west corner of the island. The Imperial Guards' attack on Singapore Island between the Sungei Kranji and the Causeway was due to take place on the evening of 9 February. The Imperial Guards' orders after landing were to swing south east to block the route between Singapore town and Changi.

Between the mouth of the Sungei Kranji and the Causeway, Brigadier Maxwell's 27th Australian Brigade was deployed on only a quarter of the frontage the 22nd Brigade had held the previous night. Maxwell's reserve unit, the 2/29th Battalion, had already been sent away to the aid of the 22nd Brigade. That morning, 9 February, Bennett's GSO 2, Major C. B. Dawkins, had assured Malaya Command that the situation was secure in the 27th Brigade's area. 'No orders had been issued to withdraw from Kranji and no such orders were going to be issued.' [36] The Sungei Kranji and its bordering swamps stretched inland for at least three miles. Thus the calamitous events that had taken place in Taylor's sector had had no immediate impact upon the 27th Brigade.

Brigadier Maxwell's headquarters was situated seven miles behind his battalions, near Bennett's Western Area headquarters. Maxwell, echoing behaviour he had exhibited on the mainland, became decidedly nervous about his left flank after he realised that the Japanese had punched Taylor's brigade inland. At 11 a.m. Maxwell requested permission to withdraw his left-hand unit, the 2/26th Battalion, from the Johore Strait to face westward. Bennett would only permit Maxwell to turn the left flank of the battalion to face the swamps of the Sungei Kranji. Around midday Maxwell again contacted Bennett's headquarters, and requested that he be allowed to withdraw both his battalions from the strait, and realign them to face west along the north-south running Woodlands Road. Bennett did not give his assent to this request, but from that point onwards Maxwell took matters into his own hands.[37]

During the afternoon Maxwell called the commanders of both his remaining units, the 2/26th and 2/30th Battalions, to a conference. The 2/26th Battalion's commander until that morning had been Lieutenat-Colonel A. H. Boyes, but Maxwell had ordered Boyes to report to AIF General Base Depot. Boyes told his assembled company commanders before departing that he had been selected to coordinate rear defences. Maxwell later said of Boyes that he 'had not been a satisfactory Battalion commander', despite the battalion's fine performance on the mainland.[38] The battalion's new commander, Lieutenant-Colonel Oakes, had only left another unit the previous day.

At the brigade conference Maxwell promptly ordered the 2/30th Battalion's Lieutenant-Colonel Galleghan to hospital as he was suffering hearing difficulties. Maxwell then took it upon himself to issue orders for his battalions to prepare to retire from the Johore Strait during the coming night. The right flank 2/30th Battalion was to pull south from the strait to a position forward of Bukit Mandai, whilst the left flank 2/26th Battalion extended the line southwards parallel to Woodlands Road. This proposed move threatened to expose the left flank of the brigade's neighbouring 11th Indian Division. Maxwell was later to claim, that so far as the 11th Division was concerned, he expected that its left-hand battalion would have to turn its left flank, but otherwise would not be affected. Maxwell had no idea that the Japanese Imperial Guards were planning to attack his brigade that evening.

With Galleghan packed off to hospital, Lieutenant R. W. Eaton, the 2/30th Battalion's intelligence officer, returned to his unit with Maxwell's orders. The battalion's new commander, Major G. E. Ramsay, was not happy at the prospect of abandoning his battalion's compact position near the Causeway. The Australians were dug into firm ground with good fields of fire. Lieutenant-Colonel Oakes of the 2/26th Battalion was ordered by Maxwell to coordinate the withdrawal of the two battalions overnight. Oakes was still unfamiliar with the brigade's sector, but he was required to undertake this task as he was senior to Major Ramsay, and Maxwell, though both his units had new commanders, continued to stay at his headquarters far to the rear.[39]

In the evening, around 9 p.m., Brigadier Maxwell visited nearby Western Area headquarters at Hillview estate. Bennett was absent and Maxwell spoke to Lieutenant-Colonel Thyer. Thyer later recalled that a very tired Maxwell had told him that

> he was a doctor in civil life and his function was to save life. Maxwell considered that what was going on on Singapore Island after the Japanese landings was senseless slaughter. Maxwell was going back to Percival to urge him to surrender.

Thyer advised Maxwell to talk to Bennett before doing anything rash.[40] Yet it is likely that Maxwell spoke to Percival later that night.[41] Whatever exactly happened that day and evening, Maxwell was finished as a commander.

As night of 9/10 February approached, Japanese artillery fire falling on the 27th Brigade increased in intensity. On the left flank of the brigade front, the 2/26th Battalion was in position behind a belt of mangroves. The mangroves had considerable depth, except at the seafront of Kranji village. Australian outposts in the mangroves kept watch on the strait.

The Japanese bombardment lifted about 8.30 p.m., and within half an hour motor barges and launches surged out of the gloom. The Imperial Guards' opening assault wave was a battalion of the 4th Guards Regiment. There was little defending artillery fire when SOS flares were shot skywards. As had been the case the previous night, the beach lights failed to make an impact. Most of the barges headed towards the 2/26th Battalion's front. The battery supporting the battalion had been ordered to pull back to a new position after dark, presumedly by Western Area headquarters, and was out of action during a critical period of the initial assault. The main Japanese landing was on the seafront of Kranji village, and straight into the teeth of the battalion's forward companies. Hand-to-hand fighting took place in the swamps, and the Japanese assault was held at the main defence line five hundred yards inland.

In the brigade's right-hand sector, near the Causeway, fire-fights broke out between men of the 2/30th Battalion and the invaders. Small groups of Japanese struggled ashore near the mouths of the streams between which the oil tanks were situated. Barges that neared the Causeway were driven off without landing. The Australians, dug in on rising ground behind the road leading to the Causeway, swept the mudflats below with machine gun fire. Shouts and screams were heard out in the darkness.

At midnight of 9/10 February communications between Brigadier Maxwell's headquarters and Lieutenant-Colonel Oakes's 2/26th Battalion were temporarily re-established. Maxwell took the opportunity to order the implementation of the withdrawal plan he had discussed with Oakes the previous afternoon. First though the Woodlands oil depot's two million gallons of fuel had to be destroyed. Lieutenant A. B. Watchorn's section of sappers arrived to carry out the task, only for a shell to set on fire the lorry carrying their explosives and equipment. The valves on the oil tanks were opened to let the oil flow down into the strait. The oil soon caught fire further to inconvenience nearby Japanese troops hugging the shore. Later Watchorn returned with more explosives to finish the job.

During the early hours of the morning of 10 February Oakes issued orders for a withdrawal.[42] In the darkness Oakes led the two Australian battalions further to the rear than Maxwell had intended. Maxwell later conceded:

'This delegation of authority [to Oakes] was again an error of judgement. I suppose I did it because I am a doctor in civil life and did not know enough of soldiering.' The 2/30th Battalion retired to a new position behind Mandai Road, roughly three miles inland from the Johore Strait. The 2/26th Battalion deployed southwards along Woodlands Road. Maxwell and his brigade-major later claimed that Western Area headquarters undertook to pass on word of their brigade's retreat to the neighbouring 11th Indian Division. But General Bennett and Lieutenant-Colonel Thyer always denied any prior knowledge of Maxwell's retirement.[43]

Despite the confusion that beset the ranks of the defenders, the Japanese assault on the brigade had come very close to failure. A report sent back to the Imperial Guards' headquarters during the night alleged that the enemy had flooded the Johore Strait with burning petroleum. The leading wave of troops was being annihilated in a sea of flames. This report was forwarded to XXV Army headquarters, now located north of Tengah aerodrome. According to Lieutenant-Colonel Tsuji, Yamashita was breakfasting on dry bread in a tent when the news arrived. On the strength of that one report, General Nishimura, a pre war rival of Yamashita's, requested permission to break off the attack. Yamashita however refused to be panicked, and called for further reports on the progress of the battle prior to making a decision. The information upon which Nishimura was basing his request proved to be greatly exaggerated. Nishimura agreed to continue the assault when he realised the mistake.[44]

That night, 9/10 February, General Percival had another opportunity to review the course of the battle for Singapore. Yet he was still satisfied that the dispatch of the 12th and 15th Indian Brigades to Western Area was sufficient reinforcement to ensure the holding of the Jurong Line. Not a single formation was withdrawn from the north-east or southern coasts. Instead Percival spoke to Generals Heath and Simmons about a provisional plan for an inner perimeter. At 12.50 a.m. on 10 February Percival issued a plan for an inner defensive ring around Singapore town that was to include Kallang aerodrome, MacRitchie and Peirce reservoirs, and Bukit Timah village. The plan was included in an instruction to Bennett, Heath and Simmons. There was nothing wrong with a staff officer making prudent provisional plans for likely future troop movements, including possible retreats. But Percival was first and foremost a commander, and it was not his place to be spreading defeatist instructions at such a crucial moment. A different man would have been planning the organization of a strong counter-attack to drive the Japanese back into Johore Strait.

# 15

# *Bukit Timah*

At daylight on 10 February, the second full day of the battle for Singapore, great clouds of oil smoke bellowed skywards from the burning depot on the island's north coast. In the north-west corner of Singapore the Japanese 5th and 18th Divisions were still strangely quiet. That morning the Imperial Guards Division, freshly landed near the Causeway, posed the most immediate threat to Singapore's defenders.

The 11th Indian Division's left flank had been exposed by the 27th Australian Brigade's mysterious withdrawal from the Causeway sector. The only warning received was a pencilled note that was sent by runner to the Gurkha unit adjoining the Australians' right flank. A Gurkha patrol was sent out to confirm that the Australians had indeed vanished. A number of casualties were lost when a detachment was dispatched further to probe the now vacant sector beyond the division's left flank. Brigadier Maxwell later claimed that his brigade's withdrawal did not alter the subsequent result of the battle at Singapore by so much as five minutes. But all of the 11th Division's problems on 10 February were the direct result of Maxwell's actions.

News of the successful Japanese landing at Kranji did not reach Bennett's Western Area headquarters until 5 a.m., 10 February. Shortly after, a report of the 27th Brigade's unexpected retreat also arrived. By 6.30 a.m. this news had been belatedly relayed through Malaya Command to the headquarters of Major-General Key's 11th Division. Key requested of Western Area that the 27th Brigade reoccupy its original position, but he was told this was not possible. Key directed his reserve, the 8th Indian Brigade, to recapture some of the high ground south of the Australians' original position along the strait. Key was the only British divisional commander at Singapore fortunate enough to have a brigade-sized reserve.

Later that morning, as the 8th Brigade advanced, patchy fighting developed across the hilly features of a series of plantation estates. Some of the Indians' objectives were taken without heavy loss, but opposition was fierce in places. The stiffest fighting befell the seven hundred strong Garhwal Rifles composite battalion, comprising the remnants of the regiment's 2nd and 5th Battalions and a liberal addition of newly arrived recruits. The Garhwalis were crossing a large clearing towards a rubber estate when they were fired on from all sides. Pinned down, casualties mounted. Lieutenant-Colonel Smith was wounded in the knee. He died in an ambush whilst being driven to the rear in a carrier. Six of the Garhwalis' British officers were killed in the engagement. As the day wore on the troops furthest forward withdrew or drifted back towards a feature on which a reserve company had been posted. The senior officer present reorganized the battalion.[1] To the south west of the 8th Brigade's units, the 27th Brigade's two Australian battalions had little contact with the Japanese during 10 February.[2]

Percival's Malaya Command Operation Instruction No. 40, the chief product of the general's overnight musing, had been distributed by the morning of 10 February. The instruction stated:

> Should it be impossible to hold the enemy on the line mentioned in paragraph 2 above [roughly those positions currently being held], GOC Malaya intends to withdraw to an inner position on which the final battle for Singapore will be fought ... Recces of Areas will be carried out at once and the plans for the movement of formations into the areas allotted to them will be prepared.[3]

At 7.30 a.m. Bennett had details of Percival's provisional plan sent out to his subordinate commanders. This had not been Percival's intention, but Bennett had not had the benefit of the verbal discussion of the plan that Percival had had with his other area commanders, Generals Heath and Simmons. Nor was Bennett familiar with the rather Byzantine piece of staff ritual whereby, as subsequently explained by Percival, an instruction marked 'Secret and Personal' was not for distribution beyond the recipient. As Percival's provisional plan required a reconnaissance of the sectors to be occupied in the final perimeter, and as such reconnaissance was best carried out by those formations concerned, it was not altogether surprising that Bennett had details of the plan sent to his subordinates as a preliminary warning.

In Bennett's Western Area, after dawn on 10 February, Taylor's 22nd Brigade retired a short distance to fill a gap in the notional Jurong Line between the 12th and 15th Brigades. To the south of the 15th Brigade, the 44th Brigade prolonged the line to the headwaters of the Jurong River. In theory the four brigades filling the Jurong Line, barely more than three miles across, was a considerable force.

At 9 a.m. an exhausted Taylor received from Bennett news of Percival's instruction concerning a final inner perimeter. By 10 a.m. Taylor had issued a brigade plan based on his misunderstanding that Percival's instructions would soon be put into effect. Taylor went to reconnoitre his brigade's

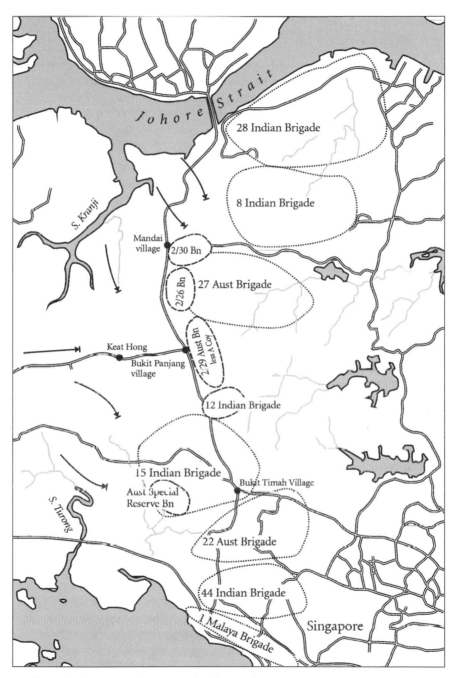

15. Strategic Position, Singapore Island, 10 February 1942.

sector in the proposed final perimeter near Reformatory Road. Taylor called
at Western Area headquarters on the way. According to Taylor:

> I saw the GOC [Bennett], who asked me why I had not reported to him before.
> I pointed out that under the circumstances I considered my place was with my
> Brigade and not at Divisional Headquarters. He then made some disparaging
> remarks in relation to my handling of the situation and about the Brigade. He
> stated that it was not his intention that the order I had received should be put
> into operation forthwith, but only under certain circumstances.[4]

Nonetheless Taylor carried on with his reconnaissance, and his brigade's
reserve – five hundred men of the 2/18th Battalion and Merrett Force (the
remnants of the 2/19th and 2/20th Battalions) – retired to Reformatory Road
later in the morning. Taylor's units still holding the front line were thus
deprived of the presence of their brigadier and supporting troops during a
vital period.

Meanwhile, at the northern end of the Jurong Line, near the headwaters
of the Kranji River, the 12th Indian Brigade was sitting astride Choa Chu
Kang Road. The 22nd Brigade's 2/29th Battalion continued the line southwards, though one of its companies and the unit's commander had become
detached during the retirement from Bulim earlier that morning. By 8 a.m.
on 10 February Japanese troops were starting to probe past the 12th Brigade's
northern flank, and the force withdrew a thousand yards behind a stream
running in front of Keat Hong village. The officer in command of the nearby
companies of the 2/29th Battalion, Major F. Hore, agreed to cooperate with
Paris's 12th Brigade. Hore shuffled his unit across to become the brigade's
lead unit on Choa Chu Kang Road.

Brigadier Paris had sent patrols beyond his brigade's right flank into what
was supposed to be the 27th Brigade's sector leading towards the Causeway.
The patrols found no Australians, and reported that Woodlands Road was
unoccupied northwards to at least Mandai village. On his own initiative Paris
withdrew the Argylls and the 2/29th Battalion to Bukit Panjang village, at
the junction of Choa Chu Kang and Woodlands Roads. Paris was worried
that a Japanese thrust south down Woodlands Road might fall upon the rear
of his brigade. These moves had been completed by early afternoon. The
Hyderabads were posted between Keat Hong and Bukit Panjang. Paris had no
authority to retire from the Jurong Line, but Paris's formation had had its
own flank endangered by the 27th Brigade's unauthorized retreat of the previous night. Each withdrawal left a neighbouring unit's flank exposed. In light
of Percival's and Bennett's failure to provide strong leadership, subordinate
brigade and battalion commanders were decidedly nervous, and reluctant
to hang on in vulnerable positions once a front had begun to crumble.

Worse was to come for the defending army. By early morning of 10 February, at the southern end of the Jurong Line, the 15th and 44th Brigades had settled in either side of Jurong Road. The ground was broken and visibility badly restricted. Brigadiers J. B. Coates and Ballentine had received Bennett's instructions regarding Percival's final perimeter about 10.30 a.m. Ballentine informed his unit commanders of the instructions, and later recounted:

> I am quite sure this order from the GOC-in-C had a psychological effect on me and, although I gave an edited version to them, on my Battalion Commanders as well. It was, I think, bound to do so especially when one considers the many precedents of withdrawal we had heard of and the one we had just participated in [away from the coast of Singapore Island]. I had never looked over either shoulder before but I think I did then. Certainly I found it unsettling.[5]

The next withdrawal, if required, would be along tracks leading south east towards the West Coast Road and Pasir Panjang village.

At 1.30 p.m. the Japanese began to advance down Jurong Road, albeit in no great strength. The right-hand company of the unit astride the road, the 44th Brigade's 6/1st Punjabis, was compelled to pull back a short distance, as also were some men and transport of the 15th Brigade's British Battalion, positioned to the immediate north of Jurong Road. Subsequently the Punjabis wrongly reported to the 44th Brigade's headquarters that units to their right were heading rearwards.[6] When Brigadier Ballentine discovered that the 15th Brigade seemed to be pulling out, he ordered a retreat for fear of being outflanked. The 44th Brigade, in accordance with their role in Percival's provisional plan for a final perimeter, fell back several miles and reached Pasir Panjang village late in the afternoon. The Indians rested in the shade of trees outside Pasir Panjang, whilst Ballentine rang General Simmons at Southern Area headquarters. Simmons told Ballentine to take up a position in the vicinity of Reformatory Road. With night falling the Indians advanced back up Reformatory Road towards its junction with Ulu Pandan Road.[7]

After the 44th Brigade had retreated, Coates's 15th Brigade was left with their flank exposed. Coates ordered his brigade to pull back eastwards along Jurong Road to milestone 9. The brigade was now only two miles from Bukit Timah village. Major A. E. Saggers's Special Reserve Battalion of the 22nd Brigade, still in position in the central sector of the Jurong Line, soon found itself isolated on both flanks, and retired during the afternoon. Saggers's men reached the 15th Brigade, and extended that brigade's line to the south of Jurong Road. The 1st Malaya Brigade stepped back along the south coast to conform with the 44th Brigade's movements. The entire Jurong Line had now been abandoned; not due to Japanese action, but mostly because a succession of confused and anxious subordinate commanders had fallen back of their own volition.

That morning of 10 February, well to the rear, Percival, accompanied by General Wavell, who had just flown into Singapore from Java, drove to visit Bennett. Percival later wrote:

> Gordon Bennett was not quite so confident as he had been up country. He had always been very certain that his Australians would never let the Japanese through and the penetration of his defences had upset him.[8]

Soon after the generals arrived at Western Area headquarters the building, a large house on a rise next to Holland Road, was straddled by a stick of bombs from a Japanese aircraft. The tell-tale collection of staff cars clustered at the top of the driveway had doubtless helped alert Japanese airmen to the importance of the target. The generals emerged unhurt from the floor of their conference room, covered with fallen plaster and dust.

Generals Percival and Wavell left Bennett to visit Generals Heath and Key. When told the full story of the 27th Brigade's decampment, Percival decided to put the formation under Key's command. With the road running south from the Causeway so vulnerable, Percival also finally ordered the creation of a reserve brigade comprising units of the 18th Division. The brigade was to assemble at the Racecourse and come under the command of Western Area. These were the first troops from coastal brigade sectors in either Northern or Southern Area to be sent to the aid of formations fighting in the western half of the island.

Early in the afternoon, Percival and Wavell returned to see Bennett. They were informed that much of the Jurong Line had been lost. Wavell insisted that it be retaken, and Percival, who was rather more capable of decisive action with Wavell at his elbow, ordered Bennett to counter-attack. That night Wavell fell from a sea wall onto rocks and wire as he was preparing to board an aircraft and leave Singapore. Wavell broke two small bones in his back, and after a few days in hospital was something of an invalid for weeks to come.

Wavell left Singapore 'without much confidence in any prolonged resistance', and issued a strongly worded order of the day before departing. The order was based on a forceful cable that Churchill had sent to Wavell. Churchill had complained that Singapore's garrison must greatly outnumber the Japanese on the island,

> and in a well-contested battle they should destroy them. There must at this stage be no thought of sparing the troops or population ... Commanders and Senior

Officers should die with their troops. The honour of the British Empire and of the British Army is at stake.

Wavell's order of the day was not well received by the garrison, nor was Percival's covering note to senior officers, which included the words:

In some units the troops have not shown the fighting spirit which is to be expected of men of the British Empire. It will be a lasting disgrace if we are defeated by an army of clever gangsters many times inferior in numbers to our men.[9]

Late in the afternoon of 10 February Bennett's headquarters issued orders for a counter-attack by the 12th, 15th, and 22nd Brigades to retake the Jurong Line. The troops were to take their objectives with a three stage advance: the first stage that evening, the second stage at dawn the next day, and the third stage later in the day. The 44th Brigade and the 18th Division's 'Tomforce' Brigade – named after its commander, Lieutenant-Colonel L. C. Thomas – were to stay in reserve. By this time the 12th, 15th, and 22nd Brigades had only 4000 infantry between them (1300, 1100 and 1500 respectively), and little organized artillery support. The Japanese force slowly but steadily moving into the gap between the headwaters of the Kranji and Jurong Rivers was considerably stronger.

After receiving orders for the counter-attack, Coates's 15th Brigade only needed to shuffle forward slightly to take their first objective. To the south of the 15th Brigade, the 22nd Brigade was faced with a long and difficult night advance from Reformatory Road to reach their first objective. Brigadier Taylor instructed X Battalion to occupy a point just south of milestone 9½ on Jurong Road. Merrett Force was ordered to advance into Sleepy Valley, a mile south of milestone 10. There was no reasonable opportunity for reconnaissance. The 2/18th Battalion and a detachment of the 2/4th Machine Gun Battalion remained in reserve near Reformatory Road.[10]

X Battalion had been assembled from 22nd Brigade men sent to the General Base Depot for re-equipping, and stragglers rounded up at many places between the north-west coast and Singapore town after the disastrous fighting of 8/9 February. As the headquarters of the 2/19th and 2/20th Battalions had been destroyed, there had been no formed unit to which men of those battalions could be returned. On the other hand, stragglers from the 2/18th Battalion could have been returned to Varley's command. Lieutenant-Colonel Boyes had been given command of X Battalion. There were 550 fit 22nd Brigade men available at the General Base Depot at 8 a.m. on 10 February, including twenty-seven officers.[11]

General Yamashita, however, had schemes of his own for the night of 10/11 February. With the bulk of XXV Army's infantry transported across the strait, Yamashita's plan was to seize the vital heights of Bukit Timah by dawn of 11 February, a special day for Japan known as *Kigensetsu*, as it was the anniversary of the accession of the first Emperor and the founding of the Japanese Empire. If the Japanese could secure Bukit Timah the defending garrison would be forced to abandon a large part of Singapore's reservoir catchment area, and much of the garrison's fuel, food and munitions. Almost a million civilians were huddling under a pall of oil smoke, amid the bomb-damaged houses and streets of Singapore Town. As artillery ammunition was in short supply, XXV Army was to attack by night with the bayonet. Its 5th Division was to advance east along Choa Chu Kang Road. The 18th Division was to simultaneously advance down Jurong Road.[12]

Astride Choa Chu Kang Road the 12th Brigade's Hyderabads came under heavy mortar fire and infantry assault shortly after dusk. The battalion rapidly faded away. Out of the darkness Japanese infantry, with tanks close behind, moved towards the 2/29th Battalion. In confused fighting two or three tanks may have been disabled, but the battalion soon pulled back to high ground 150 yards east of Bukit Panjang and Woodlands Road. The Australians withdrew down the pipeline to the Racecourse later in the night.[13]

With the cross-roads at Bukit Panjang now in their possession, Japanese tanks and infantry pushed on southwards down Woodlands Road until they reached a couple of road-blocks hastily erected by the Argylls. The leading tank was hit by gunfire but there were fifty more tanks behind. The road blocks were brushed aside. Japanese troops entered Bukit Timah village around midnight. Inexplicably Japanese tanks did not further exploit the gap they had punched in Western Area's defences, and halted at Bukit Timah.[14]

Whilst the 12th Brigade was being dispersed, X Battalion advanced into the darkness, so black at times that men had to hang onto the scabbard of the man in front to maintain direction. Jurong Road was reached after a cross-country march. Bukit Timah village was in flames in the distance. The battalion passed through the 15th Brigade, and Lieutenant-Colonel Boyes paused to confer with Major Saggers of the Special Reserve Battalion. A patrol sent on ahead found dead Indians strewn over a wide area. The advance into hostile territory was resumed with flares floating in the sky ahead. Vehicles by the roadside still smouldered, and occasional movement was detected in the surrounding scrub.

By 1 a.m. of 11 February, after travelling a short distance along a track leading south from Jurong Road, X Battalion had reached their allotted position. Close company perimeters were established. Every second man was to remain awake, but many were soon fast asleep. Battalion headquarters was located perilously close to a dump of fuel drums. Fires glowed in the distance. Boyes was not pleased by his unit's exposed location, and he warned Captain Richardson that disaster might lie ahead.[15]

Around 3.00 a.m. a report arrived at A Company's headquarters of suspicious movement out in the scrub. Soon after, shouting and shooting erupted. Incoming fire ignited the petrol near Boyes's headquarters. Exploding drums leapt high into the air. The perimeter was lit up, clearly silhouetting men to Japanese soldiers gathered in the surrounding vegetation. Heavy rifle and machine gun fire, and showers of grenades and mortar bombs, rained onto the battalion out of the darkness. Boyes was killed at an early stage. A strong party of enterprising Japanese quickly cut a passage into the heart of the Australians' perimeter. After an intense period of hand to hand combat the battle rapidly turned into a rout. Major Keegan was among the dead. In total, somewhere between 120 and 150 officers and men of X Battalion were killed that night.

Several semi-organized parties of Australians regained friendly lines, as did numerous other individuals and small groups of men. Only a handful of prisoners were taken by the triumphant Japanese. Australians scattered in all directions to reach the West Coast Road or Reformatory Road at a variety of points. Captain Richardson's party marched on a compass bearing towards the south coast. The party's wounded were packed off to hospital in transport, and the rest proceeded into town. After crossing Anderson Bridge a divisional car pulled up. A staff major accused them of being deserters, and threatened to have them arrested. Richardson intervened to explain the situation before someone did the major an injury.[16]

The better part of a mile to the south of X Battalion's last stand, the two hundred men of Merrett Force (mainly from the 2/19th and 2/20th Battalions) had formed a perimeter for the night in Sleepy Valley. In the distance tracer could be seen and firing heard, though Major Merrett's men did not know what the commotion was about. At dawn Japanese were on high ground around the perimeter, and the Australians came under machine gun fire. Merrett ordered his force to retreat to Reformatory Road. Split into two groups by skirmishing, Merrett Force lost fifty casualties fighting its way to safety. They were fortunate to escape the annihilation that befell X Battalion.[17] For the second time at Singapore, isolated 22nd Brigade units had been smashed in battle with XXV Army's main thrust.

During the night of 10/11 February, after X Battalion's rout, troops of the Japanese 18th Division probed the 15th Brigade. Brigadier Coates cancelled the attack planned for daylight, but the order did not reach Lieutenant-Colonel Cumming's composite Jat battalion. The Jats advanced on schedule and were cut off behind Japanese lines.[18]

About 6 a.m. the 15th Brigade's headquarters was attacked from the rear by Japanese who had reached Bukit Timah. Coates's brigade-major was mortally wounded, and the brigade staff took refuge with the British Battalion. Fighting was still in progress in front of the brigade, and at 7.30 a.m. Coates ordered a withdrawal across country to Reformatory Road. The brigade, organized into three columns comprising the British Battalion, the Special Reserve Battalion, and the 3/16th Punjab and other Indian detachments, set out at 9.30 a.m. After traversing a mile through a terrain of small hills, grassland, scrub and rubber, the brigade was ambushed crossing a saucer-shaped depression in Sleepy Valley. Rifle, machine gun and mortar fire from the flanks and front caused great confusion and panic.[19] Machine guns sited amongst huts blocking the brigade's path had to be attacked and cleared at considerable cost. The brigade was broken up into a number of groups, some of which reached friendly lines as formed bodies.[20]

The Australians of Major Saggers's Special Reserve Battalion, separated from other 15th Brigade troops, finished up at the Chinese High School. Roughly sixty officers and men had been killed in the morning's fighting. Apart from Saggers, there were few officers still present. In a bid to secure further orders, Saggers left his unit to report to Western Area headquarters at Tanglin Barracks. The unit's war diary, written by Saggers himself, later stated:

> Returning to the spot where he [Saggers] had left the men, his batman was the only one there. It appeared they had been led further towards Singapore, as they had been heavily shelled. The CO [Saggers] and his batman walked a mile searching for them, but were unable to find them. Subsequently he ascertained that all ranks had caught vehicles into Singapore.
> By this time it was nearly dusk, and, being completely fatigued, he and his batman entered a vacant house, found something to eat, then slept the clock around.

Saggers had only been away from his unit for an hour and a half.[21]

Whilst disaster was overtaking the 15th Brigade that morning of 11 February, a brigade-strength 'Tomforce' advanced under Bennett's orders to retake Bukit Timah and Bukit Panjang villages. It was wrongly believed that the Japanese at Bukit Timah 'were in no great strength'. The pall of oil smoke in the air was thicker than ever as the petrol depot east of Bukit Timah had been fired the previous evening. Buildings in Bukit Timah still smouldered. Overnight, prior to Tomforce's arrival, a handful of isolated British and Australian field and anti-tank guns and crews had been the only significant body of troops standing between Bukit Timah and Singapore Town.

Tomforce's 18th Reconnaissance Battalion, rearmed after their rescue from the sinking *Empress of Asia*, was ordered to advance directly up the road towards Bukit Timah, with the 4th Norfolks and 1/5th Sherwood Foresters moving in support north and south of the road. The Tomforce battalions made slow progress through patches of scrub, plantation and jungle. The brigade gradually split up as sub-units lost visual touch. The leading companies of the Reconnaissance Battalion were pinned down by machine gun fire behind a railway embankment on the outskirts of Bukit Timah.

On the Norfolks' front, north of Bukit Timah Road, troops became scattered in some very thick scrub between the road and the pipeline. South of the road one Forester company was swept away by troops retreating from another battle. Half of another company reached their objective, but withdrew as they believed they were being shelled by British guns. The Foresters' commanding officer formed a defensive perimeter near the Chinese cemetery at Reformatory Road with the remainder of his battalion.

Late in the afternoon the 18th Division's commander, Major-General Beckwith-Smith, ordered Tomforce to withdraw back to the Racecourse. It had become only too apparent that Tomforce could advance no further, and had become too dispersed to defend their front overnight. The rump of the exhausted 2/29th Battalion had spent the day in close support of Tomforce. Lieutenant-Colonel Pond's battalion also retired after dark. Clashes in the night caused the already gravely weakened unit to split up into a number of groups. Pond reported at Bennett's headquarters at Tanglin Barracks with the remnants of his Headquarters Company.

During the morning of 11 February, after ordering his headquarters to shift to Fort Canning, Percival had made Heath responsible for the front east of the Racecourse. At a 9 a.m. conference Heath had decided to form a second improvised brigade group from 18th Division units standing on the north-east coast – Brigadier T. H. Massy-Beresford's 'Massy Force'. Percival visited Massy-Beresford's headquarters during the afternoon, and told the brigadier that his main task was to push west as far as possible in support of Tomforce's right flank. The advance, however, got off to a slow start as the 4th Suffolks had left their transport in Thomson village. Marching onwards by a circuitous route in stifling heat and humidity, the Suffolks did not get to within a mile of Tomforce's immediate right flank. Percival later switched Tomforce from Bennett's command to Heath's.[22] It had taken Percival almost three days to get the main body of the 18th Division actively involved in the defence of Singapore.

To the north of the reservoir catchment area, General Key's 11th Division was still in position to block the advance of the Imperial Guards who had crossed the strait near the Causeway. That morning Key had been told by

Brigadier Maxwell that his brigade was no longer under the division's command. Maxwell then informed Key that his brigade was going to move southwards towards Bukit Panjang. Maxwell later claimed that he was acting on the orders of Malaya Command.[23] The 2/30th Battalion retired southwards in accordance with Maxwell's instructions, but lost contact with Maxwell and the 2/26th Battalion. During the afternoon the 2/30th Battalion's Major Ramsay took his unit eastwards across the reservoir catchment area. Lieutenant-Colonel Oakes of the 2/26th Battalion was also out of touch with Maxwell. Oakes was aware that the Japanese had seized Bukit Panjang with tanks, and he ordered his battalion to withdraw down the pipeline to the Racecourse. The column was split by skirmishing with Japanese patrols on the way, but the bulk of the battalion reached safety.[24] In the wake of Maxwell's confused instructions, his brigade had fallen apart completely.

South of Bukit Timah on 11 February the other Australian brigade at Singapore, the 22nd Brigade, continued to hold station along Reformatory Road with a skeleton force. Just before dawn there had been fighting around brigade headquarters as Japanese forces advanced south from Bukit Timah down Reformatory Road. A counter-attack by an improvised group of Australians and Indians stabilized the situation. Patchy fighting with troops of the Japanese 18th Division continued along Reformatory Road during the afternoon. Four hundred men of the 2/4th Machine Gun Battalion formed the apex of the brigade's line. Malaya Command sent the 2nd Gordon Highlanders across from Changi to help shore up the right flank of the Australian sector. Half of the 5th Bedfordshire and Hertfordshire (British 18th Division), and a hastily formed battalion of Royal Engineers and Indian sappers and miners, also arrived further south to help fill the gap between the 44th Brigade and the 1st Malaya Brigade astride the west coast road. Neither of these brigades came under attack that day.[25]

To add insult to injury, on 11 February Japanese aircraft dropped twenty-nine copies of a surrender demand in wooden boxes. Percival had no means of replying to the message from Yamashita, and the Japanese general's demand was premature. At Tyersall in the afternoon Japanese aircraft also bombed an Indian military hospital, housed in a hutment camp next door to a camp occupied by the remnants of the 12th Indian Brigade. The huts caught fire. Many patients and staff were rescued by Argylls and Royal Marines, but scores died of burns and shrapnel.[26]

The brunt of the fighting during the first stage of the battle for Singapore had fallen upon those Australian battalions posted on the north-west coast of the island. Some Australians coming out of disastrous battles had little confidence left in either their commanders or Singapore's future prospects.

By the late afternoon and evening of 10 February the first reliable reports had reached Malaya Command of groups of Australians in Singapore town looking for motor boats, or loitering about the Harbour Board.[27] In the wake of the Bukit Timah battle Lee Kip Lin recalled:

> We drove down Orchard Road and I remember very distinctly hundreds of these soldiers, Australians mainly, sprawled all over the road, drunk. And they broke into the shops opposite the Orchard Road Market ... And they broke into Cold Storage on the other side of the road. They were looting the place for food and liquor. And they were drinking it straight off the bottle, smashing the bottles all over the streets.[28]

On 11 February Lieutenant J. O. C. Hayes noted:

> Back in town, in the neighbourhood of the Oranje Hotel the streets were full of obvious deserters. They loitered in twos and threes, armed and shouting the news that 'they won't be long now'. A number of them were drunk and the large majority were certainly Australians ... There were NCOs among them but all shreds of discipline had gone. It did not seem as though all of these had been cut off from units.[29]

A British lieutenant-colonel claimed that an AIF soldier to whom he remonstrated threatened to throw a couple of grenades at him. When General Key and the 135th Field Regiment's Lieutenant-Colonel P. J. D. Toosey were out inspecting troops they came across a party of Australians heading in the opposite direction. Key asked them where they were going, and was told to get out of the way, 'we're fed up with this place. If you don't get out of the way we'll shoot you.' Major J. C. Westall 'personally saw cases of Australian Officers endeavouring to persuade their men to return to their units, but who flatly refused to do so'.[30]

There was of course nothing new about 'stragglers' in the Malayan campaign. In battles on the mainland thousands of soldiers from broken units had made their way southwards in large and small parties after calamitous defeats – a clear majority of the force present at some engagements. There was also nothing new about stragglers in a world war campaign. Percival later recalled that in March 1918 he had taken a detachment to clear stragglers from a French village, and had found soldiers belonging to twenty-one different units sheltering there. What made the situation unusual at Singapore, compared with other battles in Malaya, was that there were tens of thousands of rear echelon troops and influential civilians crammed inside the shrinking perimeter to record the sight of shattered formations. What made the behaviour of Australian stragglers noteworthy was their rioting and genuine aggression towards authority. By 11 February hundreds of soldiers had gathered in the dock area and town, and hundreds more were scattered elsewhere. Major Westall estimated that 80 per cent of the mass of demoralized men at the docks were Australians.[31] That was a reasonable and predictable estimate. At that stage of the battle around 80 per cent of European troops engaged and broken were Australian. Five Australian, two under strength British, and three Indian battalions had been shredded between 9 and 11 February. These units disgorged a sizeable number of stragglers, some with the intention of deserting, in addition to inspiring a degree of panic among faint-hearted members of rear echelon formations.

At Singapore's docks a number of ships had sailed since the initial Japanese landing. The *Kinta* and *Darvel* had left with a thousand servicemen aboard, including the 2/3rd Reserve Motor Transport Company. The hospital ship *Wu Sueh* had sailed with over three hundred patients. The majority of the Naval Base's civilian staff, and Europeans of the Singapore Harbour Board, had also been evacuated.[32] But on 11 February there was still plenty of shipping, large and small, gathered at Keppel Harbour.

The *Empire Star*, a large transport of almost 17,000 tons, had arrived at Singapore as far back as 27 January. On 11 February the ship began embarking over 2000 RAF personnel, European nurses, and women and children. Not surprisingly the *Empire Star* attracted the attention of the uniformed rabble that had been collecting at the docks over the previous twenty-four hours. According to the *Empire Star's* Chief Officer, Mr J. L. Dawson:

> During one period I was called to the gangway because of panic at the shore end of the gangway and on investigation found that a large number of Australian troops were panicking to get on board. I went to the gangway and told the troops that there was no need to panic and that this ship was reserved for only RAF personnel, women and children. Eventually these Australian troops quietened down and we were able to proceed with the work of getting our own people on board. During the day I noticed that Australian troops were climbing up the mooring ropes on board to the after deck and by any other means they could find.

The ship was due to leave the quay at 6 p.m., and the gangway was only raised with the assistance of military police.

As the *Empire Star* got underway Dawson went to speak to the armed Australian troops who had gathered on the after deck. A corporal told Dawson that their leader on board was a captain.

> I went down into No. 1 Tween deck, which was allocated to the women and children and shouted the Captain's name, in answer to which he came forward. When he appeared I noticed that he had even taken his shoulder 'pips' off so that he could not be recognized. We took this Captain in front of his men having already removed all their guns and revolvers.[33]

Another forty-five deserters had boarded the nearby *Gorgon* (thirty Australians and fifteen British).

In the early hours of 12 February the *Empire Star* and *Gorgon* passed through the network of minefields outside Keppel Harbour. Another dozen smaller merchant ships also left Singapore that night. By 8 a.m. the *Empire Star* had caught up with a small naval squadron. The cruiser *Durban* and other warships had sailed carrying five hundred evacuees. The *Empire Star* and *Durban* were subjected to a succession of air attacks by a total of fifty bombers. The *Empire Star* suffered three hits. There were numerous near misses, one of which almost lifted the ship out of the water. One bomber was shot down and another was seen losing height, gushing smoke from an engine.[34]

The *Empire Star* reached Batavia on the evening of 13 February. The deserters were taken off without incident, and after some vehicles and stores were unloaded, the ship headed onwards to Fremantle. The AIF's commander at Java later reported that 'one officer and approximately 175 other ranks from Singapore ... arrived in Batavia without satisfactory explanation as to why they had left Malaya'.[35] Most of those men had disembarked from the *Empire Star*.

# 16

# *Capitulation*

On 12 February the Japanese consolidated their grip on Bukit Timah, the vital centre of Singapore Island. The outnumbered and outgunned XXV Army was badly overstretched, and alarmingly short of artillery ammunition, but the inmates of Fort Canning had little inkling of these facts. General Yamashita's intention was to concentrate his forces for a final thrust into Singapore Town. In the meantime pressure would be maintained on the British perimeter slowly to choke the life out of Percival's force.

Astride Bukit Timah Road, the most direct route to Singapore town, heavy firing on 12 February began about 6.45 a.m. as Japanese infiltrated Tomforce's 4th Norfolks.[1] Confused fighting followed. As the morning progressed Tomforce retreated to the junction of Bukit Timah and Adam and Farrer Roads, almost two miles behind Racecourse village. During the retirement the 1/5th Sherwood Foresters were caught by advancing Japanese tanks and forced southwards in disorder.

By early afternoon Tomforce had taken up a new position at Hill 80, a ridge just in front of Adam Road. 'At this time', wrote the 18th Division's history, '18th Battalion Reconnaissance Corps and 4th Norfolks could each put into the line approximately 120 and 200 men respectively'.[2] A Reconnaissance Battalion officer separated from his unit went straight to Fort Canning, 'to make a report that the petrol dump near Bukit Timah had gone up in flames and burning petrol was flowing down the road faster than you can run'. In Keppel Harbour a naval party was dispatched to persuade AIF and Reconnaissance Battalion men to leave the ship *Mata Hari*. Malaya Command's war diary noted: 'Thomasforce has been surrounded and has almost disintegrated.'[3]

The Japanese did not attack down Bukit Timah Road again on 12 February. British units used the breathing space to dig in along Adam and Farrer Roads under occasional shell and mortar fire. Anti-tank guns were deployed to cover Bukit Timah Road and a subsidiary parallel road. The 1st Cambridgeshires, 3/17th Dogras and 5/11th Sikhs were deployed to shore up the sector. Towards evening the 4th Suffolks at the Golf Course were ordered to pull back to fill the gap between the force at Adam Road and the south bank of MacRitchie Reservoir.

During the day Percival had decided to withdraw Heath's and Simmon's troops from the north-east and south-east coasts to form the final perimeter around Singapore he had been thinking about since the evening of 9 February. At noon Heath ordered the 11th and 18th Divisions to start retiring from their coastal positions in Northern Area. As Bukit Timah had been lost, it was no longer possible to form a tenable perimeter that included both MacRitchie and Peirce Reservoirs. Peirce Reservoir and the northern bank of MacRitchie Reservoir were abandoned. British forces retained possession of the south bank of MacRitchie Reservoir, and the pumping station that fed water from the reservoir to Singapore town. The water supply was still assured, providing that the pipes through which the water was pumped remained intact. This was a factor over which neither Heath nor Percival had a great deal of control.[4]

In Northern Area the 11th Division's 8th Indian Brigade had begun 12 February west of Nee Soon village, south from which an important road ran along the east side of the reservoirs to Thomson village and Percival's final perimeter. At 8.30 a.m. the 2/10th Baluchis at Mandai Road reported that the 1/8th Punjabis to their right had 'vanished'. A patrol sent to the Punjabis' area failed to return. A staff officer went to the Punjabis' headquarters to discover what had happened. He was told by the acting commanding officer, Captain Finlayson, that two companies were missing. Finlayson later reported that a third company had also disappeared. Battalion headquarters and D Company was all that remained. The Punjabis had been rebuilt using 'immature boys', and had been badly shaken by a mortar barrage the previous day. A reserve battalion was rushed up to fill the gap caused by the Punjabis' disintegration.[5]

During the afternoon three Japanese tanks came down Mandai Road towards Nee Soon. The tanks were pounded by anti-tank and field guns, after which the 8th Brigade's withdrawal southwards continued without incident. The 53rd Brigade covered the final retirement of the 8th and 28th Brigades along badly congested roads. General Nishimura's plan to thrust his Imperial Guards through the reservoir catchment to cut Thomson Road behind the 11th Division was thwarted by the speed of the division's retreat.

South of Bukit Timah Road on 12 February the 22nd Australian Brigade could muster only eight hundred Australian infantry, most of whom were from the 2/4th Machine Gun Battalion and 2/18th Battalion.[6] (The brigade's three battalions and the machine gun battalion had started the Singapore battle with roughly 3400 infantry.) In fitful fighting during the day Lieutenant-Colonel J. M. Anketell of the machine gun battalion was mortally wounded. The Gordon Highlanders and the still relatively intact 2/26th Battalion played crucial front-line roles in General

Bennett's much shrunken Western Area command. Brigadier Taylor was sent to hospital after collapsing from exhaustion, but only after a final verbal confrontation with Bennett. Lieutenant-Colonel Varley was appointed the 22nd Brigade's new commander.

Bennett and his staff were planning to form an AIF perimeter around their headquarters at Tanglin Barracks. All rear echelon personnel were to be concentrated in the perimeter. The concept was arguably a prudent precaution, but it displayed a parochial lack of faith in Malaya Command. South of Bennett's force, the 44th Indian Brigade and the 1st Malaya Brigade had a relatively quiet day, except for a local Japanese attack that overran an Indian company.

13 February dawned grimly for Percival's army. By noon the 53rd Brigade had retired south down Thomson Road to take up their place in the perimeter at the eastern end of MacRitchie Reservoir. Brigadier E. H. W. Backhouse's 54th Brigade headquarters took over command of Tomforce's units astride Bukit Timah Road. Massy-Beresford's 55th Brigade was responsible for the sector between the two aforementioned brigades.

East of the reservoir catchment area, the 11th Indian Division, and the 2nd Malaya Brigade completed their withdrawals from the north-east and south-east coasts. The previous afternoon coastal batteries at Changi had been blown-up. East of Changi, a battalion of Hyderabad States Force Infantry and the 2/17th Dogras had been left behind at Bukit Pengerang in Johore, and on the island of Pulau Tekong Besar respectively. In the rush of events shipping had not been provided to bring them back to Singapore Island.

South of Bukit Timah Road and the 18th British Division, the Australians had their first relatively quiet day since the landing. Further south the 44th Indian Brigade still held a narrow front. The 1st Malaya Brigade prolonged the line towards the coast with their left flank thrown forward to rest at Pasir Panjang village.

XXV Army's main thrust for 13 February was launched against the 1st Malaya Brigade and Pasir Panjang ridge. On the brigade's left flank, the 1st Malays held Pasir Panjang village, with the 2nd Malays, 2nd Loyals and other detachments prolonging the front northwards. Pasir Panjang ridge was shelled and bombed for two hours, before an attack at 2 p.m. by the Japanese 56th Regiment made rapid progress towards Buona Vista Road, 2000 yards to the rear. A Japanese battalion advancing down the coast road attacked the 1st Malays. Both of the 1st Malays' forward companies were driven back. The 2nd Malays were also bundled rearwards, and two of their companies were overrun and scattered.[7]

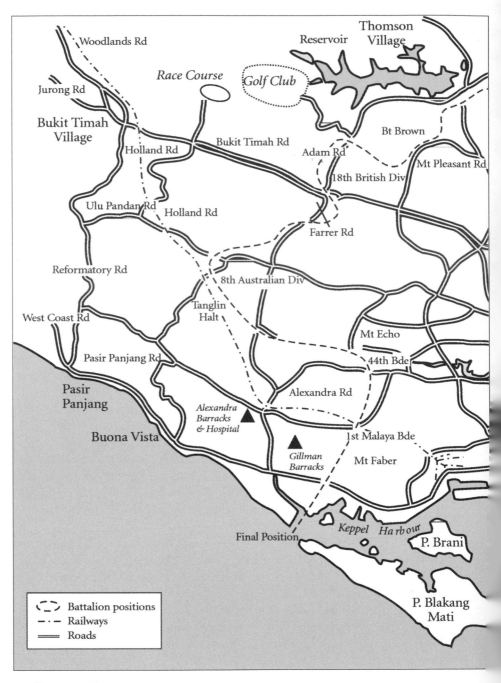

16. Singapore Town.

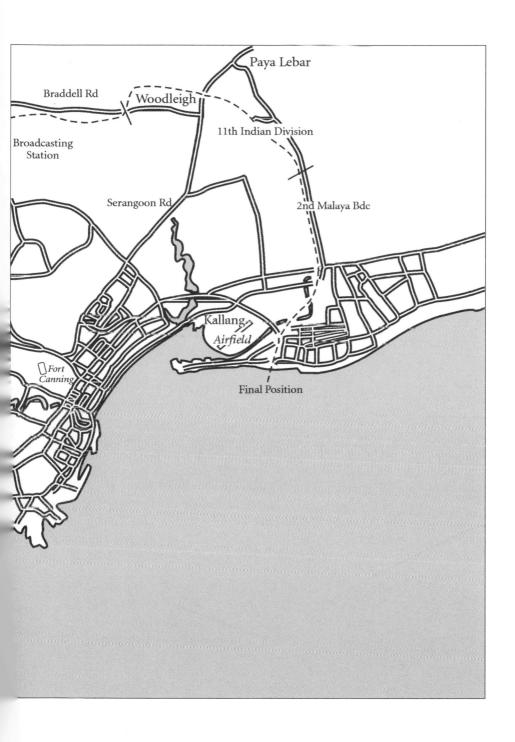

Paya Lebar

Braddell Rd

Woodleigh

Broadcasting
Station

11th Indian Division

Serangoon Rd

2nd Malaya Bde

Kallang
Airfield

Fort
Canning

Final Position

The 1st Malaya Brigade retired that evening to a new line with their left flank at Buona Vista village. The 44th Brigade withdrew as well but the 22nd Brigade did not, thus exposing their left flank for a distance of almost two miles. The Japanese, however, did not swing north east to attack the Australians' flank, and continued to focus their attention on the 1st Malaya Brigade.

Whilst the 1st Malaya Brigade was fighting for survival, senior British commanders at Singapore met at Fort Canning during the afternoon of 13 February. General Heath told the conference that he felt that the situation was hopeless and General Bennett was in agreement.[8] The Japanese had come five hundred miles down the Malayan peninsula and were now only three miles from Singapore River. Percival countered that he was not authorized by Wavell to capitulate, and added: 'I have my honour to consider and there is also the question of what posterity will think of us if we surrender this large Army and valuable fortress.' According to Percival, Heath then replied, 'You need not bother about your honour. You lost that a long time ago up in the North'.[9] Nonetheless Percival did not think the time was right to capitulate, and the defending garrison was ordered to fight on.

At Keppel Harbour the senior Royal Navy officer still at Singapore, Rear-Admiral Spooner, decided to sail all remaining small craft from Singapore that night of 13/14 February. There were over forty vessels ready to leave port with space for 3000 evacuees in addition to the crews. Percival's Fort Canning headquarters was informed of Spooner's intention and asked to help determine who should be 'officially' evacuated. Ultimately the army was allocated 1800 places, of which one hundred were for Australians. It was decided to evacuate staff officers and technicians no longer required, though more than one formation mistakenly sent combatants away. Few Indians, Malays or Chinese were among those to be evacuated. Percival said goodbye to Air Vice-Marshal Pulford that evening. Pulford was leaving with Spooner. Pulford's parting words to Percival were: 'I suppose you and I will be held responsible for this, but God knows we did our best with what little we had been given.'[10]

A number of senior staff officers left with the fleet of small ships. Two of Percival's staff at Fort Canning, Lieutenant-Colonels Phillips and Ashmore, were among those evacuated. Phillips and Ashmore left for the docks from Fort Canning with a small Malaya Command evacuation party.[11] The party crossed Singapore town by lorry and on foot. The darkened streets were full of vehicles. Groups of soldiers wandered about, and fires burnt in the distance. Warehouses full of rubber had been torched to prevent them falling into enemy hands. Broken telegraph poles, and piles of rubble from bombed buildings littered the roads. The party boarded HMS *Malacca*, and, illuminated by the glow of fires, the ship slipped out of harbour, one of the rag-tag collection of several dozen craft to sail that night.[12] Some of the ships leaving Singapore carried large numbers of passengers. The *Mata Hari* had 483 men, women and children aboard, and was fired on when it passed a broken down launch full of military personnel.

The fate of shipping leaving Singapore on the night of 13/14 February was grim. The straggling flotilla had to pass down the north coast of Sumatra in order to reach the port of Batavia on Java. Japanese warships were due to arrive off the coast of Banka Island near Sumatra during 14 February, preparatory to a sea landing the following day. Of those small British ships sailing along Sumatra's coast, most were sunk or captured. The small ships could do little to fight back, but when the *Li Wo*, a former Yangtze River paddle steamer, ran into a Japanese convoy, her commander rammed a transport before his ship was blown out of the water. Lieutenant Wilkinson was later awarded a posthumous Victoria Cross. The launch Rear-Admiral Spooner and Air Vice-Marshal Pulford were aboard was chased by a Japanese destroyer and ran aground. Shipwrecked on a malarial island, both men died in the weeks ahead. After one ship sank twenty-one Australian military nurses landed on Banka Island in a lifeboat, only to be machine gunned by their Japanese captors. Just one nurse survived the massacre to tell the tale.

The night of 13/14 February, like the previous night, was relatively quiet around the perimeter. On the south-west coast of Singapore the batteries of Faber Fire Command near Keppel Harbour were still manned and active. Malaya Command had told the commander of the batteries to treat all craft as hostile.[13] Every evening the guns of Faber Fire Command had blazed away at suspected Japanese landing and scout craft approaching Keppel Harbour. A number of ships were sunk. A British officer had watched through a telescope as on successive nights a large junk and a thousand ton tramp steamer were trapped in search lights and blown apart. As mostly Australian survivors were washed ashore it gradually became clear that the craft were carrying stragglers cut off in the western part of the island.[14] More constructively the three big 9.2 inch guns of Connaught Battery fired back over Pulau Blakang Mati towards the Japanese.

The main drama on dry land during the night of 13/14 February was Japanese infiltration of the 2nd Cambridgeshires, the left-hand battalion of the 53rd Brigade, east of Thomson village. The acting commanding officer, Major A. B. G. Stephen, and his adjutant, were killed in the fighting. At dawn the Japanese also attacked Hill 105 at the eastern tip of MacRitchie Reservoir. Troops on Hill 105, to the immediate left of the Cambridgeshires, were driven south down Thomson Road for half a mile.[15]

South of MacRitchie Reservoir the 55th Brigade's left-hand unit, the 1st Cambridgeshires, fought a steady battle against encroaching Japanese. The brigade's right-hand battalion, the 4th Suffolks, to the immediate south of the reservoir, was heavily attacked late in the afternoon. A group of tanks advanced along Sime Road and rapidly penetrated the battalion's defences. Japanese infantry followed into the gaps torn in the Suffolks' front, and after a stiff fight the battalion retreated a mile to Mount Pleasant Road, the 18th Division's reserve line. When the rolls were called the next day, the Suffolks were found to have lost 250 officers and men killed, wounded and missing.[16]

In the eastern half of Percival's perimeter, the main sensation on 14 February was the disappearance of a large part of the 2/10th Baluchis. Firing had been heard during the night, and in the morning reports had reached battalion headquarters of Japanese infiltration. But when reinforcements were sent to the threatened area they could not find C Company. The position was empty. No Japanese could be seen. A British officer's body, slashed by a sword, and those of several sepoys were discovered, but the others had gone, leaving their arms and equipment behind. A Company and much of B Company had also vanished. The Royal Rifles composite battalion was rushed forward to plug the gap without further incident. The Baluchis had probably been harangued by either Indian National Army or Japanese infiltrators and persuaded to surrender. Irrespective of what exactly had happened, the Baluchis' leadership cadre had been too weak and tired to withstand subversion.[17]

South of Bukit Timah Road the 8th Australian Division experienced another relatively quiet day on 14 February, but the 18th Japanese Division continued their drive down the south-west coast against the 1st Malaya Brigade. Overnight Brigadier G. G. R. Williams, for reasons that remain obscure, had ordered his brigade to pull right back behind Singapore River for a last ditch stand. As this would have involved abandoning Mount Faber and Keppel Harbour, in addition to fatally exposing the flank of the brigade's neighbouring formations, Southern Area's GOC, General Simmons, promptly cancelled Williams's orders when he heard news of them. All units received the cancellation but for the 122nd Field Regiment, and another detachment, both of which moved rearwards to add to the congestion and confusion in Singapore Town.[18]

The Japanese attacked the 1st Malaya Brigade throughout 14 February. The defenders' task was not helped by the fact that Bennett had directed nearby Australian artillery to fire only in support of troops under Bennett's command. As the guns could take Japanese advancing along the south coast in enfilade, this was a selfish act of no small consequence.[19] The 1st Malays'

B Company at Buona Vista village was strongly attacked early in the afternoon. Buona Vista fell later that day. C Company, sited on a low hill north of Pasir Panjang Road, was also overrun. A deep drain behind the hill was full of burning oil flowing from the damaged Normanton oil depot. Only a lieutenant and four men managed to leap over the blazing ditch to rejoin the rest of their unit. The Japanese hanged the body of Lieutenant Abnan bin Saidi upside down from a tree to celebrate their victory.

The 1st Malays' D Company had spent the day on the unit's right flank, near Alexandra brickworks. In the early evening a column of Japanese infantry came marching down the road. They were fired on at 100–150 yards range by the Malays and other British troops with devastating effect. After the ambush between ninety to a hundred bodies were counted on the road.[20]

That afternoon of 14 February, as the 1st Malaya Brigade gave ground, the Japanese had captured Alexandra military hospital. Indian troops had very likely fired on the advancing Japanese from the hospital grounds before retreating to safety. Japanese troops subsequently went on a rampage in the hospital. A Loyals corporal was bayoneted on the operating table, and a number of others killed on the spot. The patients in the wards were rounded up and taken outside. The immobile were bayoneted where they lay. About 150 patients and medical personnel were roped together in groups of four or five, and sent to servants' quarters behind the hospital. During the night some of the prisoners were led away. Screams were heard in the distance, and Japanese guards returned wiping blood from their bayonets. Only a few prisoners managed to escape. Among the dead at Alexandra hospital was Lieutenant John Brownrigg of the Sherwood Foresters. Brownrigg was the stepson of Admiral Phillips. Lady Phillips lost both a son and a husband in the brief campaign in Malaya.[21]

At 10 a.m. on 14 February Percival had met Brigadier Simson, Singapore's chief Royal Engineer, and the Municipal Water Engineer to review the water supply situation. With no frost at Singapore the water mains were not deeply buried, and many pipes running between MacRitchie Reservoir and the town had been broken by shell fire and aerial bombing. Later in the morning Percival saw the Governor at the Singapore Club. Government House, a mile north of Fort Canning, had been shelled two days previously and a number of people killed. Sir Shenton Thomas advised immediate surrender given the suffering that was being inflicted on the civilian population, but Percival felt that the worsening water situation was not quite serious enough yet to warrant capitulation.

That evening official evacuees who had missed a place on the final evacuation flotilla the previous night emerged from shelter to find boats in the harbour on which to make a late getaway. The official evacuees crossed paths with armed parties of stragglers with similar intentions and little respect for authority. The Australian Commercial Secretary in Malaya, A. N. Wootton, was in a launch that evening which took thirty-eight people out to the *Mary Rose* lying offshore in the harbour. Twenty armed Australians demanded to be taken aboard without success. Rifle shots were fired as the launch pulled away from the shore but nobody was hit. The *Mary Rose* did not leave Singapore till after light next morning, by which time only a handful of sampans, junks and launches were left in the once crowded port.[22]

The most fortunate escapees travelled in small craft whose commanders wisely cut across to western Sumatra by the shortest possible route. With a prevailing wind blowing from the north east, and many small islands dotted along the route, the journey involved relatively little risk from the elements. One boat load of soldiers stopped at Raffles Lighthouse. Looking back towards Singapore they watched as

> about thirty bombs wiped out another section of Singapore, almost twelve miles away, and the lighthouse shook with the roar of them. It was a terrible sight with nothing but flames and columns of smoke spouting into the air, and dense black smoke oozing out over the sea for miles, darkening the sky. God help the poor folk still there! [23]

Back at Singapore the deteriorating morale of the defending army was still a cause of much concern as the battle wore on towards its now inevitable conclusion. The number of stragglers littering the back areas grew as successive units were ground down and broken up by the advancing Japanese. A provost officer in Singapore town noted in his company's war diary: 'More and more soldiers in Singapore, morale very low. All imaginable excuses being made to avoid returning to the line. Arms and equipment being discarded all over Singapore. Wharves crowded with soldiers viewing chances of getting off in boats.' Brigadier Ballentine of the 44th Indian Brigade claimed that for every man who wanted to fight there were two who did not.

> There were no battle police to round up would-be deserters. When I say this I am alluding to all formations with which I was in contact. It was quite common to find 700 men immured in Changi in a unit which ended the war with perhaps 200 men in its ranks.

Lieutenant-Colonel Thyer, the Australian division's GSO 1, wrote in reference to his own countrymen: 'Ultimately, the morale deteriorated, and in the last stages only two-thirds at most of those fit to fight were manning the final perimeter.'[24] In thick terrain and amid the chaos of retreat it was not difficult to slip away.

Malaya Command authorised clumsy attempts to establish piquets at key cross-roads to round up and redirect stragglers. Many men were genuinely lost, exhausted or shocked, and in need of food, water and sleep. The heat and humidity were as stifling as ever, and there had been little rain for days. When dealing with stragglers, poorly organized provost patrols often had no idea where units, assembly areas or supplies could be found.[25] As the perimeter shrank, relatively organized units moved into the built up districts of Singapore, but there were still many soldiers in small groups wandering about and hiding in the back areas of the perimeter. During the final two or three days before Singapore's capitulation a general, shifting straggler population from all contingents may have numbered several thousands. However it needs to be emphasised that 'stragglers' were a consequence of lost battles and not the cause.

The Japanese stranglehold on the British perimeter was as tight as ever at dawn on 15 February. General Percival rose at 6.30 a.m. and had a message sent out calling a commanders' conference. The doomed garrison's leaders met at Fort Canning at 9.30 a.m. The 18th Division's General Beckwith-Smith could not attend, but he sent a report saying that his formation had been unable to contain the infiltration of its front during the night. Brigadier Simson, Singapore's chief Royal Engineer, told the assembled officers that the piped water supply might not last into the next day, and that it would take several days to restore it once it had failed. As had been the case two days previously, Percival raised the subject of continued resistance. This left it to others to argue against the proposition, in particular Heath, who felt that

> to sacrifice the lives of countless Asiatics by a failure to appreciate the true situation and face up to it would have been a deplorable blot upon the Empire which it would take more than a subsequent victory in the World War to expunge.

Percival later wrote that he 'reluctantly decided to accept the advice of the senior officers present and to capitulate'. Ammunition was perilously low, and there was no chance of a successful counter-attack. It was decided to ask the Japanese for a cease fire from 4 p.m. Wavell had granted Percival permission to capitulate prior to the conference.[26]

Brigadier Newbigging of Malaya Command's administrative branch, Mr Fraser, the Straits Settlements' Colonial Secretary, and Major C. H. D. Wild, an interpreter, left Fort Canning by car at 11.30 a.m. The vehicle could not pass the defenders' own road-block at the junction of Bukit Timah and

Adam Roads. A British captain at the road-block shoved a revolver into Newbigging's chest, and Fraser was forced to hastily explain the situation. The men continued on foot for six hundred yards carrying a Union Jack and a white flag, until stopped by a Japanese patrol and taken to a villa a hundred yards away. After a short period Colonel Sugita arrived from XXV Army headquarters. Sugita made a series of demands and gave the British delegation a very large Japanese flag. The flag was to be flown over the Cathay Building as a signal that Percival had agreed to meet Yamashita at 4 p.m. to finalize terms. The delegation was driven back towards British lines. Major Wild later recounted:

> The return journey was uneventful, except for an inaccurate burst of pistol fire, delivered at somewhat unsporting range, from a Provost Corporal of 18th Division, who opined that we were spies.

At Fort Canning Wild reported to Percival as bomb blasts disturbed the ceiling boards and sent clouds of dust into the room.[27]

In the vital Bukit Timah sector that morning of 15 February numerous troops saw Newbigging's party carrying the white flag. Rumours that 'armistice' negotiations might be underway proved unsettling in units nearby. The 1st Cambridgeshires maintained their station at Adam Park, as did the 3/17th Dogras south of Bukit Timah Road, but between those units the tired Sherwood Foresters, 4th Norfolks and 5th Suffolks struggled to hang on. By afternoon those battalions had conceded some ground.[28]

Near Mount Pleasant Road a Reconnaissance Battalion officer had seen staff cars bearing the Union Jack and white flag. 'We knew the war was over for us then and we lost all interest in the battle; the Japanese attacked us again and it was with a curiously halfhearted manner we pressed our triggers and made them retreat.' At 4 p.m., at a number of places across the 18th Division's front, the ceasefire was believed to have come into effect, although continued Japanese firing made it clear that that was not the case.[29]

On the eastern side of the perimeter Japanese activity against the 11th Indian Division and 2nd Malaya Brigade was limited. A number of units were involved in anxious skirmishes near Paya Lebar airstrip, but the situation remained relatively stable. The 7th Coast Battery had been converted to an infantry unit and attached to the 2nd Malaya Brigade. According to the battery's war diary:

> Throughout the day British troops were retiring through Rochore Road in an attempt to pick up craft to put to sea ... Four medical officers trying to get away were shot at. One killed and one severely wounded ... Two officers of an anti-tank unit were placed under arrest and sent to 2 Malaya Infantry Brigade.[30]

This is a rare recorded instance of summary action being taken against stragglers.

The 8th Australian Division had another relatively quiet day on 15 February, but on the south-west coast the 1st Malaya Brigade again came under attack. The Loyals and 1st Malays gave ground and retired to a new line in front of Mount Faber. In their new position the Loyals were reorganized into two rifle companies comprising only 130 officers and men.[31]

Back in Singapore Town the Cathay Building, III Corps's headquarters, was packed with troops and civilians. The vulnerable flank of Singapore's only skyscraper was subject to occasional shelling. At the mouth of Singapore River the Fullerton Building was being used as a hospital. In a large open room scores of stretchers lay side by side. A crowd of civilians had gathered on the lawn outside St Andrew's Cathedral, and a battery was sited on the Padang with its trails only yards from the water's edge. Smoke from burning stocks of rubber in warehouses near Keppel Harbour added to the pall overhead.

After seeing General Percival at Fort Canning, Major Wild went to III Corps headquarters to find there was still some confusion in Heath's mind regarding the timing of the yet to be arranged cease fire. Wild went to the roof of the Cathay Building to fly the Japanese flag to signal that Percival agreed to meet the Japanese. Wild then returned to Fort Canning to act as Percival's interpreter for the final meeting. Neither Percival nor Brigadiers Torrance and Newbigging responded when Wild passed on Heath's query regarding the cease fire time. According to Wild:

> Astonishing as this may sound, it was not altogether so to me, as I had become inured during the past week to seeing General Percival's painful inability to give a decision and on three occasions to make any reply whatever, when points of operational importance were referred to him, particularly by my Corps Commander.[32]

Percival's party headed up Bukit Timah Road by car. General Percival, Major Wild, Brigadier Torrance and Brigadier Newbigging were present at the discussions that began about 5.15 p.m. at the shell-damaged Ford Motor Factory near Bukit Timah village.[33] Yamashita and Percival shook hands at the start of the meeting and sat opposite each other at a table. A Japanese officer present recorded that Percival seemed 'pale and thin and ill'.

Yamashita did not waste any time in pressing Percival to surrender. In response Percival asked permission to retain a thousand of his men under arms so as to maintain order in the town. Yamashita was annoyed with this request and he told Percival through an interpreter that an attack would go forward that evening if they could not reach an agreement promptly. The

Japanese commander may have thought that the British were playing for time, though Percival had no such intention. To speed up proceedings, Yamashita impatiently banged the table with his fist: 'The time for the night attack is drawing near. Is the British Army going to surrender or not? Answer YES or NO.' (He used the English words.) But Percival again asked that a thousand of his men remain under arms. Yamashita relented and the discussion moved on to the time the capitulation was to come into force. Percival wanted a cease fire at 10 p.m. Yamashita pressed for 8.30 p.m. He subsequently claimed that an attack was timed for 10.30 p.m., and a cease fire at 10 p.m. would leave only half an hour to call it off. Percival could hardly decline Yamashita's demands and terms were signed at 6.10 p.m. The two generals rose and again shook hands.

In a quick glance at a Japanese staff officer's map, Wild saw blue pencil marks indicating that an attack might have been about to be launched between Bukit Timah Road and MacRitchie Reservoir. Wild speculated that the attack would have gone clean through to the sea, and that the surrender had come just in time to spare the civil population the consequences of Japanese troops entering the town. But with hindsight this is unlikely. The Japanese lacked the weight of numbers to force their way right through Singapore Town, and may have been planning a local attack that could have taken the Mount Pleasant area.[34]

Half an hour after the surrender came into force the Bishop of Singapore, the Rt Rev. Leonard Wilson, held a service in St Andrew's Cathedral. The nave of the church was littered with stretchers and wounded men. Several hundred mostly Asian civilians filled the choir stalls. At the front line the guns fell silent and in the distance British troops could hear triumphant banzai cries.

As news of a cease fire spread within the British perimeter numerous parties prepared to make final escape bids.[35] Major M. Ashkanasy, a member of Bennett's staff, left his division's headquarters in the afternoon aware that surrender was imminent. Ashkanasy went into town and met a group of forty English troops, including several officers, mostly from the 53rd Brigade. The party found a boat. Ashkanasy later recalled:

> The harbour as we pulled out was completely empty except for the masts and funnels of sunken ships dotted around, a few skiffs sailing out and one launch, a forty-footer which we asked for a tow, but which told us that they had engine trouble and couldn't stop. We left some time in the afternoon, about 4 p.m. I think, and by 4.30 p.m. we were away from the vicinity of the jetty. We heard the firing go on and the bombing until suddenly about 8 o'clock there was sudden silence. The city was a lurid red with a line of white smoke stretching indefinitely across the horizon.[36]

The boat was rowed into the night, and later a launch towed them from an island to Sumatra.

Major Geoffrey Rowley-Conwy (the future Lord Langford) packed the 150–160 officers and men of his 30th Anti-Aircraft Battery (3rd Heavy AA Regiment) onto a junk and a motor launch. All but a few men declined to make the voyage. Rowley-Conwy had told his officers and warrant officers of his intention to escape the previous day. A junk had been found and provisioned overnight. The junk later ran aground out at sea, but it was refloated and then abandoned for other smaller craft.[37]

The most senior officer to depart from Singapore on 15 February was the Australians' General Bennett, after the final cease fire. Bennett had been thinking of escape since late January. As early as 13 December he had written to the Australian Army's headquarters at Melbourne: 'I fear a repetition of Crete.' On the evening of 15 February, after he had destroyed his papers and packed a few belongings, Bennett handed over command to his divisional Chief of Royal Artillery, Brigadier C. A. Callaghan. Bennett did not inform General Percival or any other senior officer of his intention to leave Singapore.

Bennett headed down to the waterfront with Lieutenant Gordon Walker, his ADC, and Major Moses, a liaison officer, to join other military personnel looking to make an escape. The party found a sampan and pushed off with another eight Volunteer Force men aboard. They later transferred to a larger motor boat and reached the coast of Sumatra late on 18 February. Bennett travelled to the south coast of Sumatra by road; a flight from there to Java, and onwards to Australia, was arranged by ABDA Command's staff. Bennett reached Melbourne and Australian Army headquarters on 2 March where he was told by General Sturdee, the Chief of the General Staff, that his escape had been 'ill-advised'. The 8th Division's former commander escaped the wrath of his fellow generals, however, as Australia's political leaders decided not to take action against him.[38]

Bennett claimed that he had escaped to report on the Malayan campaign and advise how the Japanese could be beaten, but given his poor performance as a commander, and lack of previous interest in the details of jungle warfare, he was hardly the best man for the task. Hostile critics alleged that Bennett's escape was motivated by careerism, and an inability to accept his share of responsibility for the fall of Singapore. Many senior Australian officers believed that Bennett had left Singapore to secure another command. The chief Australian official historian of the war, Gavin Long, later commented: 'I believe he thought he was such a great man that we couldn't possibly win the war without him.'[39] In Australia Bennett was subsequently mailed white feathers and was even posted a pair of running shoes. In hindsight Bennett should have requested the permission of the Australian government and Malaya Command to leave Singapore. That permission would almost certainly have been refused. It is highly likely that Bennett neglected to seek permission for precisely that reason, and then went on to use his position of authority to organize his escape at a time of crisis.

Other escapees from Singapore also travelled across Sumatra by river launch, road and rail. An official report on the 'evacuation' of Singapore described the behaviour of servicemen in Sumatra as a 'disgrace' for some, 'negative and uninspiring' for many, and 'brilliant' for only a few.[40] From ports on the south coasts of Java and Sumatra a number of ships, large and small, fled ahead of the triumphant Japanese. Not all ships reached Ceylon and Australia safely. The Dutch steamer *Roosenboom* was torpedoed and sunk at night far out to sea, after leaving Padang at Sumatra on 26 February with several hundred people aboard. At dawn 130 survivors, male and female, were either in or clinging to the sides of a single lifeboat, including Brigadier Paris and three lieutenant-colonels. The boat drifted a thousand miles over twenty-six days until it reached land back in the East Indies. With little food and water, and assailed by the burning sun, most of the survivors drowned or gradually fell into a coma. Parties of men at one end of the boat, European and Asian alike, resorted to cannibalism. Only a young Chinese woman, two Javanese seaman and Sergeant W. Gibson, an Argyll, survived the ordeal.[41]

Other ships were more fortunate. The *Tenumba* sailed from Padang on the same day as the *Roosenboom* with 220 aboard, including Brigadier Coates. The warships *Danae, Hobart, Dragon, Stronghold* and *Scout* left Padang on 1 March with 890 passengers. In total about 1600 servicemen and civilians reached Ceylon and India from Sumatra and Java after escaping from Singapore and Dutch territory. Others were trans-shipped from Sumatra to Java, and some of these reached Australia. The Dutch ships *Van Dam* and *Abbekerk* sailed to Fremantle carrying over a thousand evacuees. A rather hazy official estimate of escapees to leave Singapore and reach safety in Allied countries gave a figure of three thousand.[42]

After the loss of Singapore a report on the campaign was prepared for General Wavell. The report's author was Major H. P. Thomas. Thomas had been in command of a reinforcement camp at Singapore. The report summarized information that had been taken from British officers who had reached Ceylon and India from Singapore. Wavell wrote of Thomas's report to the Chief of the Imperial General Staff: 'I have read, I think, all the principal reports which compose the evidence, and a good many others; and I consider this summary fair and accurate.' Wavell, however, was not without reservations as to the report's contents. 'I would remind you of what I know you will bear in mind, that the statements available are mainly those of comparatively junior officers with a limited view.'[43]

Thomas's report contained a great deal of rumour and gossip. In addition to much comment about lack of resources and poor leadership, specific allegations fell mainly on Australians. Major J. C. K. Marshall of the Federated Malay States Volunteer Force wrote:

> 'Scorched Earth' meant simply an excuse for looting by the Australians. The Australians were known as 'daffodils' – because beautiful to look at but yellow all through. RAF were known as 'penguins' – because only one in a thousand flew.[44]

The Australians' reputation was not enhanced by Bennett's unauthorised flight from Singapore. Bennett wrote a report on the campaign which claimed as the prime causes of failure the low morale of Indian troops, poor leadership and preparations, and the 'poor quality' of the British 18th Division. Bennett's failure to accept any blame personally, or for his formation, was very much in keeping with the reports of most escapee officers, but seemed particularly mean-spirited coming from such a senior officer.[45]

Not all news of Singapore reached Britain through official channels. One evacuated 18th Division staff officer sent a lengthy letter to his father, who was a Member of Parliament and a retired admiral. Rear-Admiral T. P. H. Beamish sent extracts from the letter to Churchill, and the file was circulated in Whitehall. Captain T. Beamish reported:

> The general behaviour and attitude of the AIF on Singapore island certainly reflects nothing but discredit on its Commander. Some people seem to think that the mere fact of being an Australian gives one a free hand to behave like a hooligan.

Gossip of this kind eventually reached the ears of staff at the Australian High Commission.[46]

Churchill wrote to thank Beamish's father for the information, and Secretary of State for War, P. J. Grigg, commented: 'I should think this is nearer to the truth than anything we have had so far.' Grigg was certainly impressed by the criticism of Australians. When General Sir Claude Auchinleck, the Middle East Commander-in-Chief, later requested London that the death penalty be reintroduced for desertion and cowardice in the field, Grigg told Churchill that he doubted whether the facts in Libya justified the request: 'On the other hand the behaviour of the Australian troops in Malaya makes a much more powerful justification.'[47] There was never an official commission of inquiry into the fall of Singapore. Indeed, there were so many major set-backs for the war effort during 1940 to 1942 that it was not practical to do so.

For the British public in general, news of Japanese triumphs in the Far East was obscured by the dramas of the latest phase of the North African campaign, and the vast conflict underway in the Soviet Union. Even closer to home, British newspapers were full of the scandalous story whereby on 12 February two German battlecruisers and a heavy cruiser, the *Gneisenau*, *Scharnhorst* and *Prinz Eugen*, had been allowed to safely sail up the English Channel from Brest in broad daylight. The Royal Navy and RAF in southern England had been caught offguard and their uncoordinated attacks had failed. *The Times* commented on 14 February: 'Nothing more mortifying to the pride of sea-power has happened in home water since the seventeenth century.' [48]

# 17

# Aftermath

At dawn on 16 February, the day after the capitulation, General Yamashita rose from his bed and went outdoors. General Suzuki, XXV Army's chief of staff, followed behind his commanding officer at a discreet distance. He watched as Yamashita stood at the edge of a wood and bowed to pray facing in the direction of the Emperor's Palace in Tokyo. That day over 100,000 men of the British Empire went into captivity, much to the surprise of the Japanese, who could not fathom how such a large force could surrender having suffered relatively few casualties. XXV Army's staff had been expecting only half as many prisoners.[1]

At the first opportunity Lieutenant-Colonel Tsuji went into Singapore to inspect the fallen city. Looking back from the roof of a building he could see a Japanese flag fluttering on the heights of Bukit Timah. Singapore was full of surrendered European and Indian servicemen. Tsuji noted:

> The British soldiers looked like men who had finished their work by contract at a suitable salary, and were now taking a rest free from the anxiety of the battlefield. They even bowed courteously to us Japanese whom they hated.[2]

Tsuji was not impressed by the defeated garrison's lack of fighting spirit.

Also on the morning of 16 February, General Key and Lieutenant-Colonel Harrison went to the headquarters of the Imperial Guards Division to obtain directions regarding the surrender of their formation. They spoke with the Guards' chief of staff in French. After the formal discussions were finished, the Japanese officer motioned to a map and said:

> We have captured Malaya and Singapore. We will shortly have captured Burma, Sumatra, Java and the Philippines. We do not want India. We do not want Australia. It is time for your Empire to compromise. What else can you do?

'What will we do?' replied Key. 'We will drive you back. We will occupy your country. That is what we will do.'[3] Key's words were a bold statement for an Englishman to make in February 1942.

The Japanese took a stern line so far as looting or any suspected seditious activity was concerned. Malaya Command's Brigadier Simson was driven through the town sitting between two Japanese officers in the back of a car.

When looters were seen in some shops, the car halted and soldiers in the front seat rose and fired into the crowd to disperse it. Near the docks, Simson saw some labourers tied up with barbed wire, of whom eight Chinese were promptly beheaded in front of a crowd. In a separate incident severed heads of Chinese were displayed in a cage outside the Cathay Building to intimidate the populace.[4] The severed heads of executed civilians were also mounted on spiked railings in another part of Singapore.

Yamashita's headquarters transferred to the Raffles Institution. News arrived at the headquarters of rejoicing in Japan at XXV Army's capture of Singapore. The general, however, told his senior commanders that the battle for Singapore was just a prelude to further operations.[5]

On the morning of 16 February a Japanese officer called on Governor Thomas at the Singapore Club and instructed him to assemble all European civilians at the nearby Padang next morning. Around three thousand European civilians, including General Heath's wife, were interned in Changi gaol. British military leaders were told by the Japanese to march all European personnel, including European officers of Asian troops, to Changi camp on 17 February. That day over 50,000 European troops marched off to internment. Changi camp was at the north-east tip of the island and was the site of a collection of barracks used to house part of Singapore's peacetime garrison. (Chinese, Malay and Eurasian personnel either merged into the civilian population, were interned, paroled, or in some cases, executed.) On the mainland European prisoners were collected at Pudu gaol in Kuala Lumpur. By July 1942 over a thousand had been housed at the gaol.[6] Towards the end of the year all European prisoners at Kuala Lumpur were sent to Singapore.

At Changi internal discipline was re-established amongst the disgruntled prisoners, who in crowded conditions were reorganzied as formed units. Rations were low but the mild equatorial climate helped the men to maintain their health. Working parties were sent into Singapore to labour for the Japanese on the wharves or clearing rubble. For propaganda purposes, the Japanese arranged for Europeans, and the physically larger Australians in particular, to sweep the streets in front of cinema cameras. For similar reasons General Yamashita inspected a full parade of prisoners, including the senior British generals. (With the capitulation of the East Indies, POW camps for British personnel were also established at Sumatra and Java.)

At Changi General Percival and other generals lived amid their army. A sympathetic biographer of Percival commented:

> the defeated GOC could be seen sitting, head in hands, outside the married quarter he now shared with seven brigadiers, a colonel, his ADC, cook sergeant

and batman. He discussed his personal feelings with few, spent hours walking around the extensive compound, ruminating on the reverse and what might have been.[7]

Percival and officers of the rank of colonel and above were transferred to north Asia in August 1942.[8] Prior to departure, Percival appointed Lieutenant-Colonel E. B. Holmes of the 1st Manchesters to command at Changi, with the AIF's Lieutenant-Colonel Galleghan as his deputy. Major-General Beckwith-Smith of the 18th Division died of an illness at Singapore in November 1942.

During late 1942 and 1943 Changi camp was emptied of most of its prisoners as work parties were sent across South-East Asia and beyond to labour for the Japanese. Many British and Australian POWs were sent to build a railway between Burma and Thailand to improve the communications of the Japanese army halted at the frontier of India. A series of camps were established along the route, and, in a region in which disease was endemic and the terrain inhospitable, the men cleared undergrowth, felled trees, dug embankments and cuttings, and built bridges across rivers. Cholera, ulcers, dysentery, overwork, mistreatment at the hands of brutal guards, limited medical care and poor diet led to many deaths among the prisoners. In some contingents the rates varied between a quarter and a half of the personnel involved. About 12,500 out of a force of 61,000 British, Australian, Dutch and United States POWs used to build the Thai-Burma railway died in the course of its construction (6318 Britains and 2815 Australians).[9] Some weakened POW survivors from the railway returned to Changi late in 1943 and early 1944.

In addition, between seventy and ninety thousand of the 270,000 Asian labourers employed on the project died. Forty-five thousand Indian labourers recruited in Malaya were among the dead.[10] With the collapse of the rubber industry in Japanese-occupied Malaya, Indian estate workers had become desperate for work. These men were hired as contract labourers but soon found themselves working under slave conditions once they arrived in Thailand.

Whilst some POW parties were being shipped by the Japanese to Thailand and Burma, other parties were sent to Borneo, Japan, Korea and elsewhere in Asia. These POWs travelled in small, crowded cargo ships. Several of these ships were sunk by American submarines as their commanders were unaware the vessels were carrying friendly personnel. For example, prisoners left Singapore in September 1944 bound for Japan in two transports, a thousand British troops in one ship and 649 Australians and 599 Britons in the other. The senior POW officer was Brigadier Varley, who had also been a prominent senior officer along the Thai-Burma railway. Off Hainan Island the ships were sunk after submarines attacked their convoy. Just eight hundred survivors were picked up, including 141 by the submarines.[11] Varley was among those who died at sea. In another major incident only six of 2400 Australian and British POWs at Borneo survived starvation, illness, beatings and exhaustion on a series of marches from Sandakan to Ranau in 1945.

An official calculation later determined that of 42,610 British POWs of the Japanese, 10,298 died in captivity.[12] Of those Australians captured by the Japanese across the Asia-Pacific region, 7777 died in captivity, of whom 123 were officers.[13] Survival rates of officers were dramatically better than other ranks. This was due to the Japanese sparing the officers a good deal of manual labour and giving them a range of minor privileges.

After the capitulation Indian prisoners were separated from their European officers, though not from their Indian officers and Viceroy's Commissioned Officers. On 17 February, whilst European troops marched to Changi, the great majority of the 45,000 Indian prisoners taken at Singapore were assembled at Farrer Park. Under the direction of Major Fujiwara, a Japanese intelligence officer Captain Mohan Singh, Fujiwara's chief Indian collaborator, harangued the troops about working with the Japanese for the cause of Indian nationalism.

There were numerous Indian officers senior to Mohan Singh among the POWs taken at Singapore. Of almost a thousand Indian Army officers captured in Malaya the majority were British, but around a quarter were Indian, including numerous medical officers. The most senior officer was Lieutenant-Colonel Naranjan Singh Gill, who had been on the staff of the 11th Division. Gill assumed command of an Indian Prisoner of War headquarters. But he soon fell reluctantly into line with Fujiwara's and Mohan Singh's plans to raise a new force from captured personnel. In March 1942 a conference was held at Tokyo to which the Japanese flew Mohan Singh, Gill and other Indian nationalist leaders in Malaya. Early in May, recruiting for the 'Indian National Army' began in earnest.

Some Indian officers believed the Japanese claim that they had come to free Asia from European colonialism.[14] Knowledge at Singapore that unrest was reaching a new peak in India across the summer of 1942 heightened nationalist consciousness. After the war, though, few Indian officers claimed that nationalist fervour was their sole reason for joining the Indian National Army. Captain P. K. Sahgal stated:

> After protracted discussions the only solution that we could think of for our country's problems was the formation of a strong and well-disciplined armed

body which should fight for the liberation of India from the existing alien rule, should be able and ready to provide protection to their countrymen against any possible molestation by the Japanese, and to resist any attempt by the latter to establish themselves as rulers of the country in place of the British.[15]

Given the scale of British defeat in Malaya, there was a possibility that the Japanese might soon be in India.

Grievances amongst Indian officers about pay and racial discrimination came to the surface in captivity, as did opportunistic desires to avoid internment and gain promotion in the new army. Some officers doubted the integrity of the Japanese, and the ability of Mohan Singh to represent their interests, but joined rather than remain uninvolved. In the INA VCOs became junior officers and this was an incentive for them to join. Postwar intelligence estimates concluded that 50 per cent of Indian officers and 25 per cent of VCOs joined the INA in 1942.[16]

The actions of Indian officers were an important influence on their men and disillusioned sepoys joined the INA by the thousands. Indian other ranks had experienced defeat and had been badly let down by their British leaders. Sepoys were told that the days of the British were over. They had no means of knowing if that was true.[17] There was also strong pressure on Indian sub-units to stay together in a time of great uncertainty. The fact that the INA controlled most POW camps made it hard for the sepoys in those camps to remain aloof. They were vulnerable to mostly subtle forms of coercion and persuasion. One senior Indian officer told a paraded battalion they could either dig latrines for the Japanese or become soldiers again.[18] Medical personnel often felt obliged to join the INA so as to continue with their work unmolested.

Those Indians who stayed out of the INA did so for a host of reasons. Some Indian officers were highly anglicized and sympathetic to the British viewpoint. Others had a long family tradition of service to the Indian Army, or believed that joining the INA was an act of desertion. There was some suspicion of the motives of those jockeying for posts in the new army. A few officers and VCOs managed to escape to India from Malaya in 1942–43. Others escaped to India from Burma having joined the INA expressly for that purpose.

At Singapore and on the mainland 55,000 Indian personnel were taken prisoner. Perhaps 20,000 enlisted in the INA soon after its creation, and another 20,000 joined between June and August 1942, leaving only 15,000 who did not join.[19] Recruitment rates varied greatly between units. Among the infantry, British intelligence officers later singled out the Gurkhas, 7/6th Rajputana Rifles, 2/10th Baluchis, and Jind, Mysore, Bahawalpur and

Hyderabad States Force battalions as having low enlistment rates; whereas the 17th Dogras, 18th Garhwalis, 4/19th Hyderabads, Kapurthala State Force, 9th Jats, and 14th and 16th Punjabis had high rates of enlistment. (Though in January 1943 many men from the 17th Dogras and 14th and 16th Punjabis left the INA.) 16,000 men were formed into an INA division. Mohan Singh wanted to raise a larger force but 16,000 was the ceiling set by the Japanese. The surplus volunteers remained as POWs.[20]

When British Indian Army officers at Changi camp heard of the INA they had mixed reactions. The senior Indian Army officer at Singapore, Lieutenant-General Heath, felt that self-interest and ignorance were the main reasons for heavy enlistments. Some British officers were furious at the perfidy of their Indian officer colleagues and subordinates. Others were more understanding, and guiltily self-aware that they had badly let down those Indians under their command. Armed INA Sikhs helped to guard European prisoners at Changi, and took delight at requiring the white men to salute and perform other subservient tasks. Early in September 1942, an Indian firing squad executed two British and two Australian soldiers who had attempted to escape. Among the squad's members was a captain of the Kapathala State Force.[21]

As 1942 drew to a close, relations between the INA's leaders and the Japanese became strained. In December both Mohan Singh and Gill were arrested by the Japanese. The INA collapsed briefly but in January 1943 a new INA administrative committee was formed. About 4000 of the INA's 16,000 men left the force at this time.

The arrival of Subhash Chandra Bose at Singapore early in July 1943 gave the stagnant INA a new lease of life. Bose was a veteran Indian nationalist politician. In 1941 he had fled to Germany via Afghanistan and the Soviet Union. In Germany Bose found Nazism attractive. He helped to raise a force for the Germans among Indian POWs held in Europe. Bose travelled to Japan by submarine in the early months of 1943. His nationalism was genuine and he had an inspiring and charismatic personality. A Provisional Government of Free India was set up at Singapore later in the year. A rejuvenated INA enlisted another 10,000 POWs. By 1945 18,000 Indian civilians in South-East Asia had also enlisted. The 20–25,000 Indian Army personnel in the INA from 1943 onwards was fewer than in 1942, but a substantial body of men nonetheless.

With Bose's blessing, part of the INA was sent to Burma, and took part in a number of dismally unsuccessful operations in 1944–45.[22] Losses in the Imphal campaign of 1944 were very heavy and the rest of the INA in Burma were mopped up early the following year. The military impact of the INA was limited and the fighting spirit of its men often abysmal.

The advancing Indian Army did not take kindly to the INA in Burma. In general, sepoys who had fought and won hard campaigns against the Japanese had little time for those who had chosen to consort with the enemy.

Of the many thousands of Indian POWs who did not join the INA, or left in the early months of its existence, thousands were sent abroad to labour for the Japanese across the Pacific theatre. Many of these Indian POWs had died by the time the war ended. Death rates were very high in some locations and at Wae Wae, on the north coast of New Guinea, starving Japanese guards resorted to cannibalising their prisoners.[23] Without doubt the death rate among those POWs who were not in the INA from 1943–45 was substantially higher than for those who were in it.[24] At the war's end, British officials determined that of 55,000 Indian POWs lost in Malaya, the INA enrolled 22,000 in their ranks from 1943 to 1945, whilst 15,000 POWs were shipped to the South-West Pacific, and another 18,000 POWs were camped elsewhere in Malaya and the East Indies.[25]

Once the war was over, the British could not treat captured INA personnel as rebels in the strictest sense of the word, given the rapidly changing constitutional situation in India. By the close of 1945 Indian self-government was not far off. (Bose was killed in an air crash in August 1945.) In so far as Indian troops taken at Singapore came from within the heart of the Indian Army's traditional recruiting grounds, many ex-INA men had relatives in the Indian Army. One INA officer had a brother who won the Victoria Cross. During the war INA agents landed in India for clandestine work were executed upon capture; but, for political and paternalist reasons, British authorities in India took a soft line towards INA men after the war. Unless a specific crime was provable, INA prisoners were released and sent home. According to one set of figures, of 23,268 captured INA ex-POW personnel, after classification by investigating officers, only 3880 were declared to be 'white', meaning that they had joined the INA either in order to desert or to infiltrate the organisation. These men were able to remain in the Indian Army. 6177 were classified as 'black', the hard core of the INA, and 13,211 were 'greys'. 'Greys' were discharged and the 'blacks' dismissed from the army.[26]

In November-December 1945 a very public court-martial of three Indian officers was held at the Red Fort in Delhi. The three officers were Captain Shah Nawaz Khan and Lieutenant G. S. Dhillon of the 1/14th Punjabis, and Captain P. K. Sahgal of the 2/10th Baluchis. All three officers were convicted of waging war against the King, and Shah Nawaz Khan was also convicted on a charge of abetment to murder. Sentences of transportation for life were remitted and the three men were cashiered. Yet the Indian political class defended the men on trial as patriots. The Red Fort trial was a public relations disaster for British officialdom. Other less public trials took place in 1946.[27]

After India's independence from British rule in 1947, ex-INA officers were offered reinstatement in the Indian Army, but only at the rank they held at the time of the fall of Singapore. Few men took advantage of this offer, and ex-INA men were not welcomed by officers who had taken part in successful world war campaigns. A number of former INA officers went on to hold high posts in the diplomatic service and politics. Those Indian officers who had remained loyal in captivity carried on with their careers after the war, and several became senior generals prior to retirement.

The Japanese had passed swiftly and lightly over the civilian population of mainland Malaya during the 1941–42 campaign. But the civilian population of Singapore Island had suffered heavily during the fighting. A post-war estimate calculated that late in January 1942, and during the first week of February, 150–200 civilians had died per day, with between six and seven thousand dying during the second week of February prior to the capitulation. Admissions to civil hospitals added up to 22,000, and many more people received treatment at first aid posts.[28]

Yet the Japanese had further horrors waiting in store for the population of Singapore. In China the Japanese had routinely conducted large-scale atrocities against those elements of the population believed to be hostile to their presence. The massacres at Nanking in 1937 are only the best-known example. XXV Army headquarters had begun planning a purge of Singapore's Chinese population midway through the campaign. After the capitulation Yamashita spoke to his staff and subordinates of the need for 'mopping-up' measures against anti-Japanese elements, looters and other trouble-makers. The office of XXV Army's chief of staff issued detailed instructions, and Lieutenant-Colonel Tsuji played an important role in organizing what became known as the *Sook Ching* – 'purification by elimination'.[29]

Soon after the capitulation Lieutenant-Colonel Masayuki Oishi, commander of No. 2 Field Kempaitai, took over offices at the Supreme Court Building. Singapore Town was broken into sectors and each placed under the control of a Kempaitai officer. The local police were used to spread the order that all males between the ages of eighteen and fifty were to assemble at designated registration centres formed by fencing streets off with barbed wire. Some men were told to bring several days' rations. At the registration centres the men were questioned with the aid of informers. Those believed to be Communists, Chinese Nationalists, members of secret societies, military personnel or criminals were led away to holding pens. At some centres the screening was carried out methodically over several days; at others the process was conducted in a random fashion in a few hours. Those released had a rubber stamp with a Chinese character stamped on their arms to show Japanese sentries.[30]

Over a period of days many truck loads of detainees were driven off to beaches on the south coast of Singapore. Chinese men were ordered to walk into the sea and machine gunned by Japanese guards. At other places mass graves were prepared and executions carried out in the vicinity. Lee Kip Lin remembered that when executions were carried out in the district, 'the whole day of that day you could hear the machine-gun firing, not only from near my house but also from the other direction towards the Seaview Hotel'.[31]

Chan Cheng Yean was a member of the Volunteer Force. On 28 February he was part of a group of ninety men taken to Bedok facing the sea, where they were shot in front of a trench. He was hit in the knee and pinned in the trench by other bodies. The trenches were covered by planks and earth but Chan Cheng Yean crawled out after the Japanese had left the scene.[32] In the months to come shallow graves on the beach were uncovered by the tide. Few detainees were seen again. A similar screening process was carried out in villages outside Singapore, and elsewhere in Malaya, particularly at Penang.

Senior Japanese officers later conceded that 5000 Chinese were executed by Kempaitai, and detachments from all three of XXV Army's divisions. Major-General Kawamura, who had been appointed Singapore garrison commander, testified after the war that on 23 February 1942 he had seen General Yamashita after receiving reports that between four and five thousand Chinese had been executed or detained for execution. Yamashita had told Kawamura to continue with the operation, as he doubted whether all anti-Japanese elements had been purged.[33] A Domei News Agency reporter, Takafumi Hishikari, was attached to XXV Army headquarters's intelligence section. He later claimed that the intelligence chief, Colonel Sugita, had told him that in the region of 25,000 people had been executed. Leaders of Singapore's Chinese community have estimated that 30–50,000 people were killed. A Chinese civilian later commented: 'The Japanese soldiers' cruelty to the people during the war suggested that they were less than human.'[34] This statement is in keeping with the views of a great many Chinese in Malaya.

The British administration at Singapore made remarkably little effort after the war to determine the extent of the *Sook Ching* death toll. It was not in the interest of the returning colonial power to draw attention to its failure to protect its subjects. The true toll was doubtless well in excess of the five thousand conceded by the Japanese. Most Singaporean Chinese families lost one or more men in the period after the capitulation.

Under Japanese occupation Singapore was renamed Shonan – 'Light of the South'. The statue of Raffles near Singapore River was taken down and a Shonan Shinto shrine erected on the heights of Bukit Timah. Shortly after the conquest Southern Army headquarters was relocated at Singapore.

During the occupation the local economy steadily collapsed. Malaya was cut off from the rubber, tin and other raw material markets that lay in the Allies' sphere of the world. The Japanese purchased some of those commodities still being produced at reduced quantities, but they did so with worthless paper currency and were unable to transport to Japan all that they did confiscate. With a ruined currency, internal trade wound down to a low level. There were food shortages in Malaya, though never the kind of famine conditions that devastated Indo-China towards the war's end (with between 600,000 and two millions perishing).[35]

The Japanese worked to induce collaboration among the Malay community, and to a lesser extent among the Indian community. Malay rulers kept their positions and the Japanese tolerated Islam. Western-trained Malay and Indian intellectuals had hoped that the Japanese would advance a nationalist agenda. But the Japanese planned to annex Malaya and there was no question of local autonomy or political independence. The purges among the Chinese ensured that Japanese-Chinese relations in Malaya were turbulent. The Chinese community was also forced to pay fines to the Japanese. Guerilla groups, mostly inspired by Communism, took to the jungle and harassed the occupiers, with some British assistance, up until the liberation of 1945. Ultimately Japanese cruelty, racial superiority, corruption, forced labour and crop and raw material confiscations ensured that the bulk of the local population were genuinely glad to see the return of the colonial rulers who had let them down in 1942.

Sumatra, Java, and the rest of the Dutch East Indies had soon fallen to the Japanese following the loss of Singapore. The 100,000 strong Dutch colonial army did not put up much resistance, even by the standards of the effort to defend Malaya. General Wavell's chief of staff, General Pownall, later noted in his diary: 'From the beginning to the end of this campaign, we have been outmatched by better soldiers.'[36] A combined fleet of British, Dutch, American and Australian cruisers and destroyers made attempts to disrupt Japanese troop convoys, but to little avail. In the one-sided Battle of the Java Sea on 27–28 February, the Allied fleet was mostly sunk. Among the ships to go down were the cruisers HMS *Exeter* and HMAS *Perth*. Around 11,500 British and Australian army and air force servicemen went into captivity at Java, including the AIF's 2/2nd Pioneer and 2/3rd Machine Gun Battalions. Those two units had been disembarked from the leading ship of the convoys carrying two Australian divisions arriving from the Middle East. Small Australian garrisons unwisely left at Ambon, Rabaul and Timor also went into the bag.

In the Philippines, over 100,000 Filipino and American servicemen and civilian refugees had been trapped in the Bataan peninsula early in January 1942. The neck of the peninsula, only fifteen miles wide, was dominated by jungle-covered mountains. The beleaguered garrison suffered from lack of food, malaria and dysentery, and was eventually reduced to eating cavalry and transport animals. Unbeknownst to the Americans, the Japanese army besieging Bataan was also debilitated by malaria. In actual fact, at this point in time, the Japanese force was less than half the strength of the army under General MacArthur's command.

On 11 March 1942 MacArthur, on President Roosevelt's orders, was spirited out of the Philippines in a speed-boat. On arrival in Australia MacArthur told the press in relation to the Philippines: 'I shall return.' But the Japanese, after reinforcements had arrived, overran Bataan early in April. On 6 May the last bastion of resistance, the island fortress of Corregidor, also fell. A grim captivity for the Filipino-American garrison began with a 'death march' to their first camps of internment. Thousands died as a consequence. Japanese losses in the campaign had been 12,000 killed and wounded, a tenth of the strength of the army they had beaten. Thanks to Japan's command of the seas, the gallant American led defence of Bataan had had little effect on the overall course of the war in South-East Asia.

Whilst the East Indies and Philippines were being overrun, Japan's Southern Army had set out on the final phase of their planned round of conquests by advancing from Thailand into Burma. Burma was the last overland supply route to the Chinese Nationalists still in Allied hands.

The need to defend Burma caused the British and Australian governments to come into conflict whilst the pain of the loss of Singapore was still fresh. The 6th and 7th Australian Divisions were among the first reinforcements to arrive in the Far East from the Middle East. It had originally been determined that the troops were bound for Sumatra and Java. But after the rapid loss of the East Indies the question arose as to their revised destination. General Wavell was in favour of diverting the Australian Corps to Burma. The Chiefs of Staff in Australia, on the other hand, wanted the divisions to defend Australia. Prime Minister Curtin told the Dominions Office in respect to Burma: 'there might be a recurrence of the experiences of the Greek and Malayan campaigns'.[37] The 7th Australian Division was within sailing distance of Rangoon in late February but, despite appeals from Churchill and

Roosevelt, the Australian government refused to allow it to be landed in Burma. (Soon afterwards, however, the Australian government agreed to let the main body of the 6th Division join the garrison of Ceylon to sooth imperial relations.) [38] Australian troops would doubtless have been a valuable improvised addition to a desperate British-Indian army in Burma. But at some point the Australian government had to allow self-interest to take precedence over the conflicting desires of a British government that refused to make the war in the Far East a priority.

On 8 March Japanese troops of XV Army entered the Burmese capital of Rangoon. A fortnight previously the 17th Indian Division defending south-east Burma had been trapped on the wrong side of a wide river, after its commander had ordered the last bridge to be demolished. The remnants swam across without most of their equipment. This was yet another fiasco for the Indian Army. British forces began a thousand mile retreat to India that only ended during May. The monsoons and the wild, mountainous jungle of north-west Burma provided a barrier behind which Allied forces could endeavour to reorganize. Civil war broke out in Burma with the entry of the Japanese. This helped to set in motion a mass exodus towards India by half a million Indian civilians. Thousands would die before their journey was over.

To complete British discomfiture in India, early in April Japan's aircraft carriers raided across the Bay of Bengal to Ceylon and the east coast of India. For the loss of a handful of Japanese aircraft, two British heavy cruisers and a small aircraft carrier were sunk. The Royal Navy withdrew its biggest ships to the coast of Africa to escape. Merchant shipping in the Bay of Bengal was paralysed. Civilians fled inland in eastern India.

In Australia, the Japanese onslaught had been a tremendous shock. Down to 1941, Australians had always looked to the 'mother country', Great Britain, for succour and protection. The New South Wales Governor, Lord Wake-hurst, wrote that 'deep in the Australian mind is embedded the belief that, come what may, Britain would look after Australia'.[39] But the fall of South-East Asia had caused a wholesale reappraisal of Australian foreign policy away from reliance on the United Kingdom. On 26 December 1941 Prime Minister Curtin had told the Australian people: 'Without any inhibitions of any kind, I make it quite clear that Australia looks to America, free of any pangs as to our traditional links or kinship with the United Kingdom.' The Japanese aircraft carrier raid on Darwin on 19 February 1942 fuelled a rising sense of panic. During March Australian commanders expected landings in the Darwin area and possibly near Port Moresby in Papua New Guinea.[40]

Once the Japanese had captured all of their objectives in South-East Asia and the western Pacific, the question posed itself, what should be done next?

Japan's leadership was in general agreement that it was necessary to continue offensive action so as to maintain momentum and initiative. The army though had only limited troops available for further operations. The bulk of the army was still deployed on the Asian mainland. Nonetheless, in preparation for further operations, Rabaul was made the major fleet base for the south-west Pacific. Light Japanese forces were landed on the north coast of New Guinea in March 1942.

Port Moresby, on the south coast of Papua New Guinea, was a port from which the Japanese might menace Australia and other smaller islands in the south-west Pacific. After some weeks' debate among army and navy staff planners, on 15 March Imperial General Headquarters in Tokyo decided to capture Port Moresby and the Solomon Islands, after which the naval staff wanted to take Fiji, Samoa and New Caledonia to isolate Australia from the United States.[41] In contrast, Admiral Yamamoto and the staff of the Combined Fleet wanted to destroy the United States Fleet in the central Pacific. Early in April Yamamoto forced a showdown with his rival commanders in Toyko. The army staff supported Yamamoto's plans as they required few troops. Eventually the naval staff gave way so long as they could continue to develop their preferred operations in the south-west Pacific. In consequence, Japan's naval forces were split at a crucial moment in the war. Japanese war planers were suffering from what would subsequently be termed 'victory disease'. Late in April Imperial Headquarters, influenced in part by the recent carrier raid on Tokyo, approved Yamamoto's plan for a major operation in the central Pacific in June.[42]

Early in May the subsidiary plan to seize Port Moresby from the sea was set in motion. But United States intelligence intercepts successfully uncovered the main features of the Japanese operation. Admiral Nimitz sent two of his four carriers to help parry the threat. In the ensuing Battle of the Coral Sea from 4 to 8 May, the Japanese and Americans each lost an aircraft carrier sunk. A second Japanese carrier was badly damaged. With the United States fleet in the south-west Pacific still intact, plans to take Port Moresby from the sea were shelved. The Coral Sea engagement more or less ended any likelihood of Australia facing serious hostile landings.

Admiral Yamamoto's central Pacific plan went ahead within a few weeks of the Coral Sea battle. The Admiral's intention to attack Midway Island, to the west of Hawaii, was designed to draw the United States fleet into a decisive battle. But United States code breakers had again discovered the outline of the Japanese plan. On 4 June four Japanese aircraft carriers were sunk. From this point the Imperial Japanese Navy was forced to adopt a defensive posture. The whole complexion of the war in the Pacific had changed.

In late July 1942 Japanese forces began to advance overland towards Port Moresby. As a supporting operation, late in August, a small Japanese force was landed at Milne Bay, on the east coast of Papua New Guinea. The six Australian battalions based at Milne Bay soundly defeated the invaders. By mid September logistical failure, illness and Australian opposition had halted the Japanese thirty miles from Port Moresby. The Japanese force was ordered to retire to its bases on the north coast of Papua. A counter-offensive in the following months by the bulk of two Australian and one United States divisions shattered the Japanese. By January 1943 13,000 Japanese servicemen had been killed or died of disease in Papua New Guinea.[43]

On 7 August 1942 the Americans took an early advantage of their victory at Midway by landing marines at Guadalcanal, at the southern end of the south-west Pacific's Solomon Islands. Fighting on land, at sea and in the air lasted at Guadalcanal until February 1943. The Japanese could not match the Americans in a war of attrition and a withdrawal from Guadalcanal was ordered. (The architect of the Pearl Harbor operation, Admiral Yamamoto, died when his aircraft was shot down in April 1943.)

In the Indian Ocean, during 1942, the British Eastern Fleet, which included two modern fleet carriers for most of the year, remained firmly on the defensive. No major ships were transferred to the south-west Pacific, despite American requests. Not until August 1944 did the British Defence Committee decide that the time was right to form a fleet in the south-west Pacific. The British Pacific Fleet finally sailed into Sydney Harbour on 10 February 1945 and later took part in operations in the north-west Pacific.[44]

Meanwhile, fighting was underway in Burma and the border area of eastern India. A British offensive launched along the Arakan coast in December 1942 ground on for six months, but achieved little. The Chindit expeditions, airlifted behind Japanese lines, were heroic in concept but had less impact in practice than had been hoped. In March 1944, Japanese forces, commanded by General Mutaguchi, the 18th Division's senior officer in Malaya, set out to invade India. After a long battle and a disastrous retreat the Japanese army was shattered. The Indian Army had finally won a great victory at the expense of the Japanese.[45]

There was further fighting in the Solomons and New Guinea across 1943–44 in a bid to neutralize Rabaul, whilst Admiral Nimitz's expanded naval forces began to advance across the central Pacific through the Gilbert, Marshall and Caroline Islands. The new American aircraft carriers that came into service from late 1943 onwards transformed the Pacific war in the Allies' favour. By late 1944 American forces from the central and south-west Pacific were ready to invade the Philippines, in what was to become the most important land and sea campaign of the Pacific war.

General Yamashita, 'The Tiger of Malaya', was in command of the Japanese area army in the Philippines. He assumed his new command of over 400,000 men on 9 October 1944, just as the Americans were poised to attack. Surprisingly, Yamashita had not played a prominent part in the war following his capture of Singapore. General Tojo had seen Yamashita as a potential rival and possible candidate for the vacant war minister's position. During 1942, Yamashita had been sent to command one of the two army groups stationed in Manchuria. Only after Tojo's resignation as Prime Minister was Yamashita recalled from Manchuria.[46] Lieutenant-General Sosaku Suzuki, Yamashita's chief of staff in Malaya, commanded XXXV Army with responsibility for the central and southern Philippines.

The first American landings were made at the island of Leyte on 20 October 1944 amid a great series of naval battles. Yamashita had wanted to make the defence of Luzon the decisive battle, but Imperial Headquarters and Field Marshal Terauchi of Southern Army ordered that Leyte be heavily reinforced to counter the invasion. By the end of 1944 Japanese forces at Leyte had been mostly destroyed by the massive firepower the Americans were able to deploy. Mopping up operations continued into 1945 and Suzuki was killed in the fighting.[47]

Luzon, the main Philippines island, was invaded on 8 January 1945. On Luzon, Yamashita had 275,000 men and freedom from Imperial Headquarters to conduct the campaign as he saw fit. The general sensibly rejected the option of bottling his forces in the Bataan peninsula, and instead concentrated his forces in three mountain strongholds. Yamashita had no intention of defending Manila. But at Manila Rear-Admiral Sanji Iwabuchi had 16,000 naval troops under his command. The admiral decided that it was his duty to deny Manila's harbour installations for as long as possible. On his own initiative he posted his men, and several thousand local army personnel, in central Manila.

Facing only light opposition, American troops reached the outskirts of Manila early in February. Street fighting lasted a month. In the battle the Japanese force was annihilated but parts of the city were demolished and an estimated 100,000 civilians died.[48] Communications between Manila and Yamashita's headquarters in northern Luzon were cut by the intervening presence of powerful Americans forces. News of events at Manila thus took some days to reach the general. Yamashita later claimed that he signalled Admiral Iwabuchi to 'withdraw at once in accordance with our original plan'. Iwabuchi refused to consider retreat and rejected further orders to withdraw.[49]

Most of the trapped civilians to die in Manila were caught by crossfire, much of which was incoming shelling by a massive assemblage of United

States artillery. However the horrors of the carnage were heightened by the behaviour of half-crazed Japanese sailors and soldiers, who committed all kinds of atrocities upon the civilians in their midst. Murder, rape and torture were commonplace within the confined space of the shrinking perimeter. Advancing American infantry came upon the evidence whilst it was still fresh.

In north Luzon, Yamashita's main force held mountain passes leading into the region from February to May 1945. There was much heavy fighting. Yamashita's army was subsequently surrounded and from June to August the pocket was driven into the harshest terrain in northern Luzon.[50] Yamashita's force was probably only a month away from final defeat and dispersal into smaller parties when the surrender came. At the war's end just 115,000 Japanese were still alive and at large in the Philippines, out of a force of 450,000.[51] There is no doubt that Yamashita's defence of Luzon displayed generalship of the highest standard.[52] A thin General Yamashita gave himself up to the Americans. He did not commit hari-kiri and was reported to have said: 'If I kill myself someone else will have to take the blame.'[53]

On 2 September 1945 in Tokyo Bay a ceremonial surrender of the Japanese government was held on the USS *Missouri*. General MacArthur accepted the Japanese surrender and he placed Generals Percival and Wainwright, the American commander MacArthur had left behind in the Philippines, behind him as the documents were signed. Percival was given one of the pens MacArthur used in the ceremony. Percival then flew to the Philippines to witness General Yamashita's formal surrender of Japanese forces at Manila. The Japanese general was unaware that his British counterpart at Singapore was going to be present. Yamashita was said to have been surprised for a moment when Percival entered the room. After the war, Percival retired in 1946 as an honorary lieutenant-general. He became life president of the Far East POWs' Association, colonel of his old regiment, deputy lieutenant of his county, and wrote a book about the campaign he had fought in 1941–42. He died on 31 January 1966.

Yamashita's fate after the war was not a happy one. He was put on trial as a war criminal by the Americans. The trial began in Manila on 29 October 1945. The main charges against the general related to his responsibility for the massacres that undoubtedly took place in Manila. There were also charges relating to Japanese reprisals against civilian populations suspected of supporting Filipino guerillas. Such actions had been routine in the war in China. Senior Japanese officers testified that Yamashita had ordered that Manila was not to be defended. Nonetheless, the general's death sentence was pronounced on 7 December, the anniversary of the bombing of

Pearl Harbor. Lieutenant-General Akira Muto, Yamashita's chief of staff, commented that he 'was executed for crimes which he knew nothing of, which his men committed regardless of what he said'.[54] Yamashita told an interviewer:

> My command was as big as MacArthur's or Lord Louis Mountbatten's. How could I tell if some of my soldiers misbehaved themselves? It was impossible for any man in my position to control every action of his subordinate commanders, let alone the deeds of individual soldiers. The charges are completely new to me. If they had happened, and I had known about them, I would have punished the wrongdoers severely. But in war someone has to lose. What I am really being charged with is losing the war. It could have happened to General MacArthur, you know.[55]

Yamashita was hanged on 23 February 1946.

The dubious legal circumstances of Yamashita's execution has garnered for him a degree of sympathy. Yet if the general had not been tried as a war criminal in Manila, he would very likely have been tried by the British in Singapore for the organized massacre of Chinese carried out by Japanese troops after their capture of the island. In October 1945, a British investigating officer had asked Yamashita about the massacres at Singapore. He had replied that the Kempaitai were responsible for the killings, and that he had not been informed of the Kempaitai's activities as they had full discretionary powers to maintain law and order as they saw fit. But it is hard to believe that such a large and protracted operation could have been undertaken by an army without its commander being aware of the fact.

As it happened, General Nishimura of the Imperial Guards, General Kawamura, the Singapore garrison commander, and Lieutenant-Colonel Oishi and four other Kempaitai officers were put on trial at Singapore in March 1947 for the atrocities of February and March 1942. There was no question as to their guilt, but only Kawamura and Oishi were executed. The other five defendants served brief terms of imprisonment. Nishimura was later tried by an Australian court for an indirect association with the Imperial Guards' actions at Parit Sulong and executed in 1951.[56]

# 18

## The Fall of Singapore

Admiral Sir Herbert Richmond summarised Britain's Far East policy prior to 1941 as resting upon 'the illusion that a Two-Hemisphere Empire can be defended by a One-Hemisphere Navy'.[1] This was a penetratingly accurate assessment. The bulk of the Royal Navy's capital ships had been scrapped after the First World War as the German fleet was no longer a threat. In the years that followed, Britain never rearmed sufficiently at sea to meet Japan's challenge in the Far East. The gradual construction of an empty naval base at Singapore during the 1920s and 1930s was no substitute for an effective imperial defence strategy.

At a diplomatic level the Far East policies of successive British governments after the First World War were also built on sand. In the early 1920s the Anglo-Japanese alliance was abandoned as it had become clear that the only likely future enemy of Japan was the United States. During the interwar period Britain and the other western powers did little to check Tokyo's territorial ambitions. In practice, Japan was granted a free hand in China.

When another war with Germany began in 1939, Britain was trapped in an exhausting conflict. Thanks to inadequate preparations, the British governments of 1939–41 lacked the means with which to construct a viable global strategy. There was never any chance of this state of affairs being rectified whilst war raged across Europe and the Middle East. Churchill's wartime government was not directly responsible for prewar military preparations, though individual ministers had been involved in the decisions of other governments and oppositions. The principal exception was of course Churchill himself, who had not held a cabinet post from 1929–39, and had spent much of that period clamouring for increased military spending.[2]

By 1941 the plight of Britain's possessions in the Far East had become extremely precarious, should Japan enter the war. The position of the British Empire in the Far East had been further undermined by the Germans' conquest of France and Holland, Britain's fellow colonists in the region.

With the outbreak of war, Japan swept across South-East Asia. Even if Singapore could have withstood a lengthy siege, the island would have inevitably lain isolated hundreds of miles behind enemy lines. There was never any likelihood of a relief expedition reaching Singapore, given the general weakness of the Royal Navy. The garrison of Malaya could have been stronger in numbers and quality, but to have placed a drastically larger force in such an exposed location would have involved taking a heavy risk. In so far as Singapore was strategically indefensible in the immediate context of 1941–42, Churchill and his advisers were probably right not to have made the island a higher priority.

Despite the failure to build the Far East into a viable scheme of imperial defence, the quite separate question remains as to why such a large British-led army was so easily beaten by a smaller Japanese force.[3] As General Heath later remarked:

> the rearguard operations on the mainland of Malaya could doubtless have been more protracted, the withdrawals more orderly, and less equipment lost. Our force should have doubtless arrived more intact at Singapore.[4]

The British Empire's failure on land and in the air was so bad that it might have undone the situation no matter how sound long-term naval preparations in the Far East might have been.

General Percival has been subjected to a good deal of abuse for the manner of the defeat at Singapore.[5] One of Percival's subordinates commented: 'What we needed there [in Malaya] was a real fighting soldier like Monty who could get right up front and say "come on no bloody nonsense".'[6] After the war Percival resented the extent to which so much of the blame for the loss of Singapore was attributed to him alone. The recriminations caused the general a degree of anguish in retirement. Percival wrote that

> with less able leadership, [we might] have lost Singapore in a month instead of two and a half months – and with it possibly other and more important parts of the British Empire.[7]

It is true that Percival was faced by a particularly difficult geographic and inter-service environment in South-East Asia. Singapore was the main British logistic base in the region, and was terribly exposed to direct attack once the Japanese had won command of the air and sea. Seldom in the Second World War was an army commander let down so badly by both the RAF and Royal Navy at the same time. Hence Percival felt obliged to divide his forces. A number of formations were retained in southern Malaya to oppose potential hostile landings, whilst the bulk of III Corps was sent to northern Malaya for the Matador operation.

Percival's handling of the campaign can, nevertheless, be fairly criticised. He later wrote that he believed his duty was to impose 'the maximum delay on the Japanese at every stage so as to gain time for the arrival and deployment of reinforcements'.[8] In accordance with this principle, Percival refused to withdraw and relieve III Corps formations on the point of collapse, a policy that finally came home to roost at Slim River. The 11th Indian Division was almost destroyed in a month-long engagement in northern and central Malaya. When the time came to fight the campaign's decisive battle in Johore, the defending army was already dangerously weak, and the main body of the British 18th Division had yet to arrive at Singapore. In consequence, there was only a limited opportunity to rebuild a stable front in southern Malaya.

When General Yamashita's army reached the north bank of the Johore Strait, Percival divided his forces and spread them around Singapore's coastal rim. Singapore's defences were especially weak in the north-west corner of the island, opposite the Johore Strait's narrowest stretch. Once the battle at Singapore was underway, not enough was done to organize a counter-attack against the main Japanese landing.

Percival's conduct was certainly influenced by his experience in the First World War, which was a poor preparation for a fast-moving campaign in dense, tropical country. In essence Percival's solution to the crisis in Malaya was to await reinforcement, much as a subordinate general in France and Flanders might have waited for General Headquarters to send a stream of reserve divisions to shore up a threatened section of the line.

In Malaya the speed of the campaign's failure was considerably accelerated by the conduct of subordinate divisional commanders, who lost several important battles in a comprehensive fashion. Murray-Lyon at Jitra, Paris at Slim River and Barstow at Layang Layang all suffered bad defeats. Indeed there were few successful British commanders anywhere in Malaya. Key has always been regarded as the main exception. III Corps's Lieutenant-General Heath had few opportunities to exercise independent judgement.[9] Of the Australian commanders, Bennett and Maxwell were unequivocal failures. Although Australia and other Dominions were critical of British generalship in the world wars, they themselves had no mechanism for producing an obviously better type of senior commander.

The troops who comprised the army defending Malaya did not emerge from the campaign with their reputations any more intact than their commanders. Yet a large majority of the British Empire's fighting men in the Far East were volunteers, regulars or reservists. The army comprised relatively few conscripts. The defenders usually outnumbered their Japanese assailants on the Malayan mainland (though this was not the case in the west of Singapore Island). British equipment was also more plentiful than that of the Japanese, particularly in terms of artillery and vehicles. The exception was tanks, but the narrow, jungle-bordered roads of Malaya, frequently intersected by streams, was excellent anti-tank country. But all too often indifferent leadership gave units and larger formations little chance to perform as well as they might otherwise have done. Likewise poor or inappropriate training, and the demoralizing impact of the defeat of British forces in the air and at sea, diminished many an individual soldier's fighting spirit and ability.

When the campaign is looked at in review, from the British perspective, there is little to be gained from pointing the finger at any particular contingent: the defeat was a team effort. Indian troops in Malaya have been heavily criticised in light of the mass desertions to the Japanese-sponsored Indian National Army after Singapore's surrender. Yet in the few profitable encounters for III Corps formations in northern and central Malaya, such as at Kota Bharu and Kampar, Indians were as well represented as British or Gurkha troops. Likewise, in Johore the underprepared 45th Indian Brigade fought no better or worse than the novice 53rd British Brigade. There is often not enough information available with which accurately to assess the losses of those Indian battalions most heavily engaged.

British units in III Corps and the Singapore garrison were minorities in larger imperial formations. This arrangement generally worked well in other campaigns and was important to the notion that all contingents belonged to a single army. The bulk of the principal British formation in Malaya, the 18th Division, only arrived at Singapore when the siege of the island was about to get underway. The men of the division were denied any real chance to prove what they could do.

As for the Australians, their battalions dominated the known casualty list. Losses are an indication of fighting spirit; at least up to the point at which a unit disintegrates, when the Australian story at Singapore had its share of dark moments.

The garrison of Malaya did not fight to the last man and the last round, but the ratio of prisoners to casualties was not dramatically different from other British campaigns of 1940–42; only the scale was extraordinary. In Malaya there was prolonged and bitter fighting in certain localities. Indeed, when the casualty list is examined,* seven battalions in particular (three British and four Australian) suffered losses at a level seldom seen among British-led ground forces anywhere in the Second World War.

It would certainly be a mistake to look upon the British defeat in Malaya as an isolated occurrence. The defeats suffered by the 8th Army in North Africa in mid-1942, culminating in the fall of Tobruk, left greater numbers of men behind on the battlefields, and were worse defeats on an operational

---

* See Appendix 2.

level. The 8th Army was supposed to be the British Empire's First Eleven. A generation earlier battles without number were grossly mismanaged during the First World War. It was the capitulation that made Singapore such a calamity. Tactical and strategic defeat combined to produce a tragic outcome. Not since the capitulation at Yorktown in 1781, presaging as it did the loss of the thirteen North American colonies, had such an catastrophe befallen British arms.

So what of the Japanese? General Yamashita had the luxury of an experienced, well-trained force, and crushing aerial and naval support. But the Japanese did not employ novel tactics in Malaya. Contrary to the impression created by endless stories (mostly imagined) of fifth columnists, Japanese intelligence and preparations were by no means as well developed as subsequently claimed by British eye-witnesses and were often improvised. At face value, Yamashita's campaign plan seems quite simple, and overly dependent on British failures for its rapid success. Still, this is not giving Yamashita enough credit. The way in which XXV Army massed force on a narrow front, and made full use of surprise and manoeuvre to punch through its enemy's line, was the essence of good generalship. Local successes were rapidly exploited to keep the British on the run, thus maximizing the likelihood of triumph in the next battle. This style of mobile warfare was not far removed from the way in which the Germans had defeated the French Army in May and June 1940. The plan for the assault on Singapore Island, whereby the bulk of XXV Army was thrown against a small part of the defending force, repeated the formula that had worked so well on the mainland. Only equally good generalship on the part of the defenders could have slowed the Japanese juggernaut.

The Japanese advance into South-East Asia in 1941–42 had the appearance of a resounding success. Southern Army had won possession of the region's raw materials, including the oil of the East Indies. The Imperial Japanese Navy was supreme at sea, not only in the western Pacific and the South China Sea but also in the Indian Ocean and the Bay of Bengal.

Yet Japanese triumphs during these several months did not crush the Allies' will to resist. No thought was ever given to negotiating with Japan. The Allied position had not been fatally damaged, as Japan's conquests had mostly consisted of peripheral colonies. Japan had not overrun or inflicted any lasting damage on the homelands of its principal enemies, nor to their main sources of manpower and industry. Likewise, Japan's advance into South-East Asia had done little to solve the war in China. It was still possible for a growing armada of American transport aircraft to fly aid to China from British bases in India.

The oil and other supplies seized by Japan in South-East Asia also proved to be less valuable than had been hoped. The oilfield installations and refineries had been demolished. The managers of rubber estates and tin mines had been evacuated or imprisoned. It took many months to restore a decent level of production. By that time the oceans of the western Pacific were swarming with American submarines. The Japanese military had proved formidable but they were not invincible. In the early months of 1942 it remained to be seen how the Japanese would fare against a well-trained and properly equipped Allied force. As events would prove, the tide turned against the Japanese very quickly as 1942 wore on.

With British forces swept from South-East Asia, London and Washington did a deal whereby the South-West Pacific command zone, which included Australia and New Zealand, became a United States fiefdom. The loss of Singapore marked the moment at which Britain and Australia began to travel diverging paths. The Indian Ocean and India remained a British responsibility. The British government wished to fight against Japan to the minimum extent until Germany had been defeated. That attitude was understandable within the context of European power politics, but the Second World War was a global conflict and the British Empire was an institution with a global reach.

Devastating as the fall of Singapore was to the British Empire, the loss made remarkably little difference to the outcome of the war. The Americans advanced across the central Pacific towards Japan without paying much attention to South-East Asia. In the circumstances of the Second World War, Singapore had only a limited significance in grand strategic terms. Malaya and Singapore were valuable centres of raw material production, and symbols of British wealth and prestige, but they proved to be expendable.

Early in 1945 the Combined Chiefs of Staff ordered Admiral Lord Louis Mountbatten, Supreme Commander South-East Asia Command, that he was to complete the reconquest of Burma, and then move directly on to liberate Malaya.[10] An operation to reinvade Malaya was due to commence on 9 September 1945. The surrender of Japan on 15 August, however, meant that Malaya was peacefully reoccupied, thus saving tens of thousands of lives, combatant and civilian. There were over 100,000 Japanese army and naval personnel in Malaya, and it might have taken months of fighting to capture a ruined Singapore. On 12 September, a ceremony was held in the Municipal Buildings of Singapore City at which Admiral Mountbatten accepted the surrender of Japanese forces in South-East Asia from senior Japanese army and naval officers.

The reoccupation of Malaya by British forces, and the resumption of British administration in the colony, opened a new chapter in the long story of Britain's involvement in the region. But the loss of South-East Asia to the Japanese during the Second World War had done terrible damage to the prestige of the British and other European colonial powers. The Europeans had ruled in east Asia partly because their claims to command had been widely believed by the local population. This belief had been shattered in 1942, along with the notion that the Europeans cared for the people they ruled. Japan may have lost the war, but it had helped to make the European empires in Asia unsustainable beyond the short term. The age of European empires was passing, to be succeeded by the Cold War. If there was one event that can be seized upon as symbolic of that passing, it is Britain's loss of Singapore to Japan. It had taken British sea power several centuries to build a great maritime Empire sprawling across the globe. At Singapore the British Empire's illusion of permanences and strength was brought crashing down in a matter of weeks.

Yet Malaya's occupation by the Japanese from 1942–45 meant little to the exact timing of the colony's eventual independence from British rule. As it happened, Britain's colonies in the Far East were among the most stable parts of east Asia over the next generation, whereas in neighbouring countries the appalling legacy left by Imperial Japan continued to yield poisonous fruit. Within Malaya a long and entirely successful campaign was fought from 1948 to 1960 to rid the colony of Communist guerillas. In the early to mid 1960s British Commonwealth forces fought another effective campaign to defeat Indonesia's threat to independent Malaysia in north-west Borneo. These postwar successes for the British in South-East Asia were more typical of the heyday of empire than the last leg of the decolonization process.

A key reason for these successes was the fact that from 1945 Malaya, whether as a British colony or since independence, has enjoyed a high degree of external security. Immensely powerful and friendly American forces have been deployed in parts of Asia to the north of Malaya since the conclusion of the Second World War. In the nineteenth century the Royal Navy had been able to dominate the Far East in a similar fashion, and thus guarantee the external integrity of the territories that were annexed to the British crown or made protectorates. But after the First World War, and until 1945, no effective system was in place to defend Malaya from foreign invasion. The disastrous Malayan campaign of 1941–42 took place in that grim context.

# APPENDIX 1

# *Operation Zipper*

The reconquest of Malaya from the Japanese was not a likely project for a long period after the fall of Singapore in February 1942. Japanese aerial and naval supremacy in South-East Asia was overwhelming during 1942–43. Nonetheless, by late 1944 the situation had changed completely. By that date United States forces had destroyed the bulk of Japan's navy and air-force. American landings on the Philippines had to some extent isolated Japanese-occupied South-East Asia. Yet, so long as the Japanese held the Burmese port of Rangoon, the reconquest of Burma was South-East Asia Command's primary objective.

On 3 February 1945 Admiral Mountbatten, South-East Asia Command's Supreme Commander, received a directive from the Combined Chiefs of Staff to complete the liberation of Burma, then liberate Malaya and open the Strait of Malacca. Logically enough, Mountbatten's Joint Planning Staff proposed that an assault landing should be made half way down the west coast of Malaya, after which the invading force would advance southwards to capture Singapore.

The beaches between Port Swettenham and Port Dickson were chosen as the initial objective. A direct attack on Singapore would have been a very risky operation. The thick minefields in the Strait of Malacca and a lack of air cover at Singapore were only two of a number of deterrent factors. Late in February 1945 the Joint Planning Staff's timetable was for the landing in Malaya, Operation Zipper, to take place in October 1945, and for the advance to Singapore, Operation Mailfist, to take place from December 1945 to March 1946.

In May 1945 Rangoon was captured and by the end of that month 14th Army headquarters had begun to move to Delhi to take control of the Zipper operation. Initially two divisions were to land on the west coast of Malaya, with two more divisions following close behind, all under the command of XXXIV Corps. Initial estimates of the Japanese garrison in Malaya and the Kra Isthmus placed the majority of Japanese troops north of Kuala Lumpur. The landing was expected to face only one enemy battalion on D-Day. If two divisions of XXXIV Corps had to defend the bridgehead, it was expected that the other two divisions could reach the Johore Strait by D+65. If three

divisions were available to advance southwards, the Johore Strait might be
reached as early as D+45.[1] By D+8 it was planned to have 118,000 men and
10,400 vehicles ashore, and by D+53 182,000 men and 17,700 vehicles.[2] Three
more divisions of XV Corps were due to land in the bridgehead about D+50
to complete the deployment of 14th Army's fighting force to Malaya. On 30
May, at Mountbatten's Delhi headquarters, 9 September was chosen as
D-Day for Operation Zipper.

The choice of troops to take part in Operation Zipper was badly disrupted
by the political decision taken in London, after the end of the war in Europe,
to repatriate British Army personnel in South-East Asia Command who had
been in the theatre for at least three years and four months. The British
component of South-East Asia Command was crippled for months by this
decision. The 2nd and 36th British Divisions could not be considered for
Zipper. Many British units serving in Indian divisions had to be replaced
by Indian units as they had been decimated by the removal of 'time-expired'
officers and men. Many British technical units at corps and army level were
also hit hard.[3] Thus the 5th, 23rd, 25th, 26th Indian Divisions, and a tank
brigade were chosen to comprise XXXIV Corps. Due to the pressure of
repatriations the force for Zipper had to be reduced from seven to six
divisions. The 7th and 20th Indian Divisions, and the 255th Brigade, were
to embark for Malaya in October. Alarmingly, by August British intelligence
estimates of Japanese strength in Malaya had risen from 52,000 to
86,000.[4]

At Singapore in 1945 the Japanese 7th Area Army commanded four armies
stretching across Malaya, Sumatra, Java and Borneo. XXIX Army headquarters at Taiping was responsible for Malaya and the Andaman and
Nicobar Islands. Japanese commanders at Singapore expected the Allies to
land on the coast of north-west Malaya in the Alor Star-Penang area late
in 1945. In northern and central Malaya XXIX Army commanded the
94th Division and the 70th Independent Mixed Brigade. (XXIX Army was
due to be reinforced by the 37th Division from Indochina late in 1945.) 7th
Area Army headquarters was responsible for the defence of Johore and
Singapore Island, and directly commanded the 46th Division, the 26th IMB,
and a large base garrison. (Between May-August 1945 the 7th Area Army's
forces on Borneo fought Australian troops landed by an American task
force).

The Japanese surrender on 15 August ended the war before Operation
Zipper could begin on 9 September. General MacArthur ordered that there
were to be no landings on occupied territory until the Japanese government
had signed the formal surrender in Tokyo Bay on 2 September. Prior to
that date British minesweepers, supplied with Japanese charts, had begun

clearing a passage through minefields in the Strait of Malacca and on the final approaches to Singapore. The first Royal Navy warships reached Singapore on 3 September, and the following day a convoy carrying the 5th Indian Division arrived. As planned, the 23rd and 25th Indian Divisions landed at Port Swettenham and Port Dickson on 9 September.

The British official historian, General Kirby, wrote of Zipper: 'There would undoubtedly have been severe fighting in Johore and Singapore Island but it could not have lasted long.'[5] After the surrender Japanese commanders gave the strength of Japanese forces at Singapore and Johore as 50,118 army and air force personnel and 26,872 naval personnel. In northern and central Malaya XXIX Army comprised about 26,000 men.[6]

What might have happened if Operations Zipper and Mailfist had been fought to a conclusion is a topic of speculation. At the time of the Japanese surrender, the American plan for the invasion of Japan was for air and naval bases to be established on the southern island of Kyushu in November 1945, preparatory to the invasion of the main Japanese island of Honshu in March 1946 to seize the Tokyo plain. If the diehard faction of the Japanese government had had their way, the war might not have ended until the fall of Tokyo in mid-1946. This would have provided enough time for the British reconquest of Singapore to be completed.

As General Kirby suggested, 14th Army would doubtless have attained their objective, but the cost would most likely have greatly exceeded expectations. By way of comparison, in the Pacific theatre, on Okinawa from March-June 1945 eight American divisions had been needed to clean up a Japanese garrison of 80,000 military personnel and 34,000 enrolled civilians. The Japanese garrison had comprised a multitude of ad hoc formations, including sizeable naval and base troop contingents. American forces lost a grand total of 49,151 battle casualties in the brief campaign. (This figure includes the thousands lost at sea to kamikaze attacks).[7]

The British were planning to invade Malaya with a smaller force (six divisions) than that used by the Americans on Okinawa to tackle a similar-sized Japanese garrison. In all likelihood the Japanese would have concentrated the bulk of their forces to contest an advance on Singapore. In the confined space of southern Johore and Singapore Island the fighting might have closely resembled that which took place in southern Okinawa. On Singapore Island there was the horrific prospect of the Japanese fighting to the death amid the ruins of the town. The central location of Singapore's reservoir catchment area would have forced the Japanese commander to make his final stand around the town, just as Percival had in February 1942. The immensely crowded districts of Singapore's Chinatown might have been demolished by massed land, air and naval bombardment. If this had happened there would have been little of Singapore left to reoccupy, and the surviving civilian population would have been deeply embittered by the circumstances of their liberation.

# APPENDIX 2

# Strengths and Casualties

## 1. Strengths

Malaya Command's summary of approximate strength at 1/12/1941 gave the following figures: British 20,900, Australian 15,160, Indian Army 36,920, colonial 1378, and Volunteers 16,851, a total of 91,209. This is probably the best estimate for 1 December 1941. Brooke-Popham later reported that at 5/12/1941 Malaya Command's strength was British 19,391, Australian 15,279, Indian 37,191, Asian 4482, and Volunteers 10,552 (British 2430, Indian 727, Asian 7395), a total of 86,895. It is unlikely that the figures issued by Brooke-Popham's very small and overworked headquarters were current Malaya Command figures. The official historians estimated that at 7/12/1941 Malaya Command's strength was British 19,600, Australian 15,200, Indian 37,000, and locally enlisted 16,800, a total of 88,600. These figures are rounded, however, and S. Woodburn Kirby's *The War Against Japan*, i (London, 1957) contains numerous inaccurate troop strength, casualty and population estimates. (WO 365/14, Malaya Command strength returns; AWM 73/5, Brooke-Popham to Lieutenant-General V. Sturdee, Australian CGS, 24/12/1941; Kirby, *War Against Japan*, i, p. 163.)

There has always been some doubt as to how many troops were lost at Singapore. In 1957 Kirby and Wigmore gave a total casualty figure for the Malayan campaign of 138,708 (British 38,496, Australian 18,490, Indian 67,340, and Malayan Volunteers 14,382). Over 130,000 British Empire servicemen were believed to have become prisoners of war. But it is clear that only somewhere in the region of 120,000 officers and men were taken prisoners, of whom thousands of local Asian personnel were released and sent to their homes. Likewise, even if the number of reinforcements arriving at Singapore during the campaign is added to a 1/12/1941 figure in the low 90,000s, the total cannot add up to 138,000. The 67,000 Indians figure published by Kirby in 1957 has always been regarded as suspect. F. A. E. Crew's *The Army Medical History*, ii (London, 1957), estimated Indian Army casualties in Malaya as 340 killed, 807 wounded, 4909 missing, and 57,682 POWs, a total of 62,931 (assuming the wounded were either among the POWs or evacuated). In Kirby's *War Against Japan*, v, p. 542, total killed, missing and POWs in the Malayan campaign were listed as 130,246, including 60,427 Indian personnel. This revised figure, published in 1969, more or less squares the arithmetic.

Kirby claimed that by 8 February the Japanese force in Malaya was 110,660 strong, including 67,660 combatants, 33,000 service troops and 10,000 air crew and service personnel. Yet it is hard to see how three under strength infantry divisions, and the tank, engineer and artillery units directly under XXV Army headquarters, could have added up to a combatant force of 67,660 (Kirby, *War Against Japan*, i, p. 527). Kirby may have felt obliged to show that Singapore had fallen to a similar-sized enemy force. British combatants in Malaya heavily outnumbered their Japanese counterparts at every stage of the campaign, however, and the scale of Japanese support troops was less generous than that accorded to British formations.

## 2. Casualties

The number of casualties lost on land in Malaya by Percival's force is another mystery. As Kirby initially claimed that 138,000 officers and men were lost in Malaya, and 130,000 taken prisoner, various authors have assumed that around 8000 British Empire army personnel died in Malaya. The figures from which that estimate is derived are wrong, but the estimate is probably not too far off the mark. 7500 killed and 10,000 wounded is this author's estimate. The low ratio of killed to wounded reflects the fierce nature of fighting at close quarters in broken terrain, and the poor chances of survival of seriously wounded men left behind to fall into Japanese hands after lost battles. The ratios of killed to wounded typical on European battlefields have no relevance to Malaya.

### 18th Division

In captivity at Changi the 18th Division's staff compiled a casualty return. 612 officers and men were listed as killed or died of wounds, 1065 missing, and 1232 wounded. Over 77 per cent of casualties were lost by the division's eleven infantry units. The casualties for these units are listed below.

|  | killed | wounded | missing |
|---|---|---|---|
| *53rd Brigade* |  |  |  |
| 2nd Cambridgeshire | 84 | 106 | 89 |
| 5th Norfolk | 77 | 101 | 44 |
| 6th Norfolk | 39 | 107 | 196 |
| *54th Brigade* |  |  |  |
| 4th Norfolk | 68 | 64 | 97 |

|  | killed | wounded | missing |
|---|---|---|---|
| 4th Suffolk | 69 | 163 | 49 |
| 5th Suffolk | 25 | 71 | 11 |
| *55th Brigade* | | | |
| 1st Cambridgeshire | 35 | 102 | 37 |
| 1/5th Sherwood Foresters | 36 | 115 | 58 |
| 5th Beds and Herts | 18 | 70 | 35 |
| *Divisional Troops* | | | |
| 18th Reconnaissance Bn | 34 | 84 | 95 |
| 9th Northumberland | 14 | 36 | 17 |

At Changi in mid-1942 it was unclear how many of the missing were dead, prisoners on the mainland, or escaped. The regimental histories (or other sources) of eight of the infantry units give final figures for their unit's dead in the Singapore campaign as follows: 1st Cambridgeshire 86, 4th Norfolk 128, 18th Recce 55, 9th Northumberland Fusiliers 22, 2nd Cambridgeshire 119, 5th Beds and Herts 45, 4th Suffolk 100, and 5th Suffolk 34. If these postwar figures are compared to the killed and missing figures of 1942, and the relationship applied to the 1942 figures for all units (in other words assuming that 75.8 per cent of those listed killed and missing in 1942 were actually killed), then the 18th Division's casualties were 1271 killed and died of wounds, and 1232 wounded. 406 of the missing are thus assumed to be prisoners or escaped, some of whom would be additional wounded. (This is of course merely an informed estimate.)

*8th Australian Division*

The final casualty figures given for the 8th Australian Division when the official history was published in 1957 were 1789 killed or died of wounds, and 1306 wounded (AWM 54, 171/11/1. Over half were from New South Wales). Earlier in the 1950s a return was prepared that itemized the losses suffered by every Australian unit, on a day by day basis (AWM 54, 171/2/27). The totals for the return added up to 1663 killed and died of wounds, and 1334 wounded. Unit breakdowns are particularly useful for the purposes of this exercise, though it should be borne in mind that they slightly underestimate the final figures.

|  | killed | wounded |
|---|---|---|
| *22nd Brigade* | | |
| 2/18th Battalion | 273 | 124 |
| 2/19th Battalion | 335 | 197 |
| 2/20th Battalion | 273 | 122 |

|                      | killed | wounded |
|----------------------|--------|---------|
| *27th Brigade*       |        |         |
| 2/26th Battalion     | 86     | 146     |
| 2/29th Battalion     | 180    | 143     |
| 2/30th Battalion     | 79     | 134     |
| *Divisional Troops*  |        |         |
| 2/4th Machine Gun    | 119    | 122     |

On the mainland six officers and 165 men were taken prisoner from all AIF units. At Singapore four officers and twenty-six men were taken prisoner prior to the final capitulation. Of the infantry's 1345 officers and men killed and died of wounds, 462 were lost on the mainland and 883 at Singapore.

|                   | mainland | Singapore |
|-------------------|----------|-----------|
| 2/18th Battalion  | 85       | 188       |
| 2/19th Battalion  | 181      | 154       |
| 2/20th Battalion  | 5        | 268       |
| 2/26th Battalion  | 23       | 63        |
| 2/29th Battalion  | 133      | 47        |
| 2/30th Battalion  | 35       | 44        |
| 2/4th Machine Gun | 0        | 119       |
| Totals            | 462      | 883       |

*III Indian Corps*

(The casualty lists of a number of Indian units are incomplete or non-existent.)

1st Leicester: eight officers and 188 other ranks killed or missing presumed dead.

2nd East Surrey: thirteen officers and 172 other ranks killed or missing presumed dead.

2nd Argyll and Sutherland Highlanders: 244 killed and missing presumed dead, and roughly 150 wounded.

5/2nd Punjab: 70 killed, 50 missing and 130 wounded prior to the unit's destruction at Slim River.

2/9th Jat: 73 killed or died of wounds (four officers, one Viceroy's Commissioned Officer, 68 Indian Other Ranks), 62 wounded (seven VCOs, 55 IORs), 202 missing (one VCO, 201 IORs), 134 died as POWs (five VCOs, 129 IORs). The missing figure would include other men who died as POWs or whilst part of the Indian National Army. Many would not have died during the campaign.

5/11th Sikhs: 100 killed and wounded.

2/12th Frontier Force Regiment: 362 killed or died as POWs, 61 wounded. Of fifteen VCOs who died, two were killed in action and thirteen died as POWs. The casualty experience of IORs was probably similar.

1/13th Frontier Force Rifles: 47 killed (four officers, two VCOs, and 41 IORs) and 114 wounded (four officers, five VCOs, and 105 IORs).

1/14th Punjab: 150 killed and missing presumed dead (three officers, nine VCOs, and 138 IORs), and 120 died as POWs.

2/18th Garhwal Rifles: 34 killed and died of wounds, 51 wounded and 76 missing presumed dead.

2/1st Gurkhas: 73 killed, 68 wounded and 115 missing presumed dead or died as POWs.

2/2nd Gurkhas: 146 killed and died as POWs.

3rd Cavalry: 70 killed and wounded.

The 1/8th Punjab, 2/10th Baluch, 5/14th Punjab, 2/16th and 3/16th Punjab, 3/17th Dogra, 4/19th Hyderabad and 2/9th Gurkhas lost an average of five or six officers killed out of a starting strength of twelve to fifteen officers. These eight battalions probably lost casualties at a level similar to other Indian units listed above, or somewhat higher in a few cases.

*Singapore Fortress*

1st Manchester: four officers and 56 other ranks killed.

2nd Gordon Highlanders: 100 killed and wounded.

2nd Loyal North Lancashire: 140 killed and wounded, and other wounded amongst those taken prisoner on the mainland.

2/17th Dogra: a handful of casualties.

1st and 2nd Malay Regiment: six British officers, seven Malay officers and 146 other ranks killed.

44th Indian Brigade: ten officers killed and two wounded; 510 VCOs and IORs killed and wounded. These figures include 82 killed and 64 wounded for the 6/1st Punjab, and a similar level of loss for the 7/8th Punjab and 6/14th Punjab.

45th Indian Brigade: the 7/6th Rajputana Rifles, 4/9th Jat and 5/18th Garhwal Rifles lost 29 of their approximately 45 officers killed in the Muar battle. Casualties among VCOs and IORs were nowhere near as high but substantial nonetheless.

The Straits Settlements Volunteer Force and the Federated Malay States Volunteer Force had four battalions each. The five Indian States Force battalions in Malaya were the 1st Bahawalpur, 1st Hyderabad, 1st Mysore, Jind and Kapurthala States Force Battalions. In general Volunteer Force and ISF casualties were not heavy.

*Japanese XXV Army*

Grand total: 3506 killed and 6150 wounded. (5th Division, 3694 killed and wounded; 18th Division, 3646 killed and wounded; Imperial Guards Division, 1579 killed and wounded.)

Malayan mainland: 1793 killed and 2772 wounded. (5th Division, 695 killed and 1292 wounded; Takumi Force, 1,000 killed and wounded; Imperial Guards Division, 900 killed and wounded; Koba Force, 100 killed and wounded.)

Singapore Island: 1713 killed and 3378 wounded. (5th Division, 541 killed and 1166 wounded; Imperial Guards Division, 211 killed and 468 wounded; 18th Division, 938 killed and 1708 wounded; other units, 23 killed and 36 wounded.) L. Allen, *Singapore, 1941–42* (London, 1977), p. 271.

# APPENDIX 3

# *Order of Battle*

## 1. *MALAYA COMMAND*
### *(as at 7 December 1941)*

### *H. Q. MALAYA COMMAND*

### *SINGAPORE FORTRESS*

*Fortress Troops*: Jind Infantry Indian States Force (I.S.F.), Kapurthala Infantry (I. S. F.), 122nd Field Regiment.

*1st Malaya Brigade*: 2nd Loyal Regiment, 1st and 2nd Malay Regiment.

*2nd Malaya Brigade*: 1st Manchester (Machine Gun Battalion), 2nd Gordon Highlanders, 2/17th Dogra.

### *III INDIAN CORPS*

*Corps Troops*: 5/14th Punjab, 1st Bahawalpur Infantry I. S. F., 1st Hyderabad Infantry I. S. F., 1st Mysore Infantry I. S. F.

*28th Indian Brigade*: 2/1st, 2/2nd and 2/9th Gurkha Rifles.

*9th Indian Division*

*Divisional Troops*: 5th and 88th Field Regiments.

*8th Indian Brigade*: 2/10th Baluch, 1/13th Frontier Force Rifles, 3/17th Dogra.

*22nd Indian Brigade*: 5/11th Sikhs, 2/12th Frontier Force Regiment, 2/18th Garhwal Rifles.

*11th Indian Division*

*Divisional Troops*: 3rd Cavalry, 137th and 155th Field Regiments, 80th Anti-Tank Regiment.

*6th Indian Brigade*: 22nd Mountain Regiment, 2nd East Surrey, 1/8th Punjab, 2/16th Punjab.

*12th Indian Brigade*: 2nd Argyll and Sutherland Highlanders, 5/2nd Punjab, 4/19th Hyderabad.

*15th Indian Brigade*: 1st Leicestershire, 2/9th Jat, 1/14th Punjab, 3/16th Punjab.

## 8th AUSTRALIAN DIVISION

*Divisional Troops*: 2/10th and 2/15th Field Regiments, 2/4th Anti-Tank Regiment.

*22nd Australian Brigade*: 2/18th, 2/19th and 2/20th Battalions.

*27th Australian Brigade*: 2/26th, 2/29th and 2/30th Battalions.

## VOLUNTEER FORCES (principal units)

1st, 2nd, 3rd, 4th Battalions, Straits Settlements Volunteer Force.

1st, 2nd, 3rd, 4th Battalions, Federated Malay States Volunteer Force.

Johore Infantry, Johore Volunteer Engineers.

## REINFORCEMENTS ARRIVING AT SINGAPORE DURING THE CAMPAIGN

*44th Indian Brigade*: 6/1st Punjab, 7/8th Punjab, 6/14th Punjab.

*45th Indian Brigade*: 7/6th Rajputana Rifles, 4/9th Jat, 5/18th Garhwal Rifles.

2/4th Machine Gun Battalion AIF.

85th British Anti-Tank Regiment.

## 18th BRITISH DIVISION

*Divisional Troops*: 118th, 135th and 148th Field Regiments, 125th Anti-Tank Regiment, 9th Northumberland Fusiliers (Machine Gun Battalion), 18th Battalion Reconnaissance Corps.

*53rd Brigade*: 5th and 6th Royal Norfolk, 2nd Cambridgeshire.

*54th Brigade*: 4th Royal Norfolk, 4th and 5th Suffolk.

*55th Brigade*: 5th Bedfordshire and Hertfordshire, 1/5th Sherwood Foresters, 1st Cambridgeshire.

## 2. *JAPANESE XXV ARMY*
### *(units deployed in Malaya)*

*XXV ARMY HEADQUARTERS: Lieutenant-General T. Yamashita*

### *3rd TANK GROUP*

*IMPERIAL GUARDS DIVISION: Lieutenant-General T. Nishimura*

3rd, 4th and 5th Guards Regiments.

*5th DIVISION: Lieutenant-General T. Matsui*

*9th Brigade:* 11th and 41st Regiments.

*21st Brigade:* 21st and 42nd Regiments.

*18th DIVISION: Lieutenant General R. Mutaguchi*

*23rd Brigade:* 55th and 56th Regiments.

114th Regiment.

(The 18th Division's *35th Brigade* headquarters and 124th Regiment landed in Borneo.)

# Notes

## Notes to Chapter 1: British Malaya

1. B. W. and L. Y. Andaya, *A History of Malaysia* (London, 1982).
2. Malcolm H. Murfett, John N. Miksic, Brian P. Farrell and Chiang Ming Shun, *Between Two Oceans: A Military History of Singapore from First Settlement to Final British Withdrawal* (Singapore, 1999), pp. 35–52.
3. Ian H. Nish, *The Anglo-Japanese Alliance* (London, 1966), p. 1.
4. J. Neidpath, *The Singapore Naval Base and the Defence of Britain's Eastern Empire, 1919–1941* (Oxford, 1981), p. 2.
5. Murfett, *Between Two Oceans*, pp. 148–50.
6. Ibid., p. 154.
7. Ibid., p. 156.
8. John G. Butcher, *The British in Malaya, 1880–1941* (Kuala Lumpur, 1979).
9. ADM 199/1472B, 'Supplementary Report on Events in the Far East, 1940–45', 25/4/1947, p. 2; CAB 101/152, Lieutenant-General Sir Lionel Bond to Captain Russell Grenfell, RN, 18/9/1950.
10. Murfett, *Between Two Oceans*, p. 169.

## Notes to Chapter 2: The Rise of the Japanese Empire

1. Ian H. Nish, *The Anglo-Japanese Alliance* (London, 1966), pp. 1–29.
2. Malcolm H. Murfett, John N. Miksic, Brian P. Farrell and Chiang Ming Shun, *Between Two Oceans: A Military History of Singapore from First Settlement to Final British Withdrawal* (Singapore, 1999), pp. 123–24.
3. P. Calvocoressi, G. Wint and J. Pritchard, *Total War*, ii (London, 1989), p. 71.
4. A. Iriye, *Origins of the Second World War in Asia and the Pacific* (London, 1987), p. 5.
5. Hata Ikuhiko, 'The Marco Polo Bridge Incident, 1937', in J. W. Morley (ed.), *The China Quagmire* (New York, 1983), pp. 254–61.
6. Ibid., pp. 265–67.
7. M. and S. Harries, *Soldiers of the Sun: The Rise and Fall of the Imperial Japanese Army, 1868–1945* (London, 1991), p. 183; Hsi-Sheng Ch'l, *Nationalist China at War* (Ann Arbor, Michigan, 1982), p. 42.
8. Iris Chang, *The Rape of Nanking* (New York, 1997), p. 139; Harries, *Soldiers of the Sun*, p. 192.
9. Harries, *Soldiers of the Sun*, p. 194.

10. Iriye, *Second World War in Asia and the Pacific*, p. 48.
11. Calvocoressi, *Total War*, ii, p. 255.
12. Harries, *Soldiers of the Sun*, pp. 197–99.
13. Calvocoressi, *Total War*, ii, p. 214.
14. Iriye, *Second World War in Asia and the Pacific*, p. 90.
15. Harries, *Soldiers of the Sun*, pp. 226–27.

*Notes to Chapter 3: The Defence of Malaya*

1. Ong Chit Chung, *Operation Matador: Britain's War Plans Against the Japanese, 1918–1941*, pp. 101–5.
2. Ibid., p. 131, W. S. Churchill, 22/11/1940.
3. Nicholas Tarling, *Britain, Southeast Asia and the Onset of the Pacific War* (Cambridge, 1996), pp. 130–31.
4. A. Iriye, *Origins of the Second World War in Asia and the Pacific* (London, 1987), p. 116.
5. W. Heinrichs, *Threshold of War* (Oxford, 1988), p. 133.
6. Lionel Wigmore, *The Japanese Thrust* (Canberra, 1957), p. 41.
7. Alanbrooke Papers, LHC, 3/A/IV, 'Notes on My Life', February 1941, p. 254.
8. W. S. Churchill, *The Second World War*, iii (London, 1950), pp. 379, 505–7, 577–78, 580–81.
9. Ong Chit Chung, *Operation Matador*, p. 170.
10. Percival Papers, IWM, P 88, Lieutenant-General Sir John Dill, HQ 1st Corps BEF, to Percival, 15/2/1940.
11. J. Smyth, *Percival and the Tragedy of Singapore* (London, 1973), pp. 17 and 259.
12. One British commanding officer complained: 'the vogue of putting the infantry last in importance was still in force. Drafts, initially selected from the bottom 50 per cent of Army intakes, milked of leader and specialist types before leaving England, were further picked over by Staff vultures in the reinforcement camps before they were allowed to join their units'. CAB 106/91, Lieutenant-Colonel I. M. Stewart, 'The Loss of Singapore: A Criticism'.
13. David Day, *The Great Betrayal: Britain, Australia and the Onset of the Pacific War, 1939–42* (London, 1988), pp. 2–7. As upwards of 95 per cent of Australians could claim descent from the British Isles, the main cleavage in 1940s Australian society, apart from class and wealth, was the religious divide between Protestants and Catholics. One complete analysis of an 8th Division battalion's religious affiliations, the 2/21st Battalion, calculated that 3.7 per cent of officers and 19.3 per cent of other ranks were Catholic, the latter figure being roughly the Catholic share of that unit's state population. Many Irish Catholics in Australia adopted to a varying extent the pro-British attitude of most Australians. Joan Beaumont, *Gull Force* (Sydney, 1988), p. 27.
14. Paul Hasluck, *The Government and the People, 1939–41* (Canberra, 1952), p. 613.
15. Ian Morrison, *Malayan Postscript* (Sydney, 1943), p. 157.
16. AWM, MS 776, Lieutenant-Colonel R. F. Oakes, 'Singapore Story', p. iii.

17. AWM 67, 1/5, Lieutenant-Colonel M. Ashkanasy, 2/8/1944.

18. AWM, MS 1370, Captain Guy Round, 13th Auxiliary Pioneer Battalion, 'The Road to Singapore', pp. 296–301.

19. Brooke-Popham Papers, LHC, V/1, Air Chief Marshal Sir Robert Brooke-Popham to General Sir H. Ismay, 26/3/1941.

20. 2/19th Battalion AIF Association, *The Grim Glory of the 2/19th Battalion AIF* (Sydney, 1975), p. 531; D. Wall, *Singapore and Beyond: The Story of the Men of the 2/20th Battalion* (Sydney, 1985), p. 3.

21. AWM 67, 3/25, part 1, Lieutenant-General H. G. Bennett, diary, 10/3/1941.

22. AWM 54, 553/5/14, Major C. B. O'Brien, 23/9/1945, p. 2; AWM 93, 50/2/23/258, Brigadier H. B. Taylor, 17/6/1952.

23. Stan Arneil, *Black Jack: The Life and Times of Brigadier Sir Frederick Galleghan* (Melbourne, 1983); AWM 67, 2/109, Brigadier D. S. Maxwell, December 1946, p. 18.

## Notes to Chapter 4: Preparations For War

1. Nicholas Tarling, *Britain, Southeast Asia and the Onset of the Pacific War* (Cambridge, 1996), p. 281.

2. A. Iriye, *Origins of the Second World War in Asia and the Pacific* (London, 1987), p. 143.

3. W. Heinrichs, *Threshold of War* (Oxford, 1988), pp. 133–35.

4. Brian Bond (ed.), *Chief of Staff: The Diaries of Lieutenant-General Sir Henry Pownall*, ii, *1940–1944* (London, 1974), pp. 30–31, 30/6/1941; John Kennedy, *The Business of War* (London, 1957), p. 142, 25/6/1941.

5. Kennedy, *Business of War*, pp. 147 and 152; Alanbrooke Papers, LHC, 3/A/IV, 'Notes on My Life', p. 282, June 1941; Bond, *Pownall*, ii, p. 41.

6. Lionel Wigmore, *The Japanese Thrust* (Canberra, 1957), p. 95.

7. Alanbrooke Papers, LHC, 3/A/V, 'Notes on My Life', p. 318.

8. Brooke-Popham Papers, LHC, V/4, Chiefs of Staff to Brooke-Popham, 17/9/1941.

9. S. Woodburn Kirby, *The War Against Japan*, i (London, 1957), p. 174.

10. Ong Chit Chung, *Operation Matador: Britain's War Plans Against the Japanese, 1918–1941* (Singapore, 1997), p. 226. When war in the Far East eventually broke out the Chiefs of Staff considered leaving Brooke-Popham in command, but pressure from Duff Cooper and others quickly put an end to that idea.

11. A. J. Marder, *Old Friends, New Enemies*, i (Oxford, 1981), pp. 370–72.

12. Ibid., pp. 365–66.

13. Ibid., p. 383.

14. M. Middlebrook and P. Mahoney, *Battleship* (London, 1977), pp. 69–71.

15. WO 365/14, Malaya Command strength returns.

16. J. Ross and W. L. Hailes, *War Services of the 9th Jat Regiment*, ii, *1937–48* (London, 1965), p. 206.

17. Brooke-Popham Papers, LHC, V/1, Brooke-Popham to Ismay, 26/3/1941.

18. F. Spencer Chapman, *The Jungle is Neutral* (London, 1949), p. 10.
19. G. R. Stevens, *The 9th Gurkha Rifles*, ii, *1937–47* (1953), p. 193; Malcolm H. Murfett, John N. Miksic, Brian P. Farrell and Chiang Ming Shun, *Between Two Oceans: A Military History of Singapore from First Settlement to Final British Withdrawal* (Singapore, 1999), p. 191.
20. IOR/L/WS/1/681 – WS 12515, CIC Far East to War Office, 1/10/1941.
21. Iriye, *Second World War in Asia and the Pacific*, p. 152.
22. Ibid., p. 161.
23. Ibid., p. 165.
24. G. W. Prange, *At Dawn We Slept* (New York, 1981), p. 278.
25. Iriye, *Second World War in Asia and the Pacific*, pp. 173–74.
26. J. D. Potter, *A Soldier Must Hang* (London, 1963), pp. 4–43; A. F. Reel, *The Case of General Yamashita* (Chicago, 1949), pp. 50–51; M. Tsuji, *Singapore: The Japanese Version* (Singapore, 1960), p. 35.
27. Tsuji, *Japanese Version*, pp. 20–24.
28. Ibid., pp. 39–43.
29. Potter, *A Soldier Must Hang*, p. 42.
30. Prange, *At Dawn We Slept*, p. 370.
31. WO 106/2528, WO to CIC FE, 29/11/1941.
32. Ong Chit Chung, *Matador*, p. 230.
33. Ibid., pp. 204–5.
34. A. J. Marder, *Old Friends, New Enemies* (Oxford, 1981–90), i, pp. 392–95; ii, pp. 7–8.
35. Tsuji, *Japanese Version*, p. 74.
36. E. R. Hall, *Glory in Chaos: The RAAF in the Far East, 1940–42* (Melbourne, 1989), p. 68.
37. Prange, *At Dawn We Slept*, p. 539.

## Notes to Chapter 5: The Japanese Onslaught

1. M. Tsuji, *Singapore: The Japanese Version* (Singapore, 1960), pp. 80–82; L. Allen, *Singapore, 1941–42* (London, 1977), p. 109.
2. Hall, *Glory in Chaos*, pp. 81–82; C. Shores, B. Cull and Yasuho Izawa, *Bloody Shambles*, i (London, 1992), p. 82.
3. K. N. V. Sastri and K. D. Bhargava, *Campaigns in South-East Asia, 1941–42* (New Delhi, 1960), pp. 132–33.
4. S. Woodburn Kirby, *The War Against Japan*, i (London, 1957), pp. 184–85. On 10 December Duff Cooper was appointed Resident Minister for Far Eastern Affairs. Duff Cooper's new duties included the establishment of a War Council which was not to interfere with the activities of the service commanders.
5. Shores, *Bloody Shambles*, i, p. 82.
6. Tsuji, *Japanese Version*, p. 96; WO 172/39, 9th Indian Division, 14/12/1941. At Machang on the morning of 13 December a two company attack by the 2/10th Baluchis cost eighteen killed, twenty-two wounded and eleven missing.

7. Shores, *Shambles*, i, pp. 88–89; Hall, *Glory in Chaos*, pp. 248–49.

8. Shores, *Shambles*, i, pp. 92–4; Hall, *Glory in Chaos*, pp. 250–51.

9. P. Elphick, *Singapore: The Pregnable Fortress* (London, 1995), pp. 74–75 and 227; P. Elphick and M. Smith, *Odd Man Out: The Story of the Singapore Traitor* (London, 1993), pp. 72–75.

10. Marder, *Old Friends*, i, pp. 414–17.

11. ADM 199/1149, Captain L. H. Bell, RN, Captain of the Fleet, Eastern Fleet, 10/12/1941.

12. Marder, *Old Friends*, i, pp. 423–24; M. Middlebrook and P. Mahoney, *Battleship* (London, 1977), p. 297.

13. Marder, *Old Friends*, i, pp. 431–32 and 454–56.

14. Shores, *Shambles*, i, pp. 100–7; Hall, *Glory in Chaos*, pp. 106–15.

15. Kirby, *War Against Japan*, i, p. 201.

16. CAB 106/157, Lieutenant-Colonel G. W. P. Fennell's notebook, pp. 48–54.

17. WO 172/38, 9th Indian Division, 21/12/1941.

18. Shores, *Shambles*, i, p. 112; Hall, *Glory in Chaos*, p. 342.

19. Middlebrook and Mahoney, *Battleship*, p. 147.

20. Marder, *Old Friends*, i, pp. 433–35.

21. Ibid., i, pp. 436–38; ii, pp. 118–36. Admiral Phillips was not the only senior officer of the Royal Navy fatally to underestimate the capabilities of Japanese aircraft. During April 1942 a fleet of Japanese carriers raided across the Bay of Bengal. The heavy cruisers *Dorsetshire* and *Cornwall* sailed from Colombo to rejoin the Eastern Fleet, but a rendezvous and course were plotted on the understanding that the range of Japanese aircraft was similar to that of British carrier aircraft. Japanese aircraft, however, had almost double the range. The cruisers steamed unnecessarily close to the Japanese carriers, and were quickly sunk by hostile aircraft on 5 April. Thanks to the warm, calm seas of the Indian Ocean, 1122 out of 1546 officers and ratings were rescued after thirty hours in the water.

22. Middlebrook and Mahoney, *Battleship*, p. 174. By 1945 King George V Class battleships had sixty-four pom-poms, ten 40mm Bofors and thirty-six 20mm Oerlikon guns. Marder, *Old Friends*, ii, p. 409.

23. Middlebrook and Mahoney, *Battleship*, pp. 181, 188 and 303.

24. Ibid., pp. 221–24 and 306; Marder, *Old Friends*, i, pp. 470–71 and 479–80.

25. Marder, *Old Friends*, i, p. 474; Middlebrook and Mahoney, *Battleship*, pp. 227–30.

26. Marder, *Old Friends*, i, pp. 474–76; Middlebrook and Mahoney, *Battleship*, p. 253.

27. Shores, *Shambles*, i, p. 123; ADM 199/1149, Flight Lieutenant T. A. Vigors, No. 453 Squadron, to CIC FE, 11/12/1941.

28. Middlebrook and Mahoney, *Battleship*, p. 274; Russell Grenfell, *Main Fleet to Singapore* (London, 1951).

29. Marder, *Old Friends*, i, pp. 488 and 499.

30. Ibid., ii, p. 9.

31. K. Attiwill, *Fortress: The Story of the Siege and Fall of Singapore* (New York, 1960), p. 42.
32. A. Duff Cooper, *Old Men Forget* (London, 1955).


*Notes to Chapter 6: Jitra*

1. WO 172/123, 3/16th Punjab; Percival Papers, IWM, P 75, Lieutenant-Colonel F. R. N. Cobley, Malaya Command, 'Typescript Report on Malayan Campaign', 1942–43, p. 50.
2. C. Mackenzie, *Eastern Epic* (London, 1951), p. 252.
3. Percival Papers, IWM, P 75, Cobley, 'Report on Malayan Campaign', pp. 52–53.
4. M. Tsuji, *Singapore: The Japanese Version* (Singapore, 1960), p. 114; AWM 54, 553/1/3, US Army Historical Division, 'Japanese Studies in World War II, No. 85: XXV Army Operations in Malaya, November 1941-March 1942', compiled from memoirs of staff officers Colonel Sugita, Lieutenant-Colonel Kunitake and Lieutenant-Colonel Hashizune, pp. 35–36. The 5th Reconnaissance Regiment comprised one company of light armour, one company of light tanks, and two companies of motorised infantry.
5. Tsuji, *Japanese Version*, p. 91.
6. IOR/L/WS/1/952 – WS 16063, Brigadier W. Carpendale, 28th Indian Brigade, 'Report on Operations of the 11th Indian Division in Kedah and Perak', p. 11; WO 172/18, Malaya Command, December 1941, appendices Y. Y and F 3.
7. WO 172/117, 15th Indian Brigade, 9/12/1941; WO 172/18, Malaya Command, December 1941, appendix L 3, GSO 1 Malaya Command to GSO 3 III Corps, 4.30 p.m., 11/12/41.
8. G. Pigot, *History of the 1st Battalion 14th Punjab Regiment* (1946), p. 197; Mohan Singh, *Soldiers' Contribution to Independence* (Delhi, 1974), p. 59.
9. WO 106/2625, 'Enemy Publication No. 278, Malayan Campaign, 1941–42', p. 18.
10. Mohan Singh, *Soldiers' Contribution*, p. 60.
11. E. V. R. Bellers, *The 1st King George V's Own Gurkha Rifles (The Malaun Regiment)*, ii, *1920–47* (Aldershot, 1956), pp. 72–75.
12. Ibid., pp. 76–79; Pigot, *14th Punjab*, pp. 199–200.
13. G. Chippington, *Singapore: The Inexcusable Betrayal* (Worcester, 1992), pp. 28–38; WO 172/117, 15th Indian Brigade, 11/12/1941.
14. IWM, 89/15/1, Lieutenant S. Abbott, 2nd East Surrey, 'Memories of the Malayan Campaign'.
15. J. Ross and W. L. Hailes, *War Services of the 9th Jat Regiment*, ii, *1937–48* (London, 1965), p. 23.
16. IOR/L/WS/1/952 – WS 16063, Carpendale, 'Report on Operations of the 11th Indian Division', p. 12; CAB 106/53, Colonel A. M. L. Harrison, 'History of 11th Indian Division', p. 17; Percival Papers, IWM, P 72, 1st Battalion the Leicestershire Regiment and the British Battalion, 11/12/1941.
17. Tsuji, *Japanese Version*, pp. 120–21.
18. CAB 106/54, Colonel A. M. L. Harrison, 'History of 11th Indian Division', pp. 6

and 19; K. N. V. Sastri and K. D. Bhargava, *Campaigns in South-East Asia, 1941–42* (New Delhi, 1960), p. 162; Ross and Hailes, *9th Jat*, ii, p. 24.

19. Tsuji, *Japanese Version*, pp. 122–24.

20. CAB 106/54, Harrison, '11th Indian Division', p. 20.

21. Ibid., p. 21; Percival Papers, IWM, P 75, Cobley, 'Report on Malayan Campaign', p. 41.

22. AWM 54, 553/1/3, p. 38.

23. Mackenzie, *Eastern Epic*, p. 257; Ross and Hailes, *9th Jat*, ii, p. 25.

24. W. E. Underhill (ed.), *The Royal Leicestershire Regiment, 1928–56* (London, 1957), p. 93; WO 172/121, 2/9th Jat, 12/12/1941.

25. WO 172/120, 1st Leicester, 12/12/1941.

26. Percival Papers, IWM, P 72, 1st Leicester and British Battalion, 12/12/1941; CAB 106/54, Harrison, '11th Indian Division', p. 28; IOR/L/WS/1/952 – WS 16063, Carpendale, 'Report on Operations of the 11th Indian Division', p. 17.

27. Underhill, *Leicestershire*, pp. 93–94.

28. WO 172/121, 2/9th Jat, 13/12/1941; Percival Papers, IWM, P 75, Cobley, 'Report on Malayan Campaign', pp. 42 and 45.

29. IOR/L/WS/1/952 – WS 16063, Major-General David Murray-Lyon, '11th Indian Division: Short Summary of Events, 7–24 December 1941', p. 2.

30. CAB 101/162, Murray-Lyon to Woodburn Kirby, 21/10/1954.

31. Tsuji, *Japanese Version*, pp. 124–26.

*Notes to Chapter 7: Retreat*

1. J. P. Lawford and W. E. Catto (eds), *Solah Punjab: The History of the 16th Punjab Regiment* (Aldershot, 1967), pp. 187–88.

2. CAB 106/90, Brigadier W. O. Lay; IOR/L/WS/1/952 – WS 16063, Brigadier W. Carpendale, 'Report on Operations of the 11th Indian Division in Kedah and Perak', pp. 17–18.

3. G. R. Stevens, *The 9th Gurkha Rifles*, ii, *1937–47* (1953), p. 144.

4. WO 172/121, 2/9th Jat; Percival Papers, IWM, P 75, Lieutenant-Colonel F. R. N. Cobley, Malaya Command, 'Typescript Report on Malayan Campaign', 1942–43, pp. 45–46.

5. CAB 106/54, Colonel A. M. L. Harrison, 'History of 11th Indian Division', p. 45.

6. Ibid., pp. 40 and 46; A. E. Percival, *The War in Malaya* (London, 1949), p. 140.

7. IOR/L/WS/1/952 – WS 16063, Major-General David Murray-Lyon, '11th Indian Division: Short Summary of Events, 7–24 December 1941', p. 4.

8. WO 172/100, 2nd East Surrey; IOR/L/WS/1/952 – WS 16063, Carpendale, 'Report on Operations of 11th Indian Division', p. 19; Percival Papers, IWM, P 75, Cobley, 'Report on Malayan Campaign', p. 56.

9. IWM, 89/15/1, Lieutenant S. Abbott, 2nd East Surrey, 'Memories of the Malayan Campaign', annex B.

10. Chye Kooi Loong, *The History of the British Battalion in the Malayan Campaign,*

*1941–42* (1984), pp. 29–30; Percival Papers, IWM, P 72, 1st Leicester and British Battalion, 13/12/1941; WO 106/2625, Enemy Publication No. 278, p. 23.

11. WO 172/43, 88th Field Regiment, 13/12/1941; CAB 106/54, Harrison, '11th Indian Division', p. 56.

12. Lawford, *16th Punjab*, pp. 187–88; Percival Papers, IWM, P 75, Cobley, 'Report on Malayan Campaign', p. 56. D Company of the 2/16th Punjab had withdrawn from Jitra down the coast. Another company had been scattered during the retreat from Jitra, and a third company under Major Emsden-Lambert was heading across country for Sungei Patani.

13. C. Mackenzie, *Eastern Epic* (London, 1951), p. 259; S. Woodburn Kirby, *The War Against Japan*, i (London, 1957), p. 215; Percival Papers, IWM, P 75, Cobley, 'Report on Malayan Campaign', p. 57.

14. IWM, 89/15/1, Abbott, 'Memories of the Malayan Campaign', p. 11.

15. Lawford and Catto, *16th Punjab*, p. 189.

16. IOR/L/WS/1/952 – WS 16063, Murray-Lyon, '11th Indian Division: Short Summary of Events', p. 5.

17. WO 172/18, Malaya Command, appendix K 6, Heath to Percival, 7 p.m., 14/12/1941, appendix N 6, Percival to GSO 2 III Corps, 9.15 p.m., 14/12/1941.

18. Lionel Wigmore, *The Japanese Thrust* (Canberra, 1957), p. 154.

19. WO 325/1, 9th Brigade, 14/12/1941; Percival Papers, IWM, P 75, Cobley, 'Report on Malayan Campaign', p. 58; WO 172/100, 2nd East Surrey, appendix D.

20. IWM, 89/15/1, Abbott, 'Memories of the Malayan Campaign', pp. 11–13.

21. IOR/L/WS/1/952 – WS 16063, Carpendale, 'Report on Operations of the 11th Indian Division', p. 18; WO 172/100, 2nd East Surrey, appendix D.

22. CAB 106/54, Harrison, '11th Indian Division', p. 63; WO 172/43, 88th Field Regiment, 15/12/1941; IOR/L/WS/1/952 – WS 16063, Carpendale, 'Report on Operations of the 11th Indian Division', pp. 21–22.

23. WO 172/43, 88th Field Regiment, 15/12/1941; G. Chippington, *Singapore: The Inexcusable Betrayal* (Worcester, 1992), pp. 78–79 and 85.

24. IOR/L/WS/1/952 – WS 16063, Carpendale, 'Report on Operations of the 11th Indian Division', pp. 21–22; K. N. V. Sastri and K. D. Bhargava, *Campaigns in South-East Asia, 1941–42* (New Delhi, 1960), pp. 174–75; CAB 106/54, Harrison, '11th Indian Division', p. 66; Chippington, *Singapore*, p. 86.

25. IOR/L/WS/1/952 – WS 16063, Murray-Lyon, '11th Indian Division: Short Summary of Events'.

26. M. Tsuji, *Singapore: The Japanese Version* (Singapore, 1960), pp. 134–35; WO 325/1, 9th Brigade, 15–16/12/1941.

27. Fujiwara Iwaichi, *F. Kikan: Japanese Army Intelligence Operations in Southeast Asia during World War II* (Hong Kong, 1983), p. xv; Chye Kooi Loong, *The History of the British Battalion in the Malayan Campaign, 1941–42* (1984), pp. 192–93; WO 172/100, 2nd East Surrey, 16/12/1941. Eight missing officers later rejoined the 2nd East Surreys. Ten officers and forty-three other ranks of the 2nd East Surreys were killed at Gurun.

28. Percival Papers, IWM, P 75, Cobley, 'Report on Malayan Campaign', p. 67.

29. I. Morrison, *Malayan Postscript* (Sydney, 1943), p. 59; AIR 2/7932, 'Report by Air Vice-Marshal Sir Paul Maltby on Air Operations in Malaya and Netherlands East Indies, 8/12/1941–17/3/1942', p. 24.

30. C. Shores, B. Cull and Yasuho Izawa, *Bloody Shambles*, i (London, 1992–93), p. 132; John Bennett, *Defeat to Victory: No. 453 Squadron RAAF* (Point Cook, Victoria, 1994), pp. 24–25 and 32–35.

31. CAB 106/36, 1st Independent Company, 14/12/1941.

32. British Borneo's defence was one of Percival's responsibilities. The small British garrison comprised the 2/15th Punjabis and local Volunteer forces. On the night of 15/16 December a Japanese invasion force arrived, including the 18th Division's 124th Regiment and the 35th Brigade's headquarters. Borneo's vast interior offered a lot of room for manoeuvre and evasive flight. The last of the 2/15th Punjabis were ordered to surrender in March 1942.

33. Noel Barber, *Sinister Twilight* (London, 1968), p. 59.

## Notes to Chapter 8: Perak and Pahang

1. NAM, 6509–14, Lieutenant-Colonel C. C. Deakin, 'The Malayan Campaign, 1941–42, 5/2nd Punjab', p. 6–11. Charles Cecil Deakin, born Shropshire 1897, educated Shrewsbury, Sandhurst 1917, India 2/67th Punjab, Waziristan, Mesopotamia, Khyber, North-West Frontier 1930, Staff College Quetta 1933, GSO 1 1st Division Australian Military Force 1937–40, CO 5/2nd Punjab 1941, DSO 16/12/1941, OBE 1942–45, brigadier Ambala 1947, retired to Australia 1948 having married an Australian prior to the war.

2. WO 172/10, Malaya Command, appendix V 8, 17/12/1941

3. Percival Collection, IWM, P 43, comments by Percival on report by Air Vice-Marshal P. C. Maltby, 23/5/1947.

4. IOR/L/WS/1/31 – WS 275B, CIC FE to WO, 16/12/1941.

5. I. Morrison, *Malayan Postscript* (Sydney, 1943), p. 95; CAB 44/178, section 5, part 1, p. 22, 25/12/1941; WO 106/2550C, Lieutenant E. L. Randle, FMSVF, 22/7/1942, pp. 2–3; WO 106/2579C, Captain S. H. D. Elias, 9/7/1942; CAB 106/157, Lieutenant-Colonel G. W. P. Fennell's notebook, p. 54.

6. CAB 106/54, Colonel A. M. L. Harrison, 'History of 11th Indian Division', p. 94; G. R. Stevens, *History of the 2nd King Edward VII's Own Goorkha Rifles (The Sirmoor Rifles)*, iii, 1921–48 (Aldershot, 1952), p. 160.

7. CAB 101/162, Murray-Lyon to Kirby, 22/8/1954. Murray-Lyon told the British official historian in 1954: 'I have not thought of the Malaya campaign for years, having dismissed it as a bad dream in which no one was interested.'

8. W. Gibson, *The Boat* (London, 1952), p. 13; CAB 106/54, Harrison, '11th Indian Division', p. 118.

9. John Bennett, *Defeat to Victory: No. 453 Squadron RAAF* (Point Cook, Victoria, 1994), p. 43; E. R. Hall, *Glory in Chaos: The RAAF in the Far East, 1940–42* (Melbourne, 1989), pp. 286–90; C. Shores, B. Cull and Yasuho Izawa, *Bloody Shambles*, i (London, 1992–93), pp. 143–46.

10. Bennett, *Defeat to Victory*, pp. 58–62; AIR 2/7932, 'Report by Air Vice-Marshal Sir Paul Maltby on Air Operations in Malaya and Netherlands East Indies, 8/12/1941–17/3/1942', p. 27.

11. WO 172/16, Malaya Command, Report 13, 'Report on Light Anti-Aircraft Artillery in Malaya', p. 4; Shores, *Shambles*, i, p. 275. The incident took place on 28 December 1941.

12. Brooke-Popham Papers, LHC, V/5, Brooke-Popham, 24/12/1941.

13. John Kennedy, *The Business of War* (London, 1957), p. 183.

14. Alanbrooke Papers, LHC, 3/A/V, 'Notes on My Life', v, pp. 331–32.

15. PREM 3/499/2, Churchill to COS Committee, 17/12/1941.

16. B. Fergusson, *Wavell: Portrait of a Soldier* (London, 1961), p. 95.

17. R. Lewin, *The Chief: Field Marshal Lord Wavell* (London, 1980), p. 140.

18. WO 172/19, Malaya Command, 27/12/1941; S. Woodburn Kirby, *The War Against Japan*, i (London, 1957), p. 146; CAB 106/70, History of 18th Division. At Singapore Duff Cooper, the Resident Minister for Far Eastern Affairs, and Sir Shenton Thomas, the Governor, had come to loathe each other. Thomas was later to write of his rival: 'A rotten judge of men, arrogant, obstinate, vain; how he could have crept into office is beyond me.'

19. CAB 106/54, Harrison, '11th Indian Division', p. 129.

20. Percival Papers, IWM, P 75, Cobley, 'Report on Malayan Campaign', p. 92; CAB 106/54, Harrison, '11th Indian Division', pp. 132–35.

21. C. Mackenzie, *Eastern Epic* (London, 1951), p. 276; Kirby, *War Against Japan*, i, pp. 244–45; CAB 106/54, Harrison, '11th Indian Division', pp. 148–50; NAM, 6509–14, Deakin, 'The Malayan Campaign', pp. 39–40.

22. WO 172/117, 15th Brigade, 31/12/1941; M. Tsuji, *Singapore: The Japanese Version* (Singapore, 1960), p. 153.

23. WO 325/1, Japanese 9th Brigade, 1/1/1942.

24. WO 172/100, 2nd East Surrey, 1/1/1942; Chye Kooi Loong, *The History of the British Battalion in the Malayan Campaign, 1941–42* (1984), pp. 95–96; WO 172/43, 88th Field Regiment, 1/1/1942.

25. W. S. Churchill, *The Second World War*, iv (London, 1951), p. 40.

26. WO 325/1, Japanese 9th Brigade, 2/1/1942; WO 172/100, 2nd East Surrey, 2/1/1942.

27. WO 172/121, 2/9th Jat, 2/1/1942; J. Ross and W. L. Hailes, *War Services of the 9th Jat Regiment*, ii (London, 1965), pp. 30–32; Chye Kooi Loong, *British Battalion*, p. 98; WO 172/100, 2nd East Surrey, 2/1/1942.

28. The British Battalion lost forty-two other ranks killed. The 1/8th Punjabis lost two officers, one VCO and thirty-three Indian other ranks killed. The 2/9th Jats lost thirteen Indian other ranks killed. Chye Kooi Loong, *British Battalion*, pp. 196–97; WO 172/19, 15th Brigade, 2/1/1942.

29. W. E. H. Condon, *The Frontier Force Rifles* (Aldershot, 1953), p. 164; WO 172/106, 1/13th Frontier Force Rifles, 18/12/1941.

30. CAB 106/157, Fennell.

31. CAB 106/192, account by Brigadier G. W. A. Painter, 22nd Indian Infantry Brigade, pp. 10–11; WO 172/38, 9th Division.

32. WO 172/19, Malaya Command, 30/12/1941; WO 172/127, 5/11th Sikh; R. B. Deedes, *Historical Records of the Royal Garhwal Rifles*, ii, *1923–47* (Dehra Dun, 1962), p. 68.

33. W. E. H. Condon, *The Frontier Force Regiment* (Aldershot, 1962), p. 362; Mackenzie, *Eastern Epic*, p. 272. Earlier in the campaign, on 13 December near Machang, three snipers had fired from behind a wood pile at Cumming as he was talking to his opposite number in the 2/10th Baluch. Cumming went to ground and lobbed a well-placed grenade. After a brief exchange of fire three dead or dying Japanese were hauled out of the wood pile for inspection.

34. CAB 106/14, 'A Colonel of the Frontier Force'; Mackenzie, *Eastern Epic*, p. 273.

35. Kirby, *War Against Japan*, i, p. 272; Condon, *Frontier Force Regiment*, p. 373; Deedes, *Garhwal Rifles*, ii, p. 68.

## Notes to Chapter 9: Slim River

1. A. E. Percival, *The War in Malaya* (London, 1949), p. 208.
2. S. Woodburn Kirby, *The War Against Japan*, i (London, 1957), pp. 272–73.
3. CAB 106/157, 'An Account of 73rd Field Battery and 5th Field Regiment in Malaya', p. 12; WO 172/42, 73rd Field Battery of 5th Field Regiment, 2/1/1942.
4. NAM, 6509–14, Lieutenant-Colonel C. C. Deakin, 'The Malayan Campaign, 1941–42, 5/2nd Punjab', pp. 59 and 72.
5. CAB 106/55, Colonel A. M. L. Harrison, '11th Indian Division, Malaya', p. 75; CAB 101/156, Brigadier I. M. Stewart, 'Comment on the Official History'.
6. NAM, 6509–14, Deakin, 'The Malayan Campaign', p. 58; CAB 106/55, Harrison, '11th Indian Division', p. 77.
7. NAM, 6509–14, Deakin, 'The Malayan Campaign', pp. 61–62.
8. Kirby, *War Against Japan*, i, p. 276; CAB 106/55, Harrison, '11th Indian Division', pp. 83–84.
9. NAM, 6509–14, Deakin, 'The Malayan Campaign', pp. 63–65.
10. L. Allen, *Singapore, 1941–42* (London, 1977), pp. 147–48; M. Tsuji, *Singapore: The Japanese Version* (Singapore, 1960), p. 173.
11. Percival Papers, IWM, P 75, Lieutenant-Colonel F. R. N. Cobley, Malaya Command, 'Typescript Report on Malayan Campaign, 1942–43', pp. 149–50; K. C. Praval, *Valour Triumphs: A History of the Kumaon Regiment* (Faridabad, Haryana, 1976), p. 107; Kirby, *War Against Japan*, i, pp. 276–77.
12. C. Mackenzie, *Eastern Epic* (London, 1951), p. 324.
13. NAM, 6509–14, Deakin, 'The Malayan Campaign', pp. 69–70; Kirby, *War Against Japan*, i, p. 277.
14. CAB 106/55, Harrison, '11th Indian Division', p. 84; CAB 106/195, Brigadier W. R. Selby, 'Slim River Battle'.
15. Percival Papers, IWM, P 75, Cobley, 'Report on Malayan Campaign', p. 152; CAB 106/55, Harrison, '11th Indian Division', p. 108.
16. CAB 101/156, Lieutenant T. Slessor to Brigadier I. M. Stewart, 6/5/1953; CAB 44/179, part 7, p. 24.

17. Tsuji, *Japanese Version*, p. 172.
18. CAB 106/55, Harrison, '11th Indian Division', p. 108.
19. Kirby, *War Against Japan*, i, p. 278; I. M. Stewart, *History of the Argyll and Sutherland Highlanders 2nd Battalion (The Thin Red Line) Malayan Campaign, 1941–42* (London, 1947), pp. 80–86.
20. CAB 106/195, Selby, 'Slim River'; CAB 101/156, Stewart, 'Comment'.
21. Percival Papers, IWM, P 75, Cobley, 'Report on Malayan Campaign', p. 153.
22. R. S. Waters, *14th Punjab Regiment: A Short History, 1939–45* (London, 1950), pp. 39–41.
23. Mackenzie, *Eastern Epic*, p. 326; G. R. Stevens, *The 9th Gurkha Rifles*, ii, *1937–47* (1953), p. 165; Percival Papers, IWM, P 75, Cobley, 'Report on Malayan Campaign', p. 154.
24. Mackenzie, *Eastern Epic*, p. 327; E. V. R. Bellers, *The 1st King George V's Own Gurkha Rifles (The Malaun Regiment)*, ii, *1920–47* (Aldershot, 1956), p. 117.
25. Percival Papers, IWM, P 75, Cobley, 'Report on Malayan Campaign', p. 157.
26. CAB 106/55, Harrison, '11th Indian Division', p. 85.
27. Ibid., p. 86.
28. Ibid., p. 88.
29. WO 172/16, Captain T. B. Clark, 'Anti-Aircraft Defence of Malaya', p. 4; Tsuji, *Japanese Version*, p. 172.
30. WO 172/16, Lieutenant-Colonel P. R. Gold, 'Notes on the History of the 155th Lanarkshire Yeomanry Field Regiment RA in Malaya 1941 and 1942', 23/3/1942; Tsuji, *Japanese Version*, p. 174.
31. Stevens, *9th Gurkha*, ii, p. 170.
32. G. R. Stevens, *History of the 2nd King Edward VII's Own Goorkha Rifles (The Simoor Rifles)*, iii (Aldershot, 1952), pp. 166–67, and Stevens, *9th Gurkha*, ii, pp. 168–70.
33. WO 172/112, 12th Brigade; CAB 106/195, Selby, 'Slim River', p. 13.
34. Percival Papers, IWM, P 75, Cobley, 'Report on Malayan Campaign', p. 161.
35. AWM, 3 DRL/1999, Lieutenant-Colonel C. C. Deakin, p. 28.
36. Ibid., p. 9.
37. WO 106/2550A, extract from *Japanese Times and Advertiser*, 8/4/1942, pp. 5–6.
38. WO 106/2550A, Brigadier I. M. Stewart, 'Records of the Malayan Campaign', p. 12.
39. CAB 101/156, Stewart, 'Comment'.
40. CAB 106/80, 'Note on the Malayan Campaign by L. M. Heath', p. 17c; CAB 101/154, 'Further Comments by Colonel A. M. L. Harrison', ch. 14, p. 4.
41. AWM 73/8, Lieutenant-General Suzuki, XXV Army chief of staff, 'Japanese Campaign in Malaya', *Japanese Times and Advertiser*, evening edition, 8/4/1942, p. 15. (The report was prepared for Suzuki by Tsuji.)
42. Bellers, *1st Gurkha*, ii, p. 120.
43. S. Woodburn Kirby, *Singapore: The Chain of Disaster* (London, 1971), p. 179; Bellers, *1st Gurkha*, ii, p. 124; Tsuji, *Japanese Version*, p. 175.
44. AWM 73/8, Japanese communiques, 9/1/1942; Tsuji, *Japanese Version*, p. 175.

45. Allen, *Singapore*, p. 150; Kirby, *War Against Japan*, i, p. 281; WO 106/2583A, CIC FE to WO, 9/1/1942.

## Notes to Chapter 10: The Road to Johore

1. B. Bond (ed.), *Chief of Staff: The Diaries of Lieutenant-General Sir Henry Pownall*, ii, *1940–44* (London, 1974), p. 76.
2. CAB 101/56, Colonel A. M. L. Harrison, '11th Indian Division, Malaya', p. 11.
3. G. Pigot, *History of the 1st Battalion 14th Punjab Regiment* (1946), pp. 214–17; WO 172/100, 2nd East Surrey, 9/1/1942.
4. C. Mackenzie, *Eastern Epic* (London, 1951), p. 334; CAB 106/56, Harrison, '11th Indian Division', p. 38.
5. R. D. Palsokar, *A Historical Record of the Dogra Regiment, 1858–1981* (Faizabad, 1982), pp. 190–92; G. R. Stevens, *The 9th Gurkha Rifles*, ii, *1937–47* (1953), pp. 173–74; J. P. Lawford and W. E. Catto (eds), *Solah Punjab: The History of the 16th Punjab Regiment* (Aldershot, 1967), p. 194.
6. WO 172/42, 73rd Field Battery, 10/1/1942.
7. WO 106/2553, Percival to ABDA Command, 12/1/1942.
8. S. Woodburn Kirby, *Singapore: The Chain of Disaster* (London, 1971), p. 205.
9. AWM 52, 8/2/22, 22nd Brigade, 3/1/1942; D. Wall, *Singapore and Beyond: The Story of the Men of the 2/20th Battalion* (Sydney, 1985), pp. 29–32.
10. WO 172/20, Malaya Command, appendix A to 'Notes on Conference Held at Segamat 10.45 a.m., 12/1/1942'. 9th Division: 2/10th Baluch 600, 1/13th Frontier Force Rifles 550, 3/17th Dogras 250, 5/11th Sikhs 500, 2/12th Frontier Force Regiment 250, 2/18th Garhwal 550 and 2nd Loyals 650.
11. J. Wyett, *Staff Wallah: At the Fall of Singapore* (Sydney, 1996); F. Legg, *The Gordon Bennett Story* (Sydney, 1965); Percival Papers, IWM, P 42, Percival, 30/11/1953, p. 2; Brigadier H. C. Duncan, psc, Seaforth Highlanders 1914, Indian Army 1918, 13th Frontier Force Regiment.
12. IWM, 92/24/1, Colonel G. T. Wards, discussions at War History Institute, Tokyo, 12–22/9/1966; M. Tsuji, *Singapore: The Japanese Version* (Singapore, 1960), pp. 186 and 190; AWM 54, 553/1/3, US Army Historical Division, 'Japanese Studies in World War II, No. 85: XXV Army Operations in Malaya, November 1941 March 1942', compiled from memoirs of staff officers Colonel Sugita, Lieutenant-Colonel Kunitake and Lieutenant-Colonel Hashizune, pp. 76–77.
13. Percival Papers, IWM, P 75, Lieutenant-Colonel F. R. N. Cobley, Malaya Command, 'Typescript Report on Malayan Campaign', 1942–43, p. 179.
14. IWM, Department of Sound Records, 6171/06, Major-General B. W. Key, p. 14; AWM 73/51, Brigadier F. G. Galleghan, 1/2/1950.
15. A. E. Percival, *The War in Malaya* (London, 1949), p. 214.
16. Percival Papers, IWM, P 48, Percival to Kirby, 4/9/1954; AWM 52, 8/3/30, 2/30th Battalion; AWM 67, 2/109, Brigadier D. S. Maxwell, December 1946, p. 55.
17. Lionel Wigmore, *The Japanese Thrust* (Canberra, 1957), p. 215; Stan Arneil,

*Black Jack: The Life and Times of Brigadier Sir Frederick Galleghan* (Melbourne, 1983), p. 85.

18. A. W. Penfold, W. C. Bayliss and K. E. Crispin, *Galleghan's Greyhounds: The Story of the 2/30th Battalion* (Sydney, 1949); AWM 52, 8/2/27, 27th Brigade, 15/1/1942; AWM 67, 3/140, Galleghan.

19. 'As soon as the two infantry companies of the Kouda Detachment crossed the bridge over the Theka Besar River at a point ten kilometres west of Gemas, the bridge was destroyed by the enemy and a volume of fire received from within the jungle'. AWM 73/8, *Japanese Times and Advertiser*, 8/4/1942, pp. 48–49; WO 325/1, Japanese 9th Brigade; AWM 54, 553/1/3, US Army Historical Division, 'Japanese Studies in World War Two, No. 85', p. 78.

20. K. Harrison, *The Brave Japanese* (Adelaide, 1966), pp. 20–25.

21. Arneil, *Galleghan*, p. 90; Penfold, *2/30th Battalion*, p. 102.

22. Harrison, *Brave Japanese*, p. 27.

23. Ibid., pp. 30–32; AWM 73/8, *Japanese Times and Advertiser*, p. 39.

24. Wigmore, *Japanese Thrust*, pp. 218–19; Penfold, *2/30th Battalion*, pp. 110 and 113.

25. Penfold, *2/30th Battalion*, p. 117; Harrison, *Brave Japanese*, pp. 36–38.

26. WO 259/63, CGS Australia to WO, 2/4/1942; Mackenzie, *Eastern Epic*, p. 337; Wigmore, *Japanese Thrust*, p. 220; Penfold, *2/30th Battalion*, p. 135.

27. Tsuji, *Japanese Version*, p. 193.

28. WO 172/141, 5/18th Garhwal Rifles, 6/1/1942; NAM 7709–62, Major S. A. Watt, 7/6th Rajputana Rifles, 'The 7th Battalion in Malaya 1942'; R. Braddon, *The Naked Island* (London, 1952), p. 57.

29. J. Ross and W. L. Hailes, *War Services of the 9th Jat Regiment*, ii, *1937–48* (London, 1965), pp. 39–40.

30. Percival Papers, IWM, P 42, Percival, 30/11/1953, p. 2.

31. NAM 7709–62, Watt, p. 6; WO 172/139, 7/6th Rajputana Rifles, 15/1/1942.

32. R. B. Deedes, *Historical Records of the Royal Garhwal Rifles*, ii, *1923–47* (Dehra Dun, 1962), pp. 82–86.

33. NAM 7709–62, Watt, pp. 9–10; S. Woodburn Kirby, *The War Against Japan*, i, (London, 1957), p. 305.

*Notes to Chapter 11: The Road from Bakri*

1. IWM, 88/34/1, Major R. Hammond.

2. AWM, PR 88/214, Sergeant A. Montfort, 4th Anti-Tank Regiment, 29/12/1941; K. Harrison, *The Brave Japanese* (Adelaide, 1966), p. 41; C. Finkemeyer, *It Happened to Us* (Melbourne, 1994), pp. 7–11; R. Christie (ed.), *A History of the 2/29th Battalion* (Melbourne, 1983), p. 45. McCure had been sacked from command of a gun troop because his crews had refused to obey a training instruction ordering that guns be carried on the back trays of trucks. The crewmen rightly believed that it was safer to tow guns behind a vehicle. McCure was thus available to take charge of the composite troop when it was formed at short notice.

3. Christie, *2/29th Battalion*, p. 43; Finkemeyer, *It Happened to Us*, pp. 11–12 and 34; Harrison, *Brave Japanese*, pp. 45–48.

4. NAM, 7709–62–7, Japanese Imperial Guard History, p. 5. Parsons was later awarded the Distinguished Conduct Medal (DCM), one of a small number of decorations granted for the campaign.

5. Harrison, *Brave Japanese*, p. 47; Finkemeyer, *It Happened to Us*, p. 25. McClure evaded capture and spent the war holed up in the jungle with Communist guerrillas.

6. AWM 73/65, Lieutenant-Colonel R. F. Oakes. Lieutenant-Colonel Anderson was a Federal Member of Parliament for the Country Party from 1949–51 and 1955–61.

7. NAM, 7709–62, Colonel J. L. Jones; Lieutenant-Colonel C. G. W. Anderson, 27 and 29/5/1947.

8. A. E. Percival, *The War in Malaya* (London, 1949), pp. 218 and 228.

9. CAB 106/126, Brigadier Blood, 'Comments on an Account of Malaya Operations', p. 14.

10. Lionel Wigmore, *The Japanese Thrust* (Canberra, 1957), pp. 231–32; Christie, *2/29th Battalion*, p. 199.

11. Finkemeyer, *It Happened to Us*, p. 38.

12. AWM 67, 11/6, 45th Brigade, 19/1/1942; AWM 73/7, Lieutenant-Colonel C. G. W. Anderson, 15/1/1953; R. Braddon, *The Naked Island* (London, 1952), p. 63.

13. AWM 73/7, Anderson, 15/1/1953.

14. J. Ross and W. L. Hailes, *War Services of the 9th Jat Regiment*, ii, 1937–48 (London, 1965), p. 42.

15. Percival Collection, IWM, P 47, Major B. E. Whitman, 13th Field Company Madras Sappers and Miners, 19/1/1942.

16. Harrison, *Brave Japanese*, p. 55; AWM, PR 88/51, Private W. Anderson, 2/29th Battalion, p. 6.

17. WO 172/144, 53rd Brigade, 19/1/1941.

18. AWM 93, 50/2/23/480, Colonel J. H. Thyer, 7/10/1951.

19. Wigmore, *Japanese Thrust*, p. 237; AWM 73/8, *Japanese Times and Advertiser*, 8/4/1942, p. 47; M. Tsuji, *Singapore: The Japanese Version* (Singapore, 1960), p. 206; 2/19th Battalion AIF Association, *The Grim Glory of the 2/19th Battalion AIF* (Sydney, 1975), p. 212.

20. Janet Uhr, *Against the Sun* (Sydney, 1998), p. 133.

21. CAB 106/163, General Percival to Generals Heath, Bennett and Simmons, 20/1/1942.

22. WO 172/89, 6th Norfolk, Captain A. R. Stacy, 20/1/1942; WO 172/123, 3/16th Punjab; C. Mackenzie, *Eastern Epic* (London, 1951), pp. 343–44.

23. S. Woodburn Kirby, *The War Against Japan*, i (London, 1957), pp. 313–15 and 320.

24. Christie, *2/29th Battalion*, pp. 53–54; Braddon, *Naked Island*, pp. 73–74.

25. Ross and Hailes, *9th Jat*, ii, p. 49; Mackenzie, *Eastern Epic*, p. 347; AWM, MS 758, Lieutenant B. C. Hackney, pp. 15–42; Braddon, *Naked Island*, pp. 97–101.

26. F. Legg, *The Gordon Bennett Story* (Sydney, 1965), p. 217.

27. R. B. Deedes, *Historical Records of the Royal Garhwal Rifles*, ii, 1923–47 (Dehra Dun, 1962), p. 94; E. W. C. Sandes, *The Indian Engineers, 1939–47* (Kirkee, 1956), p. 203; AWM 67, 3/9, Lieutenant-Colonel C. G. W. Anderson. The 13th Field Company lost sixty-four officers and men killed and sixty-two wounded. The 2/29th Battalion (less a company and a platoon) lost between 17–24 January nine officers and 113 other ranks killed, presumed dead, and died of wounds, seventy-one other ranks wounded, and forty-six other rank POWs, for a total of 239. The 2/19th Battalion (less two platoons) lost between 18–23 January nine officers and 165 other ranks killed, presumed dead, and died of wounds, three officers and seventy-six other ranks wounded, and thirty other rank POWs, for a total of 292. The 2/15th Field Regiment lost between 15–23 January, two officers and forty-two other ranks killed, presumed dead and died of wounds, three officers and thirty-six other ranks wounded, and one officer and twenty-seven other rank POWs, for a total of 109. Almost all of the 2/15th Field Regiment's casualties came from the 65th Battery.

28. Wigmore, *Japanese Thrust*, p. 316; WO 106/2625, Chief of Army Information Section, 'Enemy Publication No. 278, Malayan Campaign, 1941–42', p. 56.

29. CAB 106/162, Colonel J. H. Thyer and Brigadier C. H. Kappe, 'Report on Operations of 8th Australian Division AIF in Malaya'; CAB 101/154, Harrison to Kirby, 1/2/1954; WO 172/123, 3/16th Punjab; CAB 106/174, Lieutenant-Colonel M. Elrington, 'The Story of the 2nd Battalion The Loyal Regiment in Malaya', pp. 9–14.

30. WO 172/144, 53rd Brigade, 21–23/1/1942; WO 172/123, 3/16th Punjab, 23/1/1942; CAB 106/174, Elrington, 'Loyal Regiment in Malaya', pp. 12–15.

31. WO 106/2533, ABDA Command to WO, 16 and 19/1/1942; W. S. Churchill, *The Second World War*, iv (London, 1951), p. 42.

32. Churchill, *Second World War*, iv, p. 43; WO 106/2583A, Churchill to Ismay for Chiefs of Staff Committee, 19/1/1942.

33. AIR 8/946, Churchill to Wavell, 20/1/1942.

34. AIR 8/946, Churchill to War Cabinet, Chiefs of Staff Committee, 21/1/1942; Alanbrooke Papers, LHC, 3/A/V, 'Notes on My Life', v, 1941–42, pp. 344–46.

35. CAB 69/4, War Cabinet, Defence Committee (Operations), DC (42) 4th Meeting, 21/1/1942; D. M. Horner, *High Command* (Sydney, 1982), pp. 150–51.

36. Horner, *High Command*, p. 150.

37. Ibid., pp. 151–52.

38. Churchill, *Second World War*, iv, pp. 51–52.

*Notes to Chapter 12: The Loss of the Mainland*

1. A. W. Penfold, W. C. Bayliss and K. E. Crispin, *Galleghan's Greyhounds: The Story of the 2/30th Australian Infantry Battalion* (Sydney, 1949), pp. 148–52; C. G. T. Dean, *The Loyal Regiment (North Lancashire), 1919–53* (Preston, 1955), p. 146.

NOTES TO PAGES 185–194

2. Dean, *The Loyal Regiment*, p. 146; CAB 106/174, Lieutenant-Colonel M. Elrington, 'The Story of the 2nd Battalion The Loyal Regiment in Malaya', pp. 15–20; Stan Arneil, *Black Jack: The Life and Times of Brigadier Sir Frederick Galleghan* (Melbourne, 1983), pp. 97–99; Penfold, *2/30th Battalion*, p. 159; Lionel Wigmore, *The Japanese Thrust* (Canberra, 1957), p. 264.

3. WO 172/138, 2nd Cambridgeshire, 26/1/1942; C. Mackenzie, *Eastern Epic* (London, 1951), p. 354; CAB 106/57, Colonel A. M. L. Harrison, '11th Indian Division, Malaya', pp. 25–26.

4. CAB 106/57, Harrison, '11th Indian Division', pp. 19–21.

5. WO 172/88, 5th Royal Norfolk, 26/1/1942; CAB 106/57, Harrison, '11th Indian Division', pp. 27–28.

6. K. N. V. Sastri and K. D. Bhargava, *Campaigns in South-East Asia, 1941–42* (New Delhi, 1960), p. 284; WO 172/138, 2nd Cambridgeshire, 26/1/1942.

7. WO 172/100, 2nd East Surrey, 26–28/1/1942; S Woodburn Kirby, *Singapore: The Chain of Disaster* (London, 1971), p. 207.

8. CAB 106/57, Harrison, '11th Indian Division', p. 42.

9. I. Morrison, *Malayan Postscript* (Sydney, 1943), p. 130; A. J. Marder, *Old Friends, New Enemies*, i (Oxford, 1981), p. 427.

10. S. Woodburn Kirby, *The War Against Japan*, i (London, 1957), p. 331; E. R. Hall, *Glory in Chaos: The RAAF in the Far East, 1940–42* (Melbourne, 1989), pp. 351–70, and appendix C; C. Shores, B. Cull and Yasuho Izawa, *Bloody Shambles*, ii (London, 1992–93), pp. 17–42.

11. G. Hermon Gill, *Royal Australian Navy, 1939–1942* (Canberra, 1957), p. 560.

12. AWM 51, 144, Colonel J. H. Thyer and Brigadier C. H. Kappe, 'Report on Operations of 8th Australian Division AIF in Malaya', p. 74.

13. AWM 54, 553/5/14, Major C. B. O'Brien, p. 7.

14. AWM 51, 144, Thyer and Kappe, 'Operations of 8th Australian Division', p. 75; Janet Uhr, *Against the Sun* (Sydney, 1998), pp. 173–91; AWM, PR 85/42, Papers of Brigadier H. B. Taylor.

15. G. McCabe, *Pacific Sunset* (Hobart, 1946), p. 46.

16. J. Burfitt, *Against All Odds: The History of the 2/18th Battalion* (Sydney, 1991), pp. 52–53; AWM 52, 8/3/18, 2/18th Battalion.

17. W. Miles, *The Life of a Regiment: The Gordon Highlanders*, v, *1919–45* (Aberdeen, 1961), p. 97.

18. WO 172/38, 9th Division, appendix 44 A, Operation Instruction No. 25 to Commanders 8 and 22 Brigades, 6 p.m. 26/1/1942.

19. AWM 67, 3/25, Lieutenant-General H. G. Bennett, diary, 26–27/1/1942; H. G. Bennett, *Why Singapore Fell* (Sydney, 1944), pp. 150–51.

20. AWM 73/7, Thyer, 20/1/1953 and 6/2/1953.

21. WO 172/38, 9th Division, 27/1/1942.

22. AWM 73/7, Thyer, 19/1/1953; CAB 101/151, Kirby to Gavin Long, 15/9/1954; A. B. Lodge, *The Fall of General Gordon Bennett* (Sydney, 1986), p. 131.

23. Bennett, *Why Singapore Fell*, p. 158.

24. CAB 101/151, Kirby to Long, 15/9/1954.

25. WO 172/127, 5/11th Sikh, 26/1/1942.
26. Ibid., 27/1/1942.
27. Kirby, *War Against Japan*, i, p. 337; AWM 73/7, Thyer to Kirby, 6/2/1953.
28. Sastri and Bhargava, *South-East Asia, 1941–42*, p. 289.
29. Mackenzie, *Eastern Epic*, p. 359.
30. WO 172/127, 5/11th Sikh, 28/1/1942; CAB 101/151, Kirby to Long, 15/9/1954; CAB 106/192, account by Brigadier G. W. A. Painter, 22nd Indian Infantry Brigade, p. 26.
31. IWM, 11891/4, Captain P. E. Campbell, 2/10th Baluch.
32. Percival Collection, IWM, P 31, Brigadier W. A. Trott to Percival, 18/7/1949. Sir Charles Moses was later general manager of the Australian Broadcasting Commission. AWM 73/7, Lieutenant-Colonel C. Moses, 21/1/1953, and Brigadier W. A. Trott, 19/1/1953.
33. WO 172/38, 9th Division, 28/1/1942.
34. AWM 73/7, Trott, 19/1/1953.
35. Kirby wrote to Painter in 1952: 'I have had a long interview with your friend Brigadier Lay, particularly with reference to the events around Layang Layang.' CAB 101/156, Kirby to Painter, 12/3/1952.
36. Penfold, *2/30th Battalion*, p. 167; Wigmore, *Japanese Thrust*, pp. 275–77; Arneil, *Galleghan*, pp. 100–1.
37. AWM 73/7, Major J. W. C. Wyett to Kirby, 9/2/1953; AWM 67, 3/25, Bennett, diary, 28/1/1942; AWM 93, 50/2/23/285, Brigadier F. G. Galleghan to Wigmore, 1/3/1954; AWM 67, 3/140, Galleghan.
38. AWM 73/7, Galleghan; J. Wyett, *Staff Wallah: At the Fall of Singapore* (Sydney, 1996), p. 75.
39. F. Legg, *The Gordon Bennett Story* (Sydney, 1965), pp. 221–22; Bennett, *Why Singapore Fell*, p. 158.
40. AWM 67, 3/25, Bennett, diary, 29/1/1942; AWM 52, 8/3/26, 2/26th Battalion, 29/1/1942; CAB 106/162, Thyer and Kappe, 'Report on Operations of 8th Australian Division', pp. 79–81. The 2/26th Battalion claimed to have killed five hundred Japanese near Ayer Bemban. This was a great exaggeration.
41. Bennett, *Why Singapore Fell*, pp. 98 and 164. Throughout January a radio transmitter in Johore Bharu had been sending illegal nightly messages to an unknown destination. One of the Sultan of Johore's sons fell under suspicion. He was an officer in the armed forces with access to sensitive information. The radio set was roughly located and an Englishman was arrested on 27 January. But in the panicky context of Malaya in early 1942 the fact of a man's arrest cannot be taken as an indication of his guilt. AWM 93, 50/2/23/480, Thyer to Wigmore, 7/10/1951; CAB 106/153, excerpt from 8th Australian Division Signals War Diary, January 1942, appendix; CAB 101/150, Kirby to Percival, 17/11/1954.
42. Wyett, *Staff Wallah*, p. 82; Morrison, *Malayan Postscript*, p. 138.
43. CAB 106/192, account by Brigadier Painter, pp. 27–32; Mackenzie, *Eastern Epic*, pp. 364–69; D. Russell-Roberts, *Spotlight on Singapore* (London, 1965), p. 114.

*Notes to Chapter 13: Singapore Island*

1. The 23rd Brigade's headquarters, 2/14th Field Regiment and 2/4th Pioneer Battalion, the 8th Division's last remaining units, were still in the Northern Territory of Australia.

2. C. Shores, B. Cull and Yasuho Izawa, *Bloody Shambles*, i (London, 1992–93), pp. 290–93.

3. Ibid., pp. 324–26.

4. WO 106/2528, press communique, 10 a.m., 22/1/1942. Civilian casualties on 21 January were estimated to be 287 killed and 529 wounded.

5. Shores, *Shambles*, i, pp. 331–32; John Bennett, *Defeat to Victory: No. 453 Squadron RAAF* (Point Cook, Victoria, 1994), p. 49; E. R. Hall, *Glory in Chaos: The RAAF in the Far East, 1940–42* (Melbourne, 1989), pp. 308–9 and 435.

6. Shores, *Shambles*, i, pp. 350–61.

7. WO 365/15, Malaya Command battle casualties, 7/2/1942: 1371 killed, 2614 wounded, 15,092 missing and forty-six POWs, for a total of 19,123. 2758 were British service, 1569 AIF, 11,351 Indian Army and 3445 local forces. After the war Australian losses on the mainland were calculated as 528 killed, 461 wounded and 171 POWs. AWM 54, 553/1/3.

8. A. J. Marder, *Old Friends, New Enemies*, ii (Oxford, 1990), p. 13. The 2/4th Machine Gun Battalion arrived at Singapore about 850 strong.

9. C. G. T. Dean, *The Loyal Regiment (North Lancashire), 1919–53* (Preston, 1955), pp. 151–52; ADM 267/138, Captain A. B. Smith, SS *Empress of Asia*, 27/4/1942; IWM, 86/8//1, Lieutenant-Colonel H. S. Flowers, 9th Royal Northumberland Fusiliers; C. N. Barclay, *The History of the Royal Northumberland Fusiliers in the Second World War* (London, 1952), pp. 85–86; IWM, Misc. 155, item 2406, War Diaries of 125th Anti-Tank Regiment RA and 288th Field Company RE.

10. NAM, 7910-67-2, Lieutenant-Colonel J. D. Sainter, 'War Record of the 6th Battalion 1st Punjab Regiment', 15/6/1942; NAM, 7309-2, account of Brigadier G. C. Ballentine, 44th Indian Infantry Brigade, p. 2; S. Woodburn Kirby, *The War Against Japan*, i (London, 1957), p. 362; Lionel Wigmore, *The Japanese Thrust* (Canberra, 1957), p. 289. Kirby and Wigmore estimated Singapore's garrison to be 85,000 strong, including 15,000 base troops, but the true figure was in excess of 100,000.

11. H. W. Picken (ed.), *Nobody's Own: The History of the 3rd Cavalry and its Predecessors, 1841–1945* (1962), pp. 197–98.

12. CAB 106/156, 'FMSVF and LOC Organization: Notes on the Malayan Campaign 1941–42'.

13. NAM, 7309–2, Ballentine, p. 5.

14. WO 172/88, 5th Royal Norfolk, Lieutenant K. S. Potter, 11/5/1942; CAB 106/57, Colonel A. M. L. Harrison, 'History of 11th Indian Division', p. 41. On the mainland the 5th Norfolks lost a hundred of all ranks, the 2nd Cambridgeshire two hundred, and the 6th Norfolks thirteen officers and 213 other ranks. With

the inclusion of first line reinforcements the strengths of the three battalions were raised to eight hundred, seven hundred and six hundred respectively.

15. G. Chippington, *Singapore: The Inexcusable Betrayal* (Worcester, 1992), p. 184.
16. R. W. Christie (ed.), *A History of the 2/29th Battalion* (Melbourne, 1983), pp. 97–99; AWM 67, 3/291, Lieutenant-Colonel R. F. Oakes; 2/19th Battalion AIF Association, *The Grim Glory of the 2/19th Battalion AIF* (Sydney, 1975), p. 255.
17. AWM 54, 553/5/14, Major C. B. O'Brien, p. 10.
18. Kirby, *War Against Japan*, i, p. 359. Kirby's estimate of Singapore's peacetime population was 550,000, but this was an out of date census figure. A colonial census was only an estimate. The British administration never knew exactly how many people lived in the crowded districts of Chinatown. F. S. V. Donnison, *British Military Administration in the Far East, 1943–46* (London, 1956), p. 375. The estimate of 769,216 included 599,659 Chinese. CAB 66/22, W. P (42) 92, 'Report of the Chancellor of the Duchy of Lancaster on the Termination of his Appointment as Resident Minister', 19/2/1942, p. 3; Percival Papers, IWM, P 44, Sir Shenton Thomas, 'What Malaya Did', October 1954.
19. AWM 73/65, Colonel F. G. Brink, 17/6/1944; B. Bond (ed.), *Chief of Staff: The Diaries of Lieutenant-General Sir Henry Pownall*, ii, *1940–44* (London, 1974), p. 84; M. Tsuji, *Singapore: The Japanese Version* (Singapore, 1960), p. 187.
20. Percival Papers, IWM, P 43, 'Summary of Comments by Lord Wavell on General Percival's Despatch on Operations of Malaya Command'; A. Wavell, *Despatch by the Supreme Commander of the ABDA Area to the Combined Chiefs of Staff on the Operations in the South-West Pacific, 15/1/1942–25/2/1942* (London, 1948), p. 12.
21. WO 106/2609A, Wavell to CIGS, 17/2/1942.
22. Percival Papers, IWM, P 43, Percival, 14/12/1945, P 48, Percival, 2/12/1953.
23. Kirby, *War Against Japan*, i, p. 363; Percival, *War in Malaya*.
24. Percival Papers, IWM, P 42, Percival, 2/12/1953, P 48, Percival, December 1953, p. 2.
25. Percival Papers, IWM, P 47, Percival, 'Protracted Defence of Singapore Island', 23/1/1942, P 48, Percival, December 1953, p. 3; AWM 73/7, Colonel J. H. Thyer, 19/1/1953, p. 3.
26. CAB 101/150, Kirby to Percival, 10/10/1954; Percival Papers, IWM, P 48, Percival to Kirby, 4/2/1954.
27. Tsuji, *Japanese Version*, p. 220; Kirby, *War Against Japan*, i, p. 527. The 'rifle strength' of the Japanese force poised across the Johore Strait from Singapore was no more than 25,000.
28. Tsuji, *Japanese Version*, pp. 227–29.
29. WO 325/1, Japanese 9th Brigade, 5/2/1942; Tsuji, *Japanese Version*, pp. 232–33.
30. D. Wall, *Singapore and Beyond: The Story of the Men of the 2/20th Battalion* (Sydney, 1985), p. 52.
31. H. G. Bennett, *Why Singapore Fell* (Sydney, 1944), p. 167; AWM 93, 50/2/23/342, Captain A. H. Curlewis; AWM 73/7, Captain H. E. Jessop, 23/1/1953; AWM 67,

3/25, Lieutenant-General H. G. Bennett, diary, 1/2/1942; WO 172/21, Malaya Command, Brigadier General Staff, 7/2/1942.

32. AWM 52, 8/2/22, 22nd Brigade, 2/2/1942, appendix B, Brigadier H. B. Taylor, 3–7/2/1942; CAB 106/151, Colonel J. H. Thyer, 19/1/1953; AWM 67, 3/25, Bennett, diary, 4/2/1942; Wall, *2/20th Battalion*, p. 53; AWM 73/7, Brigadier D. S. Maxwell, 26/1/1953.

33. I. Morrison, *Malayan Postscript* (Sydney, 1943), pp. 156–57.

34. L. Allen, *Singapore, 1941–42* (London, 1977), p. 164; Percival Papers, IWM, P 49, Lieutenant-Colonel B. H. Ashmore, Malaya Command, 'Some Personal Observations of Malaya Campaign, 1940–42', Ceylon, 1942, p. 19.

*Notes to Chapter 14: Across the Johore Strait*

1. M. Tsuji, *Singapore: The Japanese Version* (Singapore, 1960), p. 235; WO 172/16, 155th Field Regiment, 8/2/1942.

2. Tsuji estimated that XXV Army had 440 large missile weapons, of which 168 were field guns. The British had 266 field guns at Singapore. Tsuji, *Japanese Version*, p. 238; Lionel Wigmore, *The Japanese Thrust* (Canberra, 1957), p. 327.

3. AWM 54, 553/5/14, Major C. B. O'Brien, pp. 11–12.

4. H. G. Bennett, *Why Singapore Fell* (Sydney, 1944), p. 173; AWM 52, 8/2/22, appendix B, Brigadier H. B. Taylor, 8/2/1942.

5. AWM 73/7, Colonel J. H. Thyer, 19/1/1953; Percival Papers, IWM, P 48, Percival, December 1953, p. 4; WO 172/21, Malaya Command, appendix D 55, 3.45 p.m., 8/2/1942.

6. AWM 67, 2/109, Brigadier D. S. Maxwell, December 1946, p. 51.

7. AWM 73/7, Thyer, 19/1/1953, p. 3.

8. AWM 52, 8/2/22, 22nd Brigade, appendix B, Taylor, 8/2/1942.

9. A. E. Percival, *The War in Malaya* (London, 1949), p. 270.

10. Percival Papers, IWM, P 43, section IV and comments on part IV, p. 3.

11. AWM 93, 50/2/23/258, Brigadier H. B. Taylor.

12. Wigmore, *Japanese Thrust*, p. 308; AWM 73/7, Brigadier H. B. Taylor, 27/1/1953.

13. AWM 52, 4/2/15, 2/15th Field Regiment, 9/2/1942.

14. AWM 52, 4/1/15, HQ RAA, 8–9/2/1942; Bennett, *Why Singapore Fell*, p. 174; AWM 93, 50/2/23/258, Taylor.

15. D. Wall, *Singapore and Beyond: The Story of the Men of the 2/20th Battalion* (Sydney, 1985), p. 52.

16. Ibid., p. 60; Wigmore, *Japanese Thrust*, pp. 311–12.

17. Wall, *2/20th Battalion*, pp. 69 and 137.

18. Ibid., pp. 67–76.

19. Wigmore, *Japanese Thrust*, pp. 313–15; J. Burfitt, *Against All Odds: The History of the 2/18th Battalion* (Sydney, 1991), pp. 61–70.

20. Wall, *2/20th Battalion*, pp. 353–57.

21. Wigmore, *Japanese Thrust*, p. 316; Wall, *2/20th Battalion*, pp. 305–7.

22. NAM, 7309–2, account of Brigadier G. C. Ballentine, 44th Indian Infantry Brigade, pp. 6–8.
23. Wigmore, *Japanese Thrust*, p. 320; AWM 52, 8/3/18, 2/18th Battalion.
24. Wall, *2/20th Battalion*, pp. 78–88.
25. *2/19th Battalion*, pp. 316–19 and 364.
26. AWM 52, 8/3/29, Lieutenant-Colonel S. A. F. Pond, 'Comment by CO and Additions to Unit War Diary', p. 7.
27. Ibid.,
28. Kirby, *War Against Japan*, i, p. 403; WO 106/2550B, extract from a letter by a Staff Officer of the 18th Division, 19/6/1942.
29. AWM 51, 144, Colonel J. H. Thyer and Brigadier C. H. Kappe, 'Report on Operations of 8th Australian Division AIF in Malaya', p. 125; AWM 52, 8/2/22, 22nd Brigade, 8 p.m., 9/2/1942.
30. AWM 51, 144, Thyer and Kappe, 'Report on Operations of 8th Australian Division', pp. 125–27; *2/19th Battalion*, p. 324; AWM 171/2/27. On 8–9 February recorded casualties for the 22nd Brigade's infantry added up to 364. The 2/18th Battalion lost three officers and seventy-nine other ranks killed or died of wounds, two officers and thirty-six other ranks wounded, and two other rank POWs, for a total of 122. The 2/19th Battalion lost four officers and fifty other ranks killed or died of wounds, forty-six other ranks wounded, and one other rank POW, for a total of 101. The 2/20th Battalion lost nine officers and eighty-one other ranks killed or died of wounds, and four officers and forty-seven other ranks wounded, for a total of 141.
31. AWM 73/7, Brigadier C. H. Kappe, 5/2/1953.
32. Percival Collection, IWM, P 48, Percival, December 1953.
33. Cabinet Office, *Principal War Telegrams and Memoranda, 1940–1943: Far East* (London, 1976), CIC South-West Pacific to WO, 4 and 10/2/1942; CAB 101/150, Percival to Kirby, 13/11/1954, Kirby to Percival, 2/12/1954.
34. Wigmore, *Japanese Thrust*, p. 324. The remaining Hurricanes at Kallang aerodrome had taken off again on 9 February for another day's fighting in the face of great odds. By dawn of the following day No. 232 Squadron had been ordered to evacuate. Flyable Hurricanes and Buffaloes left for bases in the Dutch East Indies, and the ground staff headed down to Keppel Harbour to board a ship.
35. AWM 52, 8/2/22, 22nd Brigade, 9/2/1942 and appendix B.
36. WO 172/21, Malaya Command, appendix L 56, 10.10 a.m., 9/1/1942.
37. AWM 67, 3/25, part 2; Wigmore, *Japanese Thrust*, p. 329.
38. AWM 73/7, Brigadier D. S. Maxwell, 26/1/1953, Brigadier F. G. Galleghan, 22/1/1953; AWM 67, 3/261, Brigadier D. S. Maxwell; R. Magarry, *The Battalion Story* (Brisbane, 1994), p. 130.
39. AWM 67, 3/261; AWM 93, 50/2/23/554, Wigmore to Lieutenant-Colonel R. F. Oakes, 18/10/1954.
40. AWM 73/7, Thyer, 19/1/1953. In captivity Lieutenant-Colonel A. S. Blackburn asked an unnamed brigadier how the Japanese had managed to cross the Johore Strait. 'After some time the brigadier [who could have been either

Maxwell or Taylor] said: "Look here Arthur, I'll tell you what happened. I knew it was hopeless so I drew my men back from the beaches and let the Japanese through".' AWM 67, 3/36, Lieutenant-Colonel A. S. Blackburn.

41. WO 106/2550B, report by GSO 1 HQ MC; AWM 73/7, Maxwell to Long, December 1952, Maxwell, 26/1/1953.
42. A. W. Penfold, W. C. Bayliss and K. E. Crispin, *Galleghan's Greyhounds: The Story of the 2/30th Australian Infantry Battalion* (Sydney, 1949), pp. 197–200.
43. R. R. McNicoll, *The Royal Australian Engineers, 1919 to 1945: Teeth and Tail* (Canberra, 1982), p. 131; Wigmore, *Japanese Thrust*, p. 382; AWM 73/7, Maxwell, 26/1/1953; AWM 67, 3/141, Major A. P. Garde to Maxwell, 15/12/1952.
44. Tsuji, *Japanese Thrust*, pp. 242–44.

## Notes to Chapter 15: Bukit Timah

1. R. B. Deedes, *Historical Records of the Royal Garhwal Rifles*, ii, 1923–47 (Dehra Dun, 1962), pp. 97–99.
2. A. W. Penfold, W. C. Bayliss and K. E. Crispin, *Galleghan's Greyhounds: The Story of the 2/30th Australian Infantry Battalion* (Sydney, 1949), pp. 201–4.
3. WO 172/21, Malaya Command, appendix M 57.
4. AWM 52, 8/2/22, 22nd Brigade, appendix B, Brigadier H. B. Taylor, 10/2/1942; CAB 106/151, Brigadier H. B. Taylor, 27/1/1953.
5. CAB 106/152, Lieutenant-Colonel J. G. Davis, 6/14th Punjab, and Brigadier Ballentine's answers to queries concerning movements of 44th Indian Infantry Brigade.
6. CAB 106/157, Lieutenant-Colonel J. D. Sainter to Kirby, 31/12/1958, 20/3/1960, Major S. I. Strong, 6/1st Punjab, to Sainter, 14/7/1960.
7. CAB 106/152, Brigadier G. C. Ballentine.
8. A. E. Percival, *The War in Malaya* (London, 1949), p. 275.
9. WO 259/63, WO to CIC South-West Pacific, 10/2/1942; Lionel Wigmore, *The Japanese Thrust* (Canberra, 1957), p. 341.
10. AWM 52, 8/3/18, 2/18th Battalion.
11. 2/19th Battalion AIF Association, *The Grim Glory of the 2/19th Battalion AIF* (Sydney, 1975), p. 328; AWM 52, 8/2/22, 22nd Brigade, X Battalion, 10/2/1942; D. Wall, *Singapore and Beyond: The Story of the Men of the 2/20th Battalion* (Sydney, 1985), pp. 92–93. X Battalion's twenty-seven officers included seven from the 2/20th Battalion, eleven from the 2/19th Battalion, seven from the 2/18th Battalion, one from divisional headquarters and one from the AAMC.
12. M. Tsuji, *Singapore: The Japanese Version* (Singapore, 1960), pp. 248–50 and 253–54.
13. AWM 54, 4/4/4, 2/4th Anti-Tank Regiment, 8–10/2/1942.
14. AWM 73/7, Lieutenant-General H. G. Bennett, 30/1/1953; K. N. V. Sastri and K. D. Bhargava, *Campaigns in South-East Asia, 1941–42* (New Delhi, 1960), pp. 326–27.
15. Wall, *2/20th Battalion*, pp. 93–95; AWM 52, 8/2/22, 22nd Brigade, X Battalion.

16. Wall, *2/20th Battalion*, pp. 97–99. On 11–12 February the original battalions of the 22nd Brigade lost the following casualties: 2/18th Battalion, two officers and fifty-three other ranks killed or died of wounds, one officer and nineteen other ranks wounded, and five other rank POWs: 2/19th Battalion, two officers and thirty-three other ranks killed or died of wounds, and thirty other ranks wounded; 2/20th Battalion, one officer and 144 other ranks killed or died of wounds, twenty-three other ranks wounded, and two officers and four other rank POWs. The great bulk of these casualties were lost by X Battalion and Merrett Force during the night of 11/12 February. AWM 171/2/27.
17. Wall, *2/20th Battalion*, pp. 100–1; *2/19th Battalion*, pp. 336–37.
18. CAB 106/196, Lieutenant-Colonel A. E. Cumming, pp. 1–2.
19. Wigmore, *Japanese Thrust*, p. 349.
20. J. P. Lawford and W. E. Catto (eds), *Solah Punjab: The History of the 16th Punjab Regiment* (Aldershot, 1967), p. 205; AWM 52, 8/4/16, Special Reserve Battalion; AWM, PR 85/26, 2/4th Machine Gun Battalion AIF, service history and honour roll; Chye Kooi Loong, *The History of the British Battalion in the Malayan Campaign, 1941–42* (1984), p. 139. The British Battalion lost 135 dead at Singapore Island, the bulk on 11 February.
21. AWM 52, 8/4/16, Special Reserve Battalion, 17/3/1942; AWM 51, 144, Colonel J. H. Thyer and Brigadier C. H. Kappe, 'Report on Operations of 8th Australian Division AIF in Malaya', p. 144.
22. CAB 106/173, Lieutenant-Colonel L. C. Thomas, 7/4/1942; CAB 106/70, appendix C; WO 172/145, 55th Brigade, 11/2/1942.
23. AWM 73/7, Brigadier D. S. Maxwell, 26/1/1953; AWM 52, 8/2/27, 27th Brigade, 11/2/1942; Malcolm H. Murfett, John N. Miksic, Brian P. Farrell and Chiang Ming Shun, *Between Two Oceans: A Military History of Singapore from First Settlement to Final British Withdrawal* (Singapore, 1999), pp. 232 and 245.
24. Penfold, *2/30th Battalion*, pp. 206–10.
25. NAM, 7309–2, account of Brigadier G. C. Ballentine, 44th Indian Infantry Brigade, p. 12; AWM 52, 8/3/18, 2/18th Battalion; S. Woodburn Kirby, *The War Against Japan*, i (London, 1957), pp. 358–59.
26. CO 273/671/9, Lieutenant-Colonel I. M. Stewart, New Delhi, 14/11/1942.
27. WO 172/21, Malaya Command, appendix Y 58, 6.35 p.m., 10/2/1942, Captain Bell, appendix B 59, 7.20 p.m., 10/2/1942, duty officer Southern Area, 'Report Received from "M" Sector Town Beach, 18.40 hours'.
28. National Archives Singapore, A 16/16, Lee Kip Lin.
29. ADM 199/903A, Lieutenant J. O. C. Hayes, 14/5/1942, pp. 7–8; ADM 199/357, Chief Petty Officer E. F. Sheath.
30. IWM, 12749/52, Lieutenant-Colonel P. J. D. Toosey, 135th Field Regiment, p. 177; ADM 199/607A, Major J. C. Westall, Royal Marines; WO 106/2579C, Lieutenant-Colonel DLI.
31. Percival, *War in Malaya*, p. 270; AWM 52, 18/2/21, 8th Division Provost Company, 11/2/1942.
32. F. A. E. Crew, *The Army Medical Services*, ii (London, 1957), pp. 103–4; ADM

199/1472A, C. R. T. Evans, acting foreman of yard Singapore Naval Base; ADM 199/903A, H. K. Rodgers, director Singapore Harbour Board; ADM 199/357, Lieutenant-Commander D. F. H. Chandler.

33. ADM 267/138, Mr J. L. Dawson, chief officer, M. V. *Empire Star*. The events of 11 February along the Singapore waterfront were alluded to in the Australian official history of the campaign. Lionel Wigmore wrote, 'There was, however, a residue of Australian and other troops who had become desperate and defiant of authority ... On 12th February Bowden [Australian Government Representative at Singapore] cabled that a group of Australians and others had boarded a vessel without authority and in it had sailed for the Netherlands East Indies.' John Curtin, the Australian Prime Minister, cabled to Wavell at Batavia on 13 February that the death penalty could not be imposed on the men who boarded the *Empire Star* without the authorization of the Australian government. A few days later, after the fall of Singapore, Wavell signalled to reassure Curtin: 'In absence of confirmed evidence from Singapore impossible to sustain charges of desertion.' AWM 54, 553/6/2, Curtin to Wavell, 13/2/1942, Wavell to Curtin, 18/2/1942.

34. A. J. Marder, *Old Friends, New Enemies*, ii (Oxford, 1990), p. 30.

35. AWM 54, 559/2/2, Report by Brigadier A. S. Blackburn, GOC AIF Java; AWM 54, 171/11/2; AWM 232/1. The story of the *Empire Star* deserters did not by any means end when marines and sailors from HMS *Durban* escorted 135 Australian personnel off the ship at Batavia. (Captain S. N. Capon of the *Empire Star* reported that there were 139 deserters aboard.) The Australians from the *Empire Star* do not appear to have faced any significant punishment from the authorities in Batavia. The army captain who was the party's nominal leader seems to have kept his rank. (He belonged to a rear echelon formation.) However within a few days of the *Empire Star*'s arrival at Batavia the *Orcades*, carrying Australian troops from the Middle East, reached the port. The *Orcades* arrived at Batavia on 17 February and carried the 2/2nd Pioneer and 2/3rd Machine Gun Battalions and other AIF troops. The 2/2nd Pioneer Battalion's war diary noted that as the ship berthed 'a number of deserters from Singapore [were] on [the] wharf looting stores and behaving very badly'. According to Captain John Kennedy of the 2/3rd Machine Gun Battalion: 'We knew we were in Batavia because when we arrived there the deserters from Singapore pelted our ship with tins and things. And they were Australians! My commander, Arthur S. Blackburn VC, was a hotheaded old so-and-so, and if he'd had his way he'd have gone ashore and shot them. No doubt about it he would have. Some of them were terrible scum. And, of course, they ultimately joined us as POWs, and we didn't like that very much. The officer that led them was a terrible bugger. Singapore was about to fall, and the *Empire Star* had a lot of women on board and he had forced his way on the ship with a group of men. He should have been court-martialled.' Upon disembarkation Blackburn was promoted brigadier and he set out to form all Australian army troops at Java into a unified command known as 'Blackforce'. The *Empire Star* men,

other Australian escapers from Singapore, and some stray AIF reinforcements en route for Singapore were added to Blackforce. The experiment was not a success so far as the ex-Singapore men and reinforcements were concerned. The behaviour of a minority was sufficiently disruptive to warrant their being put on a ship sailing for Australia. (Blackburn's report mentioned in the main text refers to one officer and 175 other ranks arriving at Batavia from Singapore without good cause. This presumably includes all escapers under Blackburn's command, and not just those ex-*Empire Star*.) AWM 54, 553/6/2, 'Escapees, Evacuees and Alleged Deserters from Malaya and Singapore – 1939–45 War', 'Report from HMS *Durban*, 21/2/1942'; P. Elphick, *Singapore: The Pregnable Fortress* (London, 1995), pp. 312–13 and 385; AWM 52, 8/6/2, 2/2nd Pioneer Battalion, 17–28/2/1942; Patsy Adam-Smith, *Prisoners of War* (Melbourne, 1992), p. 354. Captain Capon of the *Empire Star* noted in his report that six AIF other ranks were among those killed during Japanese air attacks. 8th Australian Division records also list six other ranks believed to have been killed at sea on the *Empire Star*. All six men were from the Australian Army Service Corps. It should be noted, however, that many 8th Division units captured at Singapore had a small number of escapers either taken prisoner at Java or among those to have reached safety in Australia. AWM 54, 171/11/2, AIF Casualties Malaya-Java-Thailand as known by 2nd Echelon AIF Malaya, 8/12/1944, forwarded to Australian Red Cross Society; AWM 232/1–2, AMF POW & Missing – Far East SWP Islands, parts 1–2; AWM, PR 00592, Captain A. Smith-Ryan, 2/4th Machine Gun Battalion.

## Notes to Chapter 16: Capitulation

1. CAB 106/70, appendix C, 12/2/1942.
2. Ibid., IWM, 90/15/1, Major P. Davies, 18th Reconnaissance Battalion, p. 4.
3. WO 172/16, report No. 7, Major W. R. Walker, G2 HQ MC; WO 172/21, Malaya Command, appendix U 61, 12.30 p.m., 12/2/1942, appendix R 61, 11.20 a.m., 12/2/1942, 'Notes on GOC's Visit to AIF, Masseyforce and III Corps, a.m. 12 February'.
4. Percival Papers, IWM, P 48, Percival, December 1953, p. 6.
5. W. S. Thatcher (ed.), *The 10th Baluch Regiment in the Second World War* (Abbottabad, 1980), p. 161; CAB 106/58, Colonel A. M. L. Harrison, 'History of 11th Indian Division', pp. 29–31.
6. AWM 52, 8/3/18, 2/18th Battalion. On 12/13 February the 2/18th Battalion comprised twenty-nine officers and 462 other ranks, including eleven officers and 201 other ranks attached. On 15 February the 2/18th Battalion comprised twenty officers and 339 other ranks, including seven officers and 103 other ranks attached.
7. J. Lunt, *Imperial Sunset* (London, 1981), pp. 378–79; IWM, 88/33/1, Lieutenant H. D. Webber, 1st Malay; Dol Ramli, *History of the Malay Regiment, 1933–1942* (Singapore, 1955), pp. 85–90.

8. Bennett later claimed that Lieutenant-Colonel Derham (8th Division's chief medical officer) and Brigadier Maxwell had been urging him to cable the Australian government to 'have the show called off'. AWM 73/7, Lieutenant-General H. G. Bennett, 30/1/1953.

9. Percival Papers, IWM, P 31, 'Proceedings of the Conference Held at HQ MC (Fort Canning) at 14.00 hours Friday 13 February 1942'.

10. A. E. Percival, *The War in Malaya* (London, 1949), p. 287.

11. Percival Papers, IWM, P 49, Lieutenant-Colonel B. H. Ashmore, Malaya Command, 'Some Personal Observations of Malaya Command, 1940–42', Ceylon 1942, pp. 25–26.

12. Percival Papers, IWM, P 49, Lieutenant-Colonel B. H. Ashmore, 'Singapore to Colombo, 1942', p. 1.

13. WO 172/21, Malaya Command, appendix M 59, 10.30 p.m., 10/2/1942.

14. WO 172/21, Malaya Command, Faber Fire Command, 10.25 p.m., 10/2/1942; WO 172/180, 13–14/2/1942; WO 172/176, HQ Fixed Defences, 12–13/2/1942; WO 172/191, 968th Battery, 16th Defence Regiment; G. Chippington, *Singapore: The Inexcusable Betrayal* (Worcester, 1992), pp. 205 and 212–13.

15. CAB 106/70, 18th Division, 14/2/1942; WO 172/145, 55th Brigade, 14/2/1942.

16. WO 172/90, 4th Suffolk, 14/2/1942.

17. P. W. Fay, *The Forgotten Army* (Ann Arbor, Michigan, 1993), pp. 68–70; P. Elphick, *Singapore: The Pregnable Fortress* (London, 1995), pp. 339–41; Thatcher, *10th Baluch*, p. 162; IWM, 11748/17, Mohammad Ismail Khan, 2/10th Baluch. The 2/10th Baluchis had not been helped by the fact that their original commanding officer and adjutant had been ordered to join the official evacuation fleet, and two other British company commanders had been killed in earlier fighting at Singapore. The Baluchis were also very short of Indian junior leaders and specialists. They were one of only a few Indian battalions not amalgamated after service on the mainland. Two Indian Commissioned Officers with the missing companies later became senior Indian National Army leaders, though the Baluchis as a whole had one of the lower rates of INA membership amongst captured Indian units.

18. CAB 106/155, Brigadier G. G. R. Williams, 14/2/1942.

19. AWM 73/7, Lieutenant-Colonel A. P. Derham, 16/2/1953; Lionel Wigmore, *The Japanese Thrust* (Canberra, 1957), p. 375.

20. IWM, 88/33/1, Lieutenant D. H. Webber, 1st Malay, pp. 32–33; Ramli, *Malay Regiment*, pp. 93–100.

21. Noel Barber, *Sinister Twilight* (London, 1968), pp. 223–24; IWM, 88/63/1, Lieutenant S. E. Bell, 2nd Loyal; M. Middlebrook and P. Mahoney, *Battleship* (London, 1977), p. 327.

22. WO 106/2550B, Brigadier H. B. Taylor; AWM 67, 3/43, A. N. Wootton, 17/10/1945.

23. AWM, PR 84/28, journal of Sergeant A. R. Rupp, 2/18th Battalion, 14/2/1942.

24. CAB 106/191, Brigadier G. C. Ballentine to Brigadier J. Blood, 26/3/1951; AWM 51, 144, Colonel J. H. Thyer and Brigadier C. H. Kappe, 'Report on Operations

of 8th Australian Division AIF in Malaya', p. 193; AWM 52, 8/3/29, 2/29th Battalion, 'Comment by CO and Additions to Unit War Diary', p. 14; AWM 52, 18/2/21, 8th Division Provost Company, 14/2/1942.

25. AWM 52, 18/2/21, 8th Division Provost Company.

26. Percival Papers, IWM, P 26, section IV, Lieutenant-General L. M. Heath, 'Note on the Capitulation', p. 3.

27. W. N. Nicholson, *The Suffolk Regiment, 1928–46* (Ipswich), pp. 205–6; CAB 106/190, Major C. H. D. Wild, GSO 2, III Corps, 'Note on the Capitulation of Singapore'.

28. CAB 106/71, Diary of Events of the 54th Brigade (18th Division) at Singapore, 15/2/1942; CAB 106/70, 18th Division, map H, 4 p.m., 15/2/1942.

29. IWM, 90/15/1, Major P. Davies, 18th Reconnaissance Battalion, p. 5; CAB 106/71, 54th Brigade, 15/2/1942.

30. WO 172/182, 7th Coast Battery, 15/2/1942; WO 172/189, 9th Coast Regiment.

31. Percival Papers, IWM, P 47, Lieutenant-Colonel M. Elrington, 1/1/1946.

32. CAB 106/190, Wild, 'Note on the Capitulation of Singapore'.

33. J. D. Potter, *A Soldier Must Hang* (London, 1963), p. 81; M. Tsuji, *Singapore: The Japanese Version* (Singapore, 1960), pp. 260–66.

34. CAB 106/190, Wild, 'Note on the Capitulation of Singapore'; L. Allen, *Singapore, 1941–42* (London, 1977), pp. 180–84.

35. CAB 106/163, CIC South-West Pacific to Percival, 15/2/1942.

36. AWM 67, 1/5, Lieutenant-Colonel M. Ashkanasy.

37. Ian Skidmore, *Escape from the Rising Sun* (London, 1973); WO 172/16, report No. 12, Major G. A. Rowley-Conwy; AWM 54, 553/6/1. Another man to make an escape attempt on the evening of 15 February was Sergeant Walter Brown of the 2/15th Field Regiment. What made Brown unusual was that he was in his mid fifties, and had won the Victoria Cross and Military Medal in the First World War. AWM, 3 DRL/366, G. W. Fletcher, 2/15th Field Regiment, pp. 3–7.

38. AWM 54, 554/1/15; Wigmore, *Japanese Thrust*, p. 154; H. G. Bennett, *Why Singapore Fell* (Sydney, 1944), p. 198; A. B. Lodge, *The Fall of General Gordon Bennett* (Sydney, 1986), pp. 174–223.

39. Lodge, *Gordon Bennett*, p. 218.

40. AWM 54, 553/6/1, Lieutenant H. M. Lindley-Jones, 'Report on Evacuation from Singapore across Sumatra, February-March 1942', New Delhi, 30/11/1942, covering note by Wavell to CIGS, 20/1/1943.

41. W. Gibson, *The Boat* (London, 1952).

42. AWM 54, 553/6/1, Lindley-Jones, 'Report on Evacuation from Singapore'. Of Lieutenant-Colonel J. R. Broadbent's official party of Australian evacuees, only thirty-nine successfully escaped from Singapore. On Sumatra Broadbent's party grew to 125 Australians. After reaching Australia on a ship sailing from Java, Broadbent estimated that he had encountered seventy-five other Australian escapers en route and 164 alleged deserters (many of whom were from the *Empire Star*). AWM 54, 553/6/2.

43. WO 32/11750, Wavell (CIC India) to CIGS, 1/6/1942.

44. WO 106/2550B, Major J. C. K. Marshall, FMSVF, 15/5/1942.
45. WO 259/63, CGS Australia to WO, 2/4/1942. Bennett was promoted to lieuten-
    ant-general and packed off to command III Corps in Western Australia. He
    retired in frustration in 1944. An October 1945 military inquiry into the
    circumstances of Bennett's departure from Singapore did not support his
    actions. The report of a public judicial inquiry conducted shortly afterwards
    also criticized Bennett, but accepted that he had acted in good faith.
46. WO 106/2613B, 'Extracts from Letter Written by Staff Officer of 18th Division
    – Singapore'; WO 106/2550A, Lieutenant-Colonel I. M. Stewart.
47. WO 106/2573C, P. J. Grigg to Churchill, 5/6/1942. British units heavily engaged
    also showed signs of the 'straggling' phenomenon. The 4th Suffolks' war diary
    recorded that the unit had 250 officers and men present at 4 p.m. on 15
    February. Yet 450 marched to Changi two days later. Over the next fortnight
    the battalion's strength rose to twenty-eight officers and 746 men. The 2nd
    Loyals had 289 officers and men (including B Echelon) present on 15 February,
    but 600 within a few weeks. The British Battalion had 265 officers and men
    (including B Echelon) present on 15 February, but over 1000 by March.
    Nicholson, *Suffolk*, p. 209; WO 172/90, 4th Suffolk; C. G. T. Dean, *The Loyal
    Regiment (North Lancashire), 1919–53* (Preston, 1955), pp. 161–63; D. S. Daniell,
    *History of the East Surrey Regiment*, iv, *1920–5* (London, 1957), p. 145; Percival
    Papers, P 75, Leicesters and British Battalion war diary, appendix V. In Bennett's
    *Why Singapore Fell*, pp. 189–90, his entry for 14 February 1942 stated: 'A return
    shows that about 4500 members of the AIF are now in the perimeter. There
    are about 3000 sick and wounded in the hospitals.' Bennett went on to imply
    that casualties were the explanation for the gap in numbers between those
    present and the AIF's strength of 16–17,000 on 8 February. Bennett published
    his figures in 1944, and their accuracy is highly suspect. In an August 1942
    press article, Keith Murdoch, head of Australia's information department, put
    the AIF's strength in its final perimeter at 5000, an estimate possibly based
    on news supplied by Bennett. If these figures are accepted as accurate, however,
    they might be interpreted as meaning that thousands of unwounded Australians
    went missing at Singapore. Elphick's *Singapore*, pp. 335–38 and 352, claims that
    those pieces of evidence are conclusive proof that 8000 Australians deserted.
    Total deserters are estimated as 12,000. The break up of several Australian
    units did make a particularly bad and enduring impression on some British
    observers. A number of damning reports by British eye-witnesses at Singapore
    were withheld from British archives until the 1990s. Elphick was wrong though
    to stitch together allegations of Australian misbehaviour selectively and to
    jump to the conclusion that desertion, and Australian desertion in particular,
    was the key to the collapse of Percival's army. The causes were a good deal
    more complex than that.
48. S. W. Roskill, *The War at Sea, 1939–1945*, ii (London, 1956).

*Notes to Chapter 17: Aftermath*

1. Not all POWs taken at Singapore were beginning their first period of captivity. The 18th Division's Brigadier Backhouse had been captured after the Battle of Le Cateau in August 1914. A number of Indian Army officers and men had been taken at Kut in Mesopotamia in 1916.

2. M. Tsuji, *Singapore: The Japanese Version* (Singapore, 1960), p. 273. Yamashita made unfavourable comments about the Imperial Guards to Southern Army headquarters. In consequence the 5th and 18th Divisions received an Emperor's Citation for the capture of Singapore, but this honour was not given to the Imperial Guards. J. D. Potter, *A Soldier Must Hang* (London, 1963), p. 96.

3. L. Allen, *Singapore, 1941–42* (London, 1977), p. 184.

4. Richard Holmes and Anthony Kemp, *Bitter End* (London, 1982), p. 183; National Archives Singapore, A 107/04, Neoh Teik Hong.

5. Tsuji, *Singapore*, p. 223.

6. F. A. E. Crew, *The Army Medical Services*, ii (London, 1957), pp. 108–10; David Nelson, *The Story of Changi* (Perth, 1974), pp. 53–54.

7. Clifford Kinvig, *Scapegoat: General Percival of Singapore* (London, 1996), p. 221.

8. When the AIF's Major-General Callaghan and Brigadier Taylor left Singapore, Brigadier Maxwell remained behind as he was recovering from dysentery. Before sailing Callaghan ordered: 'Brigadier Maxwell is to remain in Changi, and has been classified as permanently unfit. He will not exercise any command NOW or in the future.' Galleghan thus became the senior AIF officer at Singapore. Maxwell left Singapore with a POW party later in the year. AWM 3DRL/2313, 2 of 4, Brigadier F. G. Galleghan, Major-General C. A. Callaghan, 15/8/1942.

9. Lionel Wigmore, *The Japanese Thrust* (Canberra, 1957), p. 588.

10. J. Pluvier, *South-East Asia from Colonialism to Independence* (Kuala Lumpur, 1988), p. 239.

11. Wigmore, *Japanese Thrust*, pp. 614–15.

12. Crew, *Medical Services*, ii, pp. 110–14 and 133–70.

13. Wigmore, *Japanese Thrust*, p. 642.

14. P. Mason, *A Matter of Honour* (London, 1974), p. 519.

15. K. K. Ghosh, *The Indian National Army* (Meerut, 1969), pp. 71–72.

16. IWM, 88/33/1, Lieutenant-Colonel E. L. Sawyer, 'The Growth of the INA and the General Conditions of Indian POWs in Singapore from 1942 to 1945'.

17. Ghosh, *Indian National Army*, p. 59.

18. Hugh Toye, *The Springing Tiger: Subhash Chandra Bose* (Bombay, 1959) p. vii.

19. G. H. Carr, *The War of the Springing Tigers* (London, 1975), p. 116.

20. IOR/L/WS/2/45, Lieutenant-Colonel G. D. Anderson, O/C Combined Services Detailed Interrogation Centre, 'A Brief Chronological and Factual Account of the INA', 16/5/1946; Ghosh, *Indian National Army*, p. 91.

21. IWM, 88/33/1, Sawyer, 'The Growth of the INA'.

22. In the 1944 Imphal battles the 1st INA Division sent 6000 men to the front, of whom 400 were killed, 1500 died of disease or exposure, 800 surrendered, and 715 deserted or went missing. Only 2600 returned. A. J. Barker, *The March on Delhi* (London, 1963). The 2nd INA Division was captured on the road to Rangoon early in 1945. A third INA division was still forming in Malaya. S. L. Menezes, *Fidelity and Honour* (New Delhi, 1993), pp. 386–97.

23. W. E. H. Condon, *The Frontier Force Regiment* (Aldershot, 1962).

24. B. Farwell, *Armies of the Raj* (London, 1989), p. 339.

25. IOR/L/WS/1/1711.

26. Farwell, *Armies of the Raj*, p. 339.

27. Ghosh, *Indian National Army*, p. 202.

28. T. J. Danaraj, *Japanese Invasion of Malaya and Singapore: Memoirs of a Doctor* (Kuala Lumpur, 1990), p. 66.

29. I. Ward, *The Killer They Called God* (Singapore, 1992), p. 104; Cheah Boon Kheng, *Red Star Over Malaya* (Singapore, 1983), p. 21.

30. National Archives Singapore, A 152/08, Heng Chiang Ki.

31. National Archives Singapore, A 16/16, Lee Kip Lin.

32. National Archives Singapore, A 248/10, Chan Cheng Yean.

33. Ward, *The Killer They Called a God*, pp. 140–49, 162–76 and 195.

34. National Archives Singapore, A 120/15, Lan Khong Kon.

35. Pluvier, *South-East Asia*, p. 278.

36. Adrian Stewart, *The Underrated Enemy: Britain's War With Japan, December 1941-May 1942* (London, 1987), p. 115.

37. AIR 8/943, Curtin to Dominions Office, 22/2/1942.

38. It is sometimes claimed in Australia that the decision to bring the 7th Division straight back to Australia was vital in so far as that formation went on to play a prominent role in New Guinea later in 1942. But if the 7th Division had landed at Rangoon, the 6th Division would certainly have come directly to Australia instead, rather than stopping at Ceylon.

39. David Day, *The Great Betrayal: Britain, Australia and the Onset of the Pacific War, 1939–42* (London, 1988), pp. 263–64.

40. D. M. Horner, *High Command* (Sydney, 1982), p. 182.

41. Ibid., p. 181.

42. J. Costello, *The Pacific War* (New York, 1981), pp. 218–21 and 236.

43. D. McCarthy, *South-West Pacific Area: First Year, Kokoda to Wau* (Canberra, 1959), p. 531.

44. S. W. Roskill, *The War at Sea, 1939–1945*, ii (London, 1956); A. J. Marder, *Old Friends, New Enemies*, ii (Oxford, 1990), pp. 155, 341, 347–48 and 408.

45. L. Allen, *Burma: The Longest War, 1941–45* (London, 1984).

46. J. D. Potter, *A Soldier Must Hang* (London, 1963), pp. 99–100.

47. Rafael Steinberg, *Return to the Philippines* (New York, 1979); M. Hamlin Cannon, *Leyte: The Return to the Philippines* (Washington, 1954), pp. 367–68.

48. Robert Ross Smith, *Triumph in the Philippines* (Washington, 1963), pp. 97 and 307.

49. Potter, *A Soldier Must Hang*, pp. 150–51.
50. Smith, *Philippines*, pp. 578–79.
51. Ibid., pp. 651–52 and 694.
52. Ibid., p. 654.
53. Potter, *A Soldier Must Hang*, p. 166.
54. Ibid., p. 195.
55. Ibid., pp. 199–200.
56. The Japanese 5th Division's Lieutenant-General Matsui became chief of staff of the Japanese Expeditionary Force in China in 1943. The Imperial Guards' Nishimura spent the war in civil posts administering occupied territory. The ever-resilient Tsuji saw further war service at Guadalcanal, the Philippines, China and Burma. After a period in hiding after the war to avoid prosecution for war crimes, Tsuji returned to Japan. He became a popular author with his account of the Malayan campaign and other stories, and a member of the Japanese Parliament. Colonel Sugita became chief of staff of Japan's self-defence force in the early 1960s.

## Notes to Chapter 18: The Fall of Singapore

1. A. R. Millett and W. Murray (eds), *Military Effectiveness*, ii (Boston, 1988), p. 108. As Chancellor of the Exchequer from 1924–29, Churchill had played a role in the cancellation of a number of cruisers and smaller warships, but these cutbacks were trivial compared to the scrapping of many of the Royal Navy's battleships in the wake of the 1921–22 Washington Naval Conference.
2. W. S. Churchill, *The Second World War*, iv (London, 1951), p. 9.
3. Some sources estimate the Japanese to have had three hundred armoured vehicles in Malaya. Yet on the mainland the thirty tanks used at Slim River was the largest concentration sighted at any stage. It only took the efforts of a handful of anti-tank gunners near Gemas and Bakri to end the participation of tanks in the mainland phase of the campaign. At Singapore fifty tanks were sighted when the Japanese seized Bukit Timah, but only a handful of tanks were seen elsewhere on the island. On paper, after most of one regiment was diverted to the Dutch East Indies, the 3rd Tank Group had 179 tanks, but a high rate of mechanical breakdown, poor repair facilities, and the loss of those vehicles knocked out in battle, greatly reduced available strength on a day to day basis. S. Woodburn Kirby, *The War Against Japan*, i (London, 1957), p. 522.
4. AWM 51, 145a, General Heath's account of campaign, p. 76.
5. I. Morrison, *Malayan Postscript* (Sydney, 1943), pp. 156–57.
6. IWM, Department of Sound Records, 12749/52, Lieutenant-Colonel P. J. D. Toosey, 135th Field Regiment, p. 181.
7. Percival Papers, P 43, Percival, 'Comments on Admiral Sir Geoffrey Layton's Report, 13/1/1947'; CAB 106/64, 'The Malayan Campaign, 8/12/1941–15/2/1942', p. 74.

8. Percival Papers, P 42, 'Notes by General Percival on Certain Senior Commanders and Other Matters', 8/1/1954.
9. Heath was well regarded by most senior Australian officers (other than Bennett). Thyer described Heath as 'on the job' and a 'man of ability'. Galleghan wrote that Heath was 'a grand soldier', and Taylor that Heath was 'in my opinion, the most able soldier in Malaya'. AWM 93, 50/2/23/480, Colonel J. H. Thyer; AWM 73/51, Brigadier F. G. Galleghan, 1/2/1950; AWM 93, 50/2/23/258, Brigadier H. B. Taylor, 17/6/1952.
10. Kirby, *War Against Japan*, v, p. 1.

## Notes to Appendix 1

1. Kirby, *War Against Japan*, v, p. 64.
2. Ibid., pp. 69 and 80.
3. Ibid., pp. 64–65.
4. Ibid., p. 91.
5. Ibid., p. 270
6. Ibid., pp. 266 and 270.
7. Ibid., p. 123.

# Bibliography

## UNPUBLISHED SOURCES

### India Office Library, London

EUR D 1196/33, Account of the Malayan Campaign by Captain F. E. Mileham, 4/9th Jat Regiment.

EUR D 1196/34, Captain A. W. Hislop, 2/9th Jat.

L/WS/1/952 – WS 16063, Brigadier W. Carpendale, 'Report on Operations of the 11th Indian Division in Kedah and Perak'; Major-General David Murray-Lyon, '11th Indian Division: Short Summary of Events, 7–24 December 1941'; Lieutenant-Colonel A. E. Cumming, 'The Fall of Singapore'.

### National Army Museum, Archives, London

6509–14. Lieutenant-Colonel C. C. Deakin and Major G. M. S. Webb, 5/2nd Punjab Regiment.

7306 121. Lieutenant-Colonel J. Frith, 2/10th Baluch Regiment.

7309–2. Account of Brigadier G. C. Ballentine, 44th Indian Infantry Brigade.

7709–62–3. Major S. A. Watt, 'The 7th Battalion [6th Rajputana Rifles] in Malaya, 1942'.

7910–67. Lieutenant-Colonel J. D. Sainter, 'War Record of the 6/1st Punjab Regiment'.

8206–93. Major Alan Glendinning, Indian Medical Service.

### Liddell Hart Centre for Military Archives, Kings' College, London

Alanbrooke Papers. Field Marshal Lord Alanbrooke (Alan Brooke), Chief of the Imperial General Staff (CIGS), 1941–46.

Brooke-Popham Papers. Air Chief Marshal Sir Robert Brooke-Popham, Commander-in-Chief Far East, 1940–41.

## Imperial War Museum, Archives, London

Abbott, Lieutenant S., 89/15/1, 2nd East Surrey.

Benford, Lance-Bombardier E. S., 86/35/1, Royal Artillery.

Flower, Lieutenant-Colonel H. S., 86/87/1, 9th Royal Northumberland Fusiliers.

Glanfield, Lieutenant D. J., 90/15/1, 118th Field Regiment, and Davies, Major P., 18th Reconnaissance Battalion.

Goodman, Brigadier E. W., 86/67/1, Chief Royal Artillery (CRA), 9th Indian Division.

Hammond, Major H., 88/34/1, 53rd Brigade.

Hannam, Captain S., P 470, 2/26th Battalion.

Heath Papers. P 441–442, Lieutenant-General Sir Lewis Heath, GOC III Indian Corps.

Hewitt, Lieutenant T. J. L., 85/35/1, 28th Indian Brigade.

Key, Major-General B. W., P 456, 11th Indian Division.

Percival Papers. Lieutenant-General A. E. Percival, GOC Malaya Command 1941–42.

P 49, Lieutenant-Colonel B. H. Ashmore, Malaya Command, 'Some Personal Observations of Malaya Campaign 1940–1942', Ceylon, 1942.

P 75, Lieutenant-Colonel F. R. N. Cobley, Malaya Command, 'Typescript Report on Malayan Campaign', 1942–43.

Sawyer, Lieutenant-Colonel E. L., 88/33/1, Royal Artillery.

Webber, Lieutenant D. H., 88/33/1, 1st Malay Regiment.

88/63/1, 'Hospital in No Man's Land: The Atrocity at Alexandra Hospital, Singapore 14/2/1942'.

## Imperial War Museum, Department of Sound Records, London

Campbell, Major P. E., 11891/4, 2/10th Baluch.

Key, Major-General B. W., 6171/06, 11th Indian Division.

Khan, Colonel Mohammad Ismail, 11748/17, 2/10th Baluch.

Lane, Private A., 10295/11, 1st Manchester.

McKenzie, Lieutenant A. G., 90/15/1, 1st Malay Regiment.

Monteath, Captain R. B., 5264/12, 3/17th Dogra.

Payne, Lieutenant H. L., 4748/4, 137th Field Regiment.

Stitt, Lieutenant-Colonel J. H., 4771/7, 2nd Gordon Highlanders.

Stoner, Captain I. W., 12194/3, 2nd Argyll and Sutherland Highlanders, ADC to General Percival.

Sugita, Colonel Ichiji, 2839/3, Imperial Japanese Army.

Toosey, Lieutenant-Colonel P. J. D., 12749/52, 135th Field Regiment.

Wethey, Major I. H., 10813/4, 5/14 Punjab.

## Public Record Office, Kew, London

ADM – Admiralty.

AIR – Air Ministry.

CAB – Cabinet Office.

CAB 101 – Cabinet Historical Section: Official War Histories.

CAB 106 – Cabinet Historical Section: Archivist and Librarian Series.

CAB 106/53–8, Colonel A. M. L. Harrison, 'History of 11th Indian Division'.

COL – Colonial Office.

PREM – Prime Minister.

WO – War Office.

    WO 106 – Directorate of Military Operations and Intelligence.

    WO 172 – War Diaries: South-East Asia Command.

    WO 208 – Directorate of Military Intelligence.

    WO 325/1, Greater East Asia War Diary, 9th Infantry Brigade.

## Australian War Memorial, Canberra

AWM 52, War Diaries.

AWM 54, Written Records.

AWM 67, Gavin Long Records.

AWM 73, Lionel Wigmore Records.

PR, Private Records.

## PUBLISHED SOURCES

### Published Government Sources

Butler, J. R. M., *Grand Strategy*, ii (London, 1957).

Cabinet Office, *Principal War Telegrams and Memoranda, 1940–1943: Far East* (London, 1976).

Crew, F. A. E., *The Army Medical Services*, ii (London, 1957).

General Staff, Malaya Command, *Tactical Notes for Malaya, 1940* (Calcutta, 1941).

Gill, G. Hermon, *Royal Australian Navy, 1939–1942* (Canberra, 1957).

Gillson, D., *Royal Australian Air Force, 1939–1942* (Canberra, 1962).

Hasluck, P., *The Government and the People, 1939–1941* (Canberra, 1952).

Hinsley, F. H., *British Intelligence in the Second World War: Its Influence on Strategy and Operations*, ii (London, 1981).

House of Commons, *Hansard: The Parliamentary Debates*.

Kirby, S. Woodburn, *The War Against Japan*, 5 vols (London, 1957–69).

Long, Gavin, *To Benghazi* (Canberra, 1952).

Long, Gavin, *The Six Years' War* (Canberra, 1973).

Mackenzie, C., *Eastern Epic* (London, 1951).

Prasad, Sri Nandan, *Expansion of the Armed Forces and Defence Organization, 1939–45* (New Delhi, 1956).

Roskill, S. W., *The War at Sea, 1939–1945*, 3 vols (London, 1954–61).

Ross, J. M. S., *Royal New Zealand Air Force* (Wellington, 1955).

Sastri, K. N. V. and Bhargava, K. D., *Campaigns in South-East Asia, 1941–42* (New Delhi, 1960).

Wavell, Lord, *Despatch by the Supreme Commander of the ABDA Area to the Combined Chiefs of Staff on the Operations in the South-West Pacific, 15/1/42–25/2/42* (London, 1948).

Wigmore, Lionel, *The Japanese Thrust* (Canberra, 1957).

## Regimental Histories

2/19th Battalion AIF Association, *The Grim Glory of the 2/19th Battalion AIF* (Sydney, 1975).

Barclay, C. N., *The History of the Royal Northumberland Fusiliers in the Second World War* (London, 1952).

Barclay, C. N., *The History of the Sherwood Foresters (Nottingham and Derbyshire Regiment), 1919–1957* (London, 1959).

Bell, A. C., *History of the Manchester Regiment 1st and 2nd Battalions, 1922–48* (Altrincham, 1954).

Bellers, E. V. R., *The 1st King George V's Own Gurkha Rifles (The Malaun Regiment)*, ii, *1920–47* (Aldershot, 1956).

Betham, G. and Geary, H. V. R., *The Golden Galley: The Story of the 2nd Punjab Regiment, 1761–1947* (Oxford, 1956).

Birdwood, F. T., *The Sikh Regiment in the Second World War* (1953).

Burfitt, J., *Against All Odds: The History of the 2/18th Battalion* (Sydney, 1991).

Christie, R. W. (ed.), *A History of the 2/29th Battalion* (Melbourne, 1983).

Chye Kooi Loong, *The History of The British Battalion in the Malayan Campaign, 1941–42* (1984).

Condon, W. E. H., *The Frontier Force Regiment* (Aldershot, 1962).

Condon, W. E. H., *The Frontier Force Rifles* (Aldershot, 1953).

Daniell, D. S., *History of the East Surrey Regiment*, iv, *1920–52* (London, 1957).

Dean, C. G. T., *The Loyal Regiment (North Lancashire), 1919–53* (Preston, 1955).

Deedes, R. B., *Historical Records of the Royal Garhwal Rifles*, ii, *1923–47* (Dehra Dun, 1962).

Goodwin, B., *Mates and Memories: Recollections of the 2/10th Field Regiment* (Brisbane, 1995).

Graham, C. A. L., *The History of the Indian Mountain Artillery* (Aldershot, 1957).

Haron, Nadzan, *The Malay Regiment, 1933–1955* (1987).

Horner, D. M., *The Gunners: A History of Australian Artillery* (Sydney, 1995).

Jacobs, J. W. and Bridgeland, R. J. (eds), *Through: The Story of Signals 8th Australian Division and Signals AIF Malaya* (Sydney, 1949).

Kemp, P. K., *History of the Royal Norfolk Regiment*, iii, *1919–51* (Norwich, 1953).

Lawford, J. P. and Catto, W. E. (eds), *Solah Punjab: The History of the 16th Punjab Regiment* (Aldershot, 1967).

McNicoll, R. R., *The Royal Australian Engineers, 1919 to 1945: Teeth and Tail* (Canberra, 1982).

Magarry, R., *The Battalion Story* [2/26th Battalion] (Brisbane, 1994).

Medley, R. H., *Cape Badge: Story of the Four Battalions of the Bedfordshire and Hertfordshire Regiment and the Hertfordshire Regiment (Territorial Army), 1939–47* (London, 1995).

Miles, W., *The Life of a Regiment: The Gordon Highlanders*, v, *1919–45* (Aberdeen, 1961).

Nicholson, W. N., *The Suffolk Regiment, 1928–46* (Ipswich).

Palsokar, R. D., *A Historical Record of the Dogra Regiment, 1858–1981* (Faizabad, 1982).

Penfold, A. W., Bayliss, W. C. and Crispin, K. E., *Galleghan's Greyhounds: The Story of the 2/30th Australian Infantry Battalion* (Sydney, 1949).

Picken, H. W. (ed.), *Nobody's Own: The History of the 3rd Cavalry and its Predecessors, 1841–1945* (1962).

Pigot, G., *History of the 1st Battalion 14th Punjab Regiment* (1946).

Praval, K. C., *Valour Triumphs: A History of the Kumaon Regiment* (Faridabad, Haryana, 1976).

Qureshi, Muhammed Ibrahim, *History of the 1st Punjab Regiment, 1759–1956* (Aldershot, 1958).

Ramli, Dol, *History of the Malay Regiment, 1933–1942* (Singapore, 1955).

Ross, J. and Hailes, W. L., *War Services of the 9th Jat Regiment*, ii, *1937–48* (London, 1965).

Sandes, E. W. C., *The Indian Engineers, 1939–47* (Kirkee, 1956).

Sheppard, M. C., *The Malay Regiment, 1933–1947* (Kuala Lumpur, 1949).

Smith, N. C., *Tid-Apa: The History of the 4th Anti-Tank Regiment* (Melbourne, 1992).

Stevens, G. R., *History of the 2nd King Edward VII's Own Goorkha Rifles (The Sirmoor Rifles)*, iii, *1921–48* (Aldershot, 1952).

Stevens, G. R., *The 9th Gurkha Rifles*, ii, *1937–47* (1953).

Stewart, I. M., *History of the Argyll and Sutherland Highlanders 2nd Battalion (The Thin Red Line) Malayan Campaign, 1941–42* (London, 1947).

Thatcher, W. S. (ed.), *The 10th Baluch Regiment in the Second World War* (Abbottabad, 1980).

Tilbrook, J. D., *To the Warrior His Arms: A History of the Ordnance Services in the Australian Army* (Canberra, 1989).

Underhill, W. E. (ed.), *The Royal Leicestershire Regiment, 1928–56* (London, 1957).

Wall, D., *Singapore and Beyond: The Story of the Men of the 2/20th Battalion* (Sydney, 1985).

Waters, R. S., *14th Punjab Regiment: A Short History, 1939–45* (London, 1950).

Whitelocke, C. and O'Brien, G., *Gunners in the Jungle* [2/15th Field Regiment] (Sydney, 1983).

## Books

Adam-Smith, Patsy, *Prisoners of War: From Gallipoli to Korea* (Melbourne, 1992).

Allen, L., *Singapore, 1941–42* (London, 1977).

Arneil, Stan, *Black Jack: The Life and Times of Brigadier Sir Frederick Galleghan* (Melbourne, 1983).

Attiwill, K., *Fortress: The Story of the Siege and Fall of Singapore* (New York, 1960).

Barber, Noel, *Sinister Twilight* (London, 1968).

Barker, A. J., *Japanese Army Handbook, 1939–45* (London, 1979).

Beaumont, J., *Gull Force* (Sydney, 1988).

Bennett, H. G., *Why Singapore Fell* (Sydney, 1944).

Bennett, John, *Defeat to Victory: No. 453 Squadron RAAF* (Point Cook, Victoria, 1994).

Bond, B. (ed.), *Chief of Staff: The Diaries of Lieutenant-General Sir Henry Pownall*, ii, *1940–44* (London, 1974).

Braddon, R., *The Naked Island* (London, 1952).

Brooke, G., *Singapore's Dunkirk* (London, 1989).

Buck, J. H. (ed.), *The Modern Japanese Military System* (London, 1975).

Burton, Reginald, *The Road to Three Pagodas* (London, 1963).

Butcher, John G., *The British in Malaya, 1880–1941* (Kuala Lumpur, 1979).

Callahan, R., *The Worst Disaster: The Fall of Singapore* (London, 1977).

Calvocoressi, P., Wint, G. and Pritchard, J., *The Penguin History of the Second World War* (London, 1999).

Chaphekar, S. G., *A Brief Study of the Malayan Campaign, 1941–42* (Poona, 1960).

Chapman, F. Spencer, *The Jungle is Neutral* (London, 1949).

Charlton, P., *The Thirty-Niners* (Melbourne, 1981).

Cheah Boon Kheng, *Red Star over Malaya* (Singapore, 1983).

Chew, Daniel and Lim, Irene (eds), *Sook Ching* (Singapore, 1992).

Chippington, G., *Singapore: The Inexcusable Betrayal* (Worcester, 1992).

Churchill, W. S., *The Second World War*, 6 vols (London, 1948–54).

Clisby, M., *Guilty or Innocent? The Gordon Bennett Case* (Sydney, 1992).

Corr, G. H., *The War of the Springing Tiger* (London, 1975).

Danaraj, T. J., *Japanese Invasion of Malaya and Singapore: Memoirs of a Doctor* (Kuala Lumpur, 1990).

Day, David, *The Great Betrayal: Britain, Australia and the Onset of the Pacific War, 1939–42* (London, 1988).

Elphick, P. and Smith, M., *Odd Man Out: The Story of the Singapore Traitor* (London, 1993).

Elphick, P., *Singapore: The Pregnable Fortress* (London, 1995).

Falk, S. L., *Seventy Days to Singapore* (New York, 1975).

Farwell, Byron, *Armies of the Raj* (London, 1989).

Fay, P. W., *The Forgotten Army* (Ann Arbor, Michigan, 1993).

Fergusson, B., *Wavell: Portrait of a Soldier* (London, 1961).

Fikemeyer, C., *It Happened to Us* (Melbourne, 1994).

Fujiwara Iwaichi, *F. Kikan: Japanese Army Intelligence Operations in Southeast Asia during World War II* (Hong Kong, 1983).

Ghosh, K. K., *The Indian National Army* (Meerut, 1969).

Gibson, W., *The Boat* (London, 1952).

Gilchrist, A., *Malaya 1941: The Fall of a Fighting Empire* (London, 1992).

Gough, R., *The Escape From Singapore* (London, 1987).

Hall, E. R., *Glory in Chaos: The RAAF in the Far East, 1940–42* (Melbourne, 1989).

Harper, R. W. E. and Miller, H., *Singapore Mutiny* (Oxford, 1984).

Harries, M. and S., *Soldiers of the Sun: The Rise and Fall of the Imperial Japanese Army, 1868–1945* (London, 1991).

Harrison, K., *The Brave Japanese* (Adelaide, 1966).

Heinrichs, W., *Threshold of War* (Oxford, 1988).

Holmes, R. and Kemp, A., *The Bitter End* (Chichester, 1982).

Horner, D. M., *Crisis of Command: Australian Generalship and the Japanese Threat, 1941–1943* (Canberra, 1978).

Horner, D. M., *High Command* (Sydney, 1982).

Iriye, A., *Origins of the Second World War in Asia and the Pacific* (London, 1987).

Kennedy, John, *The Business of War* (London, 1957).

Kennedy, J., *British Civilians and the Japanese War in Malaya and Singapore, 1941–45* (London, 1987).

Kennedy, J., *When Singapore Fell: Evacuations and Escapes, 1941–42* (London, 1989).

Kennedy, P., *The Rise and Fall of British Naval Mastery* (London, 1976).

Keogh, E. G., *Malaya, 1941–42* (Melbourne, 1962).

Kinvig, Clifford, *Scapegoat: General Percival of Singapore* (London, 1996).

Kirby, S. Woodburn, *Singapore: The Chain of Disaster* (London, 1971).

Kratoska, Paul H. (ed.), *Malaya and Singapore during the Japanese Occupation* (Singapore, 1995).

Kratoska, Paul H., *The Japanese Occupation of Malaya* (London, 1998).

Lane, Arthur, *Lesser Gods, Greater Devils* (Stockport, 1993).

Leasor, J., *Singapore: The Battle that Changed the World* (London, 1968).

Lebra, J. C., *Japanese-Trained Armies in South-East Asia* (New York, 1977).

Lee, C., *Sunset of the Raj: Fall of Singapore, 1942* (Durham, 1994).

Lee Geok Boi, *Syonan: Singapore under the Japanese, 1942–1945* (Singapore, 1992).

Legg, F., *The Gordon Bennett Story* (Sydney, 1965).

Lewin, R., *The Chief: Field Marshal Lord Wavell* (London, 1980).

Lodge, A. B., *The Fall of General Gordon Bennett* (Sydney, 1986).

Lunt, J., *Imperial Sunset* (London, 1981).

McCabe, G., *Pacific Sunset* (Hobart, 1946).

McIntyre, W. D., *The Rise and Fall of the Singapore Naval Base, 1919–1942* (London, 1979).

Mant, Gilbert, *Grim Glory* (Sydney, 1942).

Marder, A. J., *Old Friends, New Enemies*, 2 vols (Oxford, 1981–90).

Mason, P., *A Matter of Honour* (London, 1974).

Masters, J., *Bugles and a Tiger* (London, 1956).

Menezes, S. L., *Fidelity and Honour* (New Delhi, 1993).

Middlebrook, M. and Mahoney, P., *Battleship* (London, 1977).

Millett, A. R. and Murray, W. (eds), *Military Effectiveness*, 3 vols (Boston, 1988).

Moore, Micheal, *Battalion at War: Singapore, 1942* (Norwich, 1988).

Morrison, I., *Malayan Postscript* (Sydney, 1943).

Murfett, Malcolm H., Miksic, John N., Farrell, Brian P. and Chiang Ming Shun, *Between Two Oceans: A Military History of Singapore from First Settlement to Final British Withdrawal* (Singapore, 1999).

Neidpath, J., *The Singapore Naval Base and the Defence of Britain's Eastern Empire, 1919–1941* (Oxford, 1981).

Nelson, David, *The Story of Changi* (Perth, 1974).

Omissi, D., *The Sepoy and the Raj: The Indian Army, 1860–1940* (London, 1994).

Ong Chit Chung, *Operation Matador: Britain's War Plans Against the Japanese, 1918–1941* (Singapore, 1997).

Owen, F., *The Fall of Singapore* (London, 1960).

Percival, A. E., *The War in Malaya* (London, 1949).

Perry, F. W., *The Commonwealth Armies* (Manchester, 1988).

Pluvier, J., *South-East Asia from Colonialism to Independence* (Kuala Lumpur, 1974).

Potter, J. D., *A Soldier Must Hang* (London, 1963).

Reel, A. F., *The Case of General Yamashita* (Chicago, 1949).

Robertson, J., *Australia Goes to War, 1939–1945* (Melbourne, 1981).

Rose, A., *Who Dies Fighting* (London, 1944).

Roskill, S., *Naval Policy Between the Wars* (London, 1968).

Russell-Roberts, D., *Spotlight on Singapore* (London, 1965).

Shores, C., Cull, B. and Yasuho Izawa, *Bloody Shambles*, 2 vols (London, 1992–93).

Sidhu, H., *The Bamboo Fortress* (Singapore, 1991).

Simson, I., *Singapore: Too Little, Too Late* (London, 1970).

Singh, Mohan, *Soldiers' Contribution to Independence* (Delhi, 1974).

Skidmore, Ian, *Escape From the Rising Sun* (London, 1973).

Sleeman, C. (ed.), *Trial of Gozawa Sadaichi and Nine Others* (London, 1948).

Smyth, J., *Percival and the Tragedy of Singapore* (London, 1971).

Taylor, William, *With the Cambridgeshires at Singapore* (Cambridge, 1971).

Toye, H., *Subhash Chandra Bose: The Springing Tiger* (Bombay, 1959).

Tsuji, M., *Singapore: The Japanese Version* (Singapore, 1960).

Uhr, Janet, *Against the Sun* (Sydney, 1998).

Ward, I., *The Killer They Called a God* (Singapore, 1992).

Ward, I., *Snaring the Other Tiger* (Singapore, 1996).

Wrigglesworth, D., *The Japanese Invasion of Kelantan in 1941* (Kuala Lumpur, 1991).

Wyett, J., *Staff Wallah: At the Fall of Singapore* (Sydney, 1996).

Yap Siang Yong, *Fortress Singapore: The Battlefield Guide* (Singapore, 1992).

# Index

281, 335; 2/4th Machine Gun
Battalion, 205, 210, 223, 226, 229,
243, 248, 254, 304, 308, 329; 2/4th
Pioneer Battalion, 329; 6th Battalion,
35; 2/18th Battalion, 37, 189–91, 223,
226–29, 240, 243, 254, 303–4, 308,
332–34, 336; 2/19th Battalion, 38,
163, 166–70, 172–73, 175–77, 210,
227–29, 240, 243, 245, 303–4, 308,
326, 332–34; 2/20th Battalion, 36,
217, 223, 225–27, 229, 240, 243, 245,
303–4, 308, 332–34; 2/21st Battalion,
312; 2/26th Battalion, 195, 197–99,
232–35, 248, 254, 304, 308, 328;
2/29th Battalion, 163–64, 166–70,
172–73, 175–77, 210, 229–30, 232,
240, 244, 247, 304, 308, 326; 2/30th
Battalion, 154–59, 184–85, 197–98,
233–35, 246, 304, 308; Special Reserve
Battalion, 210, 229, 241, 244, 246;
X Battalion, 243–45, 333–34
Artillery: 2/4th Anti-Tank Regiment,
153, 156–59, 164, 166, 223, 308;
2/10th Field Regiment, 308; 2/14th
Field Regiment, 329; 2/15th Field
Regiment (65th Battery), 153, 159–60,
162, 169, 224, 226, 308, 326, 338
Forces: Blackforce 335; Eastforce, 175,
183, 187, 200; Merrett Force, 240,
243, 245, 334; Westforce, 152, 154,
162, 167, 174–75, 177, 191, 193, 200
Miscellaneous: 2/3rd Reserve Motor
Transport Company, 250; 2/10th
Field Company, 229; Army Medical
Corps, 333; Army Service Corps, 210,
229, 336, General Base Depot, 230,
233, 243
Australian High Commission, London, 269
Australian Labor Party, 180
*Awagisan Maru*, Japanese transport, 62
Axis, 39, 48, 117
Ayer Bemban, 199, 328
Ayer Hitam, 183–85, 191

Babington, Air Marshal Sir J., 10, 27
Backhouse, Brigadier E. H. W., 255, 340

Badang beach, 60–61
Bakri, 160–61, 163–72, 177, 184, 210, 227, 342
Ballantine, Brigadier G. C., 231, 241, 262
Banham, Major C. F. W., 186
Banka Island, 259
Bangkok, 52, 56
*Barham*, British battleship, 117
Barstow, Major-General A. E., 34, 63, 112, 125–26, 193–97, 291
Bata, Sungei, 87, 89, 92–94, 98
Bataan, 119, 203, 281, 285
Batang Berjuntai, 130
Batavia, 2, 147, 150, 251, 259, 335–36
Bate, Major, 84–85
Bates, Lt-Colonel L. V., 91
Batu Anam, 159, 167
Batu Pahat, 161, 163, 171, 173, 175, 183–87
Batu Pakaka, 11
Batu Tiga, 150
Beamish, Captain T., 269
Beamish, Rear-Admiral T. P. H., 269
Beckwith-Smith, Major-General M. B., 209, 263, 273
Bedok, 279
Belgaum, 29
Bell, Captain L. H., 66, 72, 76
Bencoolen, 2
Benedict, Lance-Havildar J., 177
Bengal, Bay of, 282, 293, 315
Bennett, Lt-General H. G., 34–35, 37–38, 106, 148, 152–55, 159–60, 162–64, 167, 173–75, 177–78, 184–85, 191, 193–94, 199–200, 214, 217–18, 221–23, 227–28, 230–33, 235, 237–38, 240, 242–43, 246–47, 255, 258, 260, 266–69, 291, 337, 339
Benut, 183, 186–87
Berih, Sungei, 223, 228–29
Berman, Naik, 149
Bernam River, 123
Berrigan, New South Wales, 164
Betong, 79–80
Beverley, Captain F. G., 168, 172, 175
Bicycles, 133, 137, 155–56
Bidor, 122